► **Mining Google Web Services:**
Building Applications with the Google API

John Paul Mueller

Mining Google Web Services:
Building Applications with the Google API

Sybex

SYBEX

San Francisco · London

Associate Publisher: Joel Fugazzotto
Acquisitions and Developmental Editor: Tom Cirtin
Production Editor: Leslie E.H. Light
Technical Editor: Russ Mullen
Copyeditor: Cheryl Hauser
Compositor: Happenstance Type-O-Rama
Graphic Illustrator: Happenstance Type-O-Rama
Proofreaders: Laurie O'Connell, Nancy Riddiough
Indexer: Lynnzee Elze
Cover Design and Illustration: Richard Miller, Calyx Design

Library of Congress Card Number: 2003116218

ISBN: 0-7821-4333-4

Manufactured in the United States of America

10 9 8 7 6 5 4 3 2 1

To Karen Watterson,
a kindred spirit and fellow worker.

Acknowledgments

Thanks to my wife, Rebecca, for working with me to get this book completed. I really don't know what I would have done without her help in researching and compiling some of the information that appears in this book. She also did a fine job of proofreading my rough draft and page proofing the result.

Russ Mullen deserves thanks for his technical edit of this book. He greatly added to the accuracy and depth of the material you see here. Russ is always providing me with great URLs for new products and ideas. I also appreciated his hard work in testing endless versions of applications and providing input in my ideas. This book is technically challenging in that it relies on a number of programming languages, new and evolving technology, and several new products. Russ met the challenge with an efficiency that few other people could match.

A number of people read all or part of this book to help me refine the approach and to test the examples on a number of systems. These unpaid volunteers helped in ways too numerous to mention here. I especially appreciate the efforts of Eva Beattie who read the entire book and selflessly devoted herself to this project. Phillipp Lenssen provided a lot of information about both Google Web Services and Amazon Web Services. He also provided the inspiration for the combined Google and Amazon application. Osvaldo Téllez Almirall provided extensive input on international issues, making the book much better suited to international needs as a result. David Clark helped with accessibility, user interface, and PHP development issues.

Matt Wagner, my agent, deserves credit for helping me get the contract in the first place and taking care of all the details that most authors don't really consider. I always appreciate his help. It's good to know that someone wants to help.

Finally, I would like to thank Tom Cirtin, Leslie Light, Cheryl Hauser, and the rest of the editorial and production staff at Sybex for their assistance in bringing this book to print. It's always nice to work with such a great group of professionals and I very much appreciate the friendship we have built over the last two books.

Contents at a Glance

Contents

Introduction

If you wanted to know something in the ancient world, you visited one of the libraries of the time, such as the Great Library at Alexandria. Founded by Ptolemy I in 300 BC, the Great Library operated for over 700 years and contained 700,000 volumes at its peak. For its time, the Great Library was an impressive store of knowledge—more than any one person could possibly read in a lifetime. The Internet is the modern equivalent of the Great Library and it too contains an impressive store of knowledge—more than any one person is likely to need in a lifetime, much less read. Knowledge has always been the most valuable quantity in every society, and those who possess it and know how to use and manage it wield power and influence.

It's All about Information

Google is one of the best ways to find information on the Internet. This unique search engine combines simplicity and flexibility, with an elegant array of search features. You probably know that using Google to search for the information you need saves considerable time. Unfortunately, for everything Google has to offer, you still end up performing the search manually. You can still spend more time than you really have to research a topic just looking for the information. Reading and using the information seems impossible, in some cases, because the time just doesn't exist to do it. Even with Google, you're still not in full control over the Internet information store.

Fortunately, Google has a great answer to this problem in the form of Google Web Services. I wrote this book because I know from personal experience that spending 5 minutes to perform a search is better than spending a whole day. I do anything I can do to make the search process easier and more automatic. The examples in this book help you understand how to accomplish research in minutes, rather than days. With the right application, you can spend more time reading the information you find, which means you'll have an edge over everyone else who has to research the same material manually.

It wasn't until I had spent some time working with Google Web Services that I began to understand how truly flexible it is and what you can accomplish with it. For example, you can build an impressive search engine for a Web site using Google as the source of information. I'll show you how to construct site searches that makes Google into your personal site-specific search engine. Combine this functionality with a database and you can gain access to instant information about a particularly useful Web site.

You'll also find that you can combine Google with other Web services to create a greater whole. For example, you can combine Google Web Services and Amazon Web Services to create a personal store of shopping information. Whenever you're unsure about a purchase, you can learn more about the product and vendor through online links immediately. You don't need to leave the store, go home, and research the purchase anymore. In short, you can make better decisions than were previously possible in less time.

Yes, the Internet is a vast information store, but it's unmanageable without a good search engine. Google provides that search engine, and using Google Web Services can make the experience even better. This book is your key to unlocking the vast potential of the modern Great Library.

Who Should Read This Book?

I've designed this book to meet the needs of anyone who wants to use Google Web Services. You might be a corporate developer, a researcher, a college student, or a store owner running a small business who needs an Internet presence. Depending on your needs, you won't use every part of the book, but you'll find that most parts have something to offer. No matter who you are, make sure you read Chapters 1 through 4. Chapters 5 through 8 are language specific, so choose a language and read the appropriate chapter (more if you're multilingual). Chapter 9 helps anyone who wants to write an application for mobile devices. Finally, Chapters 10 and 11 will help people who want to go a little further in the development process. In short, the book has something for everyone, but you might not need to read everything.

Some people have noted that a one size fits all approach generally doesn't work. I realized this early on and made a few assumptions about your skills. You need to know something about computers—you can't pick up this book as a complete novice and expect to learn something. This book is packed with resources—many of which you'll need to locate on the Internet and read. I've assumed that you're motivated to learn what Google Web Services can do for you and will use these resources to augment the information that I've provided. That said, all of the examples include complete explanations, so you don't have to worry that this book is incomplete. In fact, you'll find many instances where the information provided here doesn't appear anywhere else.

It's possible to use this book without much programming knowledge, but you'll get a lot more out of it if you do know how to program at least a little. I've included a few examples in Chapters 2, 3, and 4 that don't require many programming skills. The VBA examples in Chapter 5 are very easy and might be the best choice if your programming skills are weak.

This book doesn't *teach* any of the programming languages it presents. It concentrates on Google Web Services and shows you how to *use* several programming languages to develop solutions of all types. Consequently, you won't want to look past the first four chapters until you've already learned to use the programming language of your choice. Because it's so important to know the language you want to use, I suggest several additional books you might want to try if you don't have the required background.

Tools Required

I've made some assumptions while writing the application programming examples in this book. During the writing of this book, I used a Windows 2000 server and two Windows XP workstations (along with other devices). I also tested many of the examples using Windows 9*x*. The test machines included SQL Server and MySQL. I also created Web server setups using Internet Information Server (IIS) and Apache. The test base was as broad as I could make it, but it wasn't possible for me to test every combination of machine and software.

I tested all of the examples in this book using the most current version of the appropriate language product. In most cases, I tell you which language version I used as part of the example description. I don't guarantee that the example will work with any older versions of the product, nor did I test using educational versions of products. Given the relative simplicity of Google Web Services, however, I'm certain that most examples will work with any newer version of the supported language.

All of the desktop and Web application examples will work on a single machine, but I tested all database applications on a two-machine setup as well to ensure you could place the database on another machine. The mobile device applications are all tested using an actual device, but I also tested them using an emulator. Chapter 9 tells you how to work with emulators and presents a number of emulators you might try when writing your application.

About the Author

John Paul Mueller is a freelance author and technical editor. He has writing in his blood, having produced 62 books and over 300 articles to date. The topics range from networking to artificial intelligence and from database management to heads down programming. Some of his current books include several C# developer guides, an accessible programming guide, a book on .NET security, and a book on Amazon Web Services. His technical editing skills have helped over 35 authors refine the content of their manuscripts. John has provided technical editing services to both *Data Based Advisor* and *Coast Compute* magazines. He's also contributed articles to magazines like *InformIT, SQL Server Professional, Visual C++ Developer, Hard Core Visual Basic, asp.netPRO,* and *Visual Basic Developer.* He's currently the editor of the .NET electronic newsletter for Pinnacle Publishing (http://www.freeenewsletters.com/).

When John isn't working at the computer, you can find him in his workshop. He's an avid woodworker and candle maker. On any given afternoon, you can find him working at a lathe or putting the finishing touches on a bookcase. He also likes making glycerin soap, which comes in handy for gift baskets. You can reach John on the Internet at `JMueller@mwt.net`. John also has a Web site at `http://www.mwt.net/~jmueller/`. Feel free to look and make suggestions on how he can improve it. One of his current projects is creating book FAQ sheets that should help you find the book information you need much faster.

Part I

▶ **Discovering** Google Web Services

Chapter 1

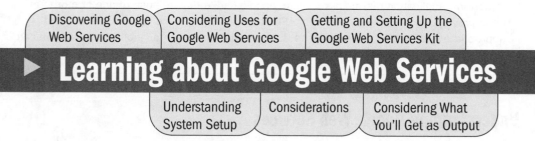

Discovering Google Web Services | Considering Uses for Google Web Services | Getting and Setting Up the Google Web Services Kit

Learning about Google Web Services

Understanding System Setup | Considerations | Considering What You'll Get as Output

Google is one of the most popular search engines around because it provides a superior number of hits. Of course, more hits don't translate into better data. The search engine is also good at providing valid information through the use of indexing and filtering so long as you specify the search criteria clearly. Given the number of ways that the Google Advanced Search (`http://www.google.com/advanced_search`) helps you look for information, providing clear direction can be overwhelming to some. The flexibility provided by the interface is part of Google's charm, however, and the reason many power users prefer Google. If you can't describe a search using this interface, you might not know what you're looking for.

Google Web Services is a means of accessing Google without going to the Web site and performing a search manually. This Web service provides essential services by helping you automate the search process and presenting data in the form that you need, rather than in the form that Google thinks you need. In this chapter, you discover how Google Web Services can help you perform searches faster and with greater accuracy. The result is that you'll reduce the time you spend searching and actually have time to do something with what you find.

It's not too amazing that Google Web Services is extremely popular—you can use it to find information located on any public Web site. In many ways, Google Web Services is superior to the manual search technique because automating a search saves both time and money. Even companies such as Macromedia (`http://www.macromedia.com/support/flash/applications/google_search/`) are getting into the act by providing tutorials and other support for Google Web Services. Google Web Services lets you look for information in many ways. For example, you could use it as the search engine for a small Web site. This chapter also discusses how you can use Google Web Services in other ways, how to download and install the kit that Google provides, and what you should expect as output.

> ▶ NOTE
>
> Various sources also refer to the Google Web Services as Google Web Application Programming Interfaces (APIs). The term *API* refers to a set of functions that a developer can call on to perform application tasks. For example, opening a file requires use of one or more functions provided by the operating system API. The term *Web service* is more specific and appropriate than API, so this book uses Google Web Services throughout. However, you can use the two terms interchangeably.

Understanding Google Web Services

Whenever a new technology appears on the scene, it's important to compare it with other technologies. The comparison process often helps you decide how this new technology differs from what you used in the past and reduces problems caused by hype. The media might try to convince you that a new product or service is something completely different, when in fact it's merely an update or a new implementation of an existing technology.

Currently, there's a lot of hype about Web services that makes them sound like something new and very complex. This section of the chapter defines Web services generally, examines Google Web Services specifically, and compares this technology to older technologies. What you'll find might surprise you because Web services are really a new implementation of an old technique.

> ▶ NOTE
>
> Don't confuse *new* with *useful*. Web services are very useful because they add new functionality to an existing idea that has worked for a long time. They're also new in that they use a different process from other technologies. However, the technology itself builds on other techniques that you have already used in some way. In sum, the implementation is new, the process is useful, but the technique is the same one you've used in the past.

What Is a Web Service?

You can look at a Web service from a number of perspectives. The easiest way to view a Web service is as a means of obtaining access to information. Essentially, you ask the server for information and the server returns that information in some form. The request and the returned information normally appear in eXtensible Markup Language (XML) form. Using XML preserves the meaning behind the information, regardless of the diversity of the platforms involved, so that you receive not only the information, but understand the context in which the information is used. The "Understanding XML Basics" section of Chapter 3 tells you more about XML. All you need to know now is that you receive information in XML format.

From a Google Web Services perspective, you request information based on any of a number of search criteria. Google supports a number of search techniques and not every technique works well for every kind of search. Chapter 2 discusses search techniques in detail. For now, just think of the search criteria as a form of request. The request defines the kind of information you want to know and how detailed that information will be. Google Web Services returns the information you request (when available) in a standardized format.

> **NOTE**

Google's database *schema* specifies the format of the information. A schema defines the organization of information in a database. Fortunately, the format of the data returned by Google is relatively simple. You only have to consider a few return types. However, the content of the return data is a different story. Learn more about the Google database schema in the "Understanding the Google Data Output" section of Chapter 4.

A Web service also performs some type of useful work. The useful work might be something as simple as interpreting your request, calculating the answer, and sending the result back. In the case of Google Web Services, the Web service accepts your request in the form of a search request, interacts with the database through a search engine to obtain the information you requested, and sends the information back to you. The search can take various forms. For example, you don't have to search all Web sites—you can concentrate on just one. You might want to look for pictures, rather than text, and might only have an interest in newsgroups. The rest of the book shows how to perform all of these tasks. The main idea is that you can submit a variety of search request types—the request type affects the information you receive back from Google.

The final consideration for a Web service (at least from the Web service user perspective) is that it executes on the remote machine, not on your machine. In short, this means you're using resources on that other machine with the permission of the machine's owner. The remote machine can set requirements for using the Web service, as well as require you to perform specific setup and security checks as part of your request. In the case of Google Web Services, you need to obtain this permission by requesting a license. You also need to download the Google Web Services Kit to ensure you follow the terms of the licensing agreement. The "Downloading and Installing the Kit" section of this chapter tells how to obtain the required permission and what this permission means to you.

> ▶ **TIP**
>
> You may find that Google Web Services is so indispensable that you'll want to work with Web services from other vendors. For example, Microsoft supports the MapPoint Web Service (`http://www.microsoft.com/mappoint/net/`). In time, standards organizations will set up directories of these Web services that you can access with ease. In the meantime, you can search for companies that offer Web services using the Web Services Finder page at `http://www.15seconds.com/WebService/`. Some people have problems using the Web Services Finder; it might produce an error instead of presenting a list of Web services. In some cases, you'll need to use a specialty Web service list such as the one at `http://www.flash-db.com/services/`. The Web services on this site are special because many of them perform one task well, such as providing you with a location based on a domain name.

How Do Web Services Work?

Many people fear new technology because they don't understand how it works, and many of those who do know how it works enjoy the mystique of knowledge too much to share it with anyone else. Web services are actually quite easy to understand if you look at them in a way that relates the task to everyday occurrences. For example, you might compare the operation of a Web service to making a withdrawal at the bank—the process really is the same. The one thing to remember is that the process a Web service uses to perform a task is always the same. No matter what technology you use to make a request or receive a response, the steps are still the same. Here are the steps that most Web services, including Google Web Services, use to complete a transaction.

1. *The client discovers the Web service.* During the act of discovery, the client might do things like download a file that tells how to interact with the Web service. This step is the same as someone walking into the bank. The person knows the bank exists and the bank teller might have noticed the person. The bank posts the rules for making a withdrawal or the teller might help a first-time customer understand the rules.

2. *The client makes a request based on the rules delivered during the discovery phase.* The rules might specify that the request has to appear in a certain form, and the client must provide specific data. This step is the same as the person walking up to the teller's window with a withdrawal request. The request must contain the person's account number, the amount they wish to withdraw, and other identifying information. The bank specifies the format of the request and the information it must contain.

3. *The server might ask the client for credentials depending on the openness of the Web service.* Google Web Services is public but still requires that you supply a developer license (account) number as identification. This step is the same as the bank teller asking you for a driver's license or other form of identification before honoring your withdrawal request.

4. *The Web service performs the work required to honor your request.* In most cases, the Web service accesses a database for information, it could enter an order, and it might even provide some level of formatting information about the original information (such as the typeface used for a word-processed document). Google Web Services performs a number of tasks depending on the request you make. The easiest request is a general search, but you can also perform checks such as making a spelling check. This step equates to the bank teller getting the money from the drawer and counting it.

5. *The Web service sends the data to the client.* The content of the information depends on the Web service. Google Web Services provides data in a very specific format based on the content of the associated database and the nature of the request. This step equates to the teller handing the person their money. In general, the teller orders the money in a specific way and counts it out to the person, rather than simply handing the money over.

6. *The client logs out of the Web service or the Web service disconnects the client after some period of inactivity.* This step equates to the person leaving the bank, money in hand. If the person doesn't leave the bank (they just hang out in the lobby), you can be sure that someone will ask them to leave.

7. *The client does something with the data it receives.* In many cases, it formats the data and presents it on screen for the user. This step equates to the person spending the money they receive from the bank.

You can add any amount of complexity needed to the individual steps, but these seven steps define the process every Web server follows. When you break a Web service down into these seven steps, the process that used to appear as magic suddenly becomes quite doable. Chapters 5 through 9 are essentially options you can use to perform these seven steps using different technologies. This book explores the seven steps using various languages and platforms—Google Web Services makes information available to just about anyone who needs it. However, it's important to remember that everything comes down to a client making a request and the Web server returning data.

Considering the Usage Requirements

There's no free lunch. Some people would have you believe that the Web service does everything for you and that the client does nothing at all. However, the client interacts with the Web service, which means the client must possess some intelligence to perform the task. To use a Web service, you must understand the usage requirements.

From a client perspective, the type of device you use to access the Web service determines the access speed, as well as what you can do with the data once you receive it. Although a PDA such as the Pocket PC can access Google Web Services just fine, you wouldn't want to use it to perform detailed searches or attempt complex activities such as converting data to another language. About the best you can hope for is to perform simple research. On the other hand, a desktop or laptop machine has all of the processing power, screen real estate, and functionality to perform any task. Google Web Services hasn't changed, but the capability of the client has.

> ▶ **NOTE**
>
> This book discusses a number of mobile devices. The Pocket PC provides additional functionality and features that make it a better target for some types of applications than devices such as the Palm. On the other hand, most Palm devices are much easier to carry and cost less than the Pocket PC. This book examines the entire range of mobile devices to ensure you understand the limitations of using a specific device to access Google Web Services. I'm not saying one device is better than another—simply that one device works better than the other for a given application.

Google Web Services also has some usage requirements and these requirements might change the way that you use your client. For example, according to the license agreement (see Appendix B for details) you can't make more than 1,000 requests per day—at least, not without special permission. The request limitation ensures the Google servers won't become overloaded, but they also mean you must provide some type of monitoring in your application to prevent abuse of the licensing terms.

> ▶ **WARNING**
>
> If you violate the licensing terms, Google Web Services simply denies your request. In addition, you might receive a message from Google requesting that you adhere to the terms of usage for the Web service.

Often, you can get around the licensing requirements for a Web service by using smart programming techniques. For example, Google doesn't require that you refresh the information you receive at any specific interval. You determine when the information you receive is too old. Using good caching techniques means that you can create applications that are lightning fast, unless the request is new or the data is old. Although it seems as if a 1,000-request limit could cause problems, you can usually satisfy far more than 1,000 requests per day by using smart data caching.

Discovering Uses for Google Web Services

Everyone associates Google with searches of various kinds. Many people use Google for simple searches. In fact, you can set browsers such as Internet Explorer to go directly to Google whenever you enter a set of search terms in the address bar. One way to do this is to use a tool such as Tweak UI to create special search entries. You could also install the Google Toolbar (`http://toolbar.google.com/`), which has the option of making your default search engine Google. However, this book doesn't go into a detailed discussion of ways to manage simple manual Google searches.

This book helps you perform complex searches quickly, more reliably, and with less effort than any manual search can provide. Power users tend to use Google for intense searches, so they usually go directly to the Google Advanced Search page at `http://www.google.com/advanced_search`. (Some power users go so far as to memorize all of the special search terms Google uses so they can type everything in the basic search field.) Figure 1.1 shows an example of this page. Notice that you can manually search for a topic using a number of criteria, such as language and file format.

FIGURE 1.1:
Use the Google Advanced Search page to get a feel for the power of the Web service.

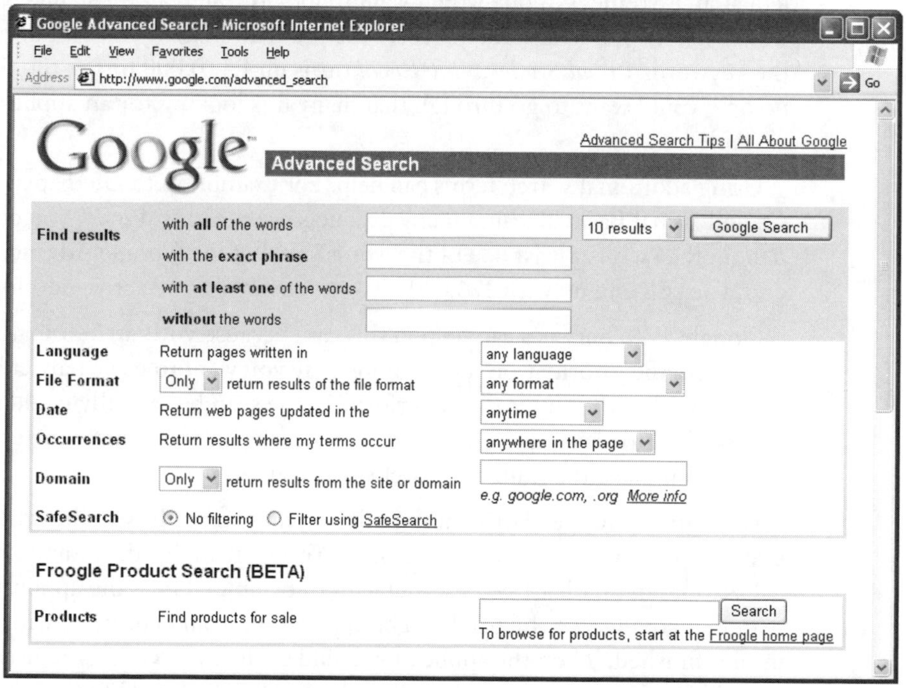

The Google Advanced Search page is useful because it helps you understand some of the power of the Google search engine. This page points to the need for some kind of automation in searching for information online. Not only does the page accept a number of inputs, but also permutations of the inputs will affect the output you see. Consequently, attempting to perform all searches manually is a time-consuming effort that many people would like to automate.

Now that you have a better idea of why you might not want to perform every search manually, it's time to consider specific ways to use Google Web Services. The following sections provide ideas on how you can improve productivity and make research easier using Google Web Services. The programming chapters of the book expand on many of these ideas by showing you how to implement them using code.

Performing Research

One of the most common uses of Google is performing research. Research searches normally begin based on keywords. The problem is that some keywords are ambiguous enough that the resulting data isn't meaningful. Try using *Windows* as a search term and you'll see this problem at an extreme. No one would want to look through all those hits. Using multiple keywords can help, but still doesn't solve the problem in many cases. For example, a search of the keywords *Visual Studio .NET Email* turns up 1,110,000 hits at the time of this writing—no one would want to go through that many hits looking for an application programming example.

Using additional search terms can help. For example, let's say that you're proficient in using C# and Visual Basic. Because many products use the term *Visual*, you could enter just *C#* and *Basic* in the "with at least one of the words" field of the Google Advanced Search page. However, you still end up with 276,000 hits—too many for the active developer to search.

Google Web Services can help in this case because you can automate multiple searches to locate specific information. For example, say you want to use a particular class or you have a special need in the application. Performing the search manually could require multiple trips to Google. However, using Web services means you could enter the criteria once and let the application make the multiple searches for you.

Even given the speed of an automatic search, you might wonder whether it's worth the effort of using Google Web Services. However, an application can do something that a manual search can't (at least not without a lot of trouble). Once the application returns from the search, it could store the results. The application would continue with each search scenario until it finished. Then the application could analyze the various returns and create a list of most likely sites based on the results. The 1,110,000 *Visual Studio .NET email* hits could suddenly become 20 or 25 hits that truly have useful information.

Conducting an Expansion Search

Expansion searches help you locate all available information on a topic by playing to the features that Google provides. For example, the order of search terms is important in the way that Google interprets a search. In addition, if you work in an acronym-laden field, expanding the acronyms is important to locate all sources of information on a given topic. Consider the following permutations of a search using the keywords *Visual Basic serial port*.

Visual Basic Serial Port   This combination returns 132,000 hits with a first site of `http://www.distiworld.com/cd-burner-to-download.htm`.

Serial Port Visual Basic   Just changing the two groups of words around reduces the number of hits to 130,000 with a first site of `http://www.lvr.com/spc.htm`.

Serial Port VB   Using the *VB* acronym reduces the number of hits further to 58,200 with a first site of `http://www.control.com/1026175817/index_html`.

VB Serial Port   You'd think that this number would be higher than the *Serial Port VB* search because of previous results. However, the number of hits is only 57,300 with a first site of `http://forums.basicmicro.net/ShowPost.aspx?PostID=7638`.

Four sets of keywords (and you could easily do more), four completely different results—it's not hard to understand why an expansion search could help you obtain the maximum benefit from Google. Manual expansion searches become cumbersome for a number of reasons. Repetition is one of the main causes, but there are others such as entry errors and result interpretation. You have to provide enough keywords to make a search specific, but each keyword adds an order of complexity to the expansion search.

Google Web Services steps in by letting you perform an expansion search automatically using code. You supply the four keywords—the code does the rest. By comparing the results of each expansion search, you can come up with an optimal group of sites. For example, you could verify that the site appears in every expansion search return, which tends to reduce the false positives. You can also rate the sites based on the number of times they appear and their position in the list. Although it's possible to perform this kind of data manipulation using a manual search, no one would want to do it.

Searching a Specific Site

Some Web sites don't provide a search engine. The site might be too small to support a search feature or hosted so the developer doesn't have access to the server's search feature. In other cases, a site does provide a search engine, but the search engine doesn't work nearly as well as Google's. You may find that the search engine fails to produce the desired results, even when you know the information exists. In both cases, you can create a site-specific search using Google Web Services.

You can perform this kind of search manually. In fact, it's not even all that time consuming. However, remembering the information you have to provide in an URL or going to Google's advanced search site every time you want to perform the search is a headache. Using Web services lets you store all of the static settings—the ones that won't change—so that all you need to know is what keywords you want to enter for that site. A site-specific search is all about convenience. Using this technique makes it easier to get the information you need without a lot of effort.

One way to use this technique is to create a search setup for your personal Web site. Many Web sites owned by individuals or the self-employed appear on hosted sites, making it impossible to add search capability with any ease. A Google Web Services application can make it easy to add a professional search service to your site, making it a lot more attractive to anyone who visits.

Another way to use this technique is to create custom search Web pages. I built one for my personal use that includes links to all my favorite coding sites. All I do now is select the site I want to search, add a few keywords, and Google Web Services takes care of all the hard work for me. Not only am I more productive, but I can stay focused on the task at hand—finding sample code. I can even make searches of multiple sites with a single click. Even though multiple searches take place in the background (a minimum of one search for each site), I only click the search button once.

Learning More about a Site

What do you really know about a Web site before you visit it? This question takes many people by surprise because they have to admit that they really don't know anything about the site. However, visiting a site implies that you're willing to open yourself to anything the site can provide within the limitations of your browser. A site that contains pornographic material or a virus when you're conducting legitimate research on parts of the human anatomy is an unwelcome surprise that you could avoid.

Google provides a number of searches you can use to verify the usefulness of a Web site before you visit it. For example, you can begin by looking for keywords in the snippet and site summary that Google provides. An examination of the links for the site, along with the Web information it provides is revealing. Figure 1.2 shows the results of an informational search on my Web site.

You can also conduct a related links search to see how the site connects to the rest of the Internet. (Chapter 2 discusses search types in detail, so don't worry if these specialized searches are unfamiliar.) If you're truly uncertain about the usefulness of the site, you can view a cached version of the page. The cached version does contain old data, but it can help you check for objectionable terms or content without exposing yourself to as much risk. The point is that with the security problems that users face today, they need a better way to assess the risk of visiting a particular site online. A fact-finding search is very useful in keeping some types of Internet risks at bay.

Unfortunately, few users are going to take the time to perform such fact-finding before visiting a site. It's simply easier to click on the URL and go there. However, you could build a Google Web Services application that would display the search results and assess the potential of a Web site before the user visits there, while maintaining single click efficiency. When the user clicks a link, your application can check the site in the background and verify that it's reasonably safe. What the user sees is the normal sequence of events that take place when they click the link.

Getting Old Data from the Cache

The Internet is constantly changing. In fact, it changes so fast sometimes that it's hard to keep all of the links updated. Anyone who spends any amount of time researching information online knows that even the links Google provides get outdated. However, seeing an error message, page not found, when you click that link isn't the end of the road. You can request cached data from Google. The cached information is old in many cases, but at least it's available and you can use it for whatever you need. Figure 1.3 shows a typical example of a cached data page.

Like many other kinds of Google searches, you can perform a cache search manually. However, you have to perform multiple keystrokes to perform the search, assuming you remember to do it. Many people simply move on to the next site without thinking when they reach an error message.

FIGURE 1.2:

Informational searches help you learn more about a Web site before you visit.

FIGURE 1.3:

Cached data searches can be very helpful, especially during research.

A Google Web Services application can reduce the problems of the dead link. It could begin by searching for the site. If the site isn't available, the application can move on to the cached page. When Google doesn't provide a cached page (a rarity), the application can move on to related links. Even if these techniques fail, the application could use some kinds of regressive searching. A regression search is one in which you begin with the result data and look for the information used to create the results. The point is the user wouldn't see an error message—a page of some kind would display and the user would then make the decision on the value of that page.

Performing Spell Checking

Interestingly, the spelling check is one of the few Google Web Services tasks that you can't perform manually. To use this feature, you send a string (up to 2,048 characters long) to Google Web Services. The Web service checks the string for spelling errors and sends the corrected string back to you.

At first, you might wonder how you would use this service. After all, it's relatively easy to find a local spell checker that won't use one or more of the 1,000 calls that Google allots to each developer per day. The answer is that you wouldn't use this service personally in most cases. However, if you're running a Web site that requests text input from users, you can use the spell checker to validate their work.

Because the data you receive as input from the user contains fewer errors, you'll also end up doing less work. For example, any database you use to maintain the user input will have fewer errors, so you'll spend less time looking for errant records.

Avoiding Pornographic Material

The Internet contains all kinds of pornographic material. No matter what your personal preferences are, this material becomes annoying at some point because it tends to get in the way of legitimate research. In addition, you don't want children to see this kind of material, and it can cause problems in the workplace. Fortunately, Google does provide a means of searching the Internet without running into too much pornographic material. In fact, you can theoretically eliminate all of it through wise keyword search choices.

Google provides an actual search feature that blocks pornographic sites based on your choice of keywords. The feature does work for the most part, unless your selection of keywords is less than perfect. For example, using *breast* as one of the keywords in a safe search produces a number of sites for cancer research and many forms of help or assistance. Using the standard search produces the expected results (13,000,000 of them). Unfortunately, figuring out which keywords to avoid isn't always easy.

Like many of the other tasks discussed in this section, you could perform this task manually and might even get good at it given enough time. However, Google Web Services can make the search process a lot more efficient. For example, you can create an application to perform a keyword translation to help you avoid the terms that produce pornographic results. When you couple this application with the safe search feature, all you'll receive is sites that contain the kind of information you need.

Downloading and Installing the Kit

Before you begin working with Google Web Services, you need to obtain the kit and a developer license. Once you have the kit, you need to install it and become familiar with its content. The following sections describe the kit-related tasks you need to perform.

Performing the Download

Downloading the kit is easy. You'll find the main Web services page at `http://www.google.com/apis/`. Figure 1.4 shows that this page contains information, along with two important links. Although the steps shown in the figure are numbered, you can perform the first two steps in any order. This chapter assumes that you want to download the Google Web Services Kit first.

FIGURE 1.4:

You can obtain
both the kit and the
developer license on
this site.

Click the download link and you'll see a page that describes the kit. This page also includes
the licensing agreement for the Google Web Services Kit. Make sure you read the licensing
agreement and understand what it means before you proceed (Appendix B provides a licensing agreement checklist you can use for your applications). Don't worry about copying the
licensing agreement to disk—the kit includes a copy of the licensing agreement you can use
for reference purposes later. Check the "I have read and agree with the Google Web APIs
license terms" option and then click Download Now. You'll see a File Download dialog box.
Click Save and you'll see a Save As dialog box. The default name of the file is GoogleAPI.ZIP,
but you can save it using another name if desired. Click Save and you'll receive the file—a
mere 666 KB in size.

Getting a License

Once you complete the download process, click the Create a Google Account link that is
available on the same page as the Google Web Services Kit download. You'll see a Web page
that requests an email address and password. This page also contains links to Google's terms
of service and privacy statements. Make sure you read both before you proceed. The Google
Web Services Kit doesn't include copies of either document, so you might want to copy the

information and save it on disk for use later. When you finish reading both documents, check the "I have read and accepted the Google Terms of Service above and Privacy Policy" option and click Create My Google Account.

> ▶ **WARNING**

The process described in this section doesn't always work as anticipated. In some cases, Google displays an error message during the email verification process. In other cases, you may think the email verification worked correctly, but never receive a confirmation email from Google containing your license key. When either of these problems occur, contact Google support at `accounts-support@google.com` for assistance. The support staff will usually send another confirmation email to your inbox that you can use to confirm your account. Never assume the process has worked until you receive the license key.

At this point, you'll see a message stating that Google will send a verification message to your email. Click on the link provided by the verification message to activate your account. After you verify your account, Google will send your developer license to your email. The license normally arrives in about an hour—you might need to wait more or less time depending on how busy Google is at the moment. Make sure you save the email message containing the developer license because you'll need it for every transaction later.

> ▶ **TIP**

You can always change the password and other information associated with your account. Simply go to the Google Accounts site at `https://www.google.com/accounts/Login`. Type your name and password to enter the site. Select the My Account link to change the account information.

Installing the Kit

The kit is actually a Zip file containing examples and documentation. If you're running Windows XP, the operating system provides a program to unpack the file for you. Otherwise, you'll need a special program that reads the compressed file and unpacks it for you such as WinZip (`http://www.winzip.com`).

You won't find any actual developer tools in the Zip file. The file does include complete path information, so you can unpack it in the root folder of your hard drive if you like. I used the D drive on my system, so the Google Web Services Kit appears in the `D:\GoogleAPI` folder.

At this point, the kit is ready for use. However, before you go any further, you need to know about two files in the \GoogleAPI folder. The LICENSE.TXT file contains a copy of the license agreement that you saw online. Make sure you retain this file so that you can refer back to the usage terms as needed.

> ▶ **NOTE**
>
> Google will eventually update their Web services package and could change the licensing agreement as well. You might wonder whether the online version of the agreement overrides the version of the agreement that comes with the Google Web Services Kit that you down-loaded. Unfortunately, Google doesn't address this concern in their license and not being a lawyer, I can't advise you. If you have questions about the terms of using Google Web Services, make sure you contact Google at api-support@google.com.

The README.TXT file contains useful information about the Google Web Services Kit and tells you where you can obtain additional information. This file is very helpful because it contains URLs where you can obtain additional examples. It also has URLs for help sites and additional information. Finally, you'll want to read this file if you want to run the examples because it contains instructions for using them. Interestingly enough, even though the kit doesn't include a Practical Extraction and Reporting Language (PERL) example, this file also includes instructions for using Google Web Services with PERL.

System Setup Considerations

Once you obtain the Google Web Services Kit and a developer license, it's easy to think that you're ready to write your first program. Theoretically, you can do just that. The problem with proceeding at this point though is that you don't know about the viability of your system configuration. For example, if you have a very fast processor and a lot of memory, it's easy to assume the page you've designed will work fine on all systems. However, once you load the resulting application on someone else's machine, it might not work very quickly (if at all).

Defining a usable development setup can save you considerable time and effort later. When you create a great development environment, you ensure that you'll see the application as the user does, which reduces the potential for deadly errors. Because the Google Web Services Kit is so accommodating, you'll need to spend a little extra time considering all of the possible usage scenarios. The following sections provide tips you can use to reduce the setup complexity.

Understanding Connectivity Requirements

You must consider three kinds of connectivity when you set up your development system. The first level of connectivity is your own machine. Make sure your machine has a connection to the Internet. Otherwise, any tests you run will fail. Remember that a Web service runs on the remote machine, not your local machine. You're borrowing the resources of that remote machine to perform useful work.

The second level of connectivity is the user's machine. If you create a Web site that simply contains links to Google's Web site, you can assume the user has a connection, but how fast is that connection? The best Web sites I've seen ask about the user's connection speed. This question allows the application to send the user the level of information that their connection can comfortably support. If you know that most users will rely on a dial-up connection for your Web site, make sure you also use a dial-up connection for testing. This additional step can greatly reduce the chances that you'll make the application too robust. Users who leave your site and don't use your application are users who are probably visiting someone else.

The third level of connectivity is the non-connected mode. You need to consider what happens when the user loses the connection or doesn't have one available. Applications can store static data locally to enable the user to continue using data they have already queried from the Web service. However, you need to observe any refresh requirements and ensure the data retains the same information the user would see online. For example, the local copy of the data must include any required copyright statements or trademarks.

> ▶ **NOTE**
>
> Google's licensing terms are flexible in that they allow you to store information as long as that information remains viable to you and you retain your relationship with Google. This flexibility means you can create user applications that only query Google when necessary, instead of for each request. It's important to note that any application you create using Google Web Services will require your license to access the site. Any queries a user makes using your application will count against your licensed access total for the day. The best policy is to ensure the user obtains a personal license from Google whenever possible. Your application can request this license information from the user so the user's access doesn't count against your total.

Programming Setups for the Non-Developer

Many of the people reading this book have marginal experience with programming or do it as a hobby. It's true that Web services rely on the resources of the remote machine, but it's also true that the client must perform work too. If you have a machine that's already marginal—

that doesn't run applications well—trying to write a Web service application for it could make matters worse. The local machine must have resources for using the Web service application.

> ▶ **NOTE**
>
> This book doesn't teach you how to program, so make sure you spend at least a little time learning one of the programming languages discussed in this book before you begin working with the examples. I do provide good descriptions of the applications, but these descriptions won't be enough if you don't understand basic programming concepts.

Depending on the kind of application you create, you'll also need local resources for the programming environment. For example, VBA users have not only the Office application of choice running, but also the VBA development environment. The addition of the VBA development environment can reduce your system performance to a crawl and give you unrealistic performance for your application.

It's also possible for you to speed things up too much. If the target platform is a 400MHz Pentium and you're using a 3GHz development machine, your application performance will look nothing like the user's performance in most cases. For a Web site, the machine performance differences might not be quite as significant as when you develop applications that run on the desktop.

Considering the User

Depending on how you use the Web application you build, user needs will take on significant importance. Many applications start out as projects that the developer is creating for personal use. Some of the best applications I've written fall into this category. However, taking shortcuts in developing the user interface, even if you're the only user, is never a good idea. At one time, I wrote rough applications that I understood but couldn't use efficiently because they were only for test purposes. After I ended up rewriting a number of the applications because I couldn't figure them out or other people asked me for copies, I began writing every program as if it were for someone else.

The applications you write with Google Web Services will likely see use from other people, even if you don't know it right now. Consequently, you need to consider what a hypothetical user will need. For example, you might need to include a few special search options. Sure, you could get the same results by typing a little extra text, but adding the functionality directly into your application makes it easier to use (faster in most cases as well).

It's also important to consider users with special needs. The "Addressing Users with Special Needs" section of Chapter 11 contains details on this topic, but you might need to perform setups before you even begin coding. For example, if you work on a Windows machine, you'll probably want to set up the Accessibility features (these features normally appear in the Control Panel and within the Start\Programs\Accessories\Accessibility folder).

Using Multiple Test Devices

If your application will appear on the Internet, you need to test using multiple devices. It's no longer safe to assume that only desktop users will have an interest in your application. You might attract Personal Digital Assistant (PDA) and cellular telephone users as well. This is especially true of a Web application that helps users find a particular kind of information quickly. People often rely on these applications when time is tight and they don't have time to look for a product themselves.

> ▶ **NOTE**
>
> Not every developer is concerned about writing applications for every platform—sometimes it's a matter of time; other times it's a matter of skill or perceived need. When an application you write falls into this category, you can still provide a modicum of support for wireless users by directing them to Google Wireless Services at http://www.google.com/options/wireless.html.

It would be nice if everyone could afford to test every application on every device, but that's not realistic for the developer. Sometimes you need to use an emulator to perform the testing because you don't have the real device handy. Fortunately, you can find a vast array of useful emulators on the Internet—everything from the Pocket PC to cellular telephones of all types. Emulators have limitations, but they do make good test devices in many cases. We'll discuss the advantages and concerns of using emulators in the "Working with Emulators" section of Chapter 9.

Sometimes it also helps to have multiple desktop machine setups. For example, you might need to consider how a Web page looks and acts in Netscape versus Internet Explorer. (Theoretically, you can run both browsers from the same machine, but doing so causes interference problems that some developers find distasteful.) Differences in how the browsers react to specific Web page designs could cause problems in your application. In some cases, you'll need multiple machines to perform this kind of testing. For example, you might need to consider how the application looks on a Macintosh versus a PC if your application has broad enough appeal. Obviously, you can still write Google Web Services applications if you don't have a multiple machine setup, but having more than one machine does make development tasks a lot easier and less error prone.

Emulating the Real World

Developers often live in a laboratory. In the laboratory, everyone has the proper equipment, fast machines, and an even faster connection. The user never disconnects unexpectedly and always knows how to get the most out of their computer. The problem with the lab is that it doesn't model the real world. In the real world, users get bored, try odd key combinations just to see what they do, don't understand their computer very well, but do know how to complain about the smallest application problems. If you want to avoid problems with the application you develop, you need to create a development environment that models the real world.

It's also easy to get lost in the development environment setup. Make sure you understand the person who uses your application. For example, it's quite possible that only desktop users will have any interest in your site on desktop machine maintenance, but you need to determine that fact in some way (online surveys work well). You also don't want to spend a lot of time testing the application to meet the needs of users who have no use for your product. Again, surveys and newsgroup polls are helpful in determining the real world environment that you must emulate with your system.

Knowing What to Expect as Output

For many developers, the idea of a Web service is easy to grasp—knowing what to expect from it is hard. The output begins with a certain amount of raw data that you'll receive from the Web service. However, the raw data doesn't really define the Web service output completely. You also need to consider quantifiable components such as the input to the Web service and that data manipulation you'll perform. In addition, there are variant elements to the output, such as the timeliness of the data. Finally, you need to consider the intangible elements. The output has some value to you, but someone else will view the output in another way. Concepts such as relevancy are difficult to quantify or even define.

Google Web Services is no different from any other Web service when it comes to output. You'll provide input, receive raw data, manipulate that data in some way, and view the output—the result of everything you have done with the Web service. The following sections discuss various elements of Web service output as they relate to Google Web Services. These sections provide an overview—the book continues to explore the subject in other chapters. However, this is the starting point—the point at which you start to consider what to expect as output from your efforts.

Limitations of Google Web Services Output

Many developers are used to working with a variety of data types when creating applications. Data types help define the kind of data you're using. For example, if a data element is a number, you might use an integer (a number without a decimal) or real number (one that has a decimal and equates to a Single or Double for Visual Basic developers). A Web service has no concept of data type when it comes to the data itself. Every data transfer is text. The XML used to transfer the data does include type information, but of the sort that's normally associated with database fields, which means you have to know the field names to make an interpretation. For example, you might receive data in a message like the one shown here.

```
<item xsi:type="ns1:ResultElement">
   <cachedSize xsi:type="xsd:string">12k</cachedSize>
   <hostName xsi:type="xsd:string" />
   <snippet xsi:type="xsd:string">
      <b>...</b> some text <b>highlight</b>) more text <b>...</b>
   </snippet>
   <directoryCategory xsi:type="ns1:DirectoryCategory">
      <specialEncoding xsi:type="xsd:string" />
      <fullViewableName xsi:type="xsd:string" />
   </directoryCategory>
   <relatedInformationPresent xsi:type="xsd:boolean">
      True
   </relatedInformationPresent>
   <directoryTitle xsi:type="xsd:string" />
   <summary xsi:type="xsd:string" />
   <URL xsi:type="xsd:string">
      http://www.mwt.net/~jmueller
   </URL>
   <title xsi:type="xsd:string"><b>DataCon Services</b></title>
</item>
```

You don't have to understand the XML portion of this message segment, but look at the data. Google Web Services sends all data as characters (as do all other Web services) and defines the data using tags (the words between the angle brackets) and attributes (extra information within the tag). For example, the line that contains <URL xsi:type="xsd:string"> http://www.mwt.net/~jmueller</URL> includes the <URL> tag that tells you that this value is http://www.mwt.net/~jmueller and that the tag type is an xsi:type="xsd:string". The tag tells you what kind of information this is. By knowing the Google database layout, you also know the data type and other information about the entry. However, the information you receive from Google is still plain text. You can see other examples of XML responses in the \GoogleAPI\soap-samples of the kit. Simply open them using Internet Explorer or another browser that supports XML. Figure 1.5 shows a typical view of one of the examples in the folder.

FIGURE 1.5:

View example files using Internet Explorer or other XML-compatible browser.

Your browser is actually very handy for viewing XML data, even if it might not make sense right now. The "Viewing XML Data in Your Browser" section of Chapter 3 discusses in detail how you can use your browser. For right now, all you need to know is that you can look at the various kinds of XML responses by opening the files in your browser.

Figure 1.5 points to another potential problem with Web service output. All of the tags and other information supplied in a request and response consume space. The file is larger than a text file with the same data because of all the tag information required. In addition, it's far more efficient to store many data types in their native format, rather than use characters. Consequently, Web service data suffers from bloat. The data uses more bandwidth than a binary message and consequently, you could experience performance problems. Because of this issue, you need to create efficient queries for your application that maximize data throughput despite the limitations of the XML format. The "Making Sensible Queries" section of the chapter discusses this issue in detail.

The results you obtain from Google are largely a matter of the input you provide in the form of a request. The "Conducting an Expansion Search" section of the chapter points out a serious flaw in making any assumptions about the return you receive from Google. The query can become quite complex because even the order of the words makes a difference in the results you receive. Google must make this assumption because most people enter the words in the order they think about them, which is usually most important to least important. Consequently, if you always assume that your first query returns all possible results, you'll find Google Web Services disappointing.

The ranking of results you receive from Google Web Services is also unlikely to be the same as the ranking you need. Google sells keywords to make some sites turn up higher in the result list. In addition, Google often bases the site ranking on criteria that won't match your own, such as the number of times that a keyword appears. The bottom line is that the output you receive from Google is "raw" output—information that you haven't filtered or organized in any way. One of the reasons to use Google Web Services is to enable you to perform tasks such as site ranking so the results appear in the order that's best for your organization.

Making Sensible Queries

Google Web Services can help you perform a number of tasks. The problem is that each request and response consumes resources. To get the most from this Web service, you need to optimize the requests and responses so that the value of the information you receive exceeds the cost of transmitting and manipulating the data.

Creating a request and then handling the response has several costs associated with it. Some of the costs are real world in that you must provide the infrastructure required to perform the task. Inefficient queries could mean adding additional bandwidth capacity or providing additional servers (if you make enough queries). Some costs are employee related—inefficient queries mean more waiting time as the computer crunches the data. Finally, inefficient queries can incur intangible costs. For example, people can become frustrated with poor query results, which affects their performance. Some of these costs are impossible to measure accurately, but they're real.

I often rely on the online search engine to help tune queries. Using the Advanced Search (`http://www.google.com/advanced_search`) page shown in Figure 1.1 can help you define and tune searches to obtain maximum data with minimal resource use. For example, computer technology is quickly outdated, so I normally provide a date range as part of my search. Using the online search to customize the date range for specific keywords can greatly enhance performance.

The Advanced Search page can help you tune keyword order—making it possible to reduce the number of keyword permutations you use on an expanded search (see the "Conducting an Expansion Search" section of the chapter for details). It also helps you decide on how to use permanent keywords. For example, a site that sells a specific product might include the product name as a permanent search term—one that is always included even if the user doesn't specify it.

One of the features the kit provides is a more complete list of special phrases and characters you can use for a search. Although the Advanced Search page will help you ferret out many of these search features, you won't find them all. For example, the Advanced Search page includes a blank for a search phrase, which is different from a keyword in that the search phrase must appear as specified on the target page (keywords can appear in any order). Fortunately, all of the special keywords and characters mentioned in the kit also work on the Advanced Search page so you can try them out. (Chapter 2 discusses search techniques in detail.) Depending on which special features you use for a search, Google Web Services output might not provide the information you imagined. Consequently, it pays to try these special features out to see what effect they have on your search results.

> **▶ TIP**
>
> You might wonder why I'm suggesting such heavy use of the Advanced Search page. Google allows you to make 1,000 requests per day using Google Web Services. The Advanced Search page doesn't have such a limit—making it easier to keep testing search techniques until you find the technique you want to use in your code. At that point, you can start making requests from Google Web Services to test your code. Don't waste calls on search techniques.

Even when you create a perfect search and properly filter the results using code, the information you receive from Google Web Services might not fulfill every need. At some point, you need to perform some level of human filtering. Users will need to state a preference or define how well a particular search result works. Only by tuning the filter can you hope to obtain specific results from Google Web Services. Tuning makes it possible to reduce search times from hours to minutes.

Defining Static and Dynamic Data

Web applications can include the concept of static and dynamic data. Dynamic data is the best type to use for Web services because it reflects changes in the Google database. An application gains important benefits by using dynamic data. For example, you won't try to access an old Web site that Google used to list because the dynamic nature of your application automatically removes the link from the list of results.

Unfortunately, dynamic data can also cause problems. For one thing, you need a connection to the Internet to work with dynamic data. When you use a desktop machine, maintaining a connection usually isn't a problem. However, many third party developers are working on applications where a connection might not be available, such as a research list application for a PDA. You download the information from Google Web Services and then use it to create a report while on the road—the connection doesn't exist while you're on the road so the data is no longer dynamic.

> ▶ **NOTE**
>
> Google does support the concept of cached data that is stored from the original Web site, but even the cached data ages at some point and becomes unavailable. Cached data does have an important use. For example, you can use cached data to obtain copies of old articles that a Web site no longer carries.

Using the term *dynamic* to refer to application data is also somewhat of a misnomer. Nothing is truly a dynamic data application. The moment the response to your query leaves the Google server, it begins to age. The data doesn't change once it leaves the Google server, so in reality it isn't truly dynamic. The only way you can achieve a dynamic presentation of sorts is to make multiple queries. You must define how often is often enough for your needs. Google doesn't provide any guidance in this case because search result viability varies by person, focus, and need.

These facts lead into the discussion of static data. Truly static data never changes at all. Most Web sites still rely on static data presentation because the information they display doesn't change often enough to warrant a dynamic presentation. When you make a single query to Google Web Services, the response you receive is static data. It's a snapshot of that particular part of the database at a specific time. The data won't change unless you make another query.

Understanding the static and dynamic nature of data is important when you design an application that relies on Google Web Services. Errors creep into the presentation you create as the data from Google Web Services ages on your system. Part of the design process for your application is to determine how much error you can accept.

Your Call to Action

If you've read the entire chapter, you know what a Web service is, how the Google Web Services fits within the general definition of a Web service, and what you can use the Google Web Services to do. You can use this knowledge to create opportunities to exercise Google as a search engine for all kinds of tasks. Data mining is increasing in importance as companies strive to gain more from the resources of the Internet—this technique accesses the needed information and discards unneeded information. At this point, you also have a machine that's setup to create a Google Web Services application of some sort and you have the Google Web Services Kit installed.

The next step of the process is to evaluate where you're going based on the content of this chapter. You need to consider what you want to do with the information Google provides, how you plan to present it, your own capabilities, and the capabilities of the person using your application. This may sound like a lot of work, but it's important to create a firm foundation for your application. When you take these preliminary steps, you begin thinking about problems and solutions to those problems.

Chapter 2 builds on the knowledge you gained in this chapter. The emphasis of Chapter 2 is on data mining—the process of using specialized search techniques to whittle search results down to just the links you need. In many cases, you can also access these search techniques using Google search page, but the emphasis of data mining is automation. Only by using the Google Web Services can you automate the search process and then display the results in the form you want, rather than rely on Google's formatting methodology.

Chapter 2

Using Typical Search Techniques · Using Special Search Techniques · Searching for Specific Files

▶ Defining a Search

Learning about the Target Web Site · Working with Cached Data · Using Filtering and Restrictions to Your Advantage · Reducing Pornography with Safe Searches

Anyone who needs an example of information overload can look no further than Google. The possibilities for searching on Google are unlimited. I've spent many hours on Google looking for information I need, and many of the products I buy now are the results of Google searches for vendors. However, the simplest Google searches can result in millions of hits and no one can possibly use that many. In short, you need another way to use Google, rather than simply typing search words in the appropriate field and clicking Google Search.

A successful Google search is one in which you obtain the information you need and, hopefully, only that information. An efficient Google search is one in which you obtain the information during the first few URL clicks. The faster you find the desired information, service, or product, the more efficient your search becomes. The focus of this chapter is the search techniques you can combine with the automation a Web service provides to get usable results quickly.

The chapter begins with a discussion of typical searches you can perform without expending a lot of energy defining search terms. It moves on to special search arguments you can add to a request that makes it more specific. For example, while a typical search can locate all occurrences of a particular body part on the Internet, many will want to limit their search to the non-pornographic sites. Limiting a search in this way requires special search techniques.

The final portions of the chapter discuss special kinds of searches that return a particular result instead of the massive quantity of unfocussed results you normally receive. For example, you might want to find files that contain certain information, such as the latest presentation on quantum computers. You might not be too interested in looking at Web sites with the same content in this case because the Web site content might include conjecture that editors removed from file. You'll also discover uses for cached data and filtering techniques. The bottom line is that you can use a multitude of ways to search for information, but locating the most efficient and practical way to perform the search is essential.

> ▶ **NOTE**
>
> This chapter and those that follow tell you that I obtained a certain number of results for a particular search phrase. Your results will likely vary from mine because Google is constantly updating its search database. I've included the result values for comparison purposes—so you can better understand the effects of using a particular search phrase.

Performing a Typical Search

The first question most people will have about this section is what constitutes a typical search. A typical search is one that you make without considering any optimization. You just enter some query words, a few special characters, and perhaps some Boolean terms, such as OR, to make the query. I consider this a typical search because most people use this kind of search until they really begin to understand Google.

> ▶ **NOTE**
>
> This book uses the term *query word* to refer to a special word that you use to make a Google query. You'll discover the query words that Google currently supports while reading this chapter. A *keyword* expresses what you want to look for with Google. For example, when you want to search for candles, you might include the word *votive* as a keyword.

You'll normally enter all of the information for a typical search on a single line. Most people begin at the Google home page (http://www.google.com/) shown in Figure 2.1. However, you can also use the Address field of your browser when you make Google your default search site or you can use one of the toolbars available at http://www.google.com/options/. Notice also that the home page lets you access the various tools that Google provides, along with the Advanced Search page.

No matter where you begin, a typical search relies on the basics to obtain a result. The following sections describe a typical search in detail.

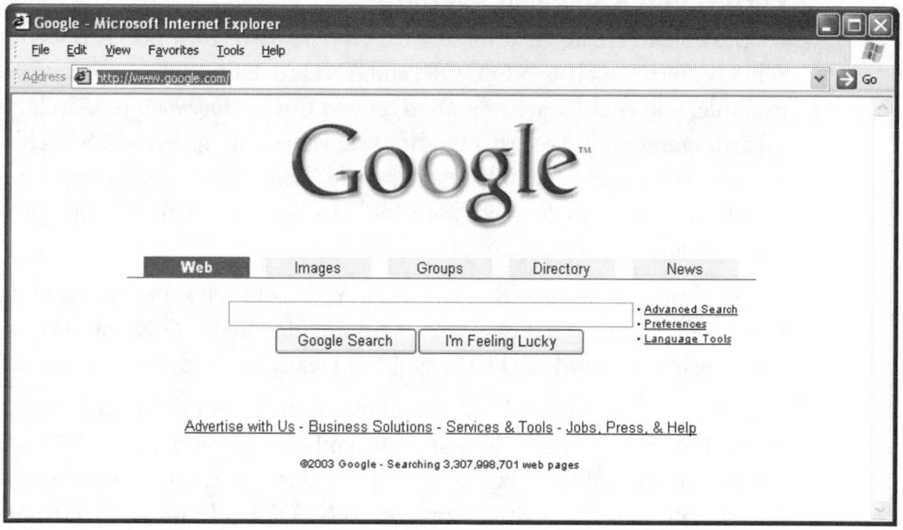

FIGURE 2.1:

FIGURE 2.1:

The Google home page provides access to a simple search as well as tools and services.

Understanding the Search Parameters

The search parameters define how Google interprets your search request. You already know from the "Conducting an Expansion Search" section of Chapter 1 that the order of the keywords is important, as are the precise terms that you use. Many people make the mistake of ordering keywords using their own priority. The goal is to obtain the correct results from Google, so experimentation helps in determining how Google will treat a specific search term. When you create an application using Google Web Services, it pays to spend time online learning what combination of position and terminology obtains the results you want.

It's frustrating to enter keywords that you think will work, but don't provide the results you want. In some cases, your choice of keywords is just fine, but other people use a synonym (a word that means about the same thing as your keyword). Google provides an undocumented synonym search (described in the "Using a Synonym Search" section of the chapter) that you can use, but the synonym search doesn't always work. When this problem occurs, you can always try an online thesaurus to help you come up with new words that mean about the same as the keyword you want. One of my favorite online thesaurus sites is Thesaurus.com at `http://thesaurus.reference.com/`.

Performing a Boolean Search

It's possible to create an argument for Google based on a Boolean search. A Boolean search relies on terms such as NOT, OR, and AND to define an interpretation of the keywords. For example, you could search for *floral bouquet* OR *arrangement* to search for floral bouquet or floral arrangement. Notice that the Boolean value is in uppercase. Searching for *floral bouquet* OR *arrangement* returns 860,000 results, while *floral bouquet or arrangement* returns only 114,000 results because Google doesn't see "or" as a Boolean term. Adding OR means that either term can exist and still return a result.

Google always assumes that you mean AND between keywords, so you never actually use the word AND in a search. However, it's important to understand that if you don't add the word OR, you're using the word AND. Using AND means that both terms must exist to return a result.

The NOT query word isn't documented and you might find that it doesn't work at some point. Google also provides a special symbol you can use for NOT—see the "Excluding Terms" section of the chapter for details. Generally, you'll want to use the special symbol and simply remember that it equates to NOT in a Boolean search. Adding NOT before a term means that Google won't include that word in the search.

Defining a Special Search

A typical search won't meet every need. In fact, the searches many people conduct are less than successful or inefficient when successful because keywords alone usually can't express a query very well. (A search with results that require half a day to process when all you need is one answer is both successful and inefficient.) Even the addition of a Boolean search won't help you locate the information you need in many cases. The problem is that you haven't defined the search criteria completely. You can test most Google special searches using the Advanced Search Page shown in Figure 2.2.

Look at the issue this way. Let's say that it takes about a minute for you to click a link in Google and decide whether the link will work or not. A minute isn't very long when you consider the time required to load the page and actually look at some of the information. A small result set of 60 links requires 60 minutes to search. Many of the search results we've discussed so far in the book contain thousands of links. Even if you eliminate many of those links by reading the snippets that Google provides, you can still spend a lot of time looking for the link you need.

Special searches can help define searches in more precise terms. In fact, careful use of search terms can reduce the number of results to the few you need. A perfect search returns just the results you need, but a less optimal result is acceptable in most cases. The idea is to reduce the number of results to a manageable level. The following sections describe various types of special search terms.

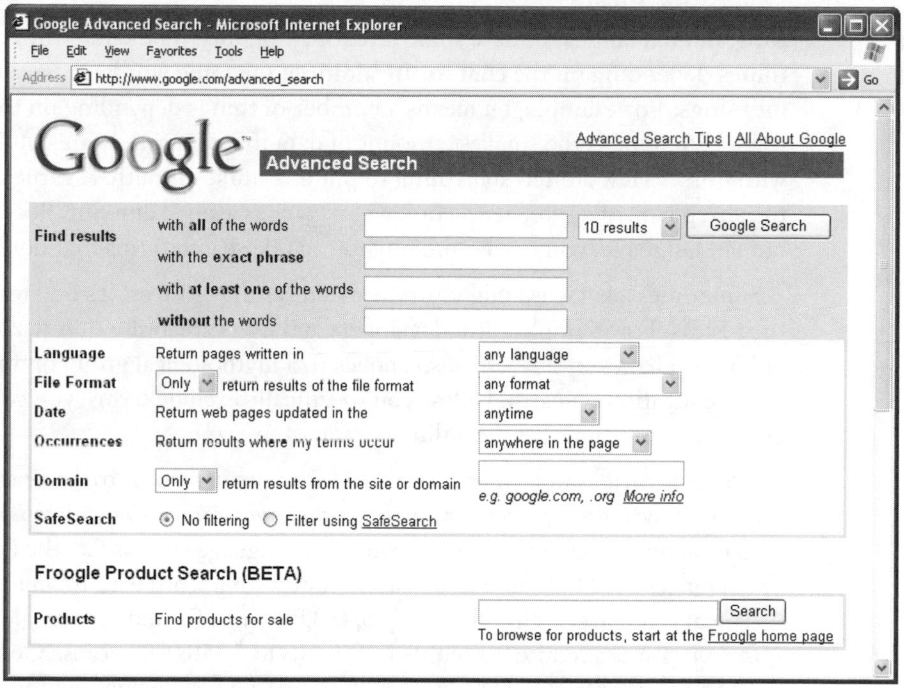

FIGURE 2.2:

The Google Advanced Search page helps you learn about special searches.

Including Terms

Google doesn't recognize common words as valid search terms. The kit refers to many of these terms as stop words. The examples include *where* and *how*. However, many terms fall into this category—terms that you might need to adequately define your search. Obviously, small words such as *the* fall into this category, as do most numbers.

Whenever you want to ensure that Google considers a stop word you provide add a + (plus) sign in front of it. For example, using a search such as *+for whom +the bell tolls* ensures that Google considers both *for* and *the* as part of the search criteria.

▶ NOTE

Always include terms carefully because adding stop words normally increases the number of search results. Unless you know that a stop word will actually improve the search results, avoid using it.

Excluding Terms

Most human languages have some level of ambiguity. The same word can mean different things depending on the context. In addition, the same word can have completely different meanings. For example, bit means a number of things depending on the context. Computer users view a bit as the smallest amount of data that you can create, while people who work with horses view a bit as something to put in a horse's mouth. A carpenter will view a bit as the sharp part of a tool, and a cook will view it as a small amount. Because of the ambiguity in human language, you need some way to exclude search terms that don't meet your needs.

Sometimes a keyword might produce odd results—at least it's odd to the person receiving the results. For example, most developers and users are aware of Amazon—the online reseller of books. However, this term also applies to a mythological group of warrior women and to a specific location on earth. Unless you specifically exclude terms, you could end up with references for everything but the online version of Amazon.

Google provides the – (minus) symbol for removing words from consideration. For example, the search term *develop computer language –program –engineering –education* helps you locate topics on computer speech, rather than a computer language such as C#, the language design process, or languages used for education. Another interesting word with too many results is *renaissance*. A typical Google search will turn up 6,410,000 hits. By adding a single exclusion, *renaissance –Harlem*, you can reduce the number of results to 5,450,000 because Google no longer displays links to pages with the word *Harlem* in them. The exclusion technique works much like a Boolean NOT—it helps you obtain everything but the excluded terms.

> ▶ **TIP**
>
> It's easy to tune the exclusion terms by creating a keyword search and looking at the results. Simply start removing the terms from the initial search results that don't fit your search criteria. In some cases, you'll actually need to open the search page to locate a word that is generic enough to remove a number of the invalid results. Of course, you have to be careful not to use an exclusion word that will remove valid results as well.

Using a Synonym Search

Google provides a poorly documented symbol you can use with a search term to find the synonyms of that term in addition to the term itself. The only place you can find the synonym symbol is on the Advanced Search page at http://www.google.com/help/refinesearch.html. Interestingly enough, it doesn't appear within the symbols defined in the Google Web Services Kit and might not work for all searches. The ~ (tilde) symbol tells Google to perform a synonym search.

In Chapter 1, you learned that the *Visual Basic Serial Port* keywords returned 132,000 results at the time of writing. Likewise, the *VB Serial Port* keywords returned 57,300 results. Google returns 1,480,000 results when using *~VB Serial Port* as a search term. When you go through the list of results, you'll see plenty of VB entries. However, you'll also see Visual Basic and VisualBASIC entries, along with other permutations such as BASIC alone.

> ▶ **TIP**
>
> Google might not provide every synonym you want or it might include a few you haven't considered. The best way to determine which synonyms Google uses is to perform a synonym search on the word *alone*, but eliminate the search word, such as *~VB –VB*. The first highlighted word in the snippet provided with the search results is the first synonym Google uses. Eliminate this word by excluding it also, such as *~VB –VB -code –ActiveX –Visual –Basic –VB6*. Eventually, Google will return an error message saying it didn't find any search results. At this point, you have all of the synonyms that Google uses for a particular search term. Now you can decide whether to add additional search terms of your own or to exclude search terms you really don't want to use.

You can use synonym searches to locate information when a Web site developer could use any of a number of terms. For example, if you use *~environment behavior* as a search term, Google also returns pages with words such as *climate* and *nature* highlighted because these terms are synonyms for environment.

It's important to use some kind of filtering with a synonym search. The *environment behavior* search returns 3,830,000 results, but the *~environment behavior* search returns 5,610,000 results, which is too many to view. For example, you could change the search *to ~environment child behavior disorders –animal –mineral –discipline*. By adding two keywords and excluding three others, you can reduce the number of results to 196,000. This is still too many results to view, but does reduce the total by 95 percent.

Using Precise Phrases

Google doesn't normally retain the order of your keywords in a search—it simply looks for the keywords wherever they might appear in the resource. Even though the order of the words in the search phrase determines the order of the results you receive, the resource need not have the words in any particular order. Generally, you can look for information this way and not experience any problems. However, when you're looking for a specific quote, a product, or reference the order of the words becomes important. When this happens, you need to search using a precise phrase.

Precise phrases appear within double quotes. For example, if you wanted to look up the precise phrase, "for whom the bell tolls," you'd enclose it in double quotes as shown. One of the advantages of using a precise phrase is that it preserves small words without using any other special symbols.

The effects of a precise phrase are easy to see. Using all the words, *+for whom +the bell tolls*, returns 86,800 results. On the other hand, the precise phrase returns only 582 results.

Performing Site Restricted Searches

Most of the noncommercial sites that I check for information lack a search engine. In many cases, it's simply because the site is on a host where the Webmaster lacks access to the server. In some cases, the site lacks a search engine because the Webmaster simply hasn't had time to create one. Even when a site includes a search engine, it might provide incomplete results or not work the way you think it should. All of these problems occur with enough regularity that you will use the site search regularly.

> ▶ **TIP**
>
> Because less skilled users usually have problems with "secret" combinations of query words and the site search is so helpful, this one search provides a significant return when using Web services. Even if you don't have a problem remembering the special query word used for a site search, the fact that you have to type the domain in for each site you want to visit can cause problems. Consequently, if you want to provide a case for using Google Web Services and need a scenario with quantifiable results—this is one of the best. A Web service that provides access to specific sites through Google can greatly reduce search times and make users more productive.

To use the site search, simply add the query word *site:* to your search, along with the domain of the search site. For example, if you wanted to search Microsoft's main Web site, you'd use *site:www.microsoft.com*. Notice that you don't include a protocol (the http or ftp portion of the URL). In addition, you can't drill down to a particular folder on the domain. Consequently, you can't directly search hosted sites using this technique, unless you use a few tricks.

One of the best methods to drill down into a particular hosted site is to combine a site search with an URL search (see the "Defining an URL Search" section for details). The combination of site search and URL search ensures you get results from just that portion of the domain.

You can also use keywords to perform the search. For example, the site might include a particular keyword as part of the title or text for every page. (See the "Defining a Title Search" section of the chapter for details.) My Web site includes my company name, DataCon Services, as part of the title for every page. Not only does this technique make it easier to find my page, it also ensures you know precisely which Web site you're visiting.

> ▶ **NOTE**

You can't include more than one site per search. Consequently, this is a great place to use Web services. A user could enter multiple sites on a form and the code associated with the form would automatically make one request per entry.

Performing Date Restricted Searches

The Internet contains old data—old in terms of some technologies such as computers. A technology that's new today is old hat in 6 months to a year. Consequently, if you want new technology solutions, you need to filter out the old solutions that the media keeps around for historical reasons. Likewise, you might actually want older information. A history buff might not want the latest information because it doesn't have the historical context of the older material. For that matter, you might simply want to locate information that you remember seeing 3 months ago and don't want to wade through newer information.

This is one case where the Google Advanced Search page doesn't reflect the realities of using Google Web Services very well. The Google Advanced Search page lets you select from: anytime, past 3 months, past 6 months, and past year. The Google Web Service is a lot more capable in this regard, because you can supply specific dates for the information you want. The only problem is you have to supply the data range as a Julian date. Supplying the *daterange* query word as *daterange:2452760-2452964* means that you want to search for pages that Google updated between 30 April 2003 and 21 November 2003.

> ▶ **NOTE**

Because the Google webbot doesn't traverse every link on the Internet every day, updates to a Web site often require a few days to appear. A webbot is essentially a software robot—it travels across the Internet looking for new information. When it finds new information, it makes a change to the Google database that you access using Google Web Services. Consequently, it's important to realize that the dates you see on Google are the dates that the Google webbot last saw a change to the affected Web page, not the date the change actually occurred.

Calculating the Julian date isn't for the faint of heart because you need to consider all kinds of issues that have occurred over the years with the calendar, such as the introduction of the Gregorian calendar we now use. Fortunately, most programming languages include a special function that helps you convert Gregorian dates to Julian dates. If your programming language or other development environment (such as a scripted Web page) is one of the few that don't support this feature, you can always use a Web site that performs the conversion for you, such as the U.S. Naval Observatory site at `http://aa.usno.navy.mil/data/docs/JulianDate.html`. Note that you should only use the integer portion of the results from this site—not the included decimal portion, which signifies the current time.

Defining a Title Search

Google actually supports two forms of title search. The first type performs a title search using just a single keyword, while the second type performs a title search using all of the keywords you've supplied. To perform a single keyword search, use the *intitle* query word. For example, if you use *intitle:VB6 program development* as a search term, Google only looks for VB6 in the title of the page. The words *program* and *development* can appear anywhere. To perform a title search with all of the keywords, use the *allintitle* query word. Google returns only two results when you use *allintitle:VB6 program development* as the search term, but returns 604 results when you use the *intitle:VB6 program development* search term.

> ▶ **TIP**
>
> You don't have to settle for an all or nothing approach to a keyword search. It's possible to use the *intitle* query word in front of any word in the search term. For example, to search for Visual Basic projects for applications that require serial port support, you could use a search term such as *intitle:Visual intitle:Basic serial port*. Google will look only in titles for Visual Basic, but will look through all parts of the Web page for serial port.

It's easy to combine a title search with other searches to locate a specific Web page. For example, you can't directly search my site using a site search because I don't have my own domain. However, you can locate information about my site by combining a site search with a title search like this: *site:www.mwt.net intitle:DataCon Services*.

Title searches aren't as successful as other search types in helping you map out sites if the site creator didn't use titles carefully. In fact, many private sites don't use titles at all, while some commercial sites use them inconsistently. For example, the search term *site:www.microsoft.com*

intitle:Windows doesn't necessarily return all of the Windows sites. The results are still useful, but Microsoft doesn't use site titles consistently. It's important to note that the search will return results for every page that does include Windows in the title, so this search will return links for products such as Windows Media Player and Windows 2000.

It's also important to remember that the keyword you supply can appear anywhere in the title, as shown in Figure 2.3. In this case, the example uses an *allintitle* search with *Visual Basic 6* as the keyword. Depending on how you phrase the search term, you can obtain very specific results using this technique, but you also need to realize that the search results might not be complete.

> ▶ **TIP**
>
> Most competent Web page developers provide a title that accurately matches the content of the page. Consequently, the title search can reduce the number of results that apply to sites with less helpful information. This technique is usually better for commercial or professional sites, rather than home or hobby sites.

FIGURE 2.3:

The Google Advanced Search page helps you learn about special searches.

Defining an URL Search

Like the title search, Google provides two forms of the URL search. The first uses just a single keyword as the basis for searching for text within an URL, while the second uses all of the keywords as the basis for the search. To perform a single keyword search, use the *inurl* query word. In this case, you must think about words that you'd see in an URL. For example, it's likely that you'll see VB6, not Visual Basic 6, as part of an URL. You can use the *allinurl* query word to perform a search with all of the keywords. In this case, you might want to perform a search for one or more subfolders of a main site. For example, you might look for *eBay* and *antique* as keywords. Figure 2.4 shows typical results for an *allinurl* query. Again, the idea is to choose words that will appear as part of an URL. Like the title search, you can also use multiple instances of the *inurl* query word to locate several words in an URL without using all of the keywords for this purpose.

Many Web sites don't have their own domain—they host space on someone else's server and have a home URL that reflects their location within another domain. For example, you can use the URL search technique to locate information on my site. All you need to do is perform a site search and combine it with an URL search like this: *site:www.mwt.net inurl:~jmueller*. The *~jmueller* portion of the URL for my home page appears as part of every URL for my Web site.

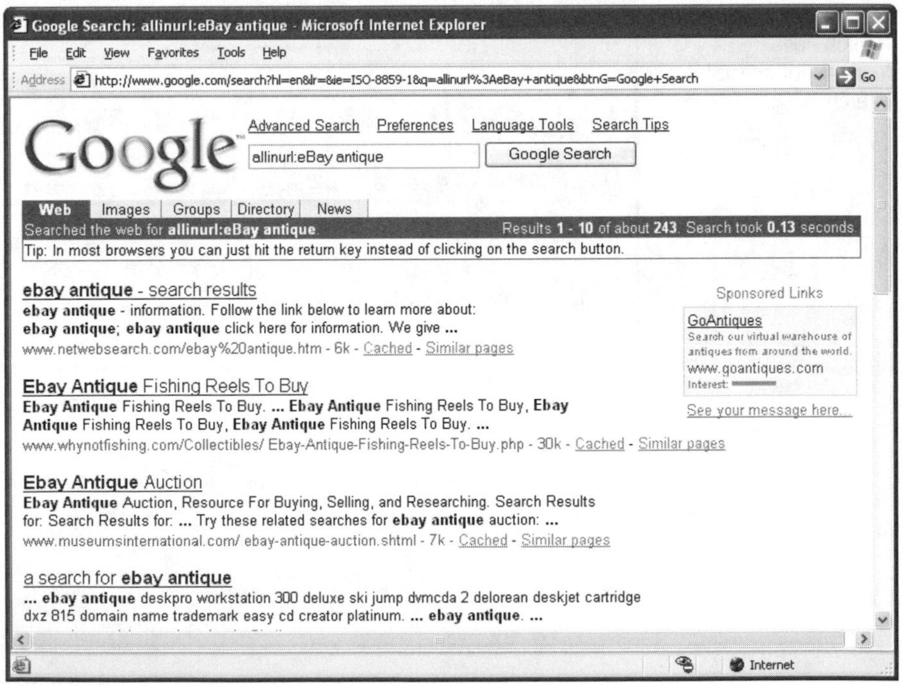

FIGURE 2.4:

Use URL searches to locate sites that have specific areas that match your keywords.

Of course, you can use a combination technique to search portions of a larger Web site. For example, you might want to visit only the Windows-specific pages on Microsoft's site. A combination search, *site:www.microsoft.com inurl:windows*, provides the results you want. A side effect of this particular search is that you'll actually build a site map of sort for just the Windows-specific URLs. In fact, if you couple Google Web Services with a graphics application, you could easily build a chart that lays out the entire Microsoft site.

> ▶ NOTE
>
> This example only returns links that have Windows in them. If you want links for Windows 2000, you need to expand the search term to include Windows 2000 like this: *site:www.microsoft.com inurl:windows OR inurl:windows2000*. An URL search can be more restricted than a title search. While the title search discussed earlier returns all Microsoft sites with the word *Windows* in the title, the URL search returns only those sites that have the word *Windows* in the URL.

Looking for Text Alone

It's possible to conduct a search where the keywords appear within the title, URL, links, or other areas of the site, but not within the text of the site itself (the area within the <body> tag). Precisely why this happens depends on the site, but often it has to do with text that you'll never see. The result of this kind of fruitless search is that you end up finding sites that have nothing to do with the research you're conducting. To avoid this problem, you can perform a text only search using the *allintext* query word.

Adding the *allintext* query word ensures that you only receive sites that actually discuss the topic you want to read about. For example, a search on *VB Serial Port* returns 57,300 results. However, using *allintext:VB Serial Port* returns only 41,100 results, which means that 16,200 of the previous results didn't have any mention of VB Serial Port in the actual text of the document.

This kind of search is especially helpful in technical or professional searches where you need to find specific words and learn how they're used. For example, developers have specific needs in this area when locating code that performs a particular task. It's hard to locate such examples because Web sites often list the terms in other areas without actually providing a coding example.

Looking for Links Alone

One of the biggest questions that developers have when asked about link searches is why anyone would want to look for a link. A link on a page doesn't really say much except that the author of the page is providing a pointer to some other location. However, links are important for a number of reasons. For example, you might want to know how many sites reference your

Web site. Sometimes it's handy to know which sites have information that relates to a particular topic. You can even use Google to discover which pages have a particular link on them. The following sections discuss all three of the link searches.

Working with Back Links

Finding Web pages that reference another Web page can be important for a number of reasons. However, many developers will use this approach to look for pages that reference a particular site. For example, you might need to verify which sites reference your site. To use this search, specify the *link* query word as part of the search term, along with the URL that you want to locate. You must use this query word alone—it doesn't work in combination with other query words.

Site references are important for a number of reasons. You might have paid to get your site mentioned on the host site (or provided some other service, such as writing content for the host site). Users of your site might complain that they can't access links found on other sites. Performing a site search helps you locate sites with old links to your site.

> ▶ **NOTE**
>
> The back link search differs from the specific link search in a very important way. When working with the back link search, you provide a specific URL for which you want to search. On the other hand, a specific link search looks for links on a page that contain a particular keyword. The keyword isn't an URL in this case, but part of an URL. Use the back link search when you need to find a particular URL and the specific link search when you need to locate URLs that contain specific keywords.

Locating Related Links

Not every piece of information on the Internet relates in some way, but connections do exist. Locating these relations can prove difficult and without help, you won't find them all. The *related* query word helps you find sites that have some kind of connection to each other based on the keyword you provide. For example, you might want to locate a site that sells classic cars based on the content of a site that you've already located. Figure 2.5 shows typical results from this kind of search.

Remember that this search locates information based on an URL that you supply. Consequently, it's important to locate a site that specifically matches your search criteria. Otherwise, Google will return results based on a less than perfect URL selection. You must use this query word alone—it doesn't work in combination with other query words.

FIGURE 2.5:

Locate related sites using the related links search.

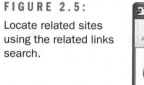

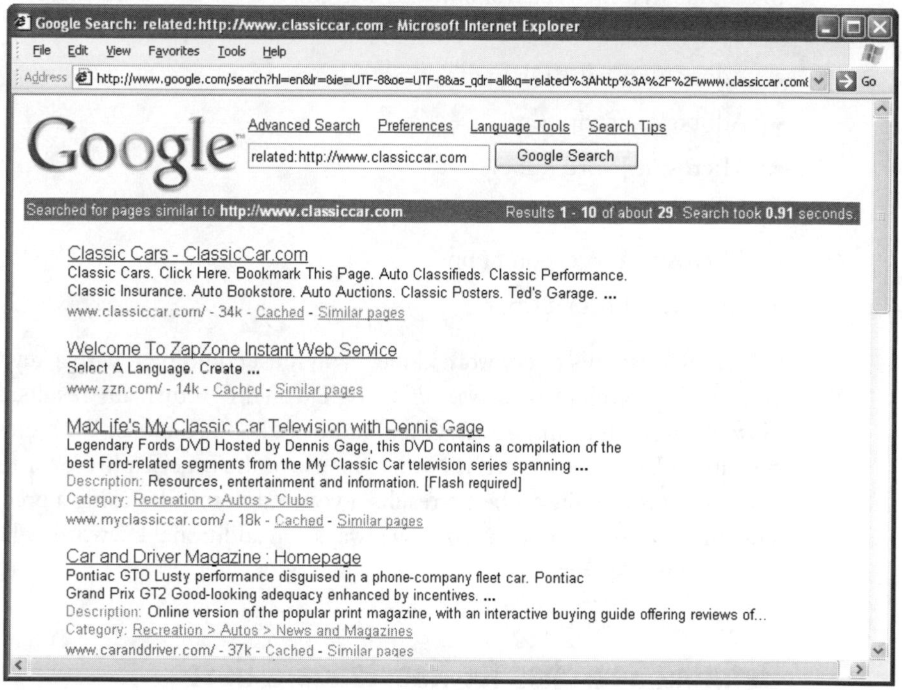

Finding Specific Links

Sometimes you need to locate pages that have a specific link on them. For example, you might want to know which sites reference support for a particular product. To search for specific keywords in links, you provide a search term that includes the *allinlinks* query word. Unfortunately, this search doesn't appear on the Advanced Search page, so the only way you can try it out is using Google Web Services.

Working with Files

Theoretically, when you view a Web page online, you're looking at a file. However, people don't tend to think of HTML as files—they tend to think of PDF and DOC data as files. Consequently, Google provides a special search you can use to locate just the kind of file you want, rather than wade through a hundred Web pages that you don't want.

To locate the file that you want, use the *filetype* query word. When you use *filetype* by itself, Google searches only for that kind of file. However, adding a minus sign (*–filetype*) tells Google to exclude that file type from the list. You add the file extension (without the period) as the search criteria. Currently, Google supports these file types:

- Adobe Acrobat PDF (.pdf)
- Adobe Postscript (.ps)
- Microsoft Word (.doc)
- Microsoft Excel (.xls)
- Microsoft Powerpoint (.ppt)
- Rich Text Format (.rtf)

You can't use this query word alone—you must combine it with a keyword. Consequently, if you use the search term *filetype:pdf*, Google wouldn't return any results. However, if you use *"Visual Basic .NET" filetype:pdf*, Google returns 4,940 results of PDF files that contain information about Visual Basic .NET. Notice the use of the precise phrase for the search term in this case. You'll normally get better results if you search for files using a precise phrase, rather than a nebulous term. Of course, you can always add additional keywords when you get too many results from a search.

Defining Searches for Nonstandard Uses

Many people assume that they can only use Google to search for current information on Web sites. It's true that most searches reveal Web sites that include the search phrases you request. However, careful use of Google lets you perform other tasks as well, such as discover whether a Web site you want to visit has potentially damaging information in the form of a virus. You might be interested in hearing how users in Spain deal with spam. The only way you can perform that kind of search is to filter out spam hits from other countries. The following sections discuss searches you can create for special reasons, such as reducing the number of hits in a language you don't understand.

Determining Web Site Information

Learning more about Web sites, especially in the virus-filled Internet of today, is essential. The "Learning More about a Site" section of Chapter 1 discussed some of the issues surrounding Web site identification and information checks. Several of the examples in the book will also discuss this very important subject from a programming perspective. However, getting the basic information you need is relatively simple. All you need to do is use the *info:* query word followed by the Web site URL. For example, to check information on my site, you'd use *info:http://www.mwt.net/~jmueller* as the search term.

Exploring Cached Data

Google is a great repository of old information. While you can always search for the latest information a Web site provides, you might need the old piece of information you saw last week. The "Getting Old Data from the Cache" section of Chapter 1 discusses the need for this kind of search in detail. To perform this kind of search, use the *cache:* query word. For example, you can locate the cached version of my Web site by using cache:*http://www.mwt.net/~jmueller* as the search term.

Understanding Filtering and Restrictions

The process of filtering and restricting data using Google Web Services doesn't work anything like the same process on the Advanced Search page. In fact, the Advanced Search page doesn't provide some of the filtering and restriction options provided by Google Web Services. (It does contain most of the options, so you can test the filtering and restrictions features out.)

Unlike many of the other search features discussed in this chapter, you don't define a restriction or a filter using a special keyword. Instead of providing these search requirements as part of the query, you include them as a special query item. Chapter 4 discusses the information you provide as part of a SOAP request in detail. For now, all you need to know is that the filter information appears as part of the `<filter>` tag of the request. Using a filter, you can tell Google to return only the first URL for returns that contain the same title and snippet information. You can also restrict sites to two return values, so you don't end up with endless links from the same site.

Google supports two kinds of restrictions. The first is a language restriction that appears as part of the `<lr>` tag of the request. This tag tells Google which language you want to view for the results. The second tag, `<restrict>`, defines the country from which you want to receive information. You can also request a special topic such as Linux.

Performing Safe Searches

Safe search techniques keep pornography at bay while you locate the actual information you need. Like other kinds of filtering, you don't define this filter as part of the search term when using Google Web Services. Chapter 4 describes the request technique you use to tell Google how to use this kind of filter. All you need to know now is that you define a safe search by setting the `<safeSearch>` tag content to true. The "Avoiding Pornographic Material" section of Chapter 1 describes in detail why you would want to use this particular feature.

Your Call to Action

This chapter discusses many ways to search for information—some people are probably yawning at this very moment after several hours of good sleep. Search techniques aren't the most exciting topic, but it's an essential topic for Google users and Google Web Services developers. Locating a topic isn't hard. All you need is a good keyword. But unless you really like going through millions of hits, you need to find the most efficient way to locate just the information you want.

It's time to try a few of these techniques on your own. One way to try them out is to use the Google Advanced Search page at `http://www.google.com/advanced_search`. Unfortunately, this technique doesn't really tell you how the information will look from a developer perspective. With this in mind, you'll also want to test the sample applications in this book. See how they work with various keyword combinations. Remember to try the keywords in more than one order because Google respects keyword order as a means for determining which results to return. Make sure you try a few of the special searches as well—including the filtering and restriction methods. It's also a good idea to try the various examples that come with the Google Web Services Kit.

> ▶ NOTE
>
> As with the examples supplied in this book, the Google examples all include a string that you replace with the developer license you request from Google. For example, in the `\GoogleAPI\soap-samples` folder, many of the files contain this string: `<key xsi:type= "xsd:string">00000000000000000000000000000000</key>`. Unfortunately, the instructions for using the Google examples don't always indicate this requirement, so you need to remember to make the change.

Some of the examples in this chapter expose the underlying XML you'll use to interact with Google Web Services. Chapter 3 goes on to the next step of working with Google Web Services—actually using XML to perform tasks. Chapter 3 discusses how XML works, shows examples of how various languages use XML, and describes some of the problems you'll encounter when using XML. For example, XML isn't secure and it causes privacy issues you'll need to consider. This next step helps you move from merely using the Web service to telling it what information you'd like to request.

Chapter 3

Discovering XML Basics | Working with Netpadd | Working with XMLwriter 2 | Presenting Information Using XSLT

▶ Working with Web Service Data

Understanding SOAP Messaging | Developing with Privacy Issues in Mind | Developing with Security Issues in Mind

All Web services rely on some form of eXtensible Markup Language (XML) to receive requests and send information. Even the Simple Object Access Protocol (SOAP) is simply a way to package information within an XML envelope, and the result looks similar to the XML that you see used in other places. This chapter isn't going to drown you in XML terminology, and it certainly won't make you an expert, but it does contain helpful information on using XML with Google Web Services.

You do need to understand some XML basics to get anything out of Google Web Services. The first section of the chapter helps you understand these basics, including the single format that Google uses to return data from requests. You'll receive enough information in this section to work with the examples in the book. However, once you start working with XML, you might find that you want to know more, so the section also includes a listing of resources (including tutorials) that you can use to increase your XML knowledge.

▶ NOTE

Because Google doesn't directly support the XML over HTTP technique of making a request, obtaining a direct view of XML in your browser is impossible. To view the XML, you normally need to write an application to capture and view the SOAP message. You can also view the raw return values using a debugger for your favorite application program. As an alternative, you can view the sample SOAP messages that Google provides.

XML isn't necessarily easy for the average human to read—it includes text mixed with tags in such a way that you can see the structure if you look hard enough, but the data isn't easy to interpret. The eXtensible Stylesheet Language Transformations (XSLT) technology can transform XML into a readable Web page. Again, this section won't make you an expert, but you'll leave the section with enough information to create basic reports and informational layouts. Like the XML section, this XSLT section contains additional information on where you can learn more about XSLT.

The SOAP section of the chapter helps you understand how SOAP works, especially how it differs from straight XML. Most serious developers consider SOAP the best way to transfer data between systems today because you gain functionality. For example, SOAP supports the Web Services Description Language (WSDL), which many IDEs can turn directly into programming information for the developer. Instead of having to learn to write complex strings to request data, the developer concentrates on the data requirements and lets the IDE perform the complex part of the task.

Finally, this chapter discusses two essential issues. The first is the problem of maintaining privacy with Web service applications. Generally, you shouldn't run into too many privacy issues with Google Web Services because you're receiving data, not sending it anywhere. However, you can run into user privacy issues because the requests your application makes reflect user needs and tastes. The second is the problem of security. Your application isn't trading sensitive information, but others might glean information about your company based on the research you perform. Consequently, keeping the request, response, and search information private is important.

Understanding XML Basics

Almost everyone has heard about and used XML in some way. If nothing else, you've seen XML extensions on some Web pages because many magazines now use XML as a fast way to present highly formatted data online. Even though your browser presents what appears to be a standard Web page, underneath the presentation the page is an XML file. XML sees more use than Web pages and Web services—it's becoming the glue that holds the Internet together. In fact, you'll find XML used for many non-Internet purposes, such as application configuration files.

In many ways, knowing XML is a way to understand the presentation and distribution of information on the Internet today. Presentation is especially important when working with Google because this search engine can help you find just the right presentation of the many sources of data you find. You might need some data presented as a table, rather than as running text. Distribution is also very important if you want to save time in sending information to other people. For example, it's often possible to find the same data distributed as a Web page, PDF file, and PowerPoint presentation. Although the following sections provide the information you need to work with Google Web Services, you'll eventually want to explore this topic further by using the resources in the "Learning More about XML" section.

Defining the Parts of an XML Message

All XML messages consist of three components: elements, attributes, and data. For all of the complexity of the examples in the previous chapters, XML doesn't contain very much in the way of complex information. In addition, XML messages consist entirely of text for the most part. Yes, you can attach encoded data, but the message itself is pure text, which makes XML quite readable. Here's a simple example that shows all three kinds of XML message components. You'll find this example in the \Chapter 03\Sample XML folder of the source code located on the Sybex Web site.

```
<?xml version="1.0" encoding="UTF-8"?>
<Hello xmlns:xsi="http://www.w3.org/2001/XMLSchema-instance">
    <Element1>Some Text 1</Element1>
    <Element2 MyAttribute="SomeValue">Some Text 2</Element2>
</Hello>
```

The first line is an element. It's a special kind of element that every XML file has—the XML heading. The <?xml?> element (or tag as some books say) defines this file as an XML file of some kind. The version attribute further defines the XML file by telling the XML parser that this is a version 1.0 file. The encoding attribute states how the data preparer formed the characters within the file. The two most popular encoding techniques in use now are UTF-8 and UTF-7. You can learn more about the Unicode Transformation Format (UTF) standard at http://www.ietf.org/rfc/rfc2152.txt and http://www.utf-8.com/.

The second line also contains an element. However, notice this element has an opening and a closing tag. The opening <Hello> tag appears first, followed by two child elements, followed by the closing </Hello> tag. Standard elements all require an opening and closing tag unless they're self-contained. You can create a self-contained tag by adding the ending slash as part of the initial tag like this <Hello />. The <Hello> element includes a special namespace attribute. You can detect namespace elements because they normally begin with xmlns, followed by a colon, followed by the name of the namespace (xsi in this case). The namespace normally has an URL attached to it. The page pointed to by the URL contains a description of the elements that the namespace defines. Whenever an XML parser sees a namespace attached to an element, it goes to the URL defined for that namespace to learn how to interpret the element, associated attributes, or data.

The <Element1> element is a child of the <Hello> element. Elements can have child/parent relationships. This element doesn't include any attributes, but it does have data in the form of Some Text 1. The value of <Element1> is Some Text 1. The XML Parser links the element to its data.

The <Element2> element is also a child of the <Hello> element and a sibling of <Element1>. This element also includes an attribute. In this case, the attribute is extra data that describes the element in some way. The value of MyAttribute appears in quotes after the attribute. To create an attribute, you must always provide a name, followed by the equals sign and a string value in quotes. An element can contain as many attributes as needed to provide a full description of its functionality.

Viewing XML Data in Your Browser

One of the problems of working with XML data is that it can become quite lengthy. The length of a Google search result can make it difficult to locate the very information you seek. Fortunately, you can see the formatted data in a browser such as Internet Explorer. The data contains indentations to show the relationships between parent and child. In addition, you can differentiate between elements, attributes, and data by looking at the colors. Finally, special elements such as processing instructions and the XML header appear in a different color.

Unless you know how a browser displays XML, you might conclude that the indentation and coloration are the only help you receive. However, browsers have a lot more to offer than that in most cases. At the very least, you can expand and collapse various levels of information. Figure 3.1 shows an example of a Google response that relies on the ability of the browser to collapse information to present a clearer picture of the response. You'll find this example in the \Chapter 03\Sample XML folder of the source code located on the Sybex Web site.

FIGURE 3.1:

Internet Explorer and other browsers can display XML files in a variety of ways.

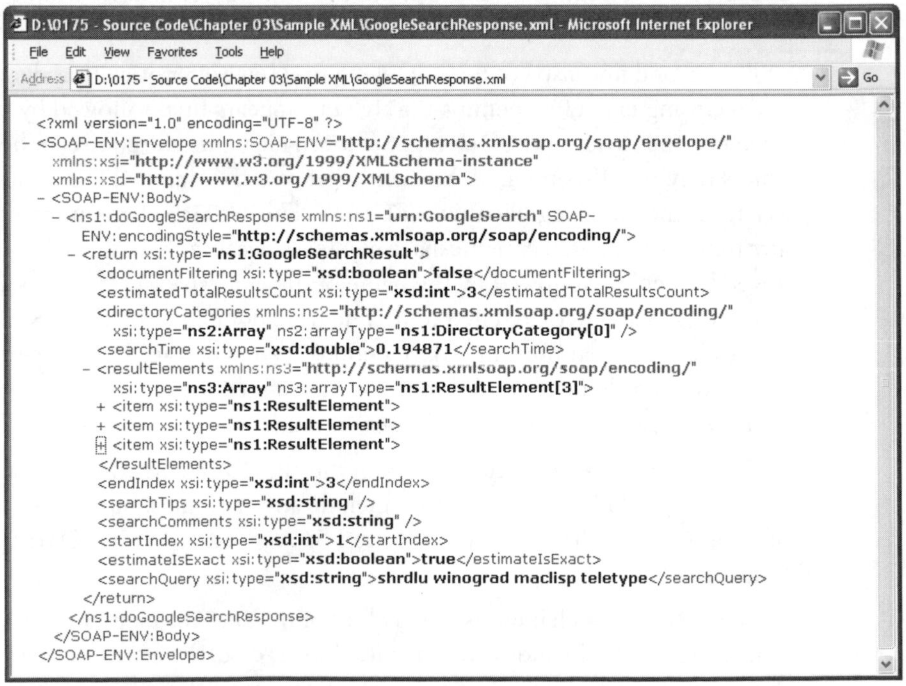

```
D:\0175 - Source Code\Chapter 03\Sample XML\GoogleSearchResponse.xml - Microsoft Internet Explorer

File   Edit   View   Favorites   Tools   Help

Address   D:\0175 - Source Code\Chapter 03\Sample XML\GoogleSearchResponse.xml                  Go

  <?xml version="1.0" encoding="UTF-8" ?>
- <SOAP-ENV:Envelope xmlns:SOAP-ENV="http://schemas.xmlsoap.org/soap/envelope/"
    xmlns:xsi="http://www.w3.org/1999/XMLSchema-instance"
    xmlns:xsd="http://www.w3.org/1999/XMLSchema">
  - <SOAP-ENV:Body>
    - <ns1:doGoogleSearchResponse xmlns:ns1="urn:GoogleSearch" SOAP-
        ENV:encodingStyle="http://schemas.xmlsoap.org/soap/encoding/">
      - <return xsi:type="ns1:GoogleSearchResult">
          <documentFiltering xsi:type="xsd:boolean">false</documentFiltering>
          <estimatedTotalResultsCount xsi:type="xsd:int">3</estimatedTotalResultsCount>
          <directoryCategories xmlns:ns2="http://schemas.xmlsoap.org/soap/encoding/"
              xsi:type="ns2:Array" ns2:arrayType="ns1:DirectoryCategory[0]" />
          <searchTime xsi:type="xsd:double">0.194871</searchTime>
        - <resultElements xmlns:ns3="http://schemas.xmlsoap.org/soap/encoding/"
              xsi:type="ns3:Array" ns3:arrayType="ns1:ResultElement[3]">
          + <item xsi:type="ns1:ResultElement">
          + <item xsi:type="ns1:ResultElement">
          ⊞ <item xsi:type="ns1:ResultElement">
          </resultElements>
          <endIndex xsi:type="xsd:int">3</endIndex>
          <searchTips xsi:type="xsd:string" />
          <searchComments xsi:type="xsd:string" />
          <startIndex xsi:type="xsd:int">1</startIndex>
          <estimateIsExact xsi:type="xsd:boolean">true</estimateIsExact>
          <searchQuery xsi:type="xsd:string">shrdlu winograd maclisp teletype</searchQuery>
        </return>
      </ns1:doGoogleSearchResponse>
    </SOAP-ENV:Body>
  </SOAP-ENV:Envelope>
```

As you can see, the entire response now fits within one screen, making it easy to get an overview of the data. Notice the minus (–) sign next to the `<resultElements>` element. This symbol indicates that you can collapse this level. The plus (+) sign that appears next to each of the `<item>` elements shows that you can expand the level to show child entries. Clicking either a minus or plus sign performs that task within the browser, so you can display any level of detail desired.

Getting XML Data Tools

A browser is a good tool for viewing XML, but you can't modify the XML using it. Because XML is pure text, you can use any editor like Notepad to edit it. However, Notepad isn't optimal because it doesn't display the XML structure. In addition, Notepad lacks tools for making the editing experience better. For example, if you want to add a new element, you must type the tag manually. Manual techniques often leave you open to data errors. Consequently, you need an editor that works well with XML files.

> ▶ **NOTE**
>
> Many of the tools mentioned in this book rely on Microsoft XML Core Services (MSXML) 4.0. In addition, some of the coding examples also rely on this library. The latest version at the time of writing is Service Pack (SP) 2, which you can download at `http://www.microsoft.com/downloads/details.aspx?familyid=3144B72B-B4F2-46DA-B4B6-C5D7485F2B42` (MSXML 4.0 is approximately 5MB, so make sure you allocate enough time to download it). Both of the editors in the sections that follow rely on MSXLM 4.0. However, Netpadd is perfectly happy using MSXML 5.0, which comes with Microsoft Office 2003. On the other hand, XMLwriter 2 specifically requests MSXML 4.0 every time you start it, even if you have MSXML 5.0 installed. Fortunately, you can install the two versions of MSXLM side by side without any ill effects.

XML editors use a number of methods for displaying the XML file. Because presentation is very important when working with XML, you should choose an XML editor that presents the information in a way that you can understand. For example, Figure 3.2 shows the tree view editor used by many XML editors such as XML Notepad and XMLSpy. In addition, XML editors cost differing amounts based on the features they provide. Some editors are very expensive because they provide automated generation features and edit a number of file types.

I chose the two XML editors presented in the sections that follow because they're simple to use and you can download them free. I'm not endorsing these editors as the only selections on the market—you should try a number of editors before you settle on one. However, because these editors provide good functionality and don't provide too many confusing features, you might want to try them as a starting point for your XML learning experience.

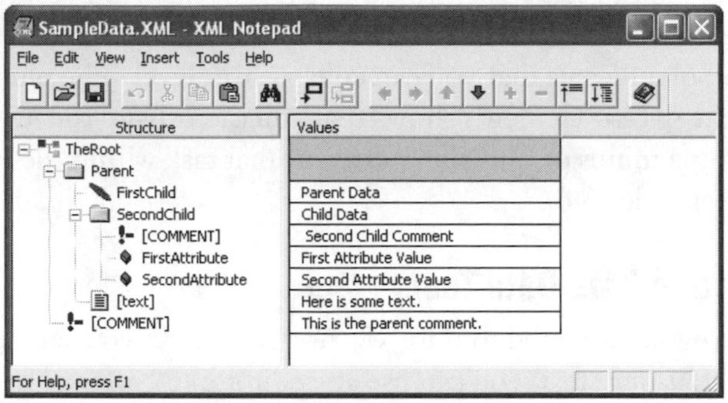

FIGURE 3.2:

Many XML editors provide a tree view display that experts like.

Using Netpadd

Netpadd (http://www.netpadd.com/) is a freeware product that has some interesting features, but is also very simple to use. To write XML using this product, you need to type all of the information manually. There's little automation in this product, so when you create an opening tag, you must create the closing tag to go with it.

The display, shown in Figure 3.3, is very much like the display you'd see in Notepad, rather than the heavily formatted display provided by products such as XMLSpy that some newer developers find confusing. (You'll find the sample file shown in Figures 3.2 and 3.3 in the \Chapter 03\Sample XML folder of the source code found on the Sybex Web site.) Netpadd does provide keyword highlighting for your XML file, which makes viewing the information a lot easier. Use the Options ➢ Hilite ➢ XML menu options to define which file types receive highlighting.

> ▶ **TIP**

One of the most popular XML editors on the market today is XMLSpy (http://www.xmlspy .com/). You can download a limited time evaluation copy of the product from the Altova Web site. Once the evaluation period ends, you must either remove XMLSpy from your system or buy a copy. Another popular choice is XML Notepad—a free download originally provided by Microsoft. Microsoft doesn't officially support XML Notepad any longer. Consequently, you can't download it from Microsoft. Some alternate download sites include WebAttack at http://www.webattack.com/get/xmlnotepad.shtml (this site has the 1.5 version) and DevHood at http://www.devhood.com/tools/tool_details.aspx?tool_id=261 (this site has the 1.0 version, which works much the same as the 1.5 version and has about the same feature set). Both of these editors provide superior handling of XML files by including special symbols and specific methods for adding data. In addition, XMLSpy works on a number of other file types and provides some task automation that you'll find helpful if you work on XML files frequently.

One of the more interesting features that Netpadd provides for XML developers is multiple data views. For example, you can use the View ➤ XML Tree command to display a tree view like the one shown in Figure 3.4. Other commands let you view the XML in other ways. Use the View ➤ XSL Transformation command to display the information as transformed by an XSL file. This particular view is very helpful when working with Google Web Services because you can fine-tune your XSL file without making numerous requests to the Web service.

You'll also like the special dialog boxes that Netpadd provides. For example, the View ➤ Special Characters command displays the Special Characters dialog box. Select the character you want to use and click either Paste or Paste as HTML to place the symbol in your document. If you've ever wasted time looking up language codes online, you'll really like the Language Codes dialog box (displayed using the View ➤ Language Codes command). Simply select the language you want to use and click Paste.

Using XMLwriter 2

XMLwriter 2 (`http://www.xmlwriter.net/`) is a try before you buy product. I won't say that this product is shareware in the strictest sense because the trial period limits use to 30 days. That said, the trial period means you can download the product and try it before making a buying decision, which makes the buying decision easier.

FIGURE 3.3:

Netpadd provides an easy to understand display of the XML file.

```
SampleData.XML - Netpadd
File  Edit  Extra  View  Options  ?
<?xml version="1.0" encoding="UTF-8"?>
<THEROOT>
    <PARENT>
        <FIRSTCHILD>Parent Data</FIRSTCHILD>
        <SECONDCHILD FIRSTATTRIBUTE="First Attribute Value" SECONDATTRIBUTE="Second Attribute Valu
            Child Data
            <!--Second Child Comment-->
        </SECONDCHILD>
        Here is some text.
    </PARENT>
    <!--This is the parent comment.-->
</THEROOT>
```

FIGURE 3.4:

View your XML files in various ways using Netpadd's View commands.

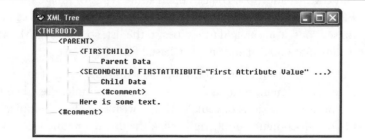

Unlike many other XML editors on the market, XMLwriter 2 also uses a Notepad-style document display for editing as shown in Figure 3.5. This product automatically assumes you want to use color-coding for keywords. You'll also find the use of automation nice. For example, when you type an opening tag, XMLwriter 2 automatically creates a closing tag for you. Load a schema for your XML file and you'll be able to choose tags directly from the TagBar displayed on the left side of the screen. The IDE also features an XML checker. Simply right-click the document and select Validate XML File from the context menu. Any errors appear in a TODO list at the bottom of the IDE.

FIGURE 3.5:

XMLwriter 2 uses a document style editor, but provides many features found in high-end products.

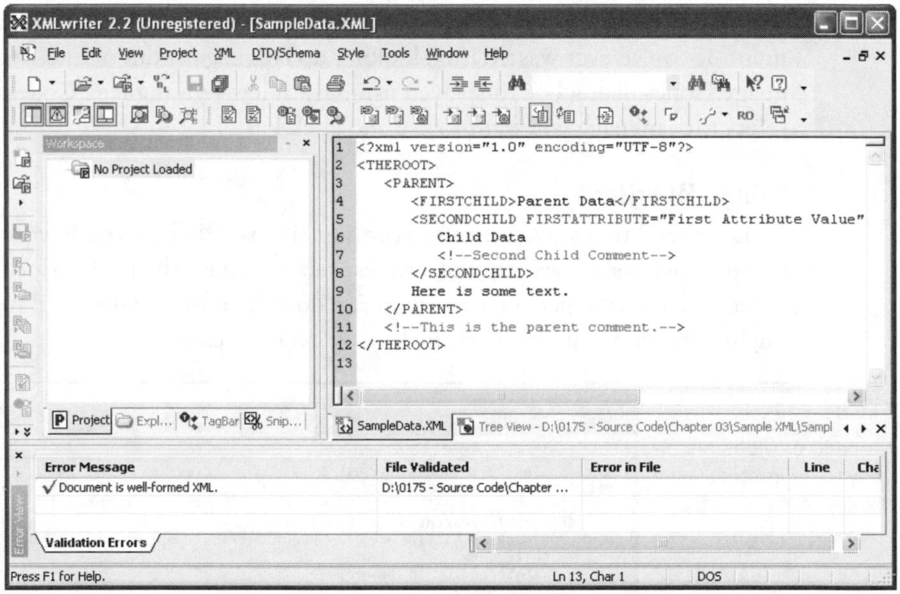

This product includes a number of features that the serious XML developer will need. For example, you can build projects using XMLwriter 2. Creating a project organizes the files and makes it easier to build the links you need. XMLwriter 2 comes with built-in support for all of the standard files—including XML, XSL, XSLT, HTML, XHTML, CSS, DTD, XSD, and text. In addition, you can open some types of image files, such as the GIF, JPG, and PNG files used by many Web sites. However, the files you can open aren't actually limited to these types. You can add new types to the list, so long as XMLwriter 2 can read them (which means that you can add any text-based file extension).

The IDE itself is fully configurable using any of the Options dialog box entries. Fortunately, the default setup is quite usable. For example, the tabbed presentation means you can see multiple versions of your XML file with ease. For example, if you want to see a tree view of your document, simply right-click the document and select View As Tree from the context menu. Figure 3.6 shows a typical example of the tree view. You can also choose a browser view for your document.

Sending Special Characters Using URL Encoding

For most people, working with Web sites is a unique experience because they encounter unexpected oddities that they haven't had to consider in the past. When you type a space into a word-processed document, nothing odd happens—the computer simply accepts the character. However, look at the word processor again. Notice how the word processor automatically looks at the space and uses it to determine where to split lines of text. The word processor does treat the space differently—it treats it as a delimiter (a fancy term that programmers use to mean a character that has a special meaning). Likewise, when you add a hyphen to a word, the computer could choose to split the sentence in the middle of the word. The hyphen acts as a delimiter.

The Internet also uses delimiters for a number of purposes, including URLs. When a Web server sees a space, it could assume that it has reached the end of the URL or the beginning of a new input parameter (or a number of other things). Consequently, you must replace spaces, question marks, and other characters with other characters that don't work as delimiters. You might have noticed this practice at work when you fill out a form on the Internet. The browser commonly replaces a space between two words with %20 or a plus sign (+). The Web server interprets these special character sequences as a space.

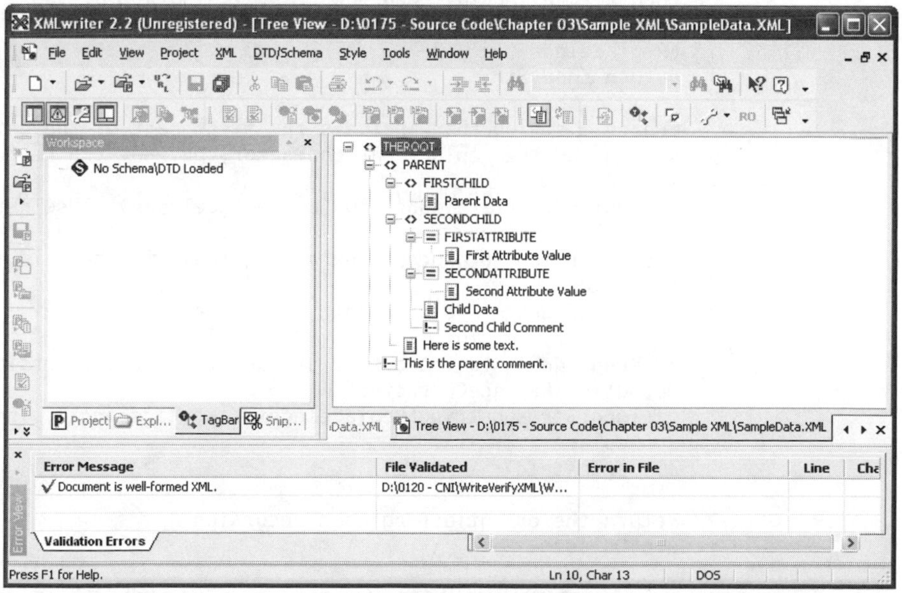

FIGURE 3.6:

Select a tree view to see the overall layout of your XML document.

At first, you might think that the character replacement is random, but there's some method to the madness. In fact, it's relatively easy to write a JavaScript function that performs the character replacement so you don't need to worry about it. Listing 3.1 shows this function. You'll find the complete source for this example in the \Chapter 03\URL Encode folder of the source code located on the Sybex Web site. Note that you can write similar functions in other languages; I'm just using this one because most people can run JavaScript using their browsers.

Listing 3.1   **Replacing Characters in a String**

```javascript
function ReplaceCharacter(InputStr, Replace, UseInstead)
{
    // Define the length of the inputs.
    var InputLength = InputStr.length;
    var ReplaceLength = Replace.length;

    // Determine whether either input has a 0 length. If so,
    // the function can't succeed. However, because this is
    // a recursive function, the function does need to return
    // the original string.
    if ((InputLength == 0) || (ReplaceLength == 0))
        return InputStr;

    // Locate the first replacement value.
    var ReplaceIndex = InputStr.indexOf(Replace);

    // If the replacement value doesn't appear within the string,
    // then return. Again, keep the recursive nature of the
    // function in mind.
    if (ReplaceIndex == -1)
        return InputStr;

    // Create a string that includes the first part of the original
    // string and the replacement character, but not the rest of the
    // string.
    var Output = InputStr.substring(0, ReplaceIndex) + UseInstead;

    // Use recursion to process the string again if there is more data
    // to process.
    if (ReplaceIndex + ReplaceLength < InputLength)

        // Keep adding to the output string after each recursion.
        Output += ReplaceCharacter(
            InputStr.substring(ReplaceIndex + ReplaceLength, InputLength),
            Replace,
            UseInstead);

    // Return the output during each recursion.
    return Output;
}
```

This might look like a lot of very complicated code, but it's actually an easy program. It uses a special technique called recursion to perform its work. In recursion, the programmer writes a program that solves the simplest form of a problem, and then has that program keep calling itself until it achieves that simple form. No matter how complex the input is, the program can solve it (given enough memory and time) because eventually the input will reach this simple solution.

In this instance, the program keeps calling itself until one of several conditions occurs. First, the program could run out of text to process. Second, the program might have some text left, but it might not contain the special character you want to replace (such as a space). If that's the case, then the program has already performed all of the required work, so it can stop.

Once the program determines there's data to process, it uses the substring() function to look for that character in the string. The substring() function returns just the first part of the string—the part that doesn't contain the special character. To this string, the code adds the replacement characters, such as %20 for a space.

It's at this point that the recursion process occurs. The code still has the other part of the string to consider—the last half. The first half of the string is free of the special character, but not the second half. When the code detects that there's still string to process, it calls itself again with the last half of the string. This process continues until the code has processed all of the input string. Figure 3.7 shows typical output from this program.

Of course, the problem is figuring out which characters to replace and what numbers to use to replace them. Unfortunately, Google doesn't publish a list of offending characters, so you'll need to experiment a little with special characters that you want to use. A space never works, and you have to exercise care with both double and single quotes. Determining what number to use is easy. Simply break out a copy of the Character Map utility that comes with Windows and you have everything you need. Figure 3.8 shows what this utility looks like.

FIGURE 3.7:

The example program shows how you can perform URL encoding.

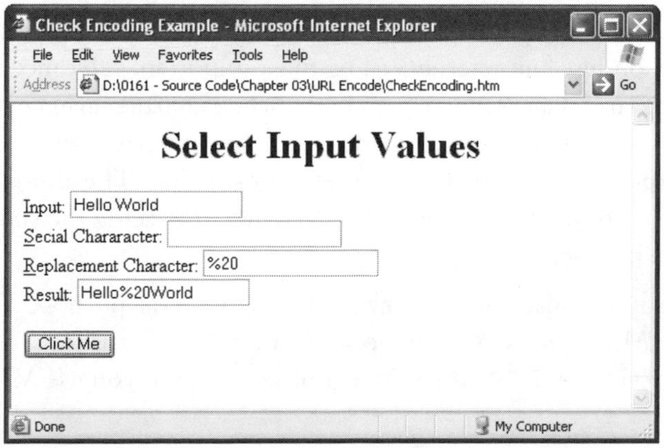

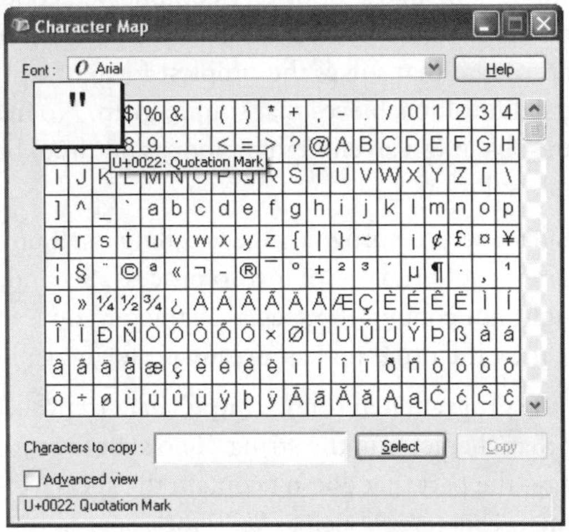

FIGURE 3.8:

Character Map makes it easy to learn the numbers associated with special characters.

Simply select the character you want and look at the number that appears at the bottom of the dialog box. This is the number you should use to replace the character in a string. You can also hover the mouse over the character and the program will display both the character name and the associated number. For example, you replace the quotation mark with %22 in an URL encoded string.

Learning More about XML

Whether you know it or not, you'll run into XML many times during your computer use. The reason is simple—XML makes a great way to exchange data between disparate systems. Fortunately, XML is relatively easy to learn. Visit the W3C Schools site at `http://www`
`.w3schools.com/xml/` to find a complete XML tutorial. You might also want to review the namespace tutorial at `http://www.zvon.org/index.php?nav_id=172&ns=34`.

Unlike many topics discussed in this book, there are multiple versions of XML so you can't rely on just one reference. The most important reference for Google Web Services appears at `http://www.zvon.org/xxl/xmlSchema2001Reference/Output/index.html`. However, make sure you also look at the references at `http://www.zvon.org/xxl/xmlSchemaReference/`
`Output/index.html` for complete information. The annotated XML reference at `http://www`
`.xml.com/axml/axml.html` is also handy for seeing the specification and expert commentary side by side.

You can also find a number of good general-purpose XML sites online. For example, the Microsoft XML Developer Center (`http://msdn.microsoft.com/nhp/default.asp?`
`contentid=28000438`) is a great place to visit if you use Microsoft products.

Using XSLT for Presentation

For many people, reading XML borders on the impossible. Using XSLT can remedy the problem to a great extent, by telling a browser or application how to interpret the information the XML file contains. Presentation can mean everything once you get past the requirements of accurate data. Unfortunately, creating Web pages by hand to achieve a combination of great presentation and accurate data consumes a lot of time, so Webmasters have looked for an easier way to create a presentation online. The combination of XML (data) and XSLT (presentation) has become more than a convenience for many organizations. Using this technique helps companies create accurate presentations with little effort. Because Google Web Services relies on XML, XSLT also provides one of the best ways for you to create a great presentation. The following sections provide a good overview of XSLT. You'll also find a section with references to other XSLT information sources.

Using a Script to Call an XSLT Page

Google doesn't know how you want to present the data they provide, so the XML you receive doesn't include any form of XSLT declaration. This declaration appears as `<?xml-stylesheet type="text/xsl" href="SearchDisplay.xsl"?>` in the XML file. The `href` attribute tells where to find the XSLT file. Without this information, the browser will never display anything but XML on screen. It would seem that the situation is hopeless. However, you have other options, such as writing a script that performs the transformation process using another technique.

The example in Listing 3.2 shows how you can download a response from Google, store the information locally, and translate it using XSLT. The result is the same as modifying the XML file to include the required linkage information, but far more automatic. You'll find the complete source for this example in the `\Chapter 03\Viewing XSLT` folder of the source code located on the Sybex Web site.

Listing 3.2 **Performing a Transformation in JavaScript**

```
function GetData(XslFile)
{
   // Get the search data.
   var TheResult = CallGoogle();

   // Place the resulting information in an XML document.
   var ProcDoc = new ActiveXObject("Msxml2.DOMDocument.4.0");
   ProcDoc.async = false;
   ProcDoc.loadXML(TheResult.context.xml);

   // Create an XSLT document and load the transform into it.
```

```
    var XSLTData = new ActiveXObject("Msxml2.DOMDocument.4.0");
    XSLTData.async = false;
    XSLTData.load(XslFile);

    // Display the output on screen.
    document.write(ProcDoc.transformNode(XSLTData));
}
```

Before the script can do anything, it must obtain the search results from Google. When using Google Web Services, you must rely on SOAP to perform this task. SOAP is extremely flexible, so you can use a number of techniques to make a request with it. The "Performing a Simple SOAP Call" section of the chapter shows one such technique. All you need to know, for the moment, is that the script obtains search results from Google using the CallGoogle() function.

The next step is a little tricky and definitely Windows specific. The code creates an instance of the Microsoft XML component. The ActiveXObject() function performs this task. The Msxml2.DOMDocument.4.0 string identifies the component. You might have to use Msxml2.DOMDocument.5.0 on newer machines with Microsoft Office 2003 or another new product loaded—the last part of the string identifies the component version number. Setting the async property to false is important because you don't want the call to load the XML to return until the browser actually receives this file. Finally, the ProcDoc.loadXML() function loads the response from Google Web Services. Notice that the code uses the loadXML() function to load text formatted as XML, rather than XML from a file.

> **NOTE**

Most versions of MSXML work fine for this example. However, you'll probably want to get MSXML Version 4.0 from http://msdn.microsoft.com/library/en-us/xmlsdk/htm/sdk_intro_6g53.asp. (MSXML Version 5.0 isn't available for download as of this writing.) The 5.0 version includes a number of features that make working with XML documents a lot easier. In addition, you'll find that the latest versions are slightly faster and contain a number of bug fixes that make your application more reliable.

The code now has a local copy of the data from Google. This local copy will disappear as soon as the function ends, so you don't have to worry about update requirements, but it's important to understand that the copy resides in memory on your machine somewhere.

At this point, the code has data to work with, but no XSLT file. The next step loads the XSLT file defined by the XslFile variable. Notice that the code uses the XSLTData.load() function because the XML appears in a file that the application must load into memory. The coupling between the XML response and the XSLT occurs in the XMLData.transformNode() function call. This call produces output that the document.write() function then sends to the current page. The result is that you see the transformed XML on screen, as shown in Figure 3.9. Notice that the URL doesn't change, even though the content differs, because you're still theoretically on the same Web page.

FIGURE 3.9:

The results of using a script to transform XML data received from Google.

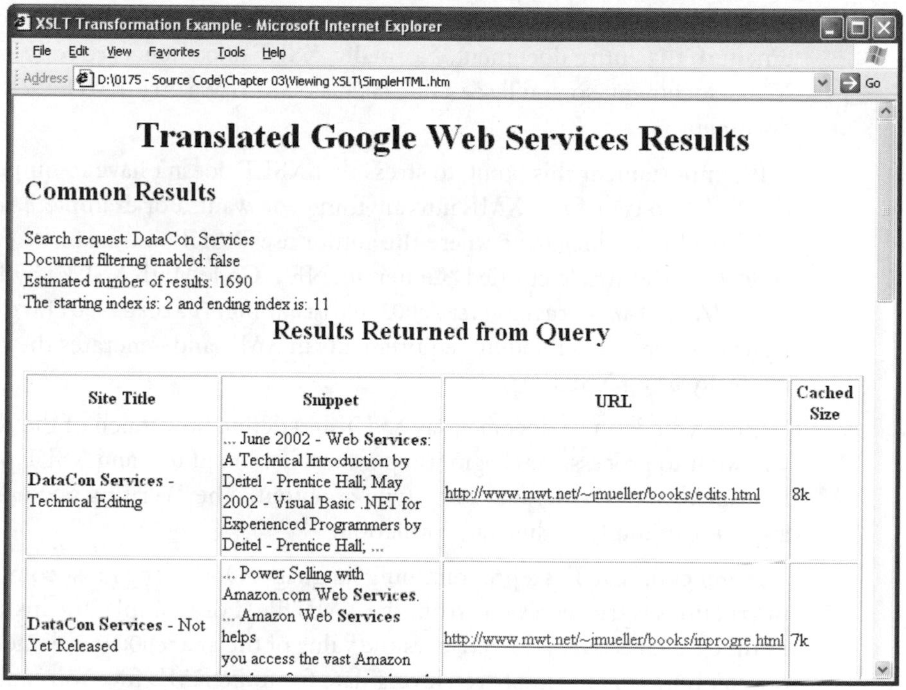

Remember that the <?xml?> element tells the XML parser that this is an XML file. The next element is an XSLT processing instruction. It tells the XML parser that this is an XSLT

Understanding How XSLT Works

Unlike an XML file, an XSLT file generates some type of presentation, using information from the XML file as input. Consequently, XSLT (or simply XSL) files often contain a combination of output text and XML. In fact, all XSLT files begin with the usual header and the special XSLT header shown here.

```
<?xml version="1.0" encoding="UTF-8"?>
<xsl:stylesheet version="1.0"
 xmlns:xsl="http://www.w3.org/1999/XSL/Transform"
 xmlns:fo="http://www.w3.org/1999/XSL/Format">
```

Remember that the <?xml?> element tells the XML parser that this is an XML file. The next element is an XSLT processing instruction. It tells the XML parser that this is an XSLT derivative of an XML file and it includes namespace pointers to Web sites that describe how to interpret XSLT. This instruction is important because otherwise the XML parser looks at this file as XML and won't have a clue what to do with all those XSLT instructions it contains.

An XSLT document describes how to transform an XML document into readable form. Therefore, the first thing it must do is tell the XML parser how much of the XML document to use for the transformation. You can choose anything from just one or two lines of the document to the entire document. Normally, XSLT documents are concerned with an entire XML document, so you'll see a line such as `<xsl:template match="/">` somewhere in the document.

It's important, at this point, to stress that XSLT doesn't have to output HTML. You can use XSLT to transform XML into anything you want. For example, I recently read an article in Visual Studio magazine where the author uses XSLT to transform XML data into program code. (See the article entitled "Generate .NET Code With XSLT" by Kathleen Dollard at `http://www.fawcette.com/vsm/2003_05/magazine/features/dollard/` for details.) That's right—she stores her coding requirements in XML and generates the required code automatically using XSLT.

Once you define a document as XSLT and define how much of the XML document input you want to process, you begin using a combination of text and XSLT processing instructions to transform the XML into some type of output. The "Writing a Simple XSLT Page" shows a specific example of this transformation.

In general, XSLT is a programming language. One of the most common programming instructions retrieves a value from the XML file. For example, the instruction `<xsl:value-of select="searchQuery"/>` retrieves the value of the `searchQuery` element. However, XSLT doesn't limit you to simply retrieving data from the XML file. You can also use functions, such as the `count()` function that returns the number of nodes in a result set, to perform data manipulation on the XML input.

You'll also find that XSLT includes a limited number of loop and logic features. For example, you can tell XSLT that you want to perform the same task with every child of the current node using the `<xsl:for-each select="ProductInfo/Request/Args/Arg">` instruction. In this case, the `select` attribute tells which node to use for processing purposes.

A final consideration for this book is that XSLT also defines something called an axis. An axis defines a way of looking at the data. For example, the at (@) symbol tells XSLT to look at the attributes of a node, rather than the element. Another common axis is `parent`, which tells XSLT to look at the parent of the current element.

Writing a Simple XSLT Page

This section describes the XSLT page used with the transformation described in the "Using a Script to Call an XSLT Page" section (see Listing 3.2). Listing 3.3 shows how to create an XSLT page that outputs HTML code. You could use the same technique to create a report or any other form of output based on the XML input received from Google. You'll find the complete source for this example in the \Chapter 03\Viewing XSLT folder of the source code located on the Sybex Web site.

Listing 3.3   **Designing an XSLT Page**

```xml
<?xml version="1.0" encoding="UTF-8"?>
<xsl:stylesheet version="1.0"
    xmlns:xsl="http://www.w3.org/1999/XSL/Transform"
    xmlns:fo="http://www.w3.org/1999/XSL/Format">
<xsl:output method="xml" indent="yes"/>
<xsl:template match="/return">
<html>
<head>
    <title>XSLT Transformation Example</title>
</head>
<body>
    <!-- Display a heading. -->
    <h1 align="center">Translated Google Web Services Results</h1>

    <!-- Display some common information. -->
    <h2>Common Results</h2>
    <label>
        Search request:
        <xsl:value-of select="searchQuery"/>
    </label><br/>
    ... Other Common Results ...

    <!-- Display the search result values. -->
    <table align="center" border="1" width="100%">
        <caption><h2>Results Returned from Query</h2></caption>
        <tbody>
            <tr>
                <th>Site Title</th>
                <th>Snippet</th>
                <th>URL</th>
                <th>Cached Size</th>
            </tr>
            <xsl:for-each select="resultElements/item">
                <tr>
                    <td>
                        <xsl:value-of select="title"
                            disable-output-escaping="yes"/>
                    </td>
```

```
<td>
    <xsl:value-of select="snippet"
        disable-output-escaping="yes"/>
</td>
<td>
    <xsl:text disable-output-escaping="yes">
        &lt;a href='
    </xsl:text>
    <xsl:value-of select="URL"/>
    <xsl:text disable-output-escaping="yes">
        '&gt;
    </xsl:text>
    <xsl:value-of select="URL"/>
    <xsl:text disable-output-escaping="yes">
        &lt;/a&gt;
    </xsl:text>
</td>
<td><xsl:value-of select="cachedSize"/></td>
                </tr>
            </xsl:for-each>
        </tbody>
    </table>

</body>
</html>
</xsl:template>
</xsl:stylesheet>
```

The code begins with the usual declarations. The `<xsl:output method="xml" indent="yes"/>` tag is important because it determines the kind of output the parser creates. You can also choose text as the output method or tell the parser that you don't want the output indented. Notice that the code also matches the `return` element using the `<xsl:template match="/return">` tag. All of the data appears within this element, so there isn't a good reason to match the root node of the XML document.

The code then outputs the heading. Notice that this is pure HTML and that the code isn't doing anything but outputting this text. The code moves on to the body where it outputs a heading.

The XSLT-specific code begins when the code outputs some of the common information returned by Google. None of this information requires special handling, so the code uses a simple `<xsl:value-of select="searchQuery"/>` tag to retrieve and display the information. The information is surrounded by descriptive text and enclosed within a `<label>` to make it easier to see.

Each return value requires special handling, so the code relies on a table. Notice the head of the table is standard HTML, but that the next selection is an `<xsl:for-each>` element. This statement tells the parser to look at all of the children of the `resultElements/item` node. The system will process each `<item>` element in turn. The next step is to use the `<xsl:value-of>` element to retrieve the name and value attributes of each `<item>` element. Because some of these entries contain the text version of the HTML tags such as > for the greater than (>) symbol, you must include `disable-output-escaping="yes"` attribute with the `<xsl:value-of>` element. Otherwise, the code will display the > symbol and not create a tag. The code ends by completing the HTML page, and then completing both the template and the stylesheet.

Learning More about XSLT

This chapter only skims the surface of what you can do with XSLT. You can perform an incredible number of tasks using this technology. One of the better places to learn about XSLT is `http://www.w3schools.com/xsl/`. You should also view the examples in the XSLT reference at `http://www.zvon.org/xxl/XSLTreference/Output/index.html`. The XSL reference at `http://www.zvon.org/xxl/xslfoReference/Output/index.html` can also come in handy when you begin creating complex XSLT pages. You can also find a good tutorial on the Web-monkey site at `http://hotwired.lycos.com/webmonkey/98/43/index2a.html?tw=authoring`.

Make sure you check out some of the better third party XSLT reference sites. For example, the XSLT.com site at `http://xslt.com/` provides links and resources for XSLT from various vendors (not just Microsoft).

It also helps to have some great books on the topic. Make sure you read books such as *Mastering XSLT* by Chuck White (Sybex, 2002). It also helps to know something about XML schemas, so check out *XML Schemas* by Chelsea Valentine, Lucinda Dykes, and Ed Tittel (Sybex, 2002).

Defining SOAP Messaging

Because Google Web Services relies so heavily on SOAP, you need to know how SOAP messaging works. The following sections describe SOAP basics, tell you about some important SOAP issues, and provide a few pointers on where you can learn more about SOAP. You'll also see a very simple SOAP example designed for use with a Web page with JavaScript.

> ▶ **NOTE**
>
> Many of the SOAP examples in this book rely on the Microsoft SOAP Toolkit. You can download this toolkit at `http://msdn.microsoft.com/nhp/default.asp?contentid=28000523`. The examples all rely on the 3.0 version of the toolkit—the latest version available at the time of writing.

Determining Which SOAP Standard to Use

SOAP has gone through three major revisions. Each revision makes SOAP a better product to use for communication purposes. Almost no one uses the SOAP 1.0 standard anymore. Few vendors used this standard because it had some significant problems that the SOAP 1.1 standard quickly solved. The SOAP 1.1 standard is popular because it works well for most communication that doesn't require security. For example, you can safely use SOAP 1.1 products for most Google Web Services tasks because you aren't passing along anything that's secret.

> ▶ **TIP**
>
> You can find many SOAP 1.1 resources now. The ZVON Web site at `http://www.zvon`
> `.org/xxl/soapReference/Output/index.html` provides a great reference you can use to
> learn more about SOAP. You'll find a SOAP tutorial at `http://www.w3schools.com/soap/`.
> The SOAP 1.1 specification appears at `http://static.userland.com/xmlRpcCom/soap/`
> `SOAPv11.htm`. Microsoft provides a SOAP testing tool that you can download at `http://`
> `msdn.microsoft.com/library/en-us/dnsoap/html/soapvalidator.asp`. Learn more
> about SOAP messages with attachments at `http://www.w3.org/TR/SOAP-attachments`.
> Finally, if you want to learn all the ins and outs of SOAP 1.1 with both Microsoft and third
> party products, get my book *Special Edition Using SOAP* (Que, 2001).

The SOAP 1.2 standard originally appeared on the scene on July 9, 2001 (`http://www.w3`
`.org/TR/2001/WD-soap12-20010709/`). However, the World Wide Web Consortium (W3C) didn't make it a recommendation until June 24, 2003 (`http://www.w3.org/TR/soap12-part1/`). Consequently, many of the products you see on the Internet today still rely on SOAP 1.1 and will probably continue to rely on this standard for some time. Even Microsoft's latest release of Visual Studio .NET still relies on SOAP 1.1.

SOAP 1.2 adds some very important features. The most important feature is added security. However, according to an *eWeek* article (`http://www.eweek.com/article2/0,4149,1137432,00`
`.asp`), the new standard includes over 400 fixes for previous problems. You can also find some interesting *InfoWorld* articles on the topic at `http://www.infoworld.com/article/03/05/07/`
`HNsoap_1.html`, `http://www.infoworld.com/article/02/12/19/021219hnsoapadvance_1`
`.html?1220fram`, and `http://www.infoworld.com/article/02/11/01/021101hnsoap12_1`
`.html?1104mnam`. The last article is especially important because it points out another reason that vendors haven't embraced SOAP 1.2—potential patent issues were involved that the standards committee had to clear up.

▶ **TIP**

> Although SOAP 1.2 resources are still a little rare, you should look at the primer at `http://www.w3.org/TR/soap12-part0/`, the framework specification at `http://www.w3.org/TR/soap12-part1/`, and the adjuncts at `http://www.w3.org/TR/soap12-part2/`. You may also want to read about test collection methods at `http://www.w3.org/TR/soap12-testcollection/`. The W3C is also working on a number of additional specifications that aren't at the recommendation stage. These specifications include SOAP 1.2 attachments (`http://www.w3.org/TR/soap12-af/`), SOAP 1.2 email bindings (`http://www.w3.org/TR/soap12-email`), and SOAP 1.2 normalization (`http://www.w3.org/TR/soap12-n11n/`).

Given the current state of SOAP, you need to consider three things when you decide which standard to use. First, you need to know whether your product of choice even supports SOAP 1.2—most don't. Second, you need to consider whether the features SOAP 1.2 offers are essential to your organization. In many cases, using SOAP 1.1 still works fine. Third, you need to consider whether the remote sites you want to work with use SOAP 1.2. Using SOAP 1.1 until your partners catch up probably makes sense. You do want to use SOAP 1.2 sometime in the future, so planning for it today is a good idea.

Understanding the Parts of a SOAP Message

To understand SOAP, you need to consider the features that make up a SOAP message. A SOAP message includes the SOAP package, the XML envelope, and the HyperText Transfer Protocol (HTTP) or Simple Mail Transfer Protocol (SMTP) transport. Think about this system in the same way that you do a letter, with SOAP acting as the letter, XML as the envelope to hold the letter, and HTTP or SMTP as the mail carrier to deliver the letter. The most common transport protocol in use today is HTTP, so that's what we'll look at in this section. Keep in mind, however, that SOAP can theoretically use any of a number of transport protocols and probably will in the future. Figure 3.10 shows a common SOAP message configuration. Notice the SOAP message formatting. This isn't the only way to wrap a SOAP message in other protocols, but it's the most common method in use today.

The HTTP portion of a SOAP message looks much the same as any other HTTP header you may have seen in the past. In fact, if you don't look carefully, you might pass it by without paying any attention. As with any HTTP transmission, there are two types of headers—one for requests and another for responses. Figure 3.10 shows examples of both types.

FIGURE 3.10:

An illustration of a typical SOAP message.

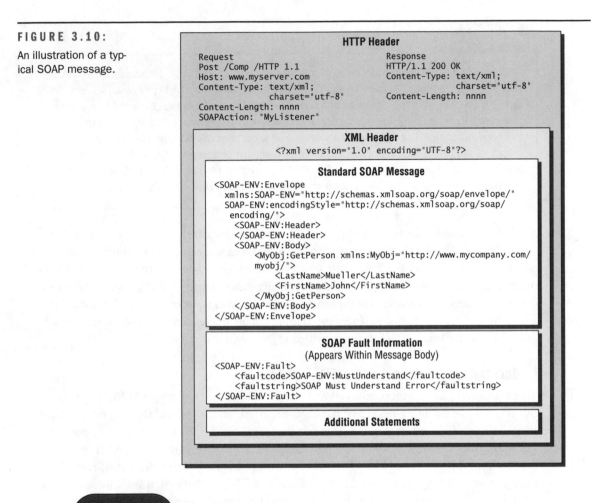

FIGURE 3.10:

An illustration of a typical SOAP message.

HTTP Header

Request
Post /Comp /HTTP 1.1
Host: www.myserver.com
Content-Type: text/xml;
          charset="utf-8"
Content-Length: nnnn
SOAPAction: "MyListener"

Response
HTTP/1.1 200 OK
Content-Type: text/xml;
          charset="utf-8"
Content-Length: nnnn

XML Header
<?xml version="1.0" encoding="UTF-8"?>

Standard SOAP Message
```
<SOAP-ENV:Envelope
  xmlns:SOAP-ENV="http://schemas.xmlsoap.org/soap/envelope/"
  SOAP-ENV:encodingStyle="http://schemas.xmlsoap.org/soap/
  encoding/">
  <SOAP-ENV:Header>
  </SOAP-ENV:Header>
  <SOAP-ENV:Body>
      <MyObj:GetPerson xmlns:MyObj="http://www.mycompany.com/
      myobj/">
          <LastName>Mueller</LastName>
          <FirstName>John</FirstName>
      </MyObj:GetPerson>
  </SOAP-ENV:Body>
</SOAP-ENV:Envelope>
```

SOAP Fault Information
(Appears Within Message Body)
```
<SOAP-ENV:Fault>
    <faultcode>SOAP-ENV:MustUnderstand</faultcode>
    <faultstring>SOAP Must Understand Error</faultstring>
</SOAP-ENV:Fault>
```

Additional Statements

► **TIP**

Working with the new capabilities provided by technologies like XML and SOAP means dealing with dynamically created Web pages. While it's nice that you can modify the content of a Web page as needed for an individual user, it can also be a problem if you need to troubleshoot the Web page. That's where a handy little script comes into play. Type **javascript:**`'<xmp>'+`**document.all(0).outerHTML+'</xmp>'** in the Address field of Internet Explorer for any dynamically created Web page and you'll see the actual HTML for that page. This includes the results of using scripts and other page construction techniques.

As with any request header, the HTTP portion of a SOAP message will contain an action (Post, in most cases), the HTTP version, a Host name, and some Content-Length information. The Post action portion of the header will contain the path for the SOAP listener. Also located within a request header is a Content-Type entry of text/xml and a charset entry of utf-8. The utf-8 entry is important right now because many SOAP toolkits don't support utf-16 or other character sets.

You'll also find the unique SOAPAction entry in the HTTP request header. It contains the Uniform Resource Identifier (URI) of the component used to parse the SOAP request. If the SOAPAction entry is "", then the server will use the HTTP Request-URI entry to locate a listener instead. This is the only SOAP-specific entry in the HTTP header—everything else we've discussed could appear in any HTTP formatted message.

The response header portion of the HTTP wrapper for a SOAP message contains all of the essentials as well. You'll find the HTTP version, status, and content length as usual. There are two common status indicators for a response header: 200 OK or 500 Internal Server Error. The SOAP specification allows use of any value in the 200 series for a positive response, but a server must return a status value of 500 for SOAP errors to indicate a server error.

Whenever a SOAP response header contains an error status, the SOAP message must include a SOAP fault section. We'll talk about SOAP faults in the "Defining Fault Tolerance in a SOAP Message" section of the chapter. All you need to know now is that the HTTP header provides the first indication of a SOAP fault that will require additional processing.

All SOAP messages use XML encoding. SOAP follows the XML specification, and you can consider it a true superset of XML. In other words, it adds to the functionality already in place within XML. Anyone familiar with XML will feel comfortable with SOAP at the outset—all you really need to know is the SOAP nuances. Although the examples in the SOAP specification don't show an XML connection (other than the formatting of the SOAP message), SOAP messages always contain an XML header similar to the one shown in Figure 3.10.

A simple SOAP message consists of an envelope that contains both a header and a body (sort of the same arrangement used by an HTML page). The header can contain information that isn't associated with the data itself. For example, the header commonly contains a transaction ID when the application needs one to identify a particular SOAP message. The body contains the data in XML format. If an error occurs, the body will contain fault information, rather than data.

SOAP is essentially a one-way data transfer protocol. While SOAP messages often follow a request/response pattern, the messages themselves are individual entities. This means that a SOAP message is stand-alone—it doesn't rely on the immediate presence of a server, nor is a response expected when a request message contains all of the required information. For example, some types of data entry may not require a response since the user is inputting information and may not care about a response.

The envelope in which a SOAP message travels, however, may provide more than just a one-way transfer path. For example, when a developer encases a SOAP message within an HTTP envelope, the request and response both use the same connection. HTTP creates and maintains the connection, not SOAP. Consequently, the connection follows the HTTP way of performing data transfer—using the same techniques as a browser uses to request Web pages for display.

Defining Fault Tolerance in a SOAP Message

Sometimes a SOAP request will generate a fault message instead of the anticipated reply. The server may not have the means to answer your request, the request you generated may be incomplete, or bad communication may prevent your message from arriving in the same state as you sent it. There are many reasons that you may receive a SOAP fault message including messages that the client produces that the server can't process, errors on the server such as a missing application, and SOAP version mismatches.

When a server returns a fault message, it doesn't return any data. Look at Figure 3.10 and you'll see a typical client fault message. Notice the message contains only fault information. With this in mind, the client-side applications you create must be prepared to parse SOAP fault messages and return the information in such a way that the user will understand the meaning of the fault.

Figure 3.10 shows the standard presentation of a SOAP fault message. Notice that the fault envelope resides within the body of the SOAP message. A fault envelope will generally contain a `faultcode` and `faultstring` element that tells you which error occurred. All of the other SOAP fault message elements are optional. The following list tells you how they're used.

`faultcode`   The `faultcode` contains the name of the error that occurred. It can use a dot syntax to define a more precise error code. The `faultcode` will always begin with a classification. For example, the `faultcode` in Figure 3.10 consists of a `SOAP-ENV` error code followed by a `MustUnderstand` subcode. This error tells you that the server couldn't understand the client request. Since it's possible to create a list of standard SOAP `faultcode`s, you can use them directly for processing purposes.

`faultstring`   This is a human-readable form of the error specified by the `faultcode` entry. This string should follow the same format as HTTP error strings. You can learn more about HTTP error strings by reading the HTTP specification at `http://www.faqs.org/rfcs/rfc2616.html`. A good general rule to follow is to make the `faultstring` entry short and easy to understand.

faultactor This element points to the source of a fault in a SOAP transaction. It contains a Uniform Resource Identifier (URI) similar to the one used for determining the destination of the header entry. According to the specification, you must include this element if the application that generates the fault message isn't the ultimate destination for the SOAP message.

detail You'll use this element to hold detailed information about a fault when available. For example, this is the element used to hold server-side component return values. This element is SOAP message body specific, which means you can't use it to detail errors that occur in other areas like the SOAP message header. A detail entry acts as an envelope for storing detail subelements. Each subelement includes a tag containing namespace information and a string containing error message information.

Understanding How WSDL Fits In

The documentation that comes with Google Web Services Kit contains examples of how to format a message using SOAP. These examples include the XML header and all of the features discussed in the "Understanding the Parts of a SOAP Message" section of the chapter. Figure 3.11 shows a typical example from the kit. However, you won't need to use these examples in most cases.

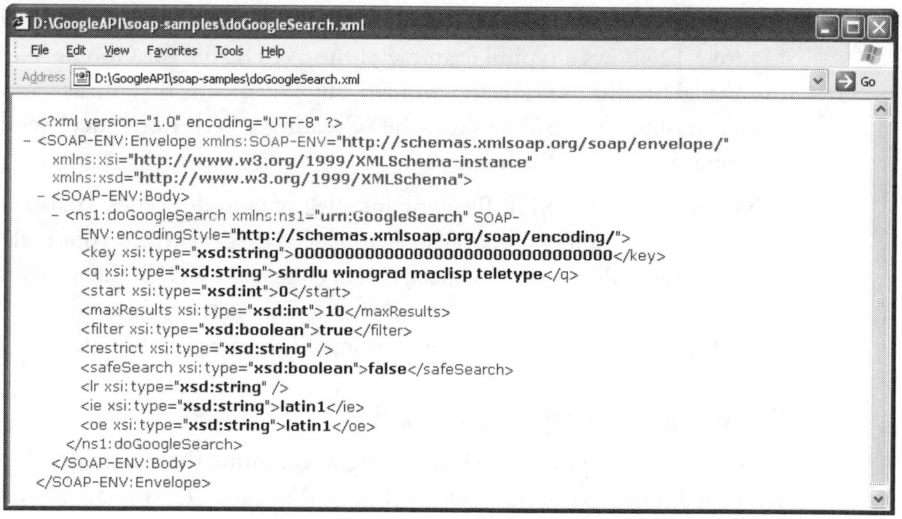

FIGURE 3.11:

The kit contains a number of SOAP message examples.

```xml
<?xml version="1.0" encoding="UTF-8" ?>
<SOAP-ENV:Envelope xmlns:SOAP-ENV="http://schemas.xmlsoap.org/soap/envelope/"
    xmlns:xsi="http://www.w3.org/1999/XMLSchema-instance"
    xmlns:xsd="http://www.w3.org/1999/XMLSchema">
  <SOAP-ENV:Body>
    <ns1:doGoogleSearch xmlns:ns1="urn:GoogleSearch" SOAP-
    ENV:encodingStyle="http://schemas.xmlsoap.org/soap/encoding/">
      <key xsi:type="xsd:string">00000000000000000000000000000000</key>
      <q xsi:type="xsd:string">shrdlu winograd maclisp teletype</q>
      <start xsi:type="xsd:int">0</start>
      <maxResults xsi:type="xsd:int">10</maxResults>
      <filter xsi:type="xsd:boolean">true</filter>
      <restrict xsi:type="xsd:string" />
      <safeSearch xsi:type="xsd:boolean">false</safeSearch>
      <lr xsi:type="xsd:string" />
      <ie xsi:type="xsd:string">latin1</ie>
      <oe xsi:type="xsd:string">latin1</oe>
    </ns1:doGoogleSearch>
  </SOAP-ENV:Body>
</SOAP-ENV:Envelope>
```

WSDL provides a means for describing a Web service so that the Integrated Development Environment (IDE) you use can create the definitions needed. Some developers originally found WSDL less than helpful, and it doesn't work with every SOAP toolkit you can download. The SOAP samples help developers who must create messages manually get the format correct. However, if you use a product such as Visual Studio .NET, the IDE downloads the WSDL from the Google Web site and you'll find that you don't actually have to worry about the construction of the SOAP message.

> ▶ **TIP**
>
> You can find a wealth of resources about WSDL on the Internet. One of the more interesting offerings includes the ZVON reference at http://www.zvon.org/xxl/WSDL1.1/Output/index.html. The W3C has a tutorial at `http://www.w3schools.com/wsdl/default.asp`. Originally, Microsoft and IBM promoted WSDL on their Web sites, but you can now find the specification on the W3C site at `http://www.w3.org/TR/wsdl`. You can find the IBM view of Web services at `http://www-106.ibm.com/developerworks/webservices/` and `http://www.alphaworks.ibm.com/tech/webservicestoolkit`. A WSDL search engine (where you can find services that rely on both SOAP and WSDL) appears at `http://www.salcentral.com/salnet/webserviceswsdl.asp`.

Like many other topics discussed, WSDL relies on XML as a basis for communication. Figure 3.12 shows a typical example of the WSDL file for Google Web Services. Note that the Visual Studio .NET IDE automatically downloads this file as part of the process of creating a reference to the Web site—the "Creating a Web Reference" section of Chapter 6 describes how to perform this task.

Notice that the WSDL file contains a list of complex types. It also contains a list of function names. You call a function such as doGoogleSearch() in your code. The IDE automatically creates code to send a doGoogleSearchRequest SOAP message and code that interprets the doGoogleSearchResponse SOAP message the application receives from the server. The WSDL file is instrumental in performing all this work automatically.

Performing a Simple SOAP Call

It's time to try the first SOAP call using a technique that many developers will employ for learning Google Web Services—a simple Web page. Listing 3.4 shows how to make a simple SOAP call using JavaScript. You'll find the complete source for this example in the \Chapter 03\Viewing XSLT folder of the source code located on the Sybex Web site.

FIGURE 3.12:

Using WSDL makes
SOAP messaging
extremely easy for the
developer.

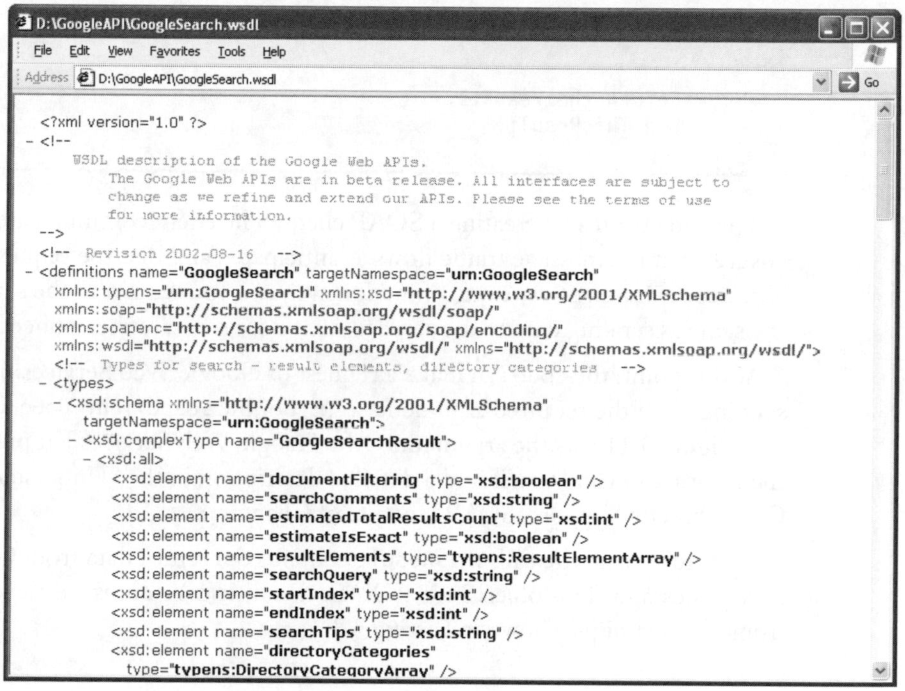

Listing 3.4   **Simple JavaScript SOAP Call**

```javascript
function CallGoogle()
{
    // Create the SOAP client.
    var SoapClient = new ActiveXObject("MSSOAP.SoapClient30");

    // Initialize the SOAP client so it can access Google
    // Web Services.
    SoapClient.MSSoapInit("http://api.google.com/GoogleSearch.wsdl",
                          "GoogleSearchService",
                          "GoogleSearchPort");

    // Make a search request.
    var ThisResult =
        SoapClient.doGoogleSearch("Your-License-Key",
                                  SubmissionForm.SearchStr.value,
                                  1,
                                  10,
                                  false,
                                  "",
                                  false,
```

```
                                 " ",
                                 " ",
                                 " ");

    // Return the results.
    return ThisResult;
}
```

The code begins by creating a SOAP client. The client communicates with the server—it ensures that the message traffic flows as anticipated and that the request is formed correctly. The SoapClient.MSSoapInit() function creates a connection to the server. This step isn't the same as sending data to the server—all it does is create the connection.

At this point, the code can make a request of Google Web Services. It performs this task by sending all of the required arguments as part of the SoapClient.doGoogleSearch() function call. Figure 3.11 lists the arguments—the Google Web Services Kit provides an overview of the information and you'll find a detailed description in the "Understanding that Google Only Directly Supports SOAP" section of Chapter 4.

On return from the call, ThisResult contains the return data from Google in the form of a SOAP message. This object isn't an XML document. You must retrieve the XML document using the technique shown in Listing 3.3.

Understanding Privacy Issues

No one sends private information across the Internet using Google unless they're looking for an individual. Google won't ask for anyone's name, address, telephone number, or other contact information. In fact, such a request would be very suspect since Google doesn't even have a use for such information—they're not selling anything, but their advertisers are. The only time you need to consider privacy issues when working with Google Web Services is if you somehow associate a request with a particular user or company. When your company is the only user of the application, you need to consider how much information you want to give away to people peeking at your communications. In some cases, you might decide to look for specific information using analysis of a general search that doesn't compromise privacy in any way.

Even though Google doesn't require the use of any personal information, you might require such information for your application. Make sure you actually need the information before you request it. You should also include a privacy policy on your Web site to ensure that everyone can use the application you created. The "Designing for Privacy Issues" section of Chapter 11 describes how to implement a privacy policy on your site.

Understanding Security Issues

The security issues for using Google are subtle. You never need to worry about using exotic encryption techniques when making a request, because nothing of direct value is exchanged. However, it's possible for someone to intercept the request and learn more about you personally or your company. When this information gathering leads to some type of valuable deduction, you have a security leak on your hand. For example, Company A might be interested in knowing whether Company B is bidding on a given project. When someone in Company A monitors the search queries users in Company B make, it becomes obvious that Company B is interested in the project and Company A takes actions to make sure their bid is accepted. The queries don't represent a security breach, but the analysis of the queries does present a problem. Company B could have protected itself by making generic queries and performing local analysis as necessary. As mentioned earlier—the security issues are subtle—perhaps too subtle for most situations.

Some security issues aren't quite as subtle. You still need to consider security for your site when it performs Web service tasks. One of the better white papers on how the standards groups are meeting security needs appears on the Microsoft site at `http://msdn.microsoft.com/library/en-us/dnwssecur/html/securitywhitepaper.asp`. This discussion also provides a road map of security services.

It's also important to consider other sources of security information. For example, the Worldwide Web Consortium (W3C) and Internet Engineering Task Form (IETF) released the XML Signature specification in 2002. An XML Signature can help a recipient validate the sender of XML data and the integrity of that data. You can read about this standard at `http://www.w3.org/TR/2002/REC-xmldsig-core-20020212/`. The W3C and IETF are still working on two other XML security standards: XML Encryption and XML Key Management.

Your Call to Action

You now know how to work with XML. This may not seem like much, but considering how important XML is to Web services, knowing how to work with XML is essential. Without knowing XML, you can't successfully build many Google Web Services applications. Viewing the XML you receive from Google helps you understand how various requests affect the information flow, which increases the chance that you'll develop efficient applications without a lot of extra effort.

This chapter is a beginning. You need to spend more time working with XML to become truly proficient with it. Make sure you visit at least some of the Web sites listed in this chapter to learn more about XML and related technologies such as SOAP and XSLT. Finally, if you don't have privacy and security policies in place, make sure you create the required documentation now, before something happens. Written policies are the best way to reduce risk. If you do have written policies, make sure you revisit them annually to ensure they still meet requirements of your organization, no matter how big or small.

Chapter 4 is the start of a new section. Rather than spending time looking at various techniques for developing applications and theoretical knowledge you need to implement a Google Web Services application, this section shows you how to perform the task. Chapter 4 presents concepts and techniques that everyone needs to work with Google Web Services. The chapters that follow begin looking at individual language requirements. In sum, Chapter 4 is the first chapter where you begin writing application code.

Part II

▶ **Writing** Google Web Services Programs

Chapter 4

Determining Which Communication Method to Use	Choosing a Platform

▶ Starting the Development Process

Choosing a Development Language	Creating Internationalized Applications

You might be one of the many people who think they can't write an application or have no interest in doing so. The applications demonstrated in Chapter 3 might not look like much, but they really are applications. Writing applications shouldn't fill you with fear or trepidation, because most people have the skills needed—all that you really need is a desire to do something and to know how to write a procedure. Coding is often more a matter of discipline and technique, art rather than science.

Designing software includes a number of tasks this chapter doesn't consider, such as how to create the user interface. In addition, the chapter won't discuss defining schedules and other tasks that don't really relate to the topic at hand—connecting to Google Web Services and using the information it provides effectively. Consequently, this chapter discusses issues you probably didn't hear about in a computer science class, read in a book, learn about in a magazine, or discuss with a friend across the street.

Web services are all about communication. Your application uses some type of communication medium to transmit a request to a remote server and receive a response. The kind of communication you use makes a great deal of difference in the way you design and optimize your application. The communication method can also change the way your application operates and can affect performance.

You also need to consider the target platform for your application and choose the best language to meet your particular needs. Google Web Services works well with a number of platforms and programming languages (as you'll see in the chapters that follow). Some developers attempt to take a one size fits all approach to selecting a language, but that's clearly not the best approach. This chapter helps you decide which platforms to target and which language to use for your specific needs.

Finally, most Web sites don't get visitors from just one country anymore. In fact, I've found that I use Google's translation service quite often now to translate sites in Japanese and German (among other languages). Often, these sites contain a bit of information I need to get a consulting job done or perform a writing task. Consequently, I understand the benefits that internationalization can provide. This final section discusses when internationalization can make your site more appealing and some of the steps you need to perform to do it.

Getting Additional Information about Application Design

This chapter doesn't discuss general application design. Make sure you augment the information in this chapter with some general design information from books such as *Designing Highly Useable Software* by Jeff Cogswell (Sybex, 2004). Another good book to consider is *Database Design for Mere Mortals: A Hands-On Guide to Relational Database Design*, Second Edition, by Michael J. Hernandez (Addison-Wesley, 2003). Finally, you might consider *Patterns of Enterprise Application Architecture* by Martin Fowler, David Rice, Matthew Foemmel, Edward Hieatt, Robert Mee, and Randy Stafford (Addison-Wesley, 2002).

Don't think that you're limited to reading books about design. You can also find a wealth of online sources for specific topics. For example, Microsoft provides a number of white papers online such as the article entitled "Modeling Your Application and Data" at `http://msdn.microsoft.com/library/en-us/vsent7/html/vxoriModelingYourApplicationData.asp`. You should also consider sources such as Rational's (now IBM) article entitled "Modeling Web Application Design with UML" at `http://www.rational.com/products/whitepapers/100462.jsp`. Sometimes online magazines provide great input. Check out the article entitled "Magic Quadrants: Business Modeling, Application Design" at `http://www4.gartner.com/pages/story.php.id.2648.s.8.jsp`—it provides some great resources you can use.

Make sure you also get any application design software you need. There are moderately priced solutions such as Microsoft Visio (`http://www.microsoft.com/office/visio/`). However, you should also consider shareware from sites such as Tucows (`http://idirect.tucows.com/`), ZDNet (`http://downloads-zdnet.com.com/2001-20-0.html`), CNET (`http://www.cnet.com/`), and Nonags (`http://nonags.com/`). If your application is small enough, you can also use simple drawing programs such as Paint Shop Pro (`http://www.jasc.com`) or create the design by hand on paper. The point is to get the design down in print so that you can refer to it.

No matter what source of information you use and how you get your design in writing, you want to avoid one of the most common mistakes that developers make—starting an application without designing it. You wouldn't consider building a house without a blueprint—developing a blueprint for your application is the same. Although this chapter doesn't provide general design information, you'll find it essential in adding the Google Web Services twist to your application design.

Choosing a Communication Method

All of the examples to this point in the book have relied on some form of communication to achieve their goals. In fact, every Google Web Services application you create will include some type of communication with the remote server unless that application relies on static data. Even then, you need to consider significant licensing issues for updates because the updated data will have to come from some source. For example, a PDA could obtain updates from a local desktop, which avoids having the PDA connect to Google Web Services, but the desktop will still need some source of updated information (usually a direct connection).

The following sections discuss the design issues surrounding the various communication choices you have. You'll find that Google Web Services isn't very flexible, which means you must exercise care in choosing a communication option. In most cases, your only choice is to use SOAP because that's what Google supports natively.

Understanding That Google Only Directly Supports SOAP

The only form of communication that Google supports directly—at least at the moment—is SOAP. Unlike other Web services, you can't use techniques such as XML over HTTP (also called REST, REpresentational State Transfer) or XML-RPC (eXtensible Markup Language Remote Procedure Call) with the current setup. However, this situation could (and probably will) change in the future. Given that Google only supports this one method of communication directly, most developers will use it rather than develop an alternative that could cause problems later.

> ▶ **NOTE**
>
> Most JavaScript applications require a separate SOAP library such as SOAPlite. However, Mozilla users can rely on the built-in SOAP support provided by their browser. This chapter doesn't discuss use of the built-in SOAP support. However, you can find the technique described and demonstrated on scottandrew.com at `http://www.scottandrew.com/weblog/googleapi`.

The Web Services Description Language (WSDL) and sample SOAP files provided with the kit show how the SOAP requests work to an extent. The WSDL file is the most reliable source, but it's completely undocumented, so you're left to figure out what each entry means. The sample SOAP files are easier to understand, but contain inaccuracies. For example, unless you read the README.TXT file that appears in the \GoogleAPI folder, rather than the SAMPLES-README.TXT file that appears with the samples in the \GoogleAPI\soap-samples folder, you won't know that Google ignores the ie and oe arguments. In this case, the sample SOAP files would lead you to believe that using the ie and oe arguments is perfectly acceptable. Unfortunately, the Google Web API Reference doesn't document these arguments clearly for a search request and doesn't include any documentation for the cached page or spelling requests. Consequently, the following sections describe these calls in detail.

Defining the Search Request Arguments

The search request asks Google for a list of links based on the search criteria you provide. Defining a complete and exact search request is so important that all of Chapter 2 focuses on this topic. However, the search criteria are just one element of the search request. The following list defines each of the search request arguments. Your application must provide these arguments in order as part of the search request. Otherwise, Google won't honor the request.

key Every request you make requires the license key you obtained from Google. When you make a request without the license key or using the key found in the Google examples, you'll receive an invalid authorization key message. Google uses a string of zeros (00000000000000000000000000000000) as the sample key—this key looks nothing like the actual key. The examples in this book use "Your-License-Key" as the sample key. In both cases, you must replace the sample key with a real key.

q This string argument contains the search request. Tests indicate that you can make search requests of any length and Google will honor them. However, Google only checks for the first 10 search terms—it ignores the remaining search terms and doesn't raise an error. Even limiting your search to 10 terms means that you can be quite specific in requesting what you want or you can make a general query and filter the data locally. The one caveat you do need to observe is that complex search specifications tend to reduce the number of results to the point that you don't get any results at all. Smart search techniques make the request specific, without attempting to locate the one result that perfectly matches a need. See Chapter 2 for a complete discussion of search request elements.

start This numeric argument contains the 0-based starting point for the search. You must couple this starting point with the number of results you request, with 10 results being the maximum. Consequently, if you want to view the third set of results and you request 10 results for each set, you would set this argument to 30. An odd problem can occur when working with Google Web Services, however. Although the results you receive are sequential, they aren't necessarily complete. The actual results might start at 1 or skip a similar result. This means you can't use a strict starting point, you must base the starting point on the returned values. The "Defining the Search Results" section describes this issue in greater detail.

maxResults Google lets you request a maximum of 10 results. However, you can specify less than that amount when you only need a few results. In addition, you may receive fewer results if the search criteria are strict enough. The benefit of requesting fewer results is that you get the response faster, so your application performs better. However, if you plan to request additional results anyway, it's probably better to request the maximum number of results and cache the additional results locally.

filter   The documentation doesn't make this particular argument very clear. You provide true or false as the input values—not the values described in the Automatic Filtering section of the Google Web API Reference. Turning filtering on means that Google looks for results that have the same title and snippet and removes them from the result set. The Web service only returns the first result and eliminates the others. In addition, Google only returns the first two results from a particular Web host. Filtering means that you have to select the start argument value carefully because Google will leave out some of the results.

restrict   This argument restricts the results you receive to a particular country of origin. Don't confuse this argument with a language restriction. For example, when you select the United States as the country of origin, you could still receive pages written in Spanish or German. However, you won't receive results from either Spain or Germany. The Restricts section of the Google Web API Reference contains a chart of country codes you must use for this argument. As with most restrictions, this argument will create holes in the result set and affect the start argument value.

safeSearch   Generally, you can use this argument to ensure you don't receive any results with pornographic content. However, the filter doesn't work all the time and some search terms will almost certainly retrieve adult content despite the use of this filter. In addition, as with most filtering, using the safe search feature may mean that you won't see some results, even though they don't contain any pornographic material. Set the argument to true when you want to avoid adult content. Contact Google at safesearch@google.com when you encounter pornographic material that you don't want. Telling Google about the problem will help refine the filter so that others don't encounter the same results.

lr   Sometimes you need a result in a specific language. This argument doesn't restrict the country that you get a result from, but it does restrict the language of the result. For example, you could tell Google that you only want results written in Japanese. The Restricts section of the Google Web API Reference contains a chart of country codes you must use for this argument. As with most restrictions, this argument will create holes in the result set and affect the start argument value.

ie   This argument is ignored. You still need to provide it as part of the SOAP message, but leave the content blank (an empty string). Google no longer offers input encoding (the use of special character sets); all output appears in 8-bit Unicode Transformation Format (UTF-8) encoding.

oe   This argument is ignored. You still need to provide it as part of the SOAP message, but leave the content blank (an empty string). Google no longer offers output encoding.

As you can see, the search request provides a number of ways to restrict the result set in addition to the search criteria. Listing 3.4 provides a simple example of how to create a SOAP search request. The search examples will increase in complexity as the book progresses.

Defining the Spelling Request Arguments

You can perform spelling checks using Google Web Services. However, simple experiments have shown so far that the spelling service only appears to work in English. Google will probably fix this limitation in the future. The actual request process is very easy. All you need supply are the two arguments shown below using the doSpellingSuggestion() method.

key   See the key argument explanation in the "Defining the Search Request Arguments" section.

phrase   This argument contains a string that you want to check. Google makes a reasonable effort to correct the spelling. However, it won't correct some types of spelling errors. For example, the spelling checker couldn't fix misspellings such as uneke (unique). The probably of getting a completely corrected string also seems to decrease as the length of this argument increases.

Listing 4.1 shows how to make a spelling request using JavaScript. You'll find the complete source for this example in the \Chapter 04\SpellingRequest folder of the source code located on the Sybex Web site.

Listing 4.1   **Spelling Request with a Browser**

```
function CallGoogle()
{
   // Create the SOAP client.
   var SoapClient = new ActiveXObject("MSSOAP.SoapClient30");

   // Initialize the SOAP client so it can access Google
   // Web Services.
   SoapClient.MSSoapInit("http://api.google.com/GoogleSearch.wsdl",
                         "GoogleSearchService",
                         "GoogleSearchPort");

   // Make a spelling request.
   SubmissionForm.CorrectStr.value =
      SoapClient.doSpellingSuggestion("Your-License-Key",
                                      SubmissionForm.SpellStr.value);
}
```

The code begins by creating a SOAP client. You must use a SOAP client to communicate with Google Web Services. The client ensures the message is properly formatted and also obtains any return values provided by the server.

Once the code creates the SOAP client, it initializes a connection to Google Web Services. Every application you create using JavaScript includes these two steps. The location of the Web Services Description Language (WSDL) doesn't change, and you'll always use the same service and port entries.

The code makes the `SoapClient.doSpellingSuggestion()` method call at this point using your license key and input string. Because this method returns a string, you can place it directly in the output label. Figure 4.1 shows typical results from this method.

Defining the Cache Request Arguments

Google provides access to cached versions of many Web sites. You can use these cached versions of a number of purposes, including obtaining information that no longer appears on a particular site. The following list describes the arguments you supply to Google to retrieve a cached page using the `doGetCachedPage()` method.

key   See the `key` argument explanation in the "Defining the Search Request Arguments" section.

url   This argument contains the URL of the site. You must make sure that Google actually has a cached version of the site using a search call or provide some form of error handling. The return value is a base 64 representation of the Web page. You can find a great description of base 64 encoding at `http://www.robertgraham.com/tools/base64coder.html` along with a tool you can use to test the results you receive from Google.

Listing 4.2 shows how to obtain the cached page from Google. You'll find the complete source for this example in the `\Chapter 04\GetCachedPage` folder of the source code located on the Sybex Web site.

FIGURE 4.1:

This example shows typical spelling check results.

Listing 4.2   **Cached Page Request with a Browser**

```
function CallGoogle()
{
   // Create the SOAP client.
   var SoapClient = new ActiveXObject("MSSOAP.SoapClient30");

   // Initialize the SOAP client so it can access Google
   // Web Services.
   SoapClient.MSSoapInit("http://api.google.com/GoogleSearch.wsdl",
                         "GoogleSearchService",
                         "GoogleSearchPort");

   // Make a cached page request.
   var TheResult =
      SoapClient.doGetCachedPage("Your-License-Key ",
                                 SubmissionForm.URLStr.value);

   for (var Counter = 0; Counter < TheResult.Length; Counter++)
   {
      document.write(TheResult[Counter].toString());
   }
}
```

Unfortunately, this listing points out a problem with JavaScript. The code fails at the for loop because of an inherent limitation in most scripting languages. The return value includes a byte array, and the version of JavaScript that comes with Internet Explorer doesn't know how to interact with it. This same limitation occurs with every JavaScript interpreter that follows the ECMAScript standard (`http://www.ecma-international.org/publications/standards/Ecma-262.htm`). To work with this data, you need to create a special object to interpret the byte array, use an existing object that might not appear on every machine that uses the application, or rely on a third party nonstandard interpreter such as the NJS JavaScript Interpreter (`http://www.bbassett.net/njs/`). Because of the issues surrounding this particular request, I recommend that you use a more advanced language, such as Visual Basic for Applications (VBA), Visual Basic, C#, PHP, or Java (among others) that do support byte arrays directly.

▶ **NOTE**

ECMA (European Computer Manufacturer's Association) is the official group tasked with maintaining the JavaScript (now called ECMAScript) standard. Most versions of JavaScript add extensions to the ECMAScript standard. For example, Microsoft's version, JScript, includes specialized support for the Windows Scripting Engine. You can find a complete list of Microsoft differences at `http://www.script-info.net/jsvbs/msscript/js56/js56jsgrpnonecmafeatures.php`.

Understanding the Google Data Output

Once you make a request, Google sends a response. Your code must interpret the response and present it to the user. The following sections provide an overview of the responses that Google sends to various requests. The sample code in the remainder of the book helps you explore this topic in greater detail.

> ▶ **TIP**
>
> It's important to remember that Google regularly changes its search algorithms to reduce the risk that some Web sites will receive more representation than they deserve. (There are other reasons for changing the search algorithm, including changes in the type of data provided on the Internet.) According to a Ziff Davis Channel Zone article (`http://www.eweek`
> `.com/article2/0,4149,1400623,00.asp?kc=EWNWS120203DTX1K0000599`), these changes occur regularly and don't always meet with Webmaster expectations. The lesson for anyone using Google Web Services is that you should expect the output of your application to change over time and prepare users for this eventuality. Make sure users don't assume that application output will remain constant.

Defining the Search Results

The search results are the most complex return that Google Web Services provides. The Search Results Format section of the Google Web API Reference discusses these results to an extent. However, it really helps to see a pictorial representation of typical results. Figure 4.2 shows a tree view of the sample SOAP response found in the `doGoogleSearchResponse.xml` file of the `\GoogleAPI\soap-samples` folder.

You should consider a few coding tricks that the documentation doesn't mention, but that become somewhat obvious when you work with Google Web Services for a while. The first is that the `startIndex` won't always be the same as the start index that you specified. Google might have removed the first result from the list. Because you can't be sure about the starting index, you should always use the `startIndex` value when telling the user which results appear on screen.

Another important coding trick is the use of the `endIndex`. Add 1 to this value and use it as the input to the next request. Otherwise, the user will receive some duplicate search results. For example, consider a case where you request 10 results starting at index 0. Google Web Services does return 10 results, but entries 1, 3, and 5 are missing because they're duplicates. Consequently, you should use a starting index of 13, rather than 10, for the next request.

FIGURE 4.2:

Use a tree view of the
Google search results
to understand the
structure of the data
you receive better.

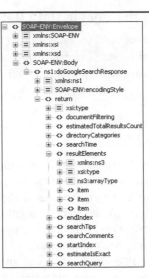

The Google Web API Reference is also unclear about some issues. For example, they never define ODP (Open Directory Project) or what it means to the user. Consequently, you don't learn about the importance of the directoryCategory element data provided with each item. When an item contains this entry, it tells you that it also appears on other search engines, such as Netscape Open Directory, Netscape What's Related, Lycos, HotBot, Dogpile, Thunderstone, Mars Society, and Linux.com Links. The additional information is helpful in determining the presence of a particular site. Once you understand ODP, you also understand the difference between a snippet and a summary element. Google always generates the snippet element, while the summary element comes from the ODP database.

> **▶ TIP**
>
> You can find a lot of interesting information about ODP online. A history of the project appears at http://www.laisha.com/zine/odphistory.html. One of the main ODP pages is at http://dmoz.org/. This page lets you test ODP out and become part of the project. Suggestions for submitting your site for admittance into the ODP appear at http://www.searchengineworld.com/misc/odp.htm. Finally, you can discuss ODP on the forum at http://www.resource-zone.com/.

Defining the Spelling Results

The spelling request results are the easiest of the responses to interpret. All that Google returns is a simple string that you can display for the user. The string contains corrections for every misspelled work in the input string. However, you need to consider a few caveats. When Google doesn't recognize a word, it leaves the misspelled version in the return string. Consequently, the user still has to interpret the results. In addition, a user could misspell a word in such a way that Google recognizes it as something else. The return word is correctly spelled, but not the word the user meant to provide.

Defining the Cached Page Results

The cached page results aren't difficult to understand conceptually—all that you get is a base 64 encoded value. Initially, this value is a string of characters that don't bear much of a resemblance to the data. Depending on the SOAP parser you use, the base 64 encoded string could appear as a byte array to the application. In short, the parser performs the essential decoding for you. However, you still can't use the resulting data.

Most application programming languages provide some means for working with the byte array. For example, the "Choosing between Current and Cached Data" section of Chapter 10 shows that C# developers can easily convert the byte array to a char array, which then acts as input for a new string. The resulting text is ready to display.

Selecting a Platform

You might think at the outset that only desktop users need the Google Web Services application you create. In some cases, you might be right. Other kinds of users might not have a need to access your application in any way because the Google search engine is freely accessible online. However, it's surprising how many applications are seeing use on alternative platforms that many people would have considered impossible even a year or two ago. The problem for developers is seeing past preconceived ideas of how users will employ an application and deciding which platforms the user could use. Once you make that determination, you have to go further and decide which platforms you want to support. The economic benefit of supporting a platform must outweigh the cost of implementing it.

The following sections discuss several platform design options. You'll find recommendations on ways to optimize your platform design decisions. These sections also contain a few surprises—things you might not have considered important. For example, the first section answers the question of whether you always need to implement a desktop application solution.

Writing Desktop Applications

Desktop applications can serve a variety of needs. You can use a desktop application for everything from a corporate library reference that incorporates information from Google Web Services to a special search engine for your Web site. If you think that no one searches the Web using a desktop application, consider the help files that Microsoft supplies with their applications. Each of these help files appears to be a desktop application, but they have an Internet connection for updates and new information.

One important consideration when using Google Web Services is that you can only search for public data. The public nature of the search engine isn't much of a problem when working with a browser-based application. However, it quickly becomes a problem when you want to create a combined local and remote search engine for your business. It's all too easy to forget that as good as Google is, you can't access any private links.

> ▶ **TIP**
>
> One of the most important additions you can make to your applications (both desktop and Web based) is a survey form. The survey should ask users questions about the usability and information content of your site. In addition, you need to know what type of device the responder used to access your site, as well as the devices the responder would like to use to access your site. The "Adding Feedback to Your Application" section of Chapter 11 discusses this issue in greater detail.

The following sections describe three kinds of desktop applications. Obviously, you can write myriad application types for a desktop machine, but these three types work well with Google Web Services. Each application type has something special to offer in the way of flexibility, usability, performance, or compatibility. It's important to weigh your choices carefully, because even desktop machines aren't a one size fits all environment.

Using Standard Applications

Many users are unaware of the communication that goes on behind the scenes with many desktop applications today. The application could rely on standard desktop application controls—the same controls that developers have always used for this kind of application. Most of the examples in Chapters 5 and 6 fall into the standard application category. (Chapter 6 does contain Web server examples that don't fall into this category.) This application doesn't look like it has any type of connectivity to the outside world, but it does use an Internet connection to retrieve data from Google Web Services.

Use standard desktop applications for corporate needs. In many cases, it isn't important that the user know the source of the information used to perform a task; they simply need to know that the information exists. This kind of application could pull data in from a number of sources in a way that helps the user perform a task quickly and with less frustration than using a number of independent applications to perform the same task. Data source hiding is an important development principle to keep in mind. Hiding the source of the data means you don't have to retrain users every time the source of the data changes.

Using Web-enabled Applications

Some developers use the term *Web-enabled* to mean any browser application that sits on the desktop. However, this description doesn't really fit today's application development products. You can easily create an application that looks like a standard desktop application, but uses a browser interface by adding one of many HTML controls to the application. The example in the "Choosing between Current and Cached Data" section of Chapter 10 falls into this category. It doesn't matter whether you use a high-end product such as Visual Studio or an Office product such as Word—the interface still looks like a standard application, but the presentation is all HTML. Microsoft actually uses this technique for most help setups in their applications today.

This kind of application can work well when you need to combine local and remote sources. For example, a research firm likely has myriad papers and other local resources generated by the company. However, when a search for a particular piece of information from a local source isn't satisfied, the search application could automatically switch to Google Web Services.

A side benefit of this approach is that you can combine sources into one page. A research firm employee might see a single page that has a list of all resources for a particular topic. The resources could include mixed local and remote sources. The employee doesn't care, as long as the search results in valid information to use as the basis for new research. The page could include mixed data types as well. For example, a link might include an associated picture so the employee could see a representation of the kind of data the source includes.

Using Browser Applications

A browser application can reside on a desktop or anywhere else for that matter. The user clicks on a link that opens Internet Explorer and takes them to the location of the application. The application could reside on a local intranet or on the Internet. A desktop browser application is usually simple compared to other kinds of browser applications. At most, the application needs to determine what type of browser the user has so that it can account for any compatibility issues.

▶ **TIP**

Part of the answer for solving browser compatibility issues is to ensure you follow World Wide Web Consortium (W3C) guidelines and validate the resulting pages. However, validation doesn't replace good testing techniques using multiple browsers. You can find an archive of most common browsers (and many uncommon browsers) on the evolt.org site at `http://browsers.evolt.org`.

It's important to consider browser compatibility because you don't know which of the many browsers available a user will choose. However, getting the vendors to tell you the facts is nearly impossible. You can find various charts that show browser compatibility issues online. One of the better charts is the Webmonkey Browser Chart at `http://hotwired.lycos.com/webmonkey/reference/browser_chart/index.html`. The advantage of using this chart is that the owner updates it regularly to reflect new browsers. Figure 4.3 shows a typical example of this chart.

As you can see, the Webmonkey Browser Chart presents a wealth of information about the features that each browser supports. Note that this chart only supports Windows browsers—Webmonkey also provides charts for the Macintosh (`http://hotwired.lycos.com/webmonkey/reference/browser_chart/index_mac.html`), Unix/Linux (`http://hotwired.lycos.com/webmonkey/reference/browser_chart/index_nix.html`), and other platforms (`http://hotwired.lycos.com/webmonkey/reference/browser_chart/index_other.html`). Make sure you consider Webmonkey's other offerings, such as a chart that shows how to create special characters and a JavaScript reference library.

FIGURE 4.3: Always check the assumptions you make about browser compatibility against a reliable chart.

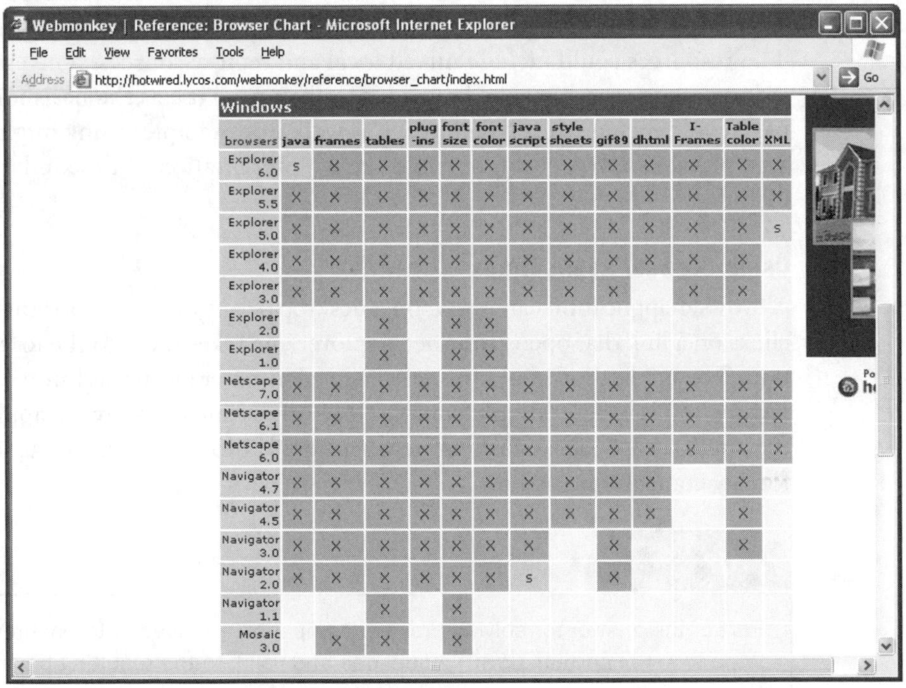

browsers	java	frames	tables	plug -ins	font size	font color	java script	style sheets	gif89	dhtml	I-Frames	Table color	XML
Explorer 6.0	S	X	X	X	X	X	X	X	X	X	X	X	X
Explorer 5.5	X	X	X	X	X	X	X	X	X	X	X	X	X
Explorer 5.0	X	X	X	X	X	X	X	X	X	X	X	X	S
Explorer 4.0	X	X	X	X	X	X	X	X	X	X	X	X	
Explorer 3.0	X	X	X	X	X	X	X	X	X		X	X	
Explorer 2.0			X		X	X							
Explorer 1.0			X		X	X							
Netscape 7.0	X	X	X	X	X	X	X	X	X	X	X	X	X
Netscape 6.1	X	X	X	X	X	X	X	X	X	X	X	X	X
Netscape 6.0	X	X	X	X	X	X	X	X	X	X	X	X	X
Navigator 4.7	X	X	X	X	X	X	X	X	X	X		X	
Navigator 4.5	X	X	X	X	X	X	X	X	X	X		X	
Navigator 3.0	X	X	X	X	X	X	X		X			X	
Navigator 2.0	X	X	X	X	X	X	S		X				
Navigator 1.1			X		X								
Mosaic 3.0		X	X		X								

Use browser applications when you think you might need to connect to other platforms. For example, using a browser application makes it much easier to move the application to the Pocket PC or even a cellular telephone. Browser applications do tend to face a variety of compatibility problems, and they're not very fast when compared to other application types, but they're the flexibility option of choice.

Writing Small Form Factor Applications

Many users now carry some type of small form factor device such as a Personal Digital Assistant (PDA). The PDA is the most popular form, but you could consider some types of notebook computers in this category too. The small form factor device is very portable, generally sees use on the road, and has limits in processing power, memory, and local storage. Notebooks and PDAs don't suffer quite the limitations of a cellular telephone, but you may still find it difficult to write a program that fits on most of these devices and delivers everything needed.

The following sections discuss two kinds of small form factor application: desktop and browser. The Pocket PC is one of the easiest and most powerful PDAs to program, so the first section discusses how you can create desktop applications for this platform. Most people use a Web application of some type for less capable devices, such as the Palm, because local storage and the difficulty of writing an application for these platforms becomes a factor.

> ▶ **TIP**

Google also provides a wireless service that you can use directly. The only problem is that the wireless service is hidden several layers down in the Web site hierarchy. Learn more about this service at `http://www.google.com/options/wireless.html`. It's important to note that this wireless service specifically excludes the Pocket PC. It does include instructions and support for many cellular telephones, the Palm, and the Handspring.

Using Pocket PC Applications

The Pocket PC provides a number of great programming options. For example, you can write directly to Windows CE or use the .NET Compact Framework. Developing a Pocket PC–specific application has many of the same advantages of creating standard desktop application. (See the "Using Standard Applications" section for details.) One of the biggest benefits of the Pocket PC application is that you don't need a Web server to host it in most cases.

> ▶ **TIP**
>
> It's possible to write a local application with a Web basis for the Pocket PC. For example, you can use products such as PocketSOAP (`http://www.pocketsoap.com/`) to write an application that relies on JavaScript to make a SOAP request locally. The PDA uses a Web interface, but it doesn't rely on contact with a server to make the request—everything occurs locally. One of the benefits of using PocketSOAP is that the vendor also makes a compatible product for desktop machines so you can use the same code base for both platforms.

Currently, many businesses favor the programmability the Pocket PC provides for applications such as remote research or product lookups (such as in order fulfillment). The user has a need for a mobile device, a laptop or notebook won't work, and the user can carry a Pocket PC in a holster. The idea is to help the user locate information as the need arises, rather than force the user to go to a special area to perform the research.

Using Generic PDA Applications

All PDAs can use a Web interface, including the Palm and Pocket PC. When you create a generic PDA application, you normally need to host it on a Web server because you can't assume anything about the processing power of the client. A host can detect the type of mobile device and provide output for that device in the form of a Web page.

From a design perspective, you need to consider the devices you want to support at the outset of the project. Everything from screen design to coding technique must consider the devices you expect to use the application. In fact, you normally need to provide settings within the application that instruct the server how to react to specific devices. A Palm might require three pages to display a Web site, while a Pocket PC can display the same information in two pages. The information is the same, but the form factor of the device is different.

One of the biggest advantages of using this approach is that you can support any device. Many users find the advanced features of the Pocket PC less than useful and the larger size of the device annoying. An office manager doesn't want to carry a Pocket PC around in a holster all day. A Palm that fits in a pocket is much better because it stays out of the way until needed.

Writing Cellular Telephone Applications

Cellular telephones are here to stay. Some people try to use them for every communication need. As cellular telephones increase in capability, it becomes easier to write Web-based applications that really do make a difference. Imagine that you're in a meeting and the boss tells you to locate information about a new technology as the result of a conversation. With the proper Google Web Services application, you could locate the information immediately and present it while the meeting is still in progress.

Although cellular telephones are extremely convenient, they also have severe limitations. You don't want to try to build an industrial strength application with one because they simply don't have the processing speed, memory capacity, or communication speed to support such an application. In short, for development purposes, consider the cellular telephone as an option for shopping list, search, or other light applications.

Writing Mixed Environment Applications

It's important to consider the fact that you might not be able to support just one device and make your Google Web Services application work. Sometimes you need to support two or even three platforms to ensure that everyone who wants to work with the application can do so. You might think that this means writing separate applications for each device, but that's not necessary anymore as long as you consider the requirements of each device before you begin writing code.

Mixed environment applications commonly work on more than one device or environment (and sometimes both). In the past, you wrote mixed environment applications using Web programming techniques because the various platforms didn't offer much in the way of commonality. For example, you can write an ASP application that detects the device type (desktop browser version, PDA model, or cellular telephone model) and outputs a page specifically tailored for that device. The essential code doesn't change and you use a single code base for every device. Only the interface changes to meet the needs of a particular device.

Today, it isn't necessary to write your application as a Web application. For example, you can use Visual Studio .NET to write an application that works on a PDA or a desktop machine. Your code base remains the same, and you need to compile the application for each kind of device. In addition, you must work within the confines of the .NET Compact Framework, rather than assume the full resources of the .NET Framework are available.

The ability to write applications that work on more than one platform or in more than one environment is so compelling that other vendors will follow suit. Eventually, you might be able to write an application that works equally well on any device without much thought. Unfortunately, although the development environment is better today, it's still not perfect—the goal of writing mixed environment applications that truly work everywhere with little effort on the developer's part is a long way off.

Picking a Development Language

Some developers have a mind-set that their particular language is the only perfect language in the world and they never plan to use anything else. I'd love to say these developers are really onto something because it would greatly reduce the efforts I go to in order to maintain proficiency with multiple languages. The sad truth is the world has yet to discover the perfect language and probably never will. Some development languages work best for one situation, and others work best in another situation. Good developers either realize the limitations of the one language they do know or have multiple languages available in their programming toolkit.

Of course, the question is how language choice affects your use of Google Web Services. Look through the examples in this book. You'll notice that all of the examples return a result from a simply constructed request. The problem is using the data you receive in some useful way. Displaying a search result with XSLT isn't a problem and you can add scripting to the resulting page to make it more flexible, but trying to build a high-end application using this technique is difficult. The sections that follow won't tell you specifically which language to use to meet your development needs, but it will help you match a language to a specific kind of project.

Choosing a Language That Meets Specific Needs

Some developers look at me rather strangely when I tell them that I develop applications in VBA (the macro language used in products such as IMSI TurboCAD, Corel Draw, and Microsoft Office) about as often as I do in other languages such as C++ or C#. I find that using VBA provides me with a way to quickly prototype Office-specific applications and reduce the user's learning curve by using an environment they already know. In addition, VBA is enough like other languages I know that I don't have a big learning curve to contend with every time I start a new project. That's also the reason you'll find a VBA chapter in this book.

In fact, the language-specific chapters (Chapters 5 through 9) each demonstrate the functionality provided by a specific language. For example, the VBA examples deal with tasks you can perform more easily in Office than you can any other environment, such as creating reports or generating lists of potential information resources. Office also makes it easy to perform some types of statistical analysis, such as the frequency of Web site appearance for given search terms. Chapter 5 shows how to perform statistical analysis and generate graphs.

However, VBA and Office don't provide the level of accessibility needed for some tasks and you definitely wouldn't want to set up a Web site that relies on VBA. The other chapters in the book cover other kinds of applications such as a Web site spelling checker, along with the information you have always provided to perform a search (keywords). The idea is to select a language that meets the needs of the application so that you don't become frustrated trying to use a hammer where a screwdriver would work better.

Considering Your Skills and Abilities

It would be easy to assume that you want and can devote hours to your Google project simply because you're reading this book. However, the fact is that many of you have time constraints and probably don't have much of an inclination to become a developer (unless you're already a professional developer). Along with considering the needs of the application, you also have to consider your skills and abilities. Trying to develop a complex analysis program when all you really know how to do is write a little HTML is going to become frustrating— you might never finish the project.

The development language you choose has to match the project, but it also has to match your skills and abilities. Often, the choice of language determines just how much you should attempt to do with Google Web Services. In other cases, you might know that you want to perform certain tasks, but that the programming language skills you possess don't quite fit in with your plans. The planning process can point out the need to call in a consultant to help with the programming part of the job. In addition, by knowing your skills and understanding the needs of the job, you can find a developer with the qualifications you need.

Honestly assessing your skills and abilities can have another effect. One person I know went back to school to learn Web application development skills. The person didn't have nearly as many time constraints as he did cash flow problems (a consultant was out of the question). Although he didn't graduate with a degree in computer science, this person now knows how to maintain a Web site that has built his business. In short, this book might help you choose a programming language that you want to learn to use Google Web Services to meet a specific need effectively.

Defining Language Limitations

Part of the design process is to understand the limitations of the language you choose. You must consider both the current application requirements and those that you need to address in the future. Moving an application from one language to another is definitely not a fun task. Consequently, you need to consider what you plan to do today and how you plan to expand the application in the future. In some cases, accomplishing this task means defining the limitations of the language.

If you choose JavaScript to create an application for your Web site, it's going to be quite flexible and most browsers won't have a problem accessing the information. In addition, you can perform most Google Web Services tasks without buying an expensive server or incurring many startup costs. JavaScript is the low-price solution for many developers. However, JavaScript is hardly the most robust programming language, and you'll find your expansion opportunities limited. For example, this probably isn't the right choice for creating complex reports, but it's a good solution if you want to offer a means to perform quick searches for products or other information.

You might think that Java or Visual Basic .NET will solve all of your development problems. They're certainly robust enough to help you perform any task you might want to do. However, I probably wouldn't use either language if my main goal were tracking product statistics. In addition, both Java and Visual Basic .NET require the skills of a good programmer to create successful applications. Good programmers don't come cheap—plan to spend quite a bit to create the Web application of your dreams.

Understanding Internationalization Issues

Many developers don't consider internationalization issues when they develop a Web application today, but it's an important issue. Unless you know that no one who speaks another language will ever have any reason to access your site, you have to consider the possibility that internationalization could benefit your site. Not every site requires internationalization, but many do. You also have to consider how to handle the internationalization of your site. In many cases, you can simply ensure that the site handles more than one type of currency; but in others, you need to provide pages in more than one language. The following sections discuss these issues as they apply to Google Web Services.

> ▶ **NOTE**
>
> Google provides support for a number of languages. However, support for non-English implementations is less than perfect. You'll find that Chinese, Japanese, and Korean requests don't work all the time. Google is aware of the problem and plans to fix it in a future release of Google Web Services.

Learning the Limits of Translation

It's important to consider not only how to internationalize your site, but also when. Sometimes the question is even "if" you should internationalize your site. Adding a second language or a second country to your site isn't a small undertaking. Even if you choose to use the least expensive approach possible, supporting two languages still means providing two sets of identical Web pages in most cases. (Some developers solve the problem by placing the language specific strings outside the application so that the content and functionality of the application are separate.) Experience shows that even with the best of intentions, one language is bound to remain behind the other in updates. Adding more languages only compounds the problem. The point is that you need to consider the monetary problems of maintaining more than one language. You need to be sure that the cost of supporting more than one language is going to result in a quantifiable gain.

The gain doesn't always have to include a monetary value. For example, you might be the librarian for your company and some employees might need to use Google Web Services in a different language. Although you can't point to a specific gain for your department, the improved performance of the employees in their department does qualify as a quantifiable gain.

However, most Google Web Services developers will need to consider the money end of things at some point. You need to perform research to discover whether the addition of another language makes sense. For example, you could include a survey on your Web site. Check for other Web sites that provide services similar to your own. In many cases, you'll see the languages these other sites support and may find that you need to support them as well to remain competitive. In most cases, you need to know that the language addition will at least pay for itself to ensure you can maintain it.

When you internationalize a site, it often means using other languages. Unless you know the target language well enough to perform the translation, you need to find someone who can translate the pages. Sometimes you can get the translation free. For example, the Free-Translation.com site at `http://www.freetranslation.com/` will accept your input and output translation in a number of languages. Figure 4.4 shows an example of such a translation from English to Spanish. The free translations on this site focus on translating English to another language, although you can find some translations that go the other direction (from Spanish to English, for example). Unfortunately, the quality of the translation on these sites varies from acceptable to poor. In many cases, you'll want to use a professional translator to ensure the quality of a translation remains high. (It's interesting to note that many of the sites providing free translation services also offer paid human translations as well.)

FIGURE 4.4:

Sometimes you can translate a limited amount of text free.

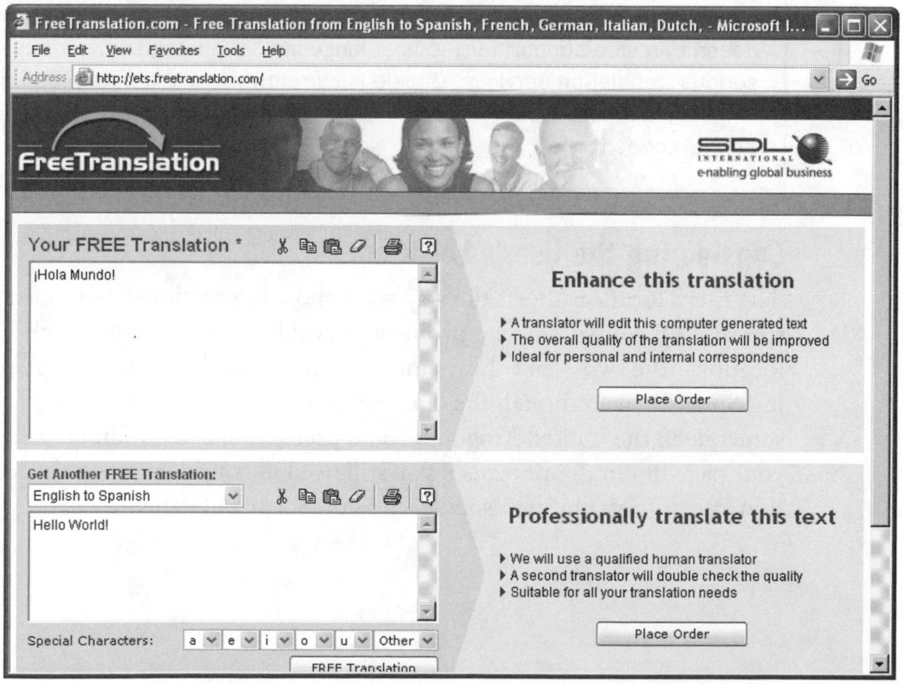

Most developers have more than just a few words to translate, and they still might not want to pay the price of using a professional translation service. You do have another option. The Google translation service works relatively well on simple Web pages. The more complicated your Web page becomes, the harder it is to get an acceptable translation. You call the Google translation service using an URL such as this:

```
http://translate.google.com/translate?hl=fr&sl=en&u=http://www.mwt.net/~jmueller
```

This URL translates my home page from English to French. All you need to supply are three items. First, you must supply the host language (the `hl` argument), which is a two-letter abbreviation such as *en* for English, *fr* for French, and *de* for German. You can find a list of standard two-letter abbreviations at `http://www.loc.gov/standards/iso639-2/englangn .html`. Make sure you use the two-letter and not the three-letter abbreviations. Second, you must provide a source language (the `sl` argument), which relies on the same two-letter code system as the host language. Finally, you must supply the URL you want to translate (the `u` argument). You can also access this service manually for both text and Web page translation at `http://www.google.com/language_tools`.

> ▶ **NOTE**
>
> Google does support most common languages, but they don't support every language. If you see the translated page in the original language, it normally means that Google doesn't provide support for the host language. In most cases, serious translations require serious translation services. Google is currently running a beta program to provide better language support—learn more about this program at `https://services.google.com/ tc/Welcome.html`.

Considering the User's Location

The user's location affects the way you handle internationalization from more than one perspective. Of course, the first problem to avoid is confusing the user's language with the user's location—the two aren't always the same. Someone in the United States could prefer speaking Spanish, even though the language spoken by most Americans is English. Likewise, someone in the United Kingdom could prefer to speak Hindi. However, even when you offer your page in Hindi or Spanish, you still need to consider the user's location because the location affects presentation issues, such as the format of dates.

> **▶ TIP**
>
> It's important to consider language issues when you develop a Web site. For example, many people have never even heard of Hindi, yet 180 million people use it as their first language and another 300 million use it as their second language (see `http://www.cs.colostate.edu/~malaiya/hindiint.html` for details).

Your Call to Action

This is the first chapter that really discussed programming techniques to the extent that you're planning for a Web site or application that relies on Google Web Services. Previous chapters have demonstrated the useful features of Google Web Services and even shown how these features work by exposing the Web service process. Completing this chapter means that you're ready to look at language-specific issues and get your application running.

Now that you've spent some time discovering the Web service process and deciding what Google Web Services can do for you, it's time to consider the design of your application. This chapter presented useful information that you need to develop a good design. However, it concentrated on Google Web Services, rather than general development principles. Now is the time to learn about these other principles, if you haven't worked with them already. In addition, you need to consider the design of your application. A written specification is nice (and required for larger companies), but just the act of thinking about what you want to do is essential.

Chapter 5 is the first language-specific chapter in the book. This chapter helps VBA users get started using Google Web Services. You'll discover how to perform specific kinds of analysis, store data for later use, and create reports based on the information you find. I chose VBA as the first language to present because many people rely on this language to work with Office and other applications. In general, Chapter 5 demonstrates that VBA is quite capable of doing amazing things with Google Web Services, and you won't find many limits of the other languages.

Chapter 5

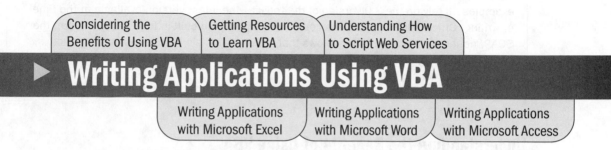

Considering the Benefits of Using VBA · Getting Resources to Learn VBA · Understanding How to Script Web Services

▶ Writing Applications Using VBA

Writing Applications with Microsoft Excel · Writing Applications with Microsoft Word · Writing Applications with Microsoft Access

Many people associate Visual Basic for Applications (VBA) with Microsoft Office. While it's true that Microsoft Office does rely on VBA as a development language, you'll find VBA used with other applications too. Microsoft provides a list of companies that have licensed VBA at `http://msdn.microsoft.com/vba/companies/company.asp`. (Make sure you read the "Other Companies That Use VBA" sidebar for additional ideas too.) Therefore, even though the examples in this chapter do rely on Microsoft products, you can use the information it contains with any product that supports VBA.

This chapter explores methods of coupling Google Web Services to an application with VBA capability. You can use Google Web Services to meet a number of needs. For example, you can track the ranking of your Web site given certain search words and then use Excel to analyze your keyword usage. Likewise, you can obtain information from Google Web Services to create a report in Word. You might use such a report to help management understand the current resources available on a particular subject—perhaps a new area the company plans to target for business.

Unfortunately, one chapter can't do everything that you normally find in a whole book. You won't learn how to use VBA in this chapter, and I'm assuming you know how to use the application in question. The chapter doesn't leave you completely in the dark, however. The "Resources for Learning VBA" section contains information on where you can learn more about VBA. Knowing how to use VBA is a prerequisite for this chapter.

> ▶ **NOTE**
>
> All of the examples in this chapter rely on the Microsoft SOAP Toolkit. You can download this toolkit at `http://msdn.microsoft.com/nhp/default.asp?contentid=28000523`. The examples all rely on the 3.0 version of the toolkit—the latest version available at the time of writing. Office 2003 applications could also rely on their built-in features to perform the SOAP requests. Experimentation shows that using the built-in features is actually a lot harder than using the Microsoft SOAP Toolkit, so this book concentrates on the Microsoft SOAP Toolkit techniques.

Understanding the Benefits of Using VBA

Most of the examples you'll see for Google Web Services outside this book probably focus on Web technologies. Developers use Google Web Services to create connections to their Web site (as a search engine) or their cellular telephone (to locate necessary information on the fly). However, VBA lets you view Google Web Services from an entirely different perspective. Instead of creating a search engine connection or researching new information, using VBA with your application lets you concentrate on data—it helps you decide how to use the data that Google provides for your own needs.

It's possible to create the kind of links described in the previous paragraph using full-fledged programming environments such as Visual Studio. You can also create a great Web environment that mimics some of these features using languages such as PHP Hypertext Processor (PHP) (yes, the acronym repeats itself—see Chapter 7 for details). However, the point is that VBA works in concert with the host application. You don't have to write a lot of the code that you normally need to write because the host application provides the required functionality for you. In fact, if you choose the right host application, writing a Google Web Services interface can become mind-numbingly simple. Just a few lines of code will help you perform tasks in seconds, rather than hours.

So, why not write every application in VBA? To say that VBA is a cure-all for every problem is incorrect. VBA answers a specific range of needs, but doesn't handle every need. In fact, the needs that VBA answers are somewhat specialized. This chapter helps you understand some of the applications where VBA can save you considerable time and expense. It also demonstrates that you can achieve truly amazing results with just a modicum of programming. The important point is to match VBA and the host application to a particular Google Web Services application need.

Resources for Learning VBA

This chapter won't teach you how to use VBA. I'm assuming that you already know enough about VBA to create your own simple applications. If you don't already have this knowledge, you can get it from a number of sources. The first place to look is my book, *VBA for Dummies*, Fourth Edition (Wiley, 2003). This book introduces you to VBA and takes you through examples using all of the major Microsoft Office applications.

Other Companies That Use VBA

Companies other than Microsoft use VBA, but you might not know about them right now. Corel makes software such as WordPerfect and Draw. WordPerfect is a word processing program, and you'll find that many legal offices still use it. One of my first professional writing jobs required use of WordPerfect. Draw is a drawing program that many professionals enjoy using. It supports a wealth of features. I drew the original versions of all of the line art in this book using Corel Draw. All of my drawing setups are performed automatically using VBA programs.

You'll also want to check out Micrografx's iGrafx Series. This product helps you create flowcharts or organizational charts. Unlike a lot of drawing tasks, both flowcharts and organizational charts are extremely repetitive—making them a perfect place to use VBA.

Another good product to check for VBA is IMSI's TurboCad. TurboCad is the drawing program I prefer to use. It's relatively inexpensive, and the VBA programs I've created for it automate many of the drawing tasks.

So, how do these products benefit from Google Web Services? Corel WordPerfect and Corel Draw are the easiest matches. You can use them to create reports, charts, and graphs based on information you retrieve from Google Web Services. Likewise, the Micrografx iGrafx product can use input from Google Web Services to create charts of various types. The question remains: how do you use a CAD application with Google Web Services? Actually, I've tried it out as a resource for finding standards. Sometimes I need to locate a particular standard for a project. All I do is highlight the number or the name of the standard that I need and ask Google Web Services to find it for me. The underlying technology is a VBA application that makes a search query from Google.

I also use Google Web Services to locate certain kinds of images. For example, say you need a connector for a drawing. You can perform a site search of the Connectivity Knowledge Platform (CKP) site at http://ckp.made-it.com/. After the search, you'll find a Connector Reference Chart at http://ckp.made-it.com/connectorchart.html. This site contains descriptions of the connectors, as well as images. With a little additional code, you can import the drawing you need into a project such as TurboCad, convert it to a raster graphic, and touch it up so it meets your needs. The process is much faster than drawing the image from scratch. Note, however, that much of the art online is copyrighted, so you need to obtain permission to use the art, in many cases, even if you modify the art to meet your specific needs.

You'll also want to look at some of the resources that Microsoft provides. For example, you'll find a Microsoft Office 2000 Resource Kit at `http://www.microsoft.com/office/ork/xp/default.htm`. This site includes some interesting tools at `http://www.microsoft.com/office/ork/2000/appndx/toolbox.htm`. Office 2003 users can find similar information on their product. You can learn about the recently released version at `http://www.microsoft.com/office/ork/2003/` and `http://office.microsoft.com/home/default.aspx`.

It's amazing to see how many third party sources you can find online for VBA. Many sites have free code, specialized examples, chat forums, tutorials, or other offerings that make your VBA experience better. For example, you can download a VBA tutorial at `http://freedownloadswindows.com/windows/Visual-Basic/656996/L-Basic.html`. Online Excel VBA tutorials appear at `http://lacher.com/toc/tutvba1.htm` and `http://lacher.com/toc/tutvba2.htm`. You might also want to check out the chat forums at `http://www.vbforums.com/` and `http://www.tek-tips.com/`.

> ▶ **NOTE**
>
> The VBA language has basic concepts that are the same across all products. A loop in Word is the same loop that you find in Excel or Corel Draw for that matter. However, every product has special objects that it includes for working with VBA. These objects vary by product, so it's usually best if you can locate a VBA tutorial for your specific product.

Don't forget to visit newsgroups with your VBA questions. Microsoft sponsors VBA newsgroups at:

- `microsoft.public.office.developer.vba`
- `microsoft.public.excel.programming`
- `microsoft.public.frontpage.programming.vba`
- `microsoft.public.office.developer.outlook.vba`
- `microsoft.public.outlook.program_vba`
- `microsoft.public.project.vba`
- `microsoft.public.visio.developer.vba`
- `microsoft.public.word.vba.addins`
- `microsoft.public.word.vba.beginners`
- `microsoft.public.word.vba.customization`

- `microsoft.public.word.vba.general`
- `microsoft.public.word.vba.userforms`
- `microsoft.public.word.word97vba`

> **▶ TIP**
>
> If you ever have a problem finding a Microsoft newsgroup, open your browser and type the name of the Microsoft news server and the name of the newsgroup. For example, if you want to access the `microsoft.public.word.vba.addins` newsgroup, type `news://news.microsoft.com/microsoft.public.word.vba.addins` in the browser's Address field and press Enter. The browser will locate the newsgroup, open your newsreader, and display that newsgroup from the Microsoft server. You can also use online resources such as Google Groups (`http://groups.google.com/`) to locate VBA newsgroups. Simply type the name of the newsgroup in the Search field, click Google Search, and you'll see a list of messages in that newsgroup.

If you noticed the overwhelming number of Word VBA newsgroups, it's because many people develop for this particular product. The `microsoft.public.word.vba.beginners` newsgroup is an exceptionally good place to start your VBA programming journey. Power-Point doesn't have a specific VBA newsgroup, so you'll need to use the general `microsoft.public.powerpoint` newsgroup instead. If you want to work with Access, be sure to look at task-specific newsgroups such as `microsoft.public.access.formscoding`.

You can also find third party newsgroups (often with better peer information, but no Microsoft help) at newsgroups such as `alt.comp.lang.vba`. Some third party products also sport their own VBA newsgroups such as AutoCAD (`autodesk.autocad.customization.vba`). In some cases, the name of the newsgroup won't be obvious, as with Corel Draw (`corel.developer.draw`).

Understanding Scripting of Web Services

In many respects, VBA is a scripting or macro language, rather than a full development language such as Visual Basic or C#. The host application interprets the VBA code when you run the macro based on an event such as selecting a menu entry, clicking a button, or opening a file. Consequently, the host application performs every task in real time—you can't decide much in advance. Although VBA is far more powerful than Web scripting languages such as JavaScript, it still has some of the benefits and problems of any scripting language. The following sections discuss how VBA scripting can affect your application and one technique for circumventing scripting issues.

Advantages and Disadvantages of VBA

VBA is a good scripting language and far more capable than VBScript (but less capable than Visual Basic). One of the biggest advantages of using VBA is that you get instant feedback. You don't have to compile the application, nor do you have to do anything fancy to see the result of your code—all you need to do is run it. This means the development cycle is much shorter and you can get your application going faster.

Unlike JavaScript and browser applications in general, most VBA environments provide good debugging. You run the program in a special environment that lets you see variables and the short-term results of operations. This is especially helpful when working with Google Web Services because you can see how your code interacts with the Web service without resorting to using on-screen data presentation or similar tricks required for browser applications in many cases.

A new developer can also learn VBA relatively quickly compared to a full-fledged programming language such as Visual Basic or C#. VBA is a subset of Visual Basic, which means it has fewer commands to learn. However, even with fewer features, VBA developers can create robust Google Web Services applications. Many of the advanced features that VBA lacks don't affect applications of this type.

The biggest disadvantage of using VBA is performance. Most interpreted languages are slower than compiled languages because an interpreter (a special program that reads the code) must convert the human-readable information into machine code during runtime. VBA developers use a variety of techniques to improve performance, but even great programming techniques can only improve performance so much. At some point, the application runs as fast as possible and you have to live with the performance implications.

From a Google Web Services perspective, VBA also presents display problems. You can only display data in the way that the host application allows. It's possible to force the application to display data in nonstandard ways, but only at the cost of long development time and poor performance. Choosing the correct application for your needs is essential when using VBA.

An Alternative to VBA

If you want to work with Google Web Services within any Office product, you need to use VBA because Google Web Services requires SOAP for access (unless you want to use a Web server or other intermediary). However, it's possible to obtain a lot of data from Google so long as you use their native format. It's possible that you can accomplish some tasks without resorting to programming by adding a simple URL to your report or other Office document. The problem, of course, is that you always give something up in order to gain simplicity. Although an embedded URL does make it easier for someone to get data from Google, the data is still in Google's format, not your preferred format.

Most versions of Office support hyperlinks in some fashion—you can even use them in Office 97 products. To create the hyperlink in an application such as Word, right-click the location in the document that you want to contain the hyperlink and choose Hyperlink from the context menu. When you see the Insert Hyperlink dialog box shown in Figure 5.1, select the Place in This Document option and type the Google search URL you want to embed. Chapter 2 discusses all of the search arguments you can use. All you need to do is combine them with the Google search URL of `http://www.google.com/search?q=`. For example, if you want to look for all occurrences of VBA on my Web site, you'd type **http://www.google.com/search?q=VBA+%22DataCon+Services%22+site%3Awww.mwt.net**. Notice that all of the special characters are escaped (see the "Sending Special Characters Using URL Encoding" section of Chapter 3 for details). Click OK. Now, whenever you Ctrl+click the hyperlink, Word will request the information from Google Web Services.

You can also create special searches using the Advanced Search page. In this case, you'll find that the search URL is longer. It's easy to figure out the pieces that you actually need and use them for a hyperlink. For example, you could also use `http://www.google.com/search?as_q=VBA&as_epq=DataCon+Services&as_sitesearch=www.mwt.net` to search for VBA topics on my Web site.

Older versions of Office might require that you use the Insert ➤ Hyperlink command to display the Insert Hyperlink dialog box shown in Figure 5.2. This dialog box works about the same as the one shown in Figure 5.1—it just doesn't include as many options. Again, type the URL that you want to receive from Google and click OK.

FIGURE 5.1:

Use the Insert Hyperlink dialog box to add a hyperlink to your application.

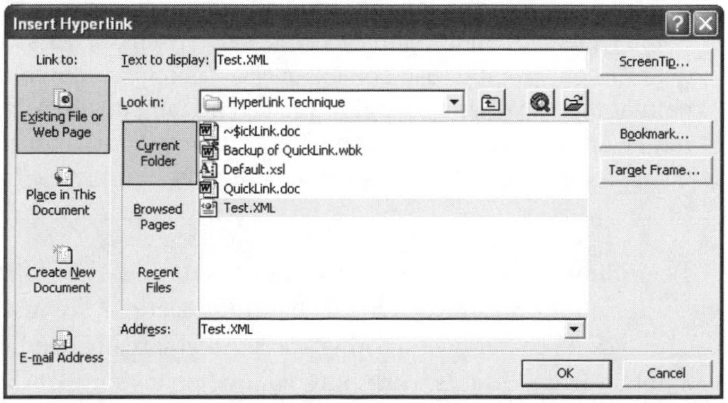

FIGURE 5.2:

Older versions of
Office might require
that you create hyper-
links using the menu
system.

FIGURE 5.2:

Older versions of
Office might require
that you create hyper-
links using the menu
system.

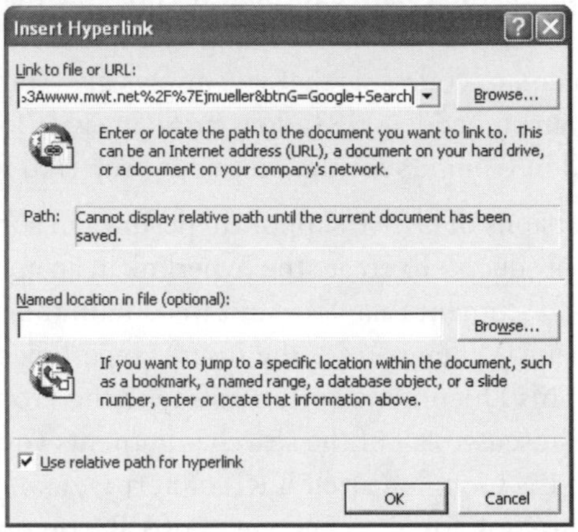

Developing with Microsoft Excel

Microsoft Excel provides a number of interesting features that can help you manipulate the
data you receive from Google Web Services. Sometimes you have to gather this data over
time. For example, you might collect changes to a list of Web sites each day at 10:00. These
Web sites could be the top 10 returns for a particular Google query, so the list would change
over time to reflect changes in Google's search algorithm, changes in the Web sites, and natural changes in the relevancy of the Web sites. After some time, you can chart this information and see how your search data is affected by changes on the Internet. For example, this
kind of statistic could help signal a need to make changes to your Web site to better compete
with other sites on the Internet.

> ▶ **TIP**
>
> Some types of statistical analysis for Google Web Services are very time sensitive. Conse-
> quently, you'll want to use something like Task Scheduler to ensure the system gathers the
> data at the same time each day. You can perform this task in a number of ways, including
> relying on the automatic document execution feature of Excel. Simply opening the document
> ensures the macro that gathers the data runs.

The following sections demonstrate ways to use Microsoft Excel with Google Web Services. It's important to remember that these sections are just examples—you can probably
use Google Web Services in other ways. All you really need is an idea of how the data you
can obtain from Google works into your company's use of the Web site. For an in-depth

treatment of the topic, see *Mastering Excel 2003 Programming with VBA* by Steven M. Hansen (Sybex, 2004).

Performing a Simple Search Using SOAP

The example in this section isn't awe inspiring, but it does provide a good starting point for working with Google Web Services from Excel. Essentially, you create a connection to Google from Excel using SOAP, just as the examples in Chapters 3 and 4 demonstrated for Web pages. However, as these sections show, Excel is far more capable than a simple Web page that relies on JavaScript. You'll find that once you gain access to the data through the application, you can perform myriad tasks.

Defining the Required References

To make this example work, you must create a reference to object libraries on your system. These object libraries have classes with methods and properties you need to work with SOAP and XML using VBA. Most of the examples you build can use any of the Microsoft XML libraries and the Microsoft SOAP Library. However, you don't have to use either of these libraries—many third party vendors create SOAP and XML libraries that work fine with VBA. The main requirement is that you have libraries that do work with SOAP and XML.

Adding a reference is easy. Open the Visual Basic editor using the Tools ➤ Macro ➤ Visual Basic Editor command. Once the IDE is visible, open the References dialog box shown in Figure 5.3 using the Tools ➤ References command.

Notice that Figure 5.3 shows the necessary libraries checked. When working with Microsoft Office 2003, you also have access to Microsoft XML Version 5.0, which has additional helpful features and bug fixes. Make sure you use the newest versions of the SOAP and XML libraries whenever possible.

FIGURE 5.3:

The References dialog box helps you add an object library reference to VBA.

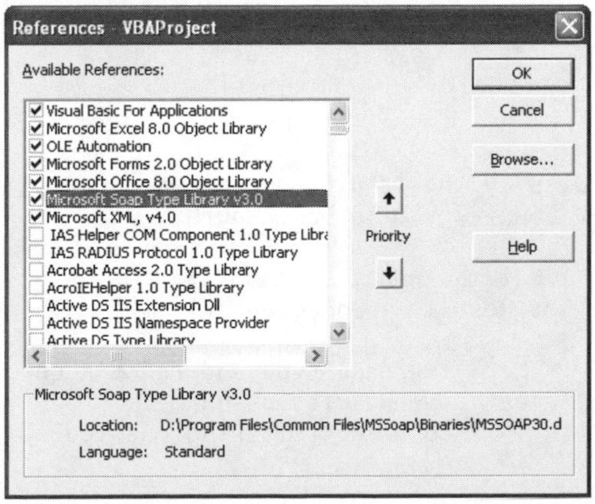

Creating the Query Code

Creating a Google query using Excel is similar to using other languages such as JavaScript, but you need to consider some definite issues, such as the format of the response data. Listing 5.1 shows the essentials of how to make a simple request using VBA from Excel. You'll find the complete source for this example in the \Chapter 05\Excel folder of the source code located on the Sybex Web site.

Listing 5.1 **Performing a Simple Google Query**

```
Public Sub SimpleQuery()
    Dim Client As SoapClient30       ' SOAP Client
    Dim Doc As IXMLDOMSelection      ' Entire Result Set
    Dim Results As IXMLDOMNode       ' Search Results
    Dim Item As IXMLDOMNode          ' Individual Item
    Dim ItemData As IXMLDOMNode      ' Item Data Element
    Dim Counter As Integer           ' Loop Counter
    Dim ItemCount As Integer         ' Counter for Item Results
    Dim DataCount As Integer         ' Data Item Count
    Dim RealData As Integer          ' Actual Item Count

    ' Create and initialize the SOAP client.
    Set Client = New SoapClient30
    Client.MSSoapInit "http://api.google.com/GoogleSearch.wsdl", _
                    "GoogleSearchService", _
                    "GoogleSearchPort"

    ' Make a search request.
    Set Doc = _
        Client.doGoogleSearch("Your-License-Key", _
                        Sheet1.Cells(1, 2), _
                        0, _
                        10, _
                        False, _
                        "", _
                        False, _
                        "", _
                        "", _
                        "")

    ' Display the results on screen.
    For Counter = 0 To Doc.Length - 1

        ' Get the node.
        Set Results = Doc(Counter)

        ' Check the node type and react accordingly.
        Select Case Results.baseName
            ' Is document filtering enabled?
```

```vb
        Case "documentFiltering"
            Sheet1.Cells(3, 2) = Results.Text

    ... Other Top Level Data ...

    ' Ending search result.
    Case "endIndex"
        Sheet1.Cells(7, 2) = Results.Text

        ' Set the real item counter.
        RealData = 0

        ' Process each item in turn.
        For ItemCount = 0 To Results.childNodes.Length - 1

            ' Get the item.
            Set Item = Results.childNodes(ItemCount)

            ' Determine whether this is a data item.
            If Item.baseName = "item" Then

                ' Process each item data element in turn.
                For DataCount = 0 To Item.childNodes.Length - 1

                    ' Get the data item.
                    Set ItemData = Item.childNodes(DataCount)

                    ' Print the required data on screen.
                    Select Case ItemData.baseName
                        Case "title"
                            Sheet1.Cells(11 + RealData, 1) = _
                                StringToText(ItemData.Text)
                        Case "URL"
                            Sheet1.Cells(11 + RealData, 2) = _
                                "=HYPERLINK(" + Chr(34) + _
                                ItemData.Text + Chr(34) + ", " + _
                                Chr(34) + ItemData.Text + Chr(34) + ")"
                        Case "cachedSize"
                            Sheet1.Cells(11 + RealData, 3) = _
                                ItemData.Text
                    End Select
                Next

                ' Update the real data counter.
                RealData = RealData + 1
            End If
        Next
    End Select
    Next
End Sub
```

If the beginning code looks similar to the JavaScript examples in the book, you're right—VBA does start by creating a SOAP client and making a call to Google. All of the input arguments are the same as those discussed in the "Defining the Search Request Arguments" section of Chapter 4. However, this is where the similarities end.

VBA provides more power for processing the data, so you have some new data types and capabilities to consider. Unlike other languages, you must use the `IXMLDOMSelection` data type to store the raw results from Google. The `Doc` object contains the entire document. The code begins by creating a loop to process the top-level elements, such as `<documentFiltering>` and `<estimatedTotalResultsCount>`, returned by Google. It places each of these nodes in the `Results` object. Getting the value of a top-level element is as easy as reading `Results.Text` property.

While these top-level entries are interesting, the information of interest appears in the `<resultElements>` node. It's at this point that you run into one of the more interesting problems posed by VBA. Even though the sample SOAP files provided with the Google Web Services Kit show that you receive at most 10 `<item>` elements as children of the `<resultElements>` node, the VBA debugger shows that this node actually contains upward of 20 children. The 10 `<item>` elements do appear in the list of children, but you have to filter them out from the null (empty) elements that VBA seems to throw in for good measure. These extra elements are the reason that the code tracks the actual number of `<item>` elements using `RealData` and requires the use of the `If` statement to verify the value of the `Item.baseName` property. This problem occurs with regularity when working with VBA, so you always have to assume you'll receive extra elements.

An individual element contains multiple children. Again, you get those null elements in with the data you want, so checking for a specific child element type is important. Some of the data, such as the `<cachedSize>` element, is in the correct format when you receive it from Google, but much of it needs tweaking. The `<title>` element is one case in point. This element includes both HTML tags and URL encoded characters. To make the title useful in VBA, you need to modify that data. The "Modifying the Google Data" section of the chapter describes the `StringToText()` function, which shows one way to handle this problem. Figure 5.4 shows typical output from this application. Notice that all the titles are completely readable.

In some cases, even though the data is perfectly usable when you receive it from Google, you can improve it so VBA users get more out of the information. For example, the `<URL>` element is completely usable when you receive it from Google. However, by adding the `HYPERLINK()` function to the URL, it becomes a link within Excel. All the user needs to do is click the resulting hyperlink to see the page directly from inside Excel. Figure 5.5 shows how the page looks when the link is clicked from within Excel. Notice that Excel actually starts a new copy of Internet Explorer to display the link.

FIGURE 5.4:

The resulting spreadsheet contains links to the sites you queried online.

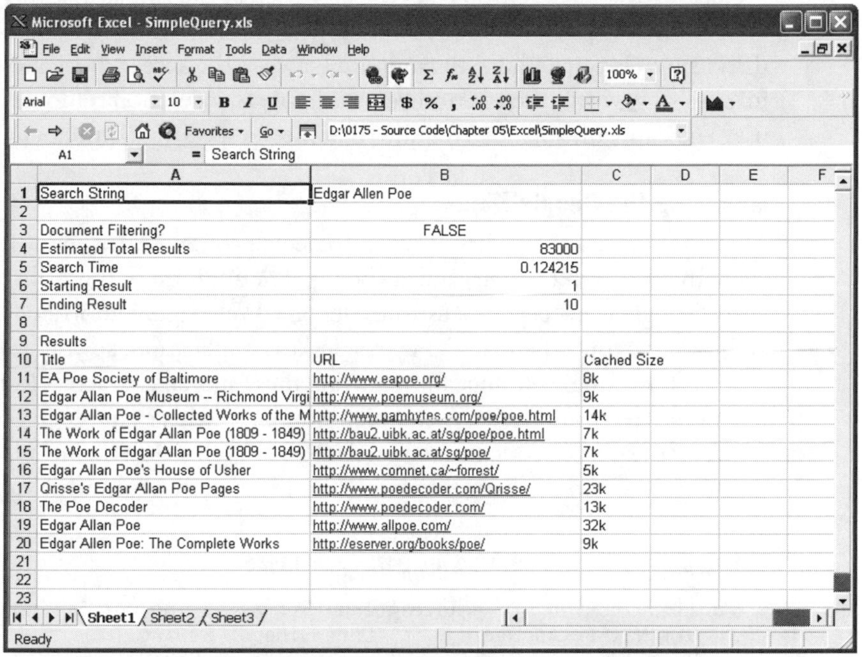

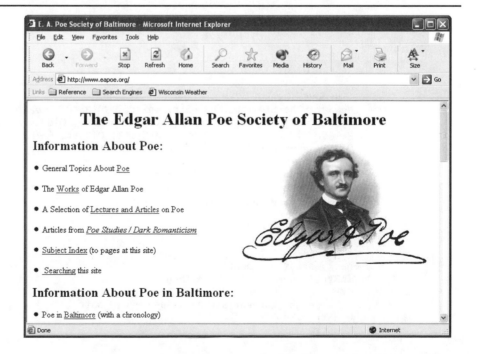

FIGURE 5.5:

Using hyperlinks within Excel makes it easy to move back and forth between spreadsheet and Internet connection.

Clicking the Back button takes the user back to the spreadsheet. When the user wants to view another link, a simple click does the job. This technique actually makes searches easier than using Google. The user can move between the spreadsheet and the Web sites. Any useful sites stay within the spreadsheet—a simple row deletion removes less useful links. The user ends up with a list of Web sites that meet a specific requirement in an easily saved form.

Modifying the Google Data

Much of the data you receive from Google will contain extra characters such as tags (especially the bold <b> tag pair) and encoding. The addition of these characters is natural considering Google expects you to use the data on a Web page. Unfortunately, these extra characters are just annoying when viewed with a desktop application, so you need to remove them. Listing 5.2 shows one technique for removing these special characters from the strings you receive from Google. You'll find the complete source for this example in the \Chapter 05\Excel folder of the source code located on the Sybex Web site. The included TestStringToText() Sub (not shown in the listing) shows how the function works with multiple ended elements.

Listing 5.2　　　**Modifying the Data Appearance**

```
Public Function StringToText(InputStr As String) As String
    Dim NewStr As String    ' Left Side of String.
    Dim OldStr As String    ' Right Side of String.

    ' Place the string in a local variable.
    OldStr = InputStr

    ' Check for bold tag.
    While Len(OldStr) > 0

        ' Remove the bold text.
        NewStr = NewStr + Left(OldStr, InStr(1, OldStr, "<b>") - 1)
        OldStr = Right(OldStr, Len(OldStr) - InStr(1, OldStr, "<b>") - 2)
        NewStr = NewStr + Left(OldStr, InStr(1, OldStr, "</b>") - 1)
        OldStr = Right(OldStr, Len(OldStr) - InStr(1, OldStr, "</b>") - 3)

        ' Check for additional bold entries.
        If InStr(1, OldStr, "<b>") = 0 Then
            NewStr = NewStr + OldStr
            OldStr = ""
        End If
    Wend

    ' Check for single quote.
    If InStr(1, NewStr, "&#39;") Then

        ' Place the current string value into OldStr.
        OldStr = NewStr
        NewStr = ""
```

```
        While Len(OldStr) > 0
            ' Exchange the encoded form for the single quote.
            NewStr = NewStr + Left(OldStr, InStr(1, OldStr, "&#39;") - 1)
            NewStr = NewStr + "'"
            OldStr = Right(OldStr, Len(OldStr) - InStr(1, OldStr, "&#39;") - 4)
            'NewStr = NewStr + OldStr

            ' Check for additional encoded entries.
            If InStr(1, OldStr, "&#39;") = 0 Then
                NewStr = NewStr + OldStr
                OldStr = ""
            End If
        Wend
    End If

    ' Return the processed string.
    StringToText = NewStr
End Function
```

The example code shows two techniques. The first technique removes a tag pair from a string. I've found that removing the tag pairs first actually works better than attempting to remove the URL encoding first. In this case, the code works on the string in a loop. It removes the beginning tag first and then the ending tag. At this point, the code determines whether there are any more tags. If so, it continues the loop.

The second technique looks for a special URL encoded character such as the single quote. It removes the escaped version of the text and then adds the real version back in. When the process is complete, the function exits and returns the converted string to the caller.

Defining Graphs and Charts

You can create a number of easy charts and graphs using Excel and Google Web Services. Look at Figure 5.4 again and you'll see all kinds of numbers. For example, you could create an application that performs an expanded search of various keywords and tracks the number of results. The number is estimated, but performing this kind of analysis will yield valuable information on how Google treats search word combinations. You could also track the time required to perform a search, analyze the cached size of the pages, and even look at the number of hits per domain. This type of research is straightforward because it comes directly from the numbers you obtain from Google Web Services.

However, you can (and possibly should) perform other kinds of analysis based on user input or personal experience. For example, you might build a page similar to the one shown in Figure 5.4 to determine which sites are most popular. One of the problems that you must solve when creating statistical information based on a Google Web Services search is how to determine the data points. Without statistical information, any chart or graph you create won't provide much value. Consequently, you need something on which to base the statistics. Unfortunately, you can't predict the results of a search before it occurs, which means creating the data points in some concrete manner is impossible. The application you design must consider the data points outside the search, which is precisely what the example in this section does. The example tracks the number of times that users select specific sites and then graphs their popularity—data you can't obtain from Google Web Services, but you must use Google Web Services to create.

> ▶ **NOTE**
>
> This example relies on special support provided by VBA for generating code dynamically (as the application runs). You need to add a reference to the Microsoft Visual Basic for Applications Extensibility component for this example. See the "Defining the Required References" section for details on adding a reference.

The Google Web Services calling code for this example is very similar to the code shown in Listing 5.1. However, it differs in one important way. This code calls on a special function to create the URL linkage as shown here.

```
Case "URL"
    CreateButtons ItemData.Text, 11 + RealData, 2
```

The `CreateButtons()` Sub starts a sequence of events that lets you track user clicks without knowing the search results in advance. Listing 5.3 shows the special code used to create the buttons on screen. You'll find the complete source for this example in the \Chapter 05\Excel folder of the source code located on the Sybex Web site.

Listing 5.3   **Generating URL Buttons**

```
Public Sub CreateButtons(ButtonURL As String, ButtonRow As Integer, _
                         ButtonCol As Integer)
    Dim NewButton As Shape        ' New Command Button for URL
    Dim SubName As String         ' Holds Button Name.
    Dim ThisModule As CodeModule  ' This Code Module

    ' Create the button.
    Set NewButton = _
        Sheet2.Shapes.AddFormControl( _
            xlButtonControl, _
            Sheet2.Cells(ButtonRow, ButtonCol).Left, _
            Sheet2.Cells(ButtonRow, ButtonCol).Top + 1, _
            Sheet2.Cells(ButtonRow, ButtonCol).Width, _
            Sheet2.Cells(ButtonRow, ButtonCol).Height - 2)

    ' The button name will have a space in it, create a name
```

```
    ' without the space.
    SubName = Left(NewButton.Name, InStr(1, NewButton.Name, " ") - 1) _
              + "_" + Right(NewButton.Name, Len(NewButton.Name) - _
              InStr(1, NewButton.Name, " ")) + "_Click"

' Create a reference to the current module.
Set ThisModule = _
Application.VBE.VBProjects(1).VBComponents("ChartsAndGraphs").CodeModule

    ' Ensure the module is visible.
    ThisModule.CodePane.Show

    ' Dynamically create the click code for the new button.
    ThisModule.InsertLines 1, _
        "Sub " + SubName + "()" + vbCrLf + _
        vbTab + "ShowLink " + Chr(34) + ButtonURL + Chr(34) + ", " + _
            CStr(ButtonRow) + ", " + CStr(ButtonCol + 2) + vbCrLf + _
        "End Sub"

    ' Configure the button caption and click action.
    NewButton.DrawingObject.Caption = ButtonURL
    NewButton.OnAction = "SimpleQuery.xls!" + SubName
End Sub
```

The code begins by creating a button and placing it on the form. Notice that the button appears in the same space as the URL text would normally appear. From a user's perspective, this technique makes it appear that the button is actually on the worksheet, even though from Excel's perspective, the button is separate from the worksheet. Figure 5.6 shows how this technique works.

When Excel creates the button, it generates a name for it automatically. The name contains a space, so you need to remove it so you can use the name for other purposes in the code. The code shows one technique for performing this task when you want to associate a click event with the button.

As previously mentioned, you have no idea of how many results Google will return, how many you'll need for your application, or even the information the links will provide. Consequently, you can't create the click events for the buttons in advance (just as you can't create the buttons in advance). This example uses dynamic code generation to create a click event handler for each button. The code is quite simple, but you must create it by obtaining a reference to the current code module. Using the `InsertLines()` method, you can generate code for the event handler. The listing shows the VBA code you create. Here's a sample of the output of that code.

```
Sub Button_1_Click()
    ShowLink "http://www.eapoe.org/", 11, 4
End Sub
```

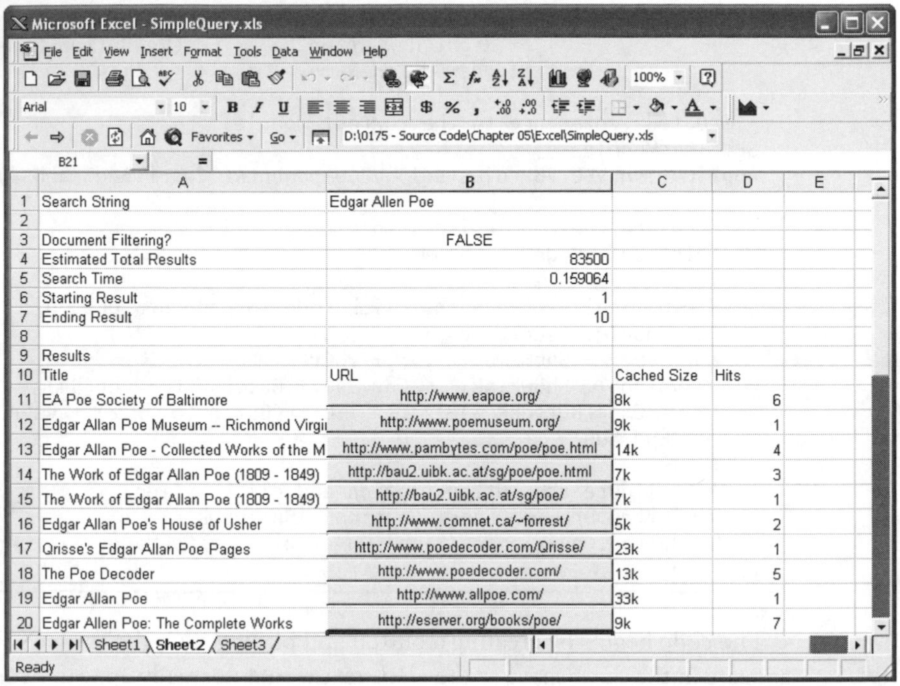

FIGURE 5.6:

Placing the buttons within the worksheet cell positions makes it look like the button is part of the worksheet.

The dynamically generated handler is specific to the button, which is based on the Google Web Services return values. This code does call a predefined Sub named ShowLink(). (The ShowLink() function is discussed later in this section.)

Once the code generates an event handler, it can associate it with the new button. The code also sets the button's Caption to match the URL returned by Google Web Services. You now have some buttons set up to use with the Google Web Services data. All of these buttons point to the ShowLink() function shown in Listing 5.4, which actually generates the statistics used for a particular URL.

Listing 5.4   Creating Statistical Data

```
Sub ShowLink(LinkValue As String, Row As Integer, Column As Integer)
    ' Update the link count.
    Sheet2.Cells(Row, Column) = Sheet2.Cells(Row, Column) + 1

    ' Follow the link.
    ThisWorkbook.FollowHyperlink Address:=LinkValue, NewWindow:=False
End Sub
```

Remember that the user is expecting the code to perform two tasks: generate statistics and display the requested page. The ShowLink() function performs both tasks using two lines of code. The first line simply increments a counter based on the location of the button on the worksheet. You can see these statistics in the Hits column shown in Figure 5.6. The second link accepts the URL provided by Google Web Services and uses the ThisWorkbook .FollowHyperlink() function to display it.

It's time to consider the actual graphing process. Like every other aspect of this example, you can't make any assumptions about the data. The worksheet contains a combination of Google-supplied data and the data you generated. Listing 5.5 shows how you can create a dynamically generated graph to display the data.

Listing 5.5   **Dynamically Creating a Chart**

```
Public Sub BuildChart()
    Dim NewChart As Chart    ' The actual chart.
    Dim TheSeries As Series  ' Holds the chart data.
    Dim DRange As Range      ' Holds the data range.
    Dim SRange As Range      ' Holds the series label range.

    ' Determine the data range.
    Sheet2.Activate
    Sheet2.Range("D11").Select
    Application.SendKeys "+^{DOWN}", True
    Set DRange = ActiveWindow.RangeSelection

    ' Determine the data range.
    Sheet2.Range("A11").Select
    Application.SendKeys "+^{DOWN}", True
    Set SRange = ActiveWindow.RangeSelection

    ' Create a new chart.
    Set NewChart = Charts.Add()

    ' Change the Name.
    NewChart.Name = "Popularity"

    ' Create a series for the chart.
    NewChart.SeriesCollection.Add _
        Source:=Worksheets("Sheet2").Range(DRange.Address)
    Set TheSeries = NewChart.SeriesCollection(1)

    ... Series Formatting ...

    ' Perform some data formatting.
    With TheSeries
        .XValues = _
            Worksheets("Sheet2").Range(SRange.Address)
```

```
        .HasDataLabels = True
        .DataLabels.Font.Italic = True
        .DataLabels.Font.Size = 13
    End With

    ... Graph Formatting ...

End Sub
```

The code for the graphing portion of the example is interesting because you have to create the graph from scratch and you can't assume anything about the graph data except a few essentials. The code begins by getting the data and series label ranges. You know the starting point for the ranges, but don't know the ending point because Google might return any number of results. In this case, the `Sheet2.Range("D11").Select` chooses the starting point. The `Application.SendKeys "+^{DOWN}", True` method call is the same as pressing Ctrl+Alt+Down Arrow, which selects the remainder of the column. Finally, with the range selected, the code places the value in the appropriate `Range` variable.

At this point, the code can add the graph to the workbook. It creates a `SeriesCollection` that holds the data range and the series label range. After some additional formatting, the code completes the graph. Figure 5.7 shows typical output from this example.

FIGURE 5.7:

The output chart shows how you can mix Google and locally created data.

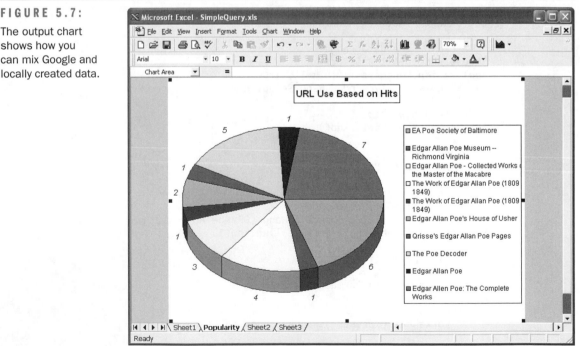

Developing with Microsoft Word

I often use Microsoft Word to create reports based on Google data. A report could include a simple list of recommended Web sites, or it might provide detailed analysis of Web site usage. You could combine data from other Office sources, such as the chart example described in the "Defining Graphs and Charts" section of the chapter. Word helps you polish the data in a report to make it look and read better. It's also easier to perform text manipulation with Word. For example, you could download the current and the cached version of a Web page, compare the two, and create a report showing the differences.

Automating Reports Using SOAP

One of the reports that I find most useful is a comparison of the current and past states of Web pages. Sometimes a vendor will try to sneak a change into a page to overcome a poor choice of words. In other cases, it's very difficult to see what actually changes because the Web page originator fails to provide any indicators such as a new item icon. Fortunately, Word makes creating such a report almost too simple. You can download the cached document from Google Web Services, import it into a Word document, and then download the new document from the vendor's Web site. Using the Tools ➢ Merge Documents command with the Track Changes feature on shows precisely where the document has changed. Listing 5.6 shows how to download and import a cached document from Google. You'll find the complete source for this example in the \Chapter 05\Word folder of the source code located on the Sybex Web site.

Listing 5.6   **Working with Cached Pages**

```
Public Sub SimpleQuery()
    Dim Client As SoapClient30 ' SOAP Client
    Dim Doc() As Byte          ' Entire Result Set
    Dim ResultStr As String    ' Converted string.
    Dim Counter As Integer     ' Loop counter.

    ' Create and initialize the SOAP client.
    Set Client = New SoapClient30
    Client.MSSoapInit "http://api.google.com/GoogleSearch.wsdl", _
                    "GoogleSearchService", _
                    "GoogleSearchPort"

    ' Make a search request.
    Doc = _
        Client.doGetCachedPage( _
            "Your-License-Key, _
            "http://www.mwt.net/~jmueller/books/inprogre.html")

    ' Convert the results to a string.
```

```
    For Counter = 0 To UBound(Doc) - 1
        ResultStr = ResultStr + Chr(Doc(Counter))
    Next

    ' Save the data as an HTML file.
    Open ThisDocument.Path + "\Temp.HTM" For Output As #1
    Write #1, ResultStr
    Close #1

    ' Send the data to screen.
    Selection.InsertFile ThisDocument.Path + "\Temp.HTM"
End Sub
```

The code begins by creating a client. The client performs communication tasks with Google Web Services. In this case, the client uses the `doGetCachedPage()` method to obtain the cached page. Notice that VBA sees the returned information as a `Byte` array, which means you can't use the data directly.

After the code gets the document from Google Web Services, it uses a `For` loop to convert the `Byte` array to a `String`. The `ResultStr` variable contains the whole Web page. Unfortunately, if you pasted `ResultStr` into the document, the results would be unreadable. Word must convert the document from HTML to make it readable.

The easiest way to perform the document conversion is to save the document to disk as an HTML file. The code uses three simple steps to perform this task. While the `Open`, `Write`, and `Close` statements might seem like old technology, they work fast and efficiently for this task. The code then uses the `Selection.InsertFile` method to import the document from disk to the current Word pane. Figure 5.8 shows typical output from this example.

> ▶ **NOTE**
>
> You can tell the `Selection.InsertFile` method to make an automatic conversion selection by setting the `ConfirmConversions` argument true. The problem with this approach is that Word doesn't always make the correct conversion choice. Letting the user ensure that Word selects HTML Document as the conversion choice ensures good application results.

Using the Web Service References Tool

The earlier examples in this chapter demonstrate that it's possible to create a reference to Google Web Services manually. However, there's an easier way to perform this task. You can use the Web Service References Tool for simple queries. A simple query is one that doesn't rely on complex data types for either the request or the response. For example, you could use this technique if your company already runs a Web service for mobile users that delivers a simple response given a simple request. You can also use it with Google Web Services, which is the method this section considers. (See the MSDN article entitled "Handling Complex SOAP Data Types in XML Web Services" at `http://msdn.microsoft.com/library/default.asp?url=/library/en-us/dnxpwst/html/odc_wsrtct.asp` for details on the complex data issues with the Web Service References Tool.)

> ► **WARNING**
>
> Due to the limitations in earlier versions of the Web Service References Tool, I don't recommend this approach for earlier versions of Office. It works marginally with Office XP and Microsoft has promised better support for Office 2003.

To use this technique, you must have the Web Service References Tool loaded on your machine. Use the Add-Ins ➤ Add-Ins Manager command to display the Add-In Manager dialog box shown in Figure 5.9. Ensure the Web Service References add-in is both loaded and started, as shown in the figure.

FIGURE 5.8:

You can easily download cached pages from Google for comparison purposes.

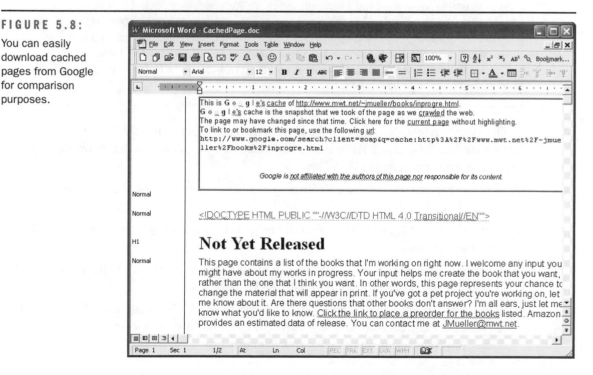

Use the Web Service
References add-in
to make using SOAP
easier.

> ▶ **NOTE**
>
> If you get an error message that VBA can't find the Web Service References Tool add-in on
> your machine, download the Microsoft Office XP Web Services Toolkit 2.0 at http://
> www.microsoft.com/downloads/details.aspx?FamilyId=4922060F-002A-4F5B-AF74-
> 978F2CD6C798&displaylang=en. (You should also check for the 2003 version if you're
> using Office 2003, but the Office XP version seems to work.) Install the toolkit, open the
> Office XP Web Services Toolkit Overview, and then Web Services Reference Tool link on the
> Welcome page to install the tool.

The Web Services Reference Tool adds new menu entries to the VBA IDE. Once you
know that the Web Service References add-in is running, you can use the following steps to
create a reference to Google Web Services.

1. Use the Tools ➤ Web Service References command to display the Web Service References Tool 2.0 dialog box.

2. Select the Web Service URL option and type **http://api.google.com/GoogleSearch
   .wsdl** in the URL field.

3. Click Search. After a few seconds (up to a minute), the Web Service References Tool 2.0
   dialog box displays information for Google Web Services.

4. Check the GoogleSearchService option and click OK. At this point, the VBA IDE will go
   a little crazy as VBA automatically creates the code required to access Google Web Services. You'd have to write this code yourself normally.

Using Microsoft Access as a Database

Sometimes, it's simply not efficient to query Google Web Services for the same information. Many users have research projects that span a week or two (and sometimes longer). They make the same queries every day and wait for Google to deliver the results. In some cases, the order of the URLs vary, making it hard to know which URLs you've already visited. For this and many other reasons, it's often easier to simply cache the data locally. The sections that follow discuss caching techniques and methodology.

Caching as a Practical Performance Enhancing Technique

You might wonder why caching will work for search applications. Many developers tend to think that every search is unique and consequently, cached searching won't work. However, most people in an environment tend to look for the same bits of information. For example, a company that provides insurance to automobile owners is unlikely to spend a lot of time researching barn roof failures in Wisconsin. In fact, such a company will have a focused search routine. The search areas of interest might encompass the automobile crashes in a single area. If you can identify a search commonality in your company or for your personal use, a cached search can be quite productive. In fact, you'll receive the following benefits from cached searches.

Faster Searches   The one benefit that everyone can agree on is that you can search more quickly using a local data store—especially if that data store is optimized for a specific use. No matter how fast your Internet connection, it can't compete with the speed of your LAN and local database. (This isn't to say that Google is slow—Google is quite fast and you'd be hard pressed to duplicate that speed, but the realities of the Internet conspire to reduce even Google's stellar performance.)

Higher Hit Rate   You can optimize a cached data store using statistics and user input. For example, some search results are almost certainly going to contain unwanted data that you can purge from the database. It's also possible to optimize the appearance of links based on hit rates and usefulness, with the better sites appearing first. In this case, better means sites that you're more likely to need, rather than the general audience that Google serves.

Search Optimization   Users often become frustrated with search engines because they don't know the required keywords. They might know a synonym of the word, but not the precise word. Google overcomes this problem by allowing synonym searches, but using this technique often results in huge return sets. By watching the keystrokes users make when entering search criteria and by knowing the typical searches for your application, the application can make word suggestions that are more appropriate and provide better results.

Offline Searches   It's impossible to perform a Google search when you don't have a connection to the Internet available. You can still perform a cached search, however, and might obtain everything you need from the offline database. As users become more mobile, the need to develop and enhance offline storage becomes more critical.

Enhanced Snippets   The Google snippets you receive are helpful, but might not be precisely what you need. It's possible to create a database that includes part Google information and part specialized information. You could store essential elements of the site when you visit it as part of an extended snippet.

Personalized Notes   Google's customer comments can become quite contagious. Storing the Google search results offers one more opportunity to include comments. The database could store localized notes about the various sites. These notes would reflect the biases, needs, and requirements of your particular organization. In short, the cached data would become value enhanced through the addition of user opinions.

Reduced Google License Usage   One of the big reasons to use a cache is so you don't eat away at the limited number of searches you can perform on Google everyday. Remember that you only get 1,000 searches per day (unless you request more and Google grants the request). Consequently, a cached search presents an opportunity to save one of the searches for that day.

> ▶ **TIP**
>
> A particular benefit of Access is that it does work well on a single machine. You can create an application that provides a personal data store of search results. Developing a personal data store means that your search data goes with you.

Creating a Cached Application

A cached application is one in which you can save data for later use. The code in this example demonstrates many of the principles you need to know in order to create a cached application. Listing 5.7 shows typical code for this kind of application. Note that this code is much shorter than the actual code in the Access database and the section doesn't describe the table layout. You'll find the complete source for this example, along with queries and table layouts, in the \Chapter 05\Access folder of the source code located on the Sybex Web site.

Listing 5.7   **Caching Google Web Services Searches**

```
Public Sub SimpleQuery()
   ' Define the Web Service variables.
   Dim Client As SoapClient30      ' SOAP Client
```

```
... Lots of Other Variables ...

' Define the database variables.
Dim SearchRec As Recordset
Dim ResultRec As Recordset

' Define the SearchQueries table field variables.
Dim Index As Integer
... Lots of Other Variables ...

' Define the Results table field variables.
Dim Title As String
... Lots of Other Variables ...

' Create the recordsets.
Set SearchRec = CurrentDb.TableDefs("SearchQueries").OpenRecordset
Set ResultRec = CurrentDb.TableDefs("Results").OpenRecordset

' Create and initialize the SOAP client.
Set Client = New SoapClient30
Client.MSSoapInit "http://api.google.com/GoogleSearch.wsdl", _
                  "GoogleSearchService", _
                  "GoogleSearchPort"

' Make a search request.
Set Doc = _
   Client.doGoogleSearch( _
     "Your-License-Key", _
     "DataCon Services site:www.mwt.net", _
     0, 10, False, "", False, "", "", "")

' Process the search information.
For Counter = 0 To Doc.Length - 1

   ' Get the node.
   Set Results = Doc(Counter)

   ' Check the node type and react accordingly.
   Select Case Results.baseName

      ' Get the original search query.
      Case "searchQuery"
         SearchQuery = Results.Text

      ' Is document filtering enabled?
      Case "documentFiltering"
         DocumentFiltering = CBool(Results.Text)

      ' Number of search results available.
      Case "estimatedTotalResultsCount"
         EstimatedTotalResults = CInt(Results.Text)

      ... Other Cases ...
```

```vba
    End Select
Next

' Begin processing the SearchQueries data.
With SearchRec

    ' Add a new record.
    .AddNew

    ' Fill it with data.
    !SearchQuery = SearchQuery

    ... Other Fields ...

    If Not SearchTips = "" Then
        !SearchTips = SearchTips
    End If

    ' Update the database to hold the record and then point to it.
    .Update
    .MoveLast

    ' Get the index for use with the results table.
    Index = !Index
End With

' Process the results.
For Counter = 0 To Doc.Length - 1

    ' Get the node.
    Set Results = Doc(Counter)

    ' Check the node type and react accordingly.
    If Results.baseName = "resultElements" Then

        ' Set the real item counter.
        RealData = 0

        ' Process each item in turn.
        For ItemCount = 0 To Results.childNodes.Length - 1

            ' Get the item.
            Set Item = Results.childNodes(ItemCount)

            ' Determine whether this is a data item.
            If Item.baseName = "item" Then

                ' Process each item data element in turn.
                For DataCount = 0 To Item.childNodes.Length - 1

                    ' Get the data item.
                    Set ItemData = Item.childNodes(DataCount)
```

```
        ' Print the required data on screen.
        Select Case ItemData.baseName
            Case "title"
                Title = StringToText(ItemData.Text)

            ... Other Cases ...

        End Select
    Next

    ' Update the real data counter.
    RealData = RealData + 1

    ' Add this record to the Results table.
    With ResultRec
        ' Add a new record.
        .AddNew

        ' Fill it with data.
        !Index = Index
        ... Other Data ...

        ' Update the database to hold the record.
        .Update
    End With
            End If
        Next
    End If
Next
```

As you can see, this is a large application and there aren't any good ways to make it shorter. The application has two tables. The first table contains all of the items that affect the results as a whole, such as the query terms and the search time. The second table contains the individual item values, including the page title and URL. The code represents these two tables as SearchRec (search items) and ResultRec (individual items). One of the first tasks the code performs is to create recordsets from these two database tables.

The code then requests the data from Google. As with other examples in this chapter, Google Web Services returns an IXMLDOMSelection object. However, unlike other examples in the chapter, you can't use a single loop to process the data—you need two loops, one for each recordset. The first loop creates the data for SearchRec. Notice the code uses VBA functions such as CBool() and CInt() to convert the data into a format the database can accept.

After the code creates all of the required values, it adds a record to SearchRec and begins filling the fields with data. Some variables, such as SearchQuery, always contain data. However, other variables, such as SearchComments, only contain data when Google Web Services sees a need to provide it. If you don't detect the empty variables as shown in the code, Access is likely to display an error and not accept the new record.

> ▶ **NOTE**
>
> You must obtain the Index field from the main record. The code uses this value to link the Results table to the SearchQueries table.

At this point, the second loop begins. The code is only concerned with the individual items this time, so it begins by searching for the `<resultElements>` element. Once found, the code processes each of the `<item>` elements in turn. Like every other VBA application, Access returns about twice as many `<item>` elements as you'd expect, with half of them containing nothing.

The code processes individual values, just as it did for the search items. However, it adds these values to the Results table after each loop. Consequently, you'll normally see 10 result records for each search record. Adding the record to the table is the same as the search values. However, if you don't include the Index value, Access will reject the record for referential integrity reasons (no matching search record).

Your Call to Action

This chapter has demonstrated how you can use VBA to write programs that use Google Web Services. It's essential to remember that the techniques in this chapter work with any application that supports VBA, not just Microsoft Office. The capabilities of the application also affect how you interact with Google Web Services. Yes, you can force a spreadsheet to act as a word processor, but the results usually aren't easy to use, flexible, or robust. Finally, this chapter demonstrates that you can do a lot more than just search using Google Web Services—it definitely provides room for all kinds of application types.

It's your turn to begin creating macro add-ons that rely on Google Web Services for your favorite application. VBA is a very flexible programming language. When you couple this language with the unique functionality provided by a specific application, you can create robust add-ons using a minimum of code and time. Of course, you can't confuse theses add-ons with full-fledged applications—the macro couples the add-on to the host application.

You might decide that you really do need a full-fledged application—that working with a specific host application just won't work for your needs. Chapter 6 discusses techniques you can use to write full-fledged applications using Visual Studio. This chapter doesn't target a specific version of Visual Studio because many people don't have the latest product. Instead, the chapter discusses several languages included with both Visual Studio 6 and Visual Studio .NET so that you can choose the language that works best for your specific need.

Chapter 6

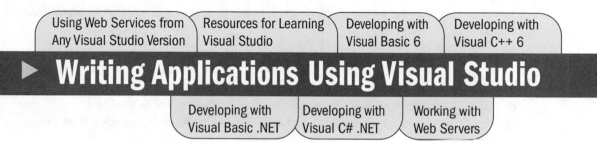

Using Web Services from Any Visual Studio Version

Resources for Learning Visual Studio

Developing with Visual Basic 6

Developing with Visual C++ 6

▶ **Writing Applications Using Visual Studio**

Developing with Visual Basic .NET

Developing with Visual C# .NET

Working with Web Servers

One of the best ways to work with Google Web Services when you want to create a free-form desktop application is to use Visual Studio. With Visual Studio, you have access to a full user interface, Web service, and database tools. Given time and resources, you can create seamless access to Google Web Services for any need, including many forms of Web application access. If you use Visual Studio .NET, mobile applications become relatively easy to create as well. In sum, this is the approach to use when you require maximum flexibility, have the required development skills, and have the time and resources to create a complete application.

The two most popular versions of Visual Studio now are Visual Studio 6.0 and Visual Studio .NET. This chapter explores both versions of Visual Studio. Visual Studio 6.0 developers will find examples for Visual C++ and Visual Basic. Visual Studio .NET developers will find examples for Visual C# and Visual Basic .NET. Most developers will find a Visual Studio flavor they like in these sections.

Visual Studio developers can create desktop or Web applications with equal ease. This chapter explores some of the differences between the two kinds of application development. You need to consider the unique issues of each environment as you create your application. For example, Web applications don't always lend themselves to extensive formatting with the same ease as desktop applications.

This chapter also considers the use of a database for various kinds of data storage, both short and long term. You might find that you need to use local storage that provides automatic data entry updates to achieve a given level of performance for your application. In some cases, you might also need to store customer or company specific short-term information as part of your application. This chapter relies on SQL Server. You can use other database managers, such as Access (see the "Using Microsoft Access as a Database" section of Chapter 5) and MySQL (see the "Using MySQL as a Database" section of Chapter 7).

Using Web Services from Any Visual Studio Version

Chapter 5 demonstrates that your best (and perhaps only) technique of working with Google Web Services is the Simple Object Access Protocol (SOAP) method. Visual Studio also relies on SOAP for access to Google Web Services. However, this environment is more robust. Visual Studio provides a number of additional tools that Office developers can only dream about.

Just because Visual Studio provides a robust development environment doesn't mean that all versions of Visual Studio are equal. You have a number of choices to consider when working with Visual Studio. The .NET version has a definite ease-of-use advantage not provided by previous editions. Instead of manually figuring out how to access the Web service, you simply add a reference to it using the technique discussed in the "Creating a Web Reference" section of the chapter.

I'd love to say that Visual Studio .NET is a positive advance in every way, but it isn't the right choice for some needs. This version of Visual Studio relies on the .NET Framework to perform tasks. The .NET Framework is a library of programming routines similar in purpose to the Windows API. The difference is that it also relies on a runtime engine in the form of the Common Language Runtime (CLR). Unless the person who needs your application has both CLR and the .NET Framework installed on their system, they can't run your application. In addition, the memory and hard drive requirements for the .NET Framework and CLR can be hefty for older systems to accommodate.

Visual Studio 6.0 has a distinct advantage in that it's familiar and you can produce native or Windows 32-bit Application Programming Interface (Win32 API) code using it. Every version of Windows can use applications created by this version of Visual Studio. Consequently, you have decisions to make when selecting which version of Visual Studio to use. Although all of the languages in this chapter can access Google Web Services, each language has features that make it better suited to specific needs.

Resources for Learning Visual Studio

This book assumes that you already know how to use Visual Studio and at least one supported language. Except as needed, I won't discuss the IDE or basic programming techniques. Of course, the chapter will discuss how to use Google Web Services in detail, but you still need to know the essentials of the IDE and language you want to use. The following sections provide some resources you can use learn Visual Studio (although these lists are by no means complete).

Using Visual Studio 6

Visual Studio is the last version of Microsoft's language product to provide full support for native applications—those that run directly from the Win32 API. Developers who don't want to adopt Microsoft's .NET strategy have continued to use this version of Visual Studio and it will probably remain viable for a long time. This book discusses the two most popular languages included with Visual Studio 6: Visual Basic 6 and Visual C++ 6. I'm assuming that you have installed the latest service pack from Microsoft (SP5 at the time of this writing).

It helps if you have a good book when learning any computer language, but especially when working with the intricacies of Visual Studio. A good starting Visual C++ book is *Beginning Visual C++ 6* by Ivor Horton (Wrox, 2003). Visual C++ developers will probably want to look at my books, *Visual C++ 6 from the Ground Up*, Second Edition (Osborne, 1998) or *Windows 2000 Programming Bible* (IDG, 1999) as their second book. Make sure you check out *Mastering C++ 6* by Michael J. Young (Sybex, 1998) as well.

For Visual Basic 6 developers, one of the best books on the market is *Visual Basic 6 for Dummies* by Wallace Wang (IDG, 1998). Another good book once you understand a few of the basics is *Mastering Visual Basic 6* by Evangelos Petroutsos (Sybex, 1998).

Make sure you also spend time looking at source code examples. For example, you can find great source code examples at Planet Source Code (`http://www.pscode.com/`). This site includes both Visual Basic and Visual C++ examples, along with helpful tutorials. Note that this site also caters to .NET users. Another good place to look for Visual Basic code is A1VBCode at `http://www.a1vbcode.com/`. The TutorGig site at `http://www.tutorgig.com/` provides tutorials for both Visual Basic and Visual C++.

Normally, I recommend spending time on Microsoft's newsgroups such as `microsoft .public.vb.bugs` or `microsoft.public.vc.database`. However, if you're a Visual Basic developer, many online forums present great information without the usual Microsoft bias. For example, the Extreme Visual Basic Forum at `http://visualbasicforum.com/` provides a number of message lists you can use to discuss issues such as adding a Windows XP interface to your application.

Using Visual Studio .NET

Visual Studio .NET promises to deliver a lot in the way of language functionality, so it's almost a shame that I only cover C# and Visual Basic in this chapter. You still have an option to use Visual C++ for development purposes. See my book *Visual C++ .NET Developer's Guide* (Osborne, 2002) for details on using this language. In fact, the inclusion of new designer tools for Visual C++ developers in Visual Studio .NET 2003 makes this language a viable choice (the first version of Visual Studio .NET didn't provide Visual C++ developers with designer support). However, I'm currently working with PERL in .NET (see `http://www.activestate` `.com/Products/Visual_Perl/` for details) and there are other choices too. You can see a list of languages at `http://msdn.microsoft.com/netframework/technologyinfo/Overview/` `default.aspx`. It's also interesting to look at the language list at `http://www.gotdotnet.com/` `team/lang/`.

> ▶ **TIP**
>
> Many of the books that you'll see online say they're for the novice, but the author has targeted them to a specific need. For example, you might see a book for database programming or using Crystal Reports. These books are helpful, but first try to find a .NET book that focuses on the language, rather than tasks you can perform with the language.

One of the best places to learn about C# is *A Programmer's Introduction to C#*, Second Edition, by Eric Gunnerson (Apress, 2001). Once you get a basic start, check out my book *Visual C# .NET Developer's Handbook* (Sybex, 2002). If you want a great .NET book that includes both Visual Basic and C#, check out *.NET Programming 10-Minute Solutions* by Russell Jones and Mike Gunderloy (Sybex, 2003).

Visual Basic .NET developers also have a wealth of information sources at their disposal. One book to try is *Beginning VB.NET* by Richard Blair, Jonathan Crossland, Matthew Reynolds, and Thearon Willis (Wrox, 2003). Many people also find *Microsoft Visual Basic .NET Step by Step* by Michael Halvorson (Microsoft Press, 2002) quite helpful. Finally, you might want to read *The Ultimate VB.NET and ASP.NET Code Book* by Karl Moore (Apress 2003).

As with any other language, seeing coding examples and trying them out on your machine is a good way to learn. One of the best places to obtain coding examples for Visual Basic .NET or Visual C++ .NET is GotDotNet (`http://www.gotdotnet.com/`). Some of the Microsoft developers frequent this site, as well as expert programmers who don't have any Microsoft affiliation. You can also learn a lot from my free .NET Tips, Trends & Technology eXTRA newsletter (sign up at `http://www.freeenewsletters.com/`). Send me your .NET questions and I'll answer them in the newsletter. I've also written a number of articles for InformIT (`http://www.informit.com/isapi/authorid~{67CBE1B0-99DC-4A19-8BFB-5D224A0F34A7}/` `authors/author.asp`). Finally, Matthew Reynolds' .NET 247 site at `http://www.dotnet247` `.com/` is packed with helpful examples and other information.

Microsoft supports a number of .NET newsgroups. The important thing to remember is that most of these newsgroups have "dotnet" in the name. For example, if you want to learn about .NET Framework interoperability problems, you should visit the `microsoft.public` `.dotnet.framework.interop` newsgroup. When you need help with Visual Basic .NET, check the `microsoft.public.dotnet.languages.vb` newsgroup. Likewise, you can visit the `microsoft` `.public.dotnet.languages.vc` newsgroup for help with Visual C++ .NET questions.

Developing with Visual Basic 6

Visual Basic 6 is still a favorite with developers today because it makes building applications easy, when they compare it to a language such as C, and still produces a native executable. Many organizations have documented the developer productivity benefits of using Visual Basic 6. You can produce both desktop and Web applications with equal ease. The design interface makes working with databases simple. In fact, if there's a problem with Visual Basic, it's that the product does too much and ends up hiding low-level functionality that developers need. Consequently, this is the language to use if you need a native code application to access Google Web Services and developer productivity is high on your list of priorities. The following sections describe how you can use Visual Basic 6 to build a Google Web Services application.

Getting the Microsoft SOAP Toolkit

Visual Studio 6 arrived on the scene well before the SOAP arrived on the scene. Consequently, none of the languages in Visual Studio 6 includes native support for SOAP. To add SOAP support, download the Microsoft SOAP Toolkit 3.0 from `http://www.microsoft` `.com/downloads/details.aspx?FamilyId=C943C0DD-CEEC-4088-9753-86F052EC8450`. Once you download the toolkit, install it on your system. Make sure you have Visual Studio 6 installed before you install the toolkit so the installation routine can make any required changes to your Visual Studio 6 setup. Note that accessing Google Web Services doesn't require all of the features provided in the Microsoft SOAP Toolkit, but it's a good idea to install everything in case you want to perform other types of SOAP development later.

> ▶ **NOTE**
>
> Microsoft still offers the Microsoft SOAP Toolkit 2.0 SP2 for download. This version of the toolkit works fine with the examples in this book. In fact, you can download this version of the toolkit from `http://www.microsoft.com/downloads/details.aspx?FamilyId=` `147ED727-0BE8-48A1-B1DA-D50B1EA582CB&displaylang=en`. However, it's better to use the newer version of the Microsoft SOAP Toolkit if possible and the version-specific information in this section reflects that toolkit's contents.

The Microsoft SOAP Toolkit contains a number of files that you need to know about before you can create an application with it. Table 6.1 provides a list of the files (including DLLs) provided in the Microsoft SOAP Toolkit. This table tells how you'll use the DLLs within an application and the utilities to create application resources or perform testing. Note that some filenames include version information that might vary from the version you have installed. In addition, you might find the files in a slightly different location and some toolkit versions could include files not listed in Table 6.1.

As you can see from Table 6.1, the library that you're going to use most often is the Microsoft SOAP Library. It contains everything you need to begin a conversation between client and server using the high-level API. What the table doesn't show is that you'll also need the latest version of the Microsoft XML Library. This library doesn't appear in the same directory as the rest of the SOAP files. The Microsoft SOAP Toolkit installation program automatically adds the latest version of the Microsoft XML Library to your System or System32 directory.

> ▶ **TIP**
>
> One of the first places you should look when experiencing client-side errors in your SOAP application is the Microsoft XML Library. My workstation has four versions of this library installed. Although the library versions are clearly marked, you could find that you selected the wrong one by mistake. The current version of the Microsoft SOAP Toolkit relies on version 4 of the Microsoft XML Library found in MSXML4.DLL.

On those few occasions where you do need low-level API access, make sure you include one of the low-level API access libraries in Table 6.1. All of the sample programs provided with the Microsoft SOAP Toolkit rely on the Windows Internet Connector Library. This doesn't make the other selections any better or worse, it simply means you'll spend a little additional time figuring out how to use them. It helps that all the low-level libraries work about the same way, contain about the same classes with the same methods, and that you could theoretically use any of the three with the same boilerplate code.

> ▶ **TIP**
>
> You might find that you have additional questions about the Microsoft SOAP Toolkit for your own needs. The microsoft.public.xml.soapsdk newsgroup is a good place to start asking questions about this product.

TABLE 6.1: Files provided with the Microsoft SOAP Toolkit

DLL Name	Location	Description
MSSOAP1.DLL and MSSOAP30.DLL	\Program Files\ Common Files\ MSSoap\Binaries	This is the first SOAP DLL that you'll use on a high-level API access client or server. Use the MSSOAP30.DLL file for version 3.0 access. The Microsoft SOAP Library contains a number of classes, but you'll always begin by creating either a SoapClient or SoapServer object. These objects support a single method call, Init(), that tells SOAP which WSDL file to use. Other classes perform tasks such as serializing data for output and reading input. This is the DLL that you'll use for simple requests with Google Web Services.
MSSOAPR.DLL and MSSOAPR3.DLL	\Program Files\ Common Files\ MSSoap\Binaries\ Resources\1033	This file contains resources for SOAP use in general and normally you won't need to reference it directly. The MSSOAPR3.DLL file contains resources specifically used by the 3.0 version of the toolkit.
MsSoapT3.EXE	\Program Files\ MSSOAP\Binaries	Use this file to start the Microsoft SOAP Trace utility. In most cases, you won't need this diagnostic tool when working with Google Web Services. However, it's helpful to know how to use it so that you can troubleshoot problems when they occur.
SOAPIS30.DLL	\Program Files\ Common Files\ MSSoap\Binaries	Use this DLL to add WSDL support to your Internet Information Server (IIS). The "Specifying an ISAPI Listener" topic of the SOAP Toolkit 3.0 help file tells how to add this file to the server. It's unlikely that you'll use this file with Google Web Services, unless you create a referral type application where a user uses a Web service application on your Web server to access Google Web Services.
WHSC30.DLL	\Program Files\ Common Files\ MSSoap\Binaries	This DLL contains the Windows HTTP SOAP Connector Library. This library provides SOAP connector service to a remote location. You'll also use this DLL to receive and send low-level SOAP messages. Use this library for complex requests, especially when working with searches, to avoid receiving unwanted data from the server. Avoid using this library with Windows 9x systems—use the Windows Internet Connector Library instead.
WISC10.DLL and WISC30.DLL	\Program Files\ Common Files\ MSSoap\Binaries	These DLLs contain the Windows Internet Connector Library. The version 3.0 toolkit includes the WISC30.DLL file. Both DLLs provide essentially the same services as the Windows HTTP Library Connector described earlier. This lower performance library works with Windows 98, Windows ME, Windows NT, and Windows 2000. As with the Windows HTTP SOAP Connector Library, use this DLL for complex requests.
WSDLGen3.DLL and WSDLGen3.EXE	\Program Files\ MSSOAP\Binaries	The WSDL generation tools create the WSDL files used to describe Web services that you create. You never need to use this tool with Google Web Services because Google provides the required WSDL file for you. This file resides at http://soap.google.com/schemas3/GoogleWebServices.wsdl for users in the United States and Japan, and http://soap-eu.google.com/schemas3/GoogleWebServices.wsdl for users in the United Kingdom and Germany.

Adding a SOAP Toolkit Reference to Visual Basic 6

Before you can develop an application using the SOAP toolkit, you need to add a reference to it in your application. The following steps tell how to perform this task.

1. Select the Project ➤ References command. You'll see a References dialog box such as the one shown in Figure 6.1.

2. Locate the Microsoft SOAP Type Library 3.0 entry in the list and check it.

3. Locate the Microsoft XML, v4.0 entry in the list and check it.

4. Click OK.

You also need to add the FlexGrid control to your application to make this example work properly. (Don't confuse the FlexGrid control with the DataGrid control—both controls use the same icon but behave differently.) To add this control, right-click the Toolbox and select Components from the context menu. Check the Microsoft FlexGrid Control 6.0 option in the Components dialog box. Click OK and you'll see the component added to your Toolbox.

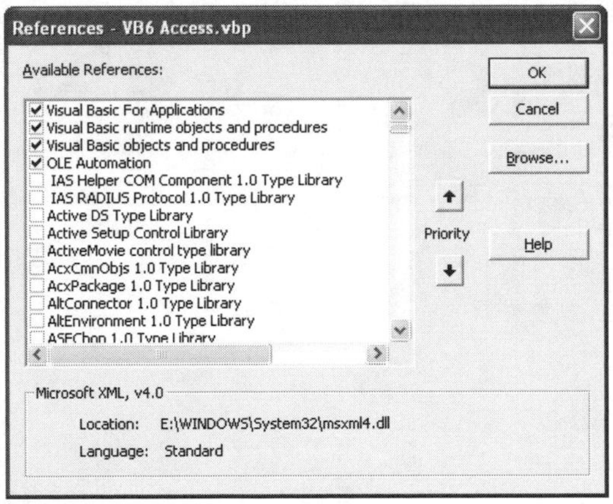

FIGURE 6.1:

Add a reference to the appropriate type libraries using this dialog box.

Performing a Search with Visual Basic 6

The Microsoft SOAP Toolkit supports two different programming strategies called the high-level Application Programming Interface (API) and the low-level API. The high-level API hides many of the details of creating an application from the developer. It requires less code to use and is easier to understand. Most language products can use the high-level API without problem. In fact, the example in this section relies on the high-level API. The low-level API requires careful construction of the SOAP message using code. You must have a very good understanding of how SOAP works to use it, but the low-level API also offers complete control over the message flow and the most flexibility. The example in the "Developing with Visual C++ 6" section of the chapter uses the low-level API to create an application that performs the same task as the Visual Basic application in this section.

> ▶ **NOTE**
>
> You must have the Microsoft SOAP Toolkit installed on your system to work with the examples in this section. Learn more about this toolkit in the "Getting the Microsoft SOAP Toolkit" section of the chapter.

Listing 6.1 shows how to create a search request using Google Web Services. This example includes support for modifying the country of origin, the language used on the Web pages, the use of filtering, and safe searching techniques. Everything is controlled as part of the application interface. You'll find the complete source for this example in the \Chapter 06\ VB6Search folder of the source code located on the Sybex Web site.

Listing 6.1   **Performing a Google Search with Visual Basic 6**

```vb
Private Sub btnTest_Click()
    Dim Client As SoapClient30        ' SOAP Client
    Dim Results As IXMLDOMSelection   ' All the results.
    Dim MainNode As IXMLDOMNode       ' High-level nodes.
    Dim ItemList As IXMLDOMNodeList   ' All the result items.
    Dim ItemNode As IXMLDOMNode       ' Result item nodes.
    Dim DataList As IXMLDOMNodeList   ' All the data items.
    Dim DataNode As IXMLDOMNode       ' One data item.

    ' Initialize the SOAP client.
    Set Client = New SoapClient30
    Client.MSSoapInit "http://api.google.com/GoogleSearch.wsdl", _
                      "GoogleSearchService", _
                      "GoogleSearchPort"

    ' Make the request.
    Set Results = Client.doGoogleSearch(txtLicense.Text, _
                                        txtKey.Text, _
                                        txtIndex.Text, _
                                        txtResults.Text, _
                                        CBool(cbFilter.Value), _
                                        txtOrigin.Text, _
                                        CBool(cbSafeSearch.Value), _
                                        txtLanguage.Text, _
                                        "", _
                                        "")
```

```
' Search through the main results.
For Each MainNode In Results

    ' Look for specific nodes.
    Select Case MainNode.baseName

        ' Update the starting index.
        Case "endIndex"
            txtIndex.Text = CStr(CInt(MainNode.Text) + 1)

        ' Display the total estimated results.
        Case "estimatedTotalResultsCount"
            txtEstResults = MainNode.Text

        ' Determine whether the results are exact.
        Case "estimateIsExact"
            cbEstExact.Value = CBool(MainNode.Text)

        ' Get all of the result items.
        Case "resultElements"
            Set ItemList = MainNode.childNodes

            ' Process each item in turn.
            For Each ItemNode In ItemList

                ' Make sure the element is an item.
                If ItemNode.baseName = "item" Then

                    ' Enter each of the column values.
                    Set DataList = ItemNode.childNodes
                    For Each DataNode In DataList

                        ' Process each data item.
                        Select Case DataNode.baseName

                            ' Get the title.
                            Case "title"
                                fgOutput.Col = 0
                                fgOutput.Text = StringToText(DataNode.Text)

                            ' Get the snippet or summary.
                            Case "snippet"
                                fgOutput.Col = 2
                                fgOutput.Text = StringToText(DataNode.Text)
                            Case "summary"
                                fgOutput.Col = 2
                                If fgOutput.Text = "" Then
                                    fgOutput.Text = _
                                        StringToText(DataNode.Text)
                                End If
```

```
                    ... Other Columns ...
                End Select
            Next

            ' Create a new row.
            fgOutput.AddItem " "
            fgOutput.Row = fgOutput.Row + 1
         End If
       Next
    End Select
  Next
End Sub
```

The code begins by creating a SOAP client using the `MSSoapInit()` method. You must supply the location of the WSDL file, the service name, and the service port as part of the input. The example shows how to use the online version of the WSDL file. This is the best option because it ensures the WSDL file is always up-to-date. You can also provide the location of the WSDL file that comes with the Google Web Services Kit. Using the local hard drive copy is the best solution when you want to troubleshoot the message traffic between Google Web Services and your application (see the "Dealing with Difficult Languages" section of the chapter for details).

The Client calls the `doGoogleSearch()` method using all of the available arguments. However, the client automatically detects empty arguments and passes a blank request element to Google Web Services. Notice that you must convert the check-box values, such as `cbFilter`, to a Boolean using the `CBool()` function before you pass the information to the client. The return value from this call is an `IXMLDOMSelection` object, `Results`, which you can treat as a collection in Visual Basic.

Because Visual Basic 6 treats most XML objects as collections, you can use the `For Each` structure to process them. Using this technique reduces code and also makes errors less likely because you don't have to keep track of loop counter variables. The code uses three processing loops: upper or main level nodes, result item level nodes, and result data level nodes.

The return value is always text and always appears in the `Text` property. Each of the loops looks at the `baseName` property to determine the node type, and then uses the `Text` property to process the node. The use of a text means you must perform data transformations in some cases. For example, when you want to determine the next index value, you must convert the text into a number, perform a math calculation, and then turn it back into text for display on screen using a combination of the `CStr()` and `CInt()` functions.

The application uses simple design elements, such as textboxes, for the main data elements. However, it uses an `MSFlexGrid` object to display the search results, including the page title and URL. The use of a grid means keeping track of the cursor position within the grid. As you can see from the code, the application uses the `Col` and `Row` properties of `fgOutput` to track cursor position. However, this approach might not always work when you need to create complex displays, so you need to use external variables as necessary. Because Google doesn't leave any of the result items blank, you can simply use the `fgOutput.AddItem()` method shown to add a new row after processing each item. Figure 6.2 shows typical output from this application.

This example includes one additional feature. Notice the call to `StringToText()` for some of the data elements. This function performs approximately the same task as the VBA examples in Chapter 5. The only difference is that this version of the function is slightly more capable than the VBA version and detects more tag types. See Listing 5.2 and its associated explanation in the "Modifying the Google Data" section of Chapter 5 for details.

FIGURE 6.2:

Typical output for a Google search when using this application

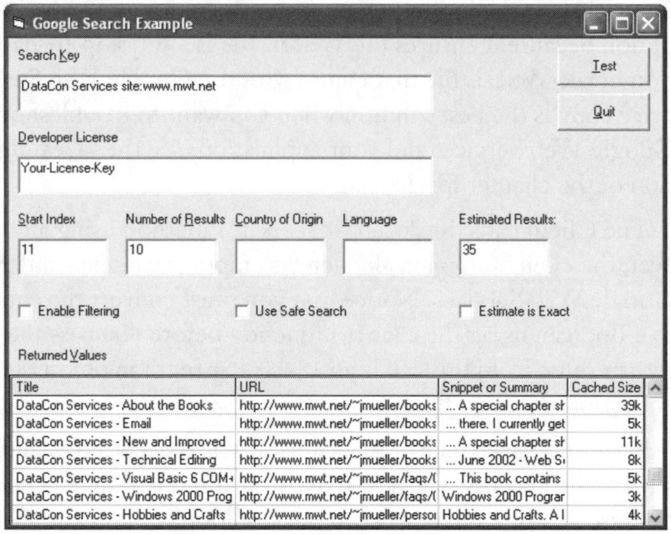

Developing with Visual C++ 6

Most developers who use Visual C++ 6 are looking for low-level flexibility and application execution speed. Given the flexibility this environment provides, some types of data manipulations are much simpler than with a product such as Visual Basic. The problem with Visual C++ 6 is that you pay a price in developer productivity when using it. A Google Web Services application can take two or three times longer to build than with Visual Basic, given applications of the same capability. In addition, building database support into a Visual C++ 6 application is more difficult and time consuming than when you use Visual Basic. Visual C++ 6 is the language of choice when you value flexibility and performance over ease of use and productivity.

> ▶ **NOTE**
>
> You must have the Microsoft SOAP Toolkit installed on your system to work with the examples in this section. Learn more about this toolkit in the "Getting the Microsoft SOAP Toolkit" section of the chapter.

Adding a SOAP Toolkit Reference to Visual C++ 6

You really need to know the location and names of the SOAP Toolkit files when working with Visual C++ because the IDE doesn't perform any hand-holding. This lack of support is one reason that Table 6.1 is so important. The following steps will help you install the SOAP Toolkit, XML, and FlexGrid support required for this example.

1. Use the Project ➤ Add to Project ➤ Components and Controls command to display the Components and Controls dialog box shown in Figure 6.3.

2. Double-click the Registered ActiveX Controls folder. Locate the Microsoft FlexGrid Control, and then click Insert. Visual C++ will ask if you want to insert this component.

3. Click OK. You'll see a Confirm Classes dialog box similar to the one shown in Figure 6.4. Normally, you don't have to change any of the entries on this dialog box. However, you may need to change the names if there's a conflict with another class.

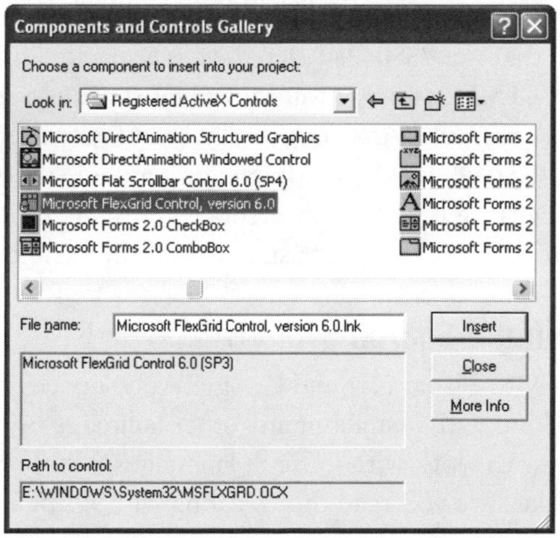

FIGURE 6.3:

Use the Components and Controls dialog box to add SOAP, XML, and FlexGrid support.

FIGURE 6.4:

The Confirm Classes dialog box shows which classes the IDE adds to support the FlexGrid.

4. Click OK. Visual C++ adds the new classes to your application and you'll see the new control in the Toolbox.

5. Click Close to close the Components and Controls dialog box.

You add the XML and SOAP reference to the application by adding code to the file. In general, you'll use the following code to add the SOAP toolkit and XML references.

```
// You must change these locations to match your setup!
#import "MSXML4.DLL"
using namespace MSXML2;
#import "E:\Program Files\Common Files\MSSoap\Binaries\MSSOAP30.DLL" \
    exclude("IStream", "IErrorInfo", "ISequentialStream", \
    "_LARGE_INTEGER", "_ULARGE_INTEGER", "tagSTATSTG", "_FILETIME")
using namespace MSSOAPLib30;
```

Notice that the MSSOAP30.DLL file has a specific directory attached because it doesn't appear in the \Windows\System32 folder. You must change this folder to match your system or the code won't compile. Also, notice that the #import reference excludes a number of elements from the MSSOAP30.DLL file. If you don't include these exclusions, the code probably won't compile because it will detect errors with existing files. The IDE automatically adds the support required by the #import statements when you build the application the first time.

Performing a Search with Visual C++ 6

Working with Visual C++ and Google Web Services does require a lot more patience and code than working with just about any other language in the book. In fact, this example demonstrates how to work with difficult languages—those that don't work well with some Web services. Make sure you read the "Dealing with Difficult Languages" section for details on this issue. Listing 6.2 shows how to create a Google search application similar to the Visual Basic 6 example using Visual C++. This example requires substantially more code than shown. You'll find the complete source for this example in the \Chapter 06\VC6Search folder of the source code located on the Sybex Web site.

Listing 6.2   **Performing a Google Search with Visual C++ 6**

```cpp
void CVC6SearchDlg::OnTest()
{
    // SOAP variables.
    ISoapConnectorPtr    Connector;      // Connection to Web Service.
    ISoapSerializerPtr   DataSend;       // Sends data to Google.
    ISoapReaderPtr       DataReceive;    // Receives data from Google.

    // XML variables
    IXMLDOMElement    *RpcElement;       // Holds entire RPC result.
    IXMLDOMNodeList   *Results;          // All the results.
    IXMLDOMNode       *MainNode;         // High-level nodes.
    ... Other XML Variables ...

    // Variables used to hold the form data.
    CString  txtLicense;     // Developer license value.
    int      lSafeSearch;    // Perform a safe search?
    ... Other Form Data Variables ...

    // Other variables.
    int      MainCount;  // Main loop counter.
    ... A Number of Miscellaneous Variables ...

    // Get the data from the window.
    m_License.GetWindowText(txtLicense);
    lSafeSearch = m_SafeSearch.GetCheck();
    ... Other Window Data Statements ...

    // Initialize the COM environment.
    CoInitialize(NULL);

    // Create a connection to Google.
    Connector.CreateInstance(__uuidof(HttpConnector30));
    Connector->Property["EndPointURL"] =
        "http://api.google.com/search/beta2";
    Connector->Connect();

    // Tell Google that the application is sending a request.
    Connector->Property["SoapAction"] =
        "urn:GoogleSearchAction";
    Connector->BeginMessage();

    // Associate the data serializer with the connection.
    DataSend.CreateInstance(__uuidof(SoapSerializer30));
```

```
DataSend->Init(_variant_t((IUnknown*)Connector->InputStream));

// Create the envelope and associated namespaces. Don't
// include namespaces that Visual C++ already includes.
DataSend->StartEnvelope("", "NONE", "UTF-8");
//DataSend->SoapAttribute("xmlns:SOAP-ENV", "",
//              "http://schemas.xmlsoap.org/soap/envelope/", "");
//DataSend->SoapAttribute("xmlns:xsi", "",
//              "http://www.w3.org/1999/XMLSchema-instance", "");
//DataSend->SoapAttribute("xmlns:xsd", "",
//              "http://www.w3.org/1999/XMLSchema", "");

// Create the SOAP body.
DataSend->StartBody("NONE");


// Start creating the request.
DataSend->StartElement("ns1:doGoogleSearch", "", "STANDARD", "");
DataSend->SoapAttribute("xmlns:ns1", "", "urn:GoogleSearch", "");
//DataSend->SoapAttribute("SOAP-ENV:encodingStyle", "",
//              "http://schemas.xmlsoap.org/soap/encoding/", "");

// Add the developer key information.
DataSend->StartElement("key", "", "NONE", "");
DataSend->SoapAttribute("SOAPSDK1:type", "", "xsd:string", "");
DataSend->WriteString(txtLicense.AllocSysString());
DataSend->EndElement();

... Other Standard Inputs ...

// Add the country restriction.
DataSend->StartElement("restrict", "", "NONE", "");
DataSend->SoapAttribute("SOAPSDK1:type", "", "xsd:string", "");
if (txtOrigin.GetLength() > 0)
   DataSend->WriteString(txtOrigin.AllocSysString());
DataSend->EndElement();

// Add the safe search requirement.
DataSend->StartElement("safeSearch", "", "NONE", "");
DataSend->SoapAttribute("SOAPSDK1:type", "", "xsd:boolean", "");
if (lSafeSearch)
   DataSend->WriteString("true");
else
   DataSend->WriteString("false");
DataSend->EndElement();

// Add the language restriction.
DataSend->StartElement("lr", "", "NONE", "");
DataSend->SoapAttribute("SOAPSDK1:type", "", "xsd:string", "");
if (txtLanguage.GetLength() > 0)
   DataSend->WriteString(txtLanguage.AllocSysString());
```

```
DataSend->EndElement();

// Not used, but you must send the empty element.
DataSend->StartElement("ie", "", "NONE", "");
DataSend->SoapAttribute("SOAPSDK1:type", "", "xsd:string", "");
//DataSend->WriteString("");
DataSend->EndElement();

// Not used, but you must send the empty element.
DataSend->StartElement("oe", "", "NONE", "");
DataSend->SoapAttribute("SOAPSDK1:type", "", "xsd:string", "");
//DataSend->WriteString("");
DataSend->EndElement();

// Close all of the open tags.
DataSend->EndElement();
DataSend->EndBody();
DataSend->EndEnvelope();

// Tell Google the request is complete.
Connector->EndMessage();

// Receive the response from Google.
DataReceive.CreateInstance(__uuidof(SoapReader30));
DataReceive->Load(_variant_t((IUnknown*)Connector->OutputStream), "");

// Build the output value.
DataReceive->get_RpcResult(&RpcElement);
RpcElement->get_childNodes(&Results);

// Set the data grid row.
CurrDGRow = 1;

// Search through the main results.
for (MainCount = 0; MainCount < Results->length; MainCount++)
{
   // Get the current node.
   Results->get_item(MainCount, &MainNode);

   // Get the node's name.
   BaseName = (const char*)MainNode->baseName;

   // Update the starting index.
   if (BaseName == "endIndex")
     m_Index.SetWindowText((const char*)MainNode->text);

   ... Other Main Node Data Items ...

   // Get all of the result items.
   if (BaseName == "resultElements")
   {
```

```cpp
MainNode->get_childNodes(&ItemList);

// Process each item in turn.
for (ItemCount = 0; ItemCount < ItemList->length; ItemCount++)
{
    ItemList->get_item(ItemCount, &ItemNode);

    // Make sure the element is an item.
    ItemName = (const char*)ItemNode->baseName;
    if (ItemName == "item")
    {

        // Enter each of the column values.
        ItemNode->get_childNodes(&DataList);
        for (DataCount = 0; DataCount < DataList->length; DataCount++)
        {
            // Process each data item.
            DataList->get_item(DataCount, &DataNode);
            DataName = (const char*)DataNode->baseName;

            // Get the title.
            if (DataName == "title")
            {
                m_Output.SetCol(0);
                m_Output.SetText((const char*)DataNode->text);
            }

            ... Other Cells ...

            // Get the cached size.
            if (DataName == "cachedSize")
            {
                m_Output.SetCol(3);
                m_Output.SetText((const char*)DataNode->text);
            }
        }

        // Add a new row.
        CurrDGRow++;
        itoa(CurrDGRow, DGRowTxt.GetBuffer(10), 10);
        DGRowTxt.ReleaseBuffer(-1);
        m_Output.AddItem("", _variant_t(DGRowTxt));
        m_Output.SetRow(CurrDGRow);
    }
  }
 }

}

// Release the COM objects.
```

```
      Connector.Release();
      DataSend.Release();
      DataReceive.Release();

      // Uninitialize the COM environment.
      CoUninitialize();
   }
```

The code includes a lot of variables—I've shortened the list to display the main types that you need to consider when working with the low-level API. Notice that instead of a client, you now need to create a connection using ISoapConnectorPtr, a method of sending a request using ISoapSerializerPtr, and a way to read the response using ISoapReaderPtr. The data handling mechanism is also different. You now receive a single element—the root node of the response in the form of an IXMLDOMElement object. However, at this point, the processing takes a familiar turn. You still use a combination of node lists (IXMLDOMNodeList objects) and nodes (IXMLDOMNode objects) to perform the task.

Before the code can do anything else, it must perform some initialization tasks. It begins by retrieving the input arguments from the form and also initializing the COM environment using the CoInitialize(NULL) function.

Creating a connection to Google Web Services is a two-part process. First, the code creates a connection. Notice the method used to define the EndPointURL property. You define most connector properties using this technique. The connection is complete when the code calls Connector->Connect(). The next step is to tell Google Web Services to expect a message. You must define the SoapAction property and call Connector->BeginMessage() to perform this task.

The presence of a connection doesn't mean you can send data. To create a serializer—an object used to send the data—you must create an instance of the SoapSerializer30 object and initialize it to use the Connector->InputStream. This two-step process will associate the serializer with the connection so Google Web Services actually receives the message you build.

Remember that you must build the message from scratch, which means defining the SOAP envelope and body, in addition to creating the content located in the body. The only problem is that the Microsoft SOAP Library makes some strange assumptions about what you do and don't want. You can control these assumptions by providing the correct input arguments, but it takes time to figure out which ones to use in some cases. For example, Google Web Services doesn't want you to provide encoding style information as part of the envelope, and you must specifically tell Google Web Services that the message is formatted using UTF-8. Consequently, the code creates the envelope using the DataSend->StartEnvelope("", "NONE",

"UTF-8") method call with the arguments shown. The envelope should include several attributes according to the Google examples. However, the SOAP library provides these arguments for you, so the listing shows these attributes as commented out.

The next step is to create the body and its content. The `DataSend->StartBody("NONE")` call tells the SOAP Library to create a body that doesn't include encoding information. Notice that the encoding information does finally appear as part of the root node declaration for the body content. In this case, the code uses the `DataSend->StartElement("ns1:doGoogle-Search", "", "STANDARD", "")` method.

Because most of the arguments you must send to Google Web Services are straight text, all you need to do is create an element, define a data type using the `SoapAttribute()` method, write the data using the `WriteString()` method, and finally end the element using the `EndElement()` method. However, some arguments, such as the `<safeSearch>` element, require special handling. In this case, you must test the input argument value and write true or false as needed. It's also important to test whether optional arguments include any data. In many cases, they don't, so you'll just write the beginning and ending of the element. The message ends by closing all of the open tags and then sending the message using `Connector->EndMessage()`.

At this point, you can receive the response from Google Web Services. To perform this task, the code creates a parser—an object that retrieves the data from the Web service. Again, this is a two-step process where the code creates `DataReceive` and then associates it with the connection using the `Connector->OutputStream` property. The code actually loads the output stream into the parser.

Building the data output begins by placing the XML into a node using the `get_RpcResult()` method. This is the root node of the data, so all you need is a single element.

Like the Visual Basic example in Listing 6.1, this example displays the main output using simple controls such as a textbox and the individual results (including title and URL) using a `MSFlexGrid` object. Unlike Visual Basic, Visual C++ views the incoming data as a series of pointers, not a collection. In addition, you can't track the position of the cursor on the `MSFlexGrid` object very easily. Consequently, you end up writing a lot more code to track all of this information. However, once you get past these differences, the code works conceptually the same as the Visual Basic example. In fact, the output looks the same as the Visual Basic example shown in Figure 6.2.

The code must perform two additional tasks before the application exits. First, the code must release the three objects used to communicate with Google Web Services or the application will incur a memory leak. Second, the application must uninitialize the COM environment.

Dealing with Difficult Languages

Sometimes, a language won't work with Google Web Services in the way that you originally anticipated. The precise cause of the problem isn't important—all you know is that you need some working code. Visual C++ is such a language. While I was able to use the high-level interface provided with the Microsoft SOAP Toolkit with Visual Basic 6 and even JavaScript (see the examples in Chapters 3 and 4 for details), Visual C++ defied all attempts to make life simple. Consequently, you'll notice the example in this section uses the low-level interface. Yes, it's harder to build the example this way, but you gain considerable flexibility and control.

Despite my best efforts, Visual C++ still proved stubborn. Code that worked fine with other Web services failed to work with Visual C++. However, this is where you can begin using a few tricks of the trade to gain an appreciation for SOAP. Many of the tools you use will create the message one piece at a time. Consequently, you need to know how the message looks, what actually works, and how to use tools that make it easier to troubleshoot the actual message. The Microsoft SOAP Toolkit comes with the Trace Utility, but you can also use tools such as the TpcTrace tool found on the PocketSOAP site at http://www .pocketsoap.com/tcptrace/.

To begin whittling this problem down to size, you need to start the SOAP interception tool (such as the Trace Utility) and configure it for use. I'll use the Trace Utility in this section because it comes with Microsoft SOAP Toolkit, but the same techniques work with any other SOAP interception tool on the market. Create a session using the File ➢ New ➢ Formatted Trace command. You'll see a Trace Setup dialog box. Type **api.google.com** in the Destination Host field and click OK. The Trace Utility is now listening for SOAP requests.

Even though the Trace Utility is listening for requests, it doesn't mean it will actually receive any. You must change your code slightly to ensure the Trace Utility receives requests. The change is simple. All you need to do is use localhost as an endpoint as shown here.

```
// Create a connection to Google.
Connector.CreateInstance(__uuidof(HttpConnector30));
Connector->Property["EndPointURL"] =
    "http://localhost:8080/search/beta2";
Connector->Connect();
```

Notice that the EndPointURL property now points to localhost using port 8080—the same settings as the input to the Trace Utility. The Trace Utility receives the request, displays the information on screen, changes the domain, and passes it to Google Web Services. When Google Web Services sends a response, the Trace Utility intercepts it, displays the information on screen, and passes the information to the application. Figure 6.5 shows a typical message session.

FIGURE 6.5:

Use the Trace Utility to discover the true form of messages passed between your application and Google.

Now that you can see the real message traffic, you know that you need to make a few changes to the way Visual C++ uses the SOAP Toolkit to create the message. For example, this display points out the need to remove some namespaces that the SOAP library creates automatically. It also shows the need to modify a few namespace settings for the variables. You don't use xsi:type as shown in the Google Web Services Kit examples—you use SOAPSDK1:type instead because the SOAP library automatically generates this namespace. All of these adjustments help make a difficult language more manageable.

Not every language relies on the low-level API. Sometimes, you need to tweak the output of a high-level API application as well. In this case, you must modify the application to point to a copy of the WSDL file on your local hard drive. For example, here is how I modified the XSLT example in Chapter 3 (see Listing 3.4 in the "Performing a Simple SOAP Call" section for details). You'll find the complete source for this example in the \Chapter 06\ Trace Utility folder of the source code located on the Sybex Web site.

```
// Initialize the SOAP client so it can access Google
// Web Services.
SoapClient.MSSoapInit("D:\\\\Temp\\\\GoogleSearch.wsdl",
                      "GoogleSearchService",
                      "GoogleSearchPort");
```

Once you point `MSSoapInit()` to the local copy, you can modify the WSDL file to work with the Trace Utility. You need to make a single change to the endpoint information in the WSDL file as shown here.

```
<!-- Endpoint for Google Web APIs -->
<service name="GoogleSearchService">
  <port name="GoogleSearchPort" binding="typens:GoogleSearchBinding">
    <soap:address location="http://localhost/search/beta2"/>
  </port>
</service>
```

This entry appears near the end of the file. Once you make this change, you can use the Trace Utility with a high-level API application, just as you did with the low-level API application. The example code folder includes the resulting request in the `WorkingRequest.XML` file. Figure 6.6 shows a typical high-level API request. Notice that the high-level API uses unique namespaces and it also doesn't include type information for the input arguments. The omission of type information could cause problems with future releases of Google Web Services, but doesn't appear to make a difference now.

FIGURE 6.6:

The high-level API automatically generates a request very similar to low-level API request you can create manually.

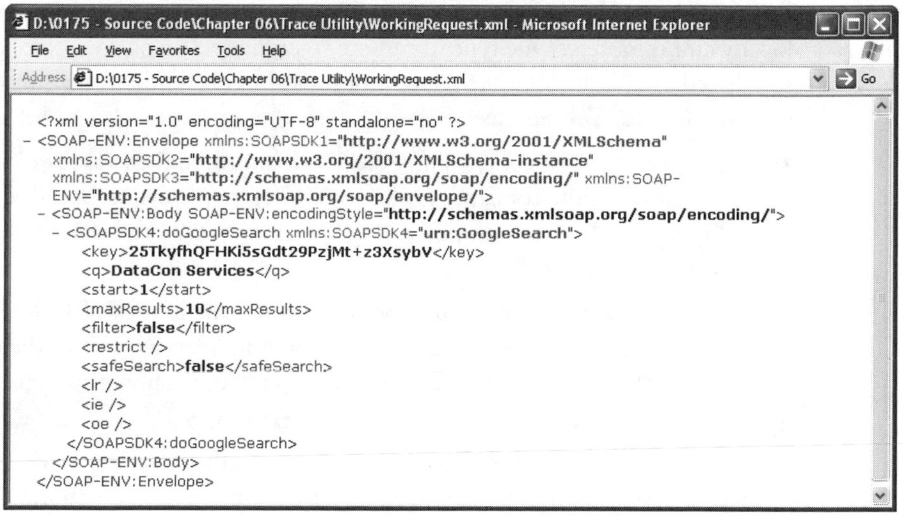

Developing with Visual Basic .NET

Visual Basic .NET isn't the same language as Visual Basic 6—the two are so different that many developers gave up trying to move code from one to the other. Many of the changes in Visual Basic .NET are actually advantageous, especially for Google Web Services application designers. For example, you have better access to the low-level details of your application. In addition, Visual Basic .NET comes with many Web service support items built in. The following sections discuss how to use Visual Basic .NET to work with Google Web Services.

> ▶ **TIP**
>
> If you don't own Visual Studio .NET, but would like to try it out, you can find a 60-day demonstration version at `http://msdn.microsoft.com/vstudio/productinfo/trial/default.aspx`. All you need to do is order the CD and install it. You can also find an online trial of Visual Studio .NET at `http://msdn.microsoft.com/vstudio/tryit/`. In general, the 60-day trial version is a better option when working with Google Web Services.

Creating a Web Reference

Visual Studio .NET introduces a number of automation features. One of these features is the ability to create a reference to a DLL, EXE, service, or other form of executable code both locally and remotely. One type of remote reference relies on Web services. You'll see this feature listed as a Web Reference in Solution Explorer. Use the following steps to create a reference to Google Web Services.

1. Right-click the project entry in Solution Explorer and choose Add Web Reference from the context menu. You'll see an Add Web Reference dialog box similar to the one shown in Figure 6.7. Notice that this dialog box already has the URL for Google Web Services WSDL file entered.

2. Type `http://api.google.com/GoogleSearch.wsdl` in the URL field as shown in Figure 6.7. Click Go. After a few minutes, the Add Web Reference dialog box will display a list of methods available on Google Web Services as shown in Figure 6.8.

3. Type a new name for the reference in the Web Reference Name field if desired. The only time you need to perform this task is when you think your application could experience a naming conflict or you want to change the name to match your application better. The examples in this chapter will use the default name of `com.Google.api`.

4. Click Add Reference. After a few moments, you'll see a new reference added to Solution Explorer like the one shown in Figure 6.9.

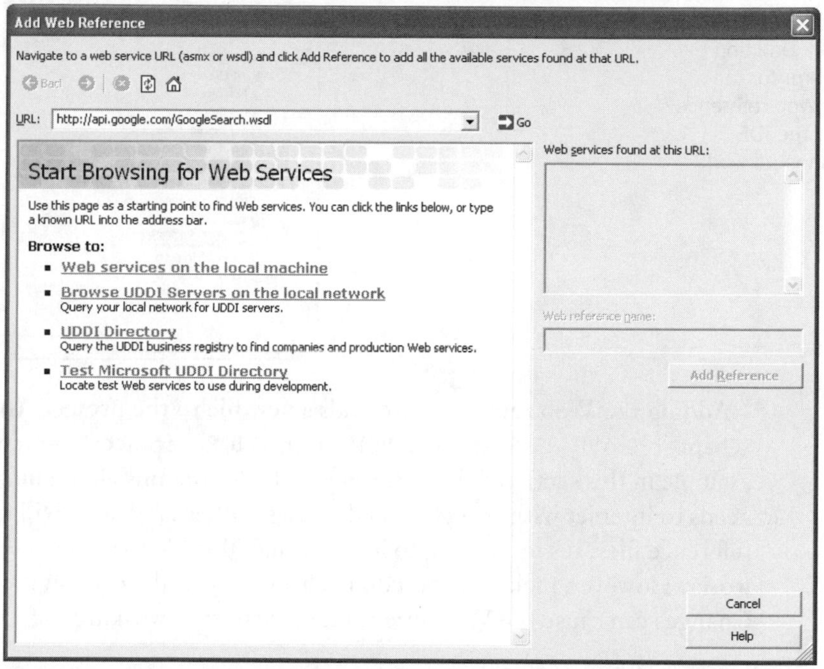

FIGURE 6.7:

The Add Web Reference dialog box helps you create a connection to Google Web Services.

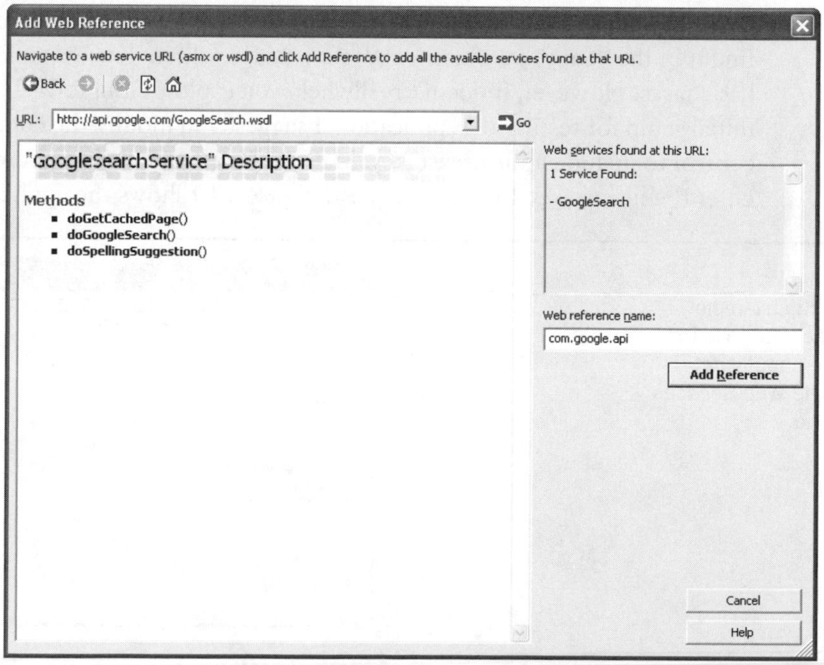

FIGURE 6.8:

Scroll through the list of Google Web Services methods to learn more about it.

FIGURE 6.9:

Check Solution Explorer for the new Web reference once the IDE finishes its work.

Adding the Web reference also adds a new file to the project. You'll find this file in the \Chapter 06\VB_NETSearch\VB_NETSearch\Web References\com.google.api folder for the example in this section. The References.VB file contains all the information your application needs to interact with Google Web Services. Other languages will create similar folders and reference files. It's interesting to look through this file to see how the Web service reference works. However, make sure you don't change any of the code in the file if you do open it. Changes can cause the Web service interface to stop working.

Using the Google Visual Basic .NET Example

The Google Web Services Kit comes with a Visual Basic .NET example application. You'll find it in the \GoogleAPI\dotnet\Visual Basic folder. The example shows how to perform basic tasks. However, it doesn't really help you exploit Google Web Services. As part of the initial setup for testing the application, I suggest you modify the content of the txtLicenseKey control to include your license key. Making this change means you won't have to constantly enter the license key for every request. Figure 6.10 shows the application.

FIGURE 6.10:

Use the example application to learn more about what Google Web Services can do.

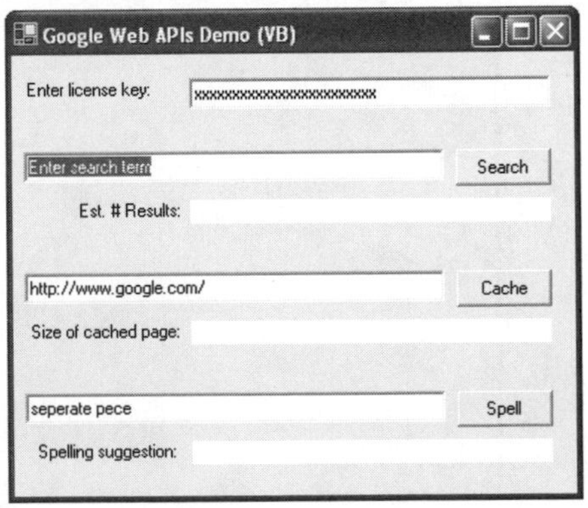

The example does test the three major features of Google Web Services: search, spelling check, and cached page display. It doesn't do much with the data. However, you can use the search feature to quickly check the number of results you receive for a particular search string. I found the test application to be faster for testing various combinations of keywords than using the standard interface.

Defining a Search with Visual Basic .NET

Creating a search application with Visual Basic .NET is relatively easy compared to the other languages described in the book. The .NET Framework provides a lot of automation that makes the code easier to create and debug. Listing 6.3 shows a typical example of a search application. You'll find the complete source for this example in the \Chapter 06\VB_NETSearch folder of the source code located on the Sybex Web site.

Listing 6.3   **Making a Search Request**

```
Private Sub btnTest_Click(ByVal sender As System.Object, _
                          ByVal e As System.EventArgs) _
                          Handles btnTest.Click
   Dim Service As GoogleSearchService   ' Search service routine access.
   Dim Result As GoogleSearchResult     ' All of the results.
   Dim Items As ResultElement()         ' All of the search items.
   Dim Item As ResultElement            ' A single result.
   Dim DR As DataRow                    ' Output data.

   ' Create the search service.
   Service = New GoogleSearchService

   ' Make the call.
   Result = Service.doGoogleSearch(txtLicense.Text, _
                                   txtKey.Text, _
                                   Convert.ToInt32(txtIndex.Text), _
                                   Convert.ToInt32(txtResults.Text), _
                                   cbFiltering.Checked, _
                                   txtCountry.Text, _
                                   cbSafeSearch.Checked, _
                                   txtLanguage.Text, _
                                   "", "")

   ' Process the main nodes.
   txtIndex.Text = Convert.ToString(Result.endIndex + 1)
   txtEstResults.Text = Result.estimatedTotalResultsCount.ToString()
   cbEstExact.Checked = Result.estimateIsExact

   ' Clear the dataset of previous results.
   dsGoogle.Tables("SearchResults").Clear()

   ' Process the result elements.
   Items = Result.resultElements
```

```
    For Each Item In Items
        ' Add a row.
        DR = dsGoogle.Tables("SearchResults").NewRow()

        ' Add the data to the row.
        DR("Title") = StringToText(Item.title)
        DR("URL") = Item.URL
        If (Item.snippet.Length > 0) Then
            DR("SnippetOrSummary") = StringToText(Item.snippet)
        Else
            DR("SnippetOrSummary") = StringToText(Item.summary)
        End If
        DR("CachedSize") = Item.cachedSize

        ' Display the row on screen.
        dsGoogle.Tables("SearchResults").Rows.Add(DR)
    Next
End Sub
```

The code begins by creating a Google client. However, Visual Basic .NET creates a specific client when you create the reference to Google Web Services. This client knows about all of the functions and provides a lot of help in making the call. You'll notice that some of the arguments rely on the `Convert.ToInt32()` method to convert the text data in the form to an `Int32`. The IntelliSense for the `Service.doGoogleSearch()` automatically alerts you to this requirement.

Unlike many of the other examples in the book, you don't need to use loops to process the main elements of `Result`. The code accesses these values directly using properties created as the result of reading the Google Web Services WSDL file. You do need to convert some properties for display. For example, the `estimatedTotalResultsCount` property requires conversion using the `ToString()` method. You can also use the `Convert.ToString()` method when needed to accommodate a calculation as shown for the `endIndex` property.

The individual result items do require loop process. However, you can place the `resultElements` property in an array and process the data in a `For Each...Next` loop as shown. Processing the array as a collection ensures you don't have to worry about counter variables.

The example uses a `DataSet`, `dsGoogle`, to store values. The `DataGrid` on the form is linked to `dsGoogle`, so all of the changes appear automatically. Make sure you view the `dsGoogle` `Tables` property to see how the dataset for a Google search is constructed. Notice the special handling the code employs for the `Item.snippet` property. You can use this technique whenever you need to make a decision about which Google return values to display on screen.

Like many of the other examples in the book, you need to modify the strings that Google provides to Visual Basic .NET. The strings contain special encoding for HTML pages that doesn't work well with desktop applications. Listing 6.4 shows one way to handle the string modifications.

Listing 6.4   Modifying the Google String

```vb
Private Function StringToText(ByVal Input As String) As String
    ' Check for bold tag.
    Input = Input.Replace("<b>", "")
    Input = Input.Replace("</b>", "")

    ' Check for the single quote.
    Input = Input.Replace("&#39", "'")

    ' Check for the <br> tag.
    Input = Input.Replace("<br>", "")
    Input = Input.Replace("<br/>", "")
    Input = Input.Replace("<br />", "")

    ' Return the results.
    Return Input
End Function
```

As you can see, all you need is the Replace() method to correct the problem in this case—no loops or odd string manipulations required. You could place these strings into an XML file, read the file into memory when the application loads, and process the HTML strings in a loop. Using this technique would let you add new strings to the list without recompiling the program. However, the list of strings shown will cover most Google search results. Figure 6.11 shows typical output from this application.

FIGURE 6.11:

Typical output for the Visual Basic .NET Search example

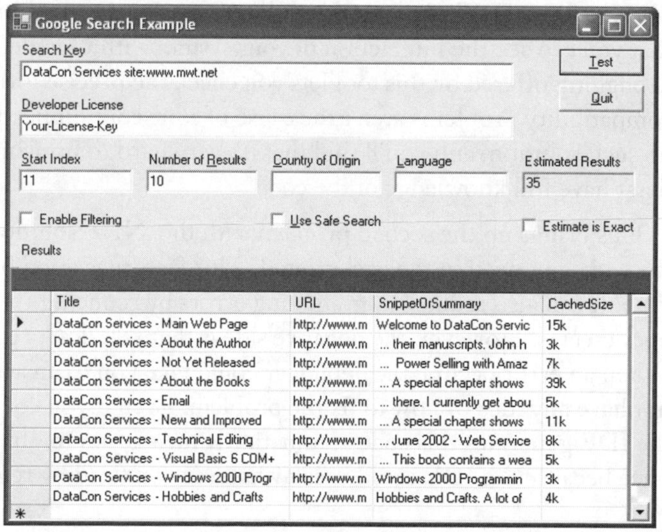

It's important to note a few features this application has that most of the previous applications don't provide. First, you can sort the results by clicking the associated column in the DataGrid. The control provides this feature by default, so you don't need to provide any extra coding. Second, this application includes full accessibility support—something that requires a lot of extra coding when using other languages. By adding custom setups to the DataGrid, you could also present the data in other ways.

Understanding the .NET Difference

Once you build a few Google Web Services applications with Visual Studio 6 and Visual Studio .NET, you begin to notice the .NET difference. Most developers find that Visual Studio .NET languages as a whole reduce the labor required to work with Google Web Services and present the data in a pleasing way. Microsoft went through a lot of effort to increase developer productivity and reduce labor-intensive actions. It would seem that an upgrade to Visual Studio .NET would instantly reap large rewards for any developer making the change.

The problem is that the decision isn't nearly as easy as Microsoft would have you believe. Other sections of the chapter have already discussed obvious benefits of using Visual Studio 6, such as the ability to output native code whenever you need it. Not every Windows machine has the .NET Framework installed and many won't ever have the .NET Framework, which means a .NET application is useless on these machines. However, you must consider several subtle issues when considering the .NET difference.

One of the most important issues is the matter of debugging. You'll notice that the Microsoft SOAP Toolkit contains a Transmission Control Protocol (TCP) tracing tool so that you can see the interaction of your system with Google Web Services. The low-level debugging offered by this tool lets you check the precise format of the message and ensure compatibility problems aren't the cause of a miscommunication. The .NET package offers no such solution, and you'll find that it's very hard to implement such a solution because you don't have full knowledge of the code.

This brings up the second problem with the .NET solution. The IDE generates a lot of the code you need in the background. This feature is good because it decreases development time. It can also reduce programming errors by reducing the amount of custom code a developer creates. However, the negative side is that you don't really know much about that code. When an error occurs, the debugger could take you to an area of that code and you might not have any idea of how to fix the problem. Even if you could fix the problem, the fact that the IDE generates this code automatically means you might revisit the problem more than once because the IDE could break whatever you fixed by regenerating the code.

Whether the .NET solution is the one you need depends on what you want out of your Google Web Services programming experience. The .NET solution is definitely better in more ways that this book will discuss. For example, you can't easily generate the applications found in Chapter 9 using Visual Studio 6—it just doesn't include the required projects and support. However, it's important to weigh the cost. This chapter shows both kinds of development side by side so that you can make a good decision on which programming language product to use for your Google Web Services application.

Developing with Visual C# .NET

Visual C# .NET is a new language that made its appearance as part of Visual Studio .NET. The language combines the flexibility of C++ with some of the programmer productivity benefits of using Visual Basic. In addition, it bears a striking resemblance to Java in many ways. In fact, many developers say that C# is Microsoft's attempt to create something as useful as Java.

No matter how you feel about C#, it's a capable language that lets you perform some tasks that Visual Basic .NET doesn't. For example, Visual Basic doesn't let you create unsafe code—that is, code that contains unmanaged pointers. C# lets you create such code so that you can perform some low-level tasks that Visual Basic isn't designed to perform. From a Google Web Services perspective, the two languages are probably equivalent and the choice of language comes down to coding style. However, it's important to keep the differences between Visual Basic and C# in mind if you plan to create a complex application. The following sections show how to create a basic C# Google Web Services application.

Using the Google C# Example

The Google Web Services Kit comes with an example application written in C#. You'll find it in the \GoogleAPI\dotnet\CSharp folder. The example demonstrates how to use Google Web Services, but doesn't do much with the data. This application is essentially the same as the Visual Basic version of the application. See the "Using the Google Visual Basic .NET Example" section of the chapter for additional information.

Defining a Search with Visual C# .NET

Creating a search with Visual C# is about the same as working with Visual Basic. The two languages do have differences though, so you need to exercise care in assuming they're interchangeable. Listing 6.5 shows a typical search application written in Visual C#. You'll find the complete source for this example in the \Chapter 06\C_SharpSearch folder of the source code located on the Sybex Web site.

Listing 6.5   **Creating a Search with Google**

```csharp
private void btnTest_Click(object sender, System.EventArgs e)
{
    GoogleSearchService   Service; // Search service routine access.
    GoogleSearchResult    Result;  // All of the results.
    ResultElement[]       Items;   // All of the search items.
    DataRow               DR;      // Output data.

    // Create the search service.
    Service = new GoogleSearchService();

    // Make the call.
    Result = Service.doGoogleSearch(txtLicense.Text, txtKey.Text,
                            Convert.ToInt32(txtIndex.Text),
                            Convert.ToInt32(txtResults.Text),
                            cbFiltering.Checked,
                            txtCountry.Text,
                            cbSafeSearch.Checked,
                            txtLanguage.Text,
                            "", "");

    // Process the main nodes.
    txtIndex.Text = Convert.ToString(Result.endIndex + 1);
    txtEstResults.Text = Result.estimatedTotalResultsCount.ToString();
    cbEstExact.Checked = Result.estimateIsExact;

    // Clear the dataset of previous results.
    dsGoogle.Tables["SearchResults"].Clear();

    // Process the result elements.
    Items = Result.resultElements;
    foreach (ResultElement Item in Items)
    {
        // Add a row.
        DR = dsGoogle.Tables["SearchResults"].NewRow();

        // Add the data to the row.
        DR["Title"] = StringToText(Item.title);
        DR["URL"] = Item.URL;
        if (Item.snippet.Length > 0)
            DR["SnippetOrSummary"] = StringToText(Item.snippet);
        else
            DR["SnippetOrSummary"] = StringToText(Item.summary);
        DR["CachedSize"] = Item.cachedSize;

        // Display the row on screen.
        dsGoogle.Tables["SearchResults"].Rows.Add(DR);
    }
}
```

The code begins by creating a GoogleSearchService object. This object contains references to all of the Google Web Services functions. The code uses the Service.doGoogleSearch() method to create a GoogleSearchResult object that contains all of the search results.

As with Visual Basic, you can read the top-level nodes, such as estimateIsExact, directly using properties. The resultElements property requires loop processing using a foreach structure.

The example stores the individual rows in dsGoogle, a DataSet that is connected to the dgGoogle DataGrid. Changes in dsGoogle automatically appear on screen. The code begins by creating a new row in dsGoogle using the NewRow() method. The resulting DataRow object, DR, contains all of the columns in the table. The code adds individual data values to each column, and then adds the data into the table using the dsGoogle.Tables["SearchResults"].Rows.Add() method. The results look similar to the Visual Basic .NET application output shown in Figure 6.11.

Using SQL Server as a Database

Using a cache to hold your Google search data is a good idea for a number of reasons. For example, using a cache helps you improve application performance. For more information on how to use caching, see the "Caching as a Practical Performance Enhancing Technique" section of Chapter 5. The example in this section relies on SQL Server to provide caching functionality. However, you could easily adapt the example to use any Database Management System (DBMS). In fact, you don't have to use a DBMS at all—a simple XML file (or even a text file) works fine for personal needs.

The SQL database for this example contains two tables. The first stores the main node results, such as the estimated number of links for a particular search. The second stores the links the application retrieved for the search. The database links the two tables using an automatically incremented index. You'll find the SQL script and data for the example in the \Chapter 06\SQL Data folder on the Sybex Web site.

The example concentrates on making searches as efficient as possible. However, you must also age the data found in the database to ensure you don't get bad results from your search. Consequently, the application checks the age of the data before it makes a request. Listing 6.6 shows how to perform multiple requests with data aging. You'll find the complete source for this example in the \Chapter 06\SQL Storage folder of the source code located on the Sybex Web site.

Listing 6.6 **Caching Google Web Services Data**

```
private void btnTest_Click(object sender, System.EventArgs e)
{
   SqlCommand    Query;   // Asks for the search data.
```

```csharp
SqlDataReader   DatRead; // Contains search results.
Object[]        Results; // An array of result values.
DataRow         DR;      // Output data.
DateTime        Scan;    // The scan date.
String          SrchNum; // Search number field data.

// Clear the dataset of previous results.
dsGoogle.Tables["SearchResults"].Clear();

// Look for the requested search.
Query =
   new SqlCommand("SELECT * FROM SearchQueries WHERE SearchQuery='"
      + txtKey.Text + "';", connGoogleData);

// Open the database connection and make the query.
connGoogleData.Open();
DatRead =
   Query.ExecuteReader(System.Data.CommandBehavior.SingleRow);

// If the data is available, read it into a result array.
if (DatRead.Read())
{

   Results = new Object[DatRead.FieldCount];
   DatRead.GetValues(Results);

   // Make sure you close the database connection.
   connGoogleData.Close();

   // Verify the data isn't too old.
   Scan = Convert.ToDateTime(Results[8].ToString());
   if (Scan.AddHours(24) < DateTime.Now)
   {
      // Get the search number.
      SrchNum = Results[0].ToString();

      // Remove the old search record.
      connGoogleData.Open();
      Query =
         new SqlCommand("DELETE FROM SearchQueries WHERE "
            "SearchNumber='" + SrchNum + "';", connGoogleData);
      Query.ExecuteNonQuery();

      // Remove the old results records.
      Query =
         new SqlCommand("DELETE FROM Results WHERE SearchNumber='" +
         SrchNum + "';", connGoogleData);
      Query.ExecuteNonQuery();
      connGoogleData.Close();

      // If it is, then update the database.
      Results = GetGoogleData();
   }
}
```

```
else
{
    // Close the database connection so we can add data.
    connGoogleData.Close();

    // Otherwise, request the data from Google.
    Results = GetGoogleData();
}

// Process the main nodes.
txtScanDate.Text = Results[8].ToString();
... Other Main Nodes ...

// Process the result nodes.
Query =
    new SqlCommand("SELECT * FROM Results WHERE SearchNumber='" +
        Results[0] + "';", connGoogleData);

// Open the database connection and make the query.
connGoogleData.Open();
DatRead = Query.ExecuteReader();

// Configure the array to hold the results data.
Results = new Object[DatRead.FieldCount];

// Process each of the result rows in turn.
while (DatRead.Read())
{
    // Get the current data.
    DatRead.GetValues(Results);

    // Add a row.
    DR = dsGoogle.Tables["SearchResults"].NewRow();

    // Add the data to the row.
    DR["Title"] = Results[1].ToString();
    ... Other Rows ...

    // Display the row on screen.
    dsGoogle.Tables["SearchResults"].Rows.Add(DR);
}

// Close the connection when finished.
connGoogleData.Close();
}
```

The code begins by clearing the old data from the form. The dsGoogle DataSet is connected to the data grid on the form. The dsSQLStorage DataSet interacts with the database. The reason the application uses two DataSet objects is that one is typed (for the SQL database) and the other is untyped.

The next step is to open the database and search for the keyword string. In this case, the code creates a `SqlCommand` object, `Query`, and uses it to execute a SQL query. Notice that you must open the database connection before using it. The example uses two tables to store information—the `SearchQueries` table contains the keywords used to create the search, while the `Results` table contains the individual page information (including title and URL).

When the query is successful, the `DatRead.Read()` method returns true. This method also fills the `DatRead` object with one row of data that you can process. The `DatRead.Read()` method continues to return true so long as there are rows to process. You can't read these values directly. The code uses the `DatRead.GetValues()` method to place the values in an `Object` array named `Results`.

It's possible, at this point, to check the scan date of the data. This step is where data aging comes into play. The `Results[8]` object contains the scanned date. The code places this information into Scan, adds 24 hours to the current value, and compares it to the current date. If the data is too old, then the code clears the information from the database and calls `GetGoogleData()` (discussed as part of Listing 6.7) to make a query to Google Web Services. Suppose for a moment that this is the first time the user has made a particular query. In this case, the code closes the database connection and calls `GetGoogleData()` immediately.

> **▶ NOTE**
>
> Make sure you use the `Query.ExecuteNonQuery()` method to delete records from the database. The `Query.ExecuteReader()` method returns a result and there isn't a result when you delete records. The `Query.ExecuteNonQuery()` method does return the number of records affected by the call, so you can verify the command worked as intended.

No matter how the code eventually satisfied the first step of obtaining the `SearchQueries` table data, the code can now display top-level information such as the total estimated number of records. The code displays this information on screen. Because the data is already clean of HTML tags and encoded characters, all the code needs to do is transfer the data from the `Results` array to the individual form controls.

It's time to get the result nodes—the ones that have the title and URL information. This step should always succeed because the `GetGoogleData()` method always places the result information in the `Results` table. The code relies on `Query` again to store the SQL statement and execute it against the database. As with the `SearchQueries` table, the `Results` table query relies on a `Query.ExecuteReader()` method call to fill `DatReader` with information. The code reads each of the results in a loop and places them in `dsGoogle`, which also displays the data on screen.

No matter how you work with Google Web Services, you need to create a client and call one of the supported methods at some point. This aspect of working with Google Web Services won't change. However, what you do to prepare for the call and how you handle the data once you receive it will change. This application requires special handling because you need to get the data from Google Web Services to your database cache. Listing 6.7 shows one way to perform this task.

Listing 6.7   **Getting the Google Data**

```csharp
private Object[] GetGoogleData()
{
    GoogleSearchService  Service;    // Search service routine access.
    GoogleSearchResult   Result;     // All of the results.
    ResultElement[]      Items;      // All of the search items.
    DataRow              SrchStore;  // Row for Search storage.
    DataRow              ResStore;   // Row for Result storage.
    Int32                SrchNum;    // SrchStore search number.

    // Create the search service.
    Service = new GoogleSearchService();

    // Make the call.
    Result = Service.doGoogleSearch(txtLicense.Text, txtKey.Text,
                        0, 10, cbFiltering.Checked,
                        txtCountry.Text,
                        cbSafeSearch.Checked,
                        txtLanguage.Text, "", "");

    // Create the new search query record.
    SrchStore = dsSQLStorage.Tables["SearchQueries"].NewRow();

    // Insert the new data into the DataRow.
    SrchStore["SearchQuery"] = txtKey.Text;
    SrchStore["DocumentFiltering"] =
        Result.documentFiltering;
    ... Other Data Entries ...
    SrchStore["DateScanned"] = DateTime.Now;

    // Add the new search query record to the database.
    dsSQLStorage.Tables["SearchQueries"].Rows.Add(SrchStore);
    daSearchQueries.Update(dsSQLStorage, "SearchQueries");

    // Save the new search number.
    SrchNum = Convert.ToInt32(SrchStore["SearchNumber"]);

    // Process the result elements.
    Items = Result.resultElements;
    foreach (ResultElement Item in Items)
    {
```

```
            // Create the new results record.
            ResStore = dsSQLStorage.Tables["Results"].NewRow();

            // Add the data to the row.
            ResStore["SearchNumber"] = SrchNum;
            ResStore["Title"] = StringToText(Item.title);
            ... Other Data Entries ...
            ResStore["CachedSize"] = Item.cachedSize;

            // Add the new results record to the dataset.
            dsSQLStorage.Tables["Results"].Rows.Add(ResStore);
        }

        // Update the database with all the new results records.
        daResults.Update(dsSQLStorage, "Results");

        // Return the search query results.
        return SrchStore.ItemArray;
    }
```

The code begins by creating a client and calling the doGoogleSearch() as discussed in other examples in this chapter. The example begins with the first result and obtains 10 results from Google. You can add the capability of retrieving the entire result set or some portion of it (as shown in the other examples in this chapter). The reason I limited the result set was to focus on the caching portion of the application.

Unlike other examples in this chapter, this example doesn't immediately display the data on screen. Instead, it begins by placing the top-level data in the SearchQueries table. The code adds a row using the NewRow() method, fills the resulting DataRow with information, and updates the table using the daSearchQueries.Update() method.

▶ **WARNING**

You must update the SearchQueries table before you proceed to the Results table. The SrchStore["SearchNumber"] property doesn't receive the correct value until after the update. Consequently, if you don't perform the update, the code will always add new results to SearchNumber 0, not the current SearchNumber value.

Processing of the Result.resultElements property works much as it does for the other examples. The difference, in this case, is that the data is placed in dsSQLStorage and eventually moved to the database. Notice that the code adds all of the data rows before it calls the daResults.Update() method. This technique ensures you get optimal performance from the application. Figure 6.12 shows typical output from this application.

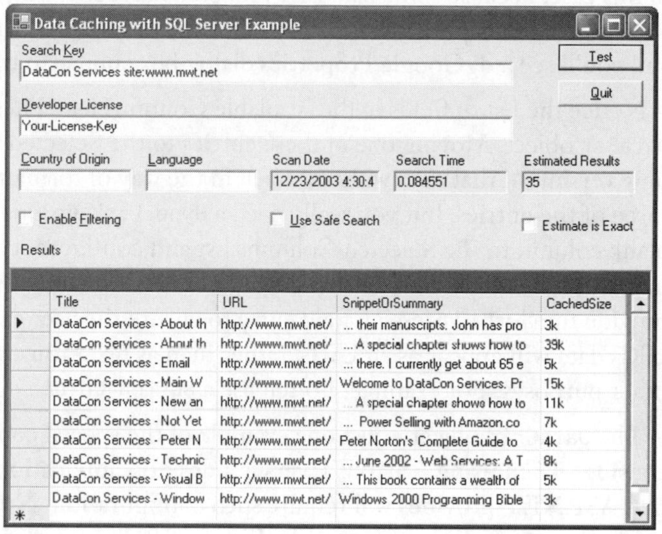

FIGURE 6.12:

Output from the caching application demonstrates that a local cache is faster than calling Google Web Services.

Working with Web Servers

You can easily create desktop applications that access Google Web Services. In many cases, a desktop application is the right solution. However, you might find that a Web application can do the job more efficiently or with fewer problems. For example, your company might decide that it needs to support more than one platform. In this case, a Web application is a good answer because you can write a single application to support multiple platforms. This chapter can't provide a full discussion of the merits of using Web applications versus desktop applications, but both have their place. The following sections provide details on using ASP.NET to create a Google Web Services application for your IIS server.

Creating an ASP.NET Application

Visual Studio .NET makes it relatively easy to create an ASP.NET application based on the same code you might use for a desktop application. In fact, I often use my desktop trial application as a starting point for the ASP.NET version because the desktop version is easier to debug. However, you can't say the two environments are precisely the same—the code is different, as is the application setup. Let's begin with the application setup.

You can use a `DataGrid` control for your output, just as you would for a desktop application. However, the `DataGrid` requires some special configuration. Microsoft assumes you want to automatically generate the columns for the `DataGrid`, but that strategy won't work, in this case, because some data isn't rendered correctly using the default setup. Set the Auto-GenerateColumns property to False. Click the ellipses button on the Columns property field and you'll see a dgGoogle Properties dialog box similar to the one shown in Figure 6.13.

Notice the list of fields in the Available Columns list. These fields appear in the dsGoogle DataSet object. Moving one of these entries to the Selected Columns list produces a text-only version of that data without much in the way of formatting. This field type works for three of the entries, but you really need a HyperLink Column object for the URL. Move a blank column to the Selected Columns list and configure it as shown in Figure 6.13. You must provide the Text Field and URL Field entries as a minimum, but I suggest that you also provide the Sort Expression field entry to ensure the user can sort on this column. Now the URL data will appear as an URL, rather than as text. You can use other column types for other purposes. For example, I often use a Button Column object for Boolean fields.

The DataGrid object is just one example of the special configuration issues you need to consider when using ASP.NET versus a desktop application. Most of the special controls that ASP.NET provides will require such configuration. Now that the application is configured, it's time to discuss some code. Listing 6.8 shows a typical example of an ASP.NET application for searching with Google Web Services. You'll find the complete source for this example in the \Chapter 06\ASP_NET_Example folder of the source code located on the Sybex Web site.

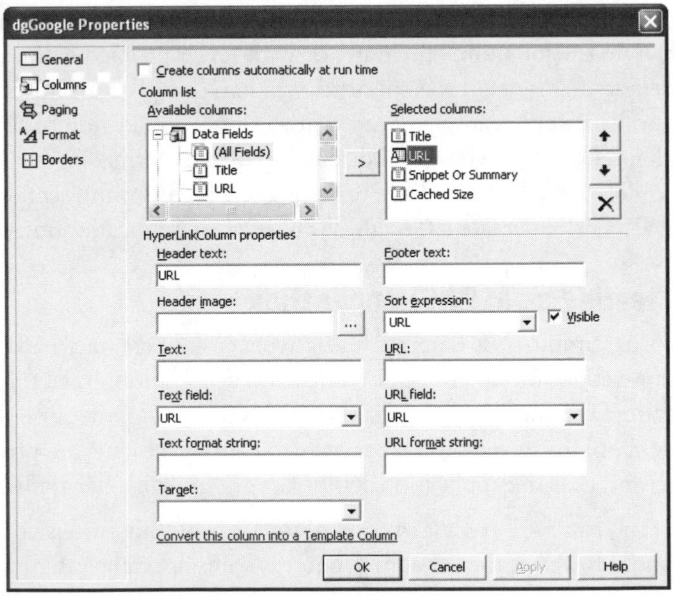

FIGURE 6.13:

Use the dgGoogle Properties dialog box to configure the DataGrid columns.

⊃ **Listing 6.8**　　　**Defining an ASP.NET Search**

```
private void btnRequest_Click(object sender, System.EventArgs e)
{
    GoogleSearchService  Service; // Search service routine access.
    GoogleSearchResult   Result;  // All of the results.
    ResultElement[]      Items;   // All of the search items.
    DataRow              DR;      // Output data.

    // Create the search service.
    Service = new GoogleSearchService();

    // Make the call.
    Result = Service.doGoogleSearch(txtLicense.Text, txtKey.Text,
                                    0, 10, false, "", false, "",
                                    "", "");

    // Process the main nodes.
    txtEstResults.Text = Result.estimatedTotalResultsCount.ToString();
    txtEstResults.Visible = true;
    lblEstResults.Visible = true;

    // Clear the dataset of previous results.
    dsGoogle.Tables["SearchResults"].Clear();

    // Process the result elements.
    Items = Result.resultElements;
    foreach (ResultElement Item in Items)
    {
        // Add a row.
        DR = dsGoogle.Tables["SearchResults"].NewRow();

        // Add the data to the row.
        DR["Title"] = StringToText(Item.title);
        DR["URL"] = Item.URL;
        if (Item.snippet.Length > 0)
            DR["SnippetOrSummary"] = StringToText(Item.snippet);
        else
            DR["SnippetOrSummary"] = StringToText(Item.summary);
        DR["CachedSize"] = Item.cachedSize;

        // Display the row on screen.
        dsGoogle.Tables["SearchResults"].Rows.Add(DR);
    }

    // Make the DataGrid and associated label visible.
    lblResults.Visible = true;
    dgGoogle.Visible = true;

    // Bind the DataGrid to the DataSet.
    dgGoogle.DataBind();
}
```

As you can see from the source code, many of the mechanics of working with Google Web Services are the same whether you create a desktop or Web-based application. For example, you still need to create a Web reference to access Google Web Services and the code still creates a client that uses the doGoogleSearch() method to make the call. However, you should notice some interesting differences as well.

One of the more important differences is that the application doesn't automatically display the output fields. Notice that most of these fields are invisible and you must set the Visible property to True at runtime. I've found that this practice tends to reduce user confusion and enhances application performance, especially when a user relies on a dial-up connection.

Another issue to consider is that you must bind the DataGrid to the DataSet, even though you set DataSource and DataMember properties during setup. Binding occurs when the code calls dgGoogle.DataBind(). You must perform the data binding process every time the data in the DataSet changes. This means calling dgGoogle.DataBind() when you perform tasks such as clearing the DataSet or modify the DataSet as part of a caching operation. Although the mechanics of the application are the same, the output also differs. Figure 6.14 shows a typical example of the output from this application.

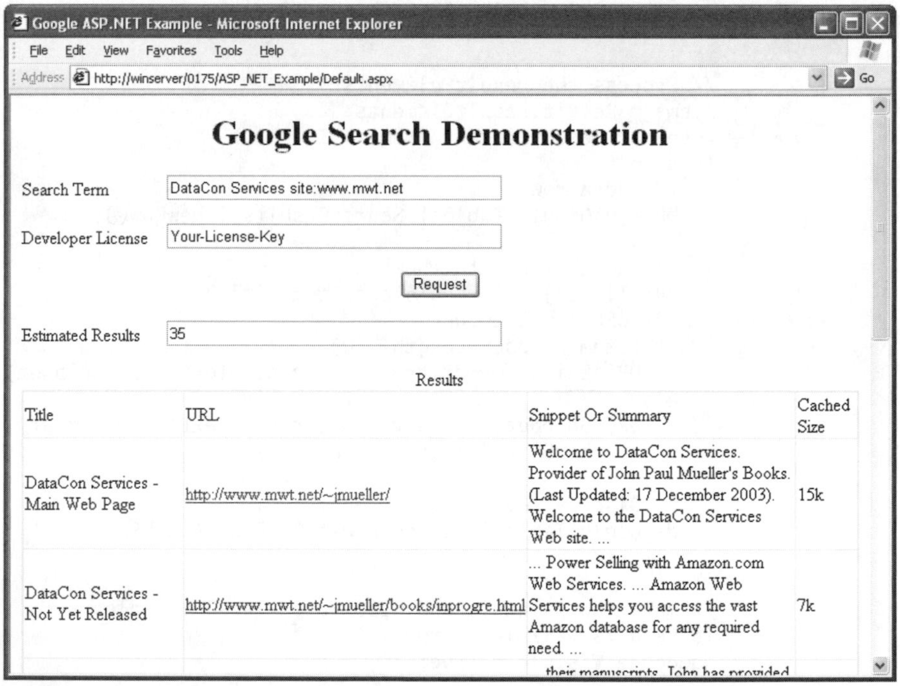

FIGURE 6.14:
ASP.NET can produce an application with an appearance similar to a desktop application.

Using the ASP.NET Applications in this Book

All of the ASP.NET applications in this book follow the same pattern as the example in the "Creating an ASP.NET Application" section of the chapter. You'll find two folders associated with every example on the Sybex Web site. The first folder, such as \Chapter 06\ASP_NET_ Example, contains the files that you should place on your development machine. The second folder, such as \Chapter 06\ASP_NET_Example (Server), contains the files that you should place on your Web server in the appropriate \Inetpub\wwwroot folder.

Once you place the files on your system, open the SLN (Solution) file for the project using a plain text editor such as Notepad. The top of this file will contain several lines of information similar to the ones shown here:

```
Microsoft Visual Studio Solution File, Format Version 8.00
Project("{FAE04FC0-301F-11D3-BF4B-00C04F79EFBC}") = "ASP_NET_Example",
"http://winserver/0161/Chapter6/ASP_NET_Example/ASP_NET_Example.csproj"
```

Change the URL on the third line to match the location of the files on your Web server. Once you make this change, save and close the file. When you open the SLN file, the Visual Studio .NET will automatically open the correct project files on your Web server. This technique lets you use a single machine by changing the Web server to localhost if desired. Make sure you recompile the application using the Rebuild Solution option to ensure that all of the compiled references also match your server setup.

Your Call to Action

This chapter demonstrates various techniques you can use to access Google Web Services using Visual Studio products such as Visual C++, Visual Basic, Visual Basic .NET, and Visual C#. Most developers will select one of these languages to create most applications, but all of them work well. The choice of language depends on personal taste and existing application infrastructure as much as the techniques for accessing Google Web Services. You also learned how to mix Visual Studio applications with SQL Server. In most cases, you'll use SQL Server for short-term storage of intermediate results or customer data. However, you can use SQL Server with Google as you would any other database application. The use of a database simply makes it easier to manipulate and analyze the data.

It's time to consider how you'll use Visual Studio to create applications to access Google Web Services. The choice of language is important because each language does excel in specific areas. Visual C++ is a great choice when application performance and flexibility are prime considerations, but Visual Basic provides the best database access for many purposes. Visual

C# and Visual Basic both provide superior database access and developer productivity. However, the cost of using these products is that every machine that uses the resulting application must have the .NET Framework loaded. Because .NET is a relatively new programming technology, you can't make assumptions about the user's machine unless you have control over the machine configuration.

Chapter 7 is the first Web-specific chapter in the book. It demonstrates techniques for accessing Google Web Services using PHP. You'll find that working with PHP is relatively easy and that support for PHP is very good. Many developers create all of their Web applications in PHP because the language is so popular and short-term costs so low. Whether PHP is the right solution for your Google Web Services application or not depends on how you plan to work with Google Web Services in the long term. Chapter 7 can help you make a good decision about the viability of using PHP for your Google Web Services project.

Chapter 7

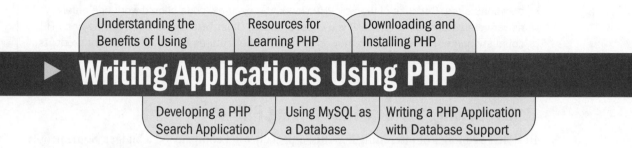

Understanding the Benefits of Using | Resources for Learning PHP | Downloading and Installing PHP

▶ **Writing Applications Using PHP**

Developing a PHP Search Application | Using MySQL as a Database | Writing a PHP Application with Database Support

Many developers have learned to use PHP over the years because it's a good solution for creating Web pages and the price is right. The PHP acronym is like many other new acronyms for the Internet—the acronym is recursive (refers back to itself). PHP stands for *PHP Hypertext Processor*. This general-purpose HTML scripting language works much like Active Server Pages (ASP) (see Chapter 6) or other page description languages you might have used. Essentially, you mix HTML with scripting information. When the PHP process sees HyperText Markup Language (HTML), it sends the text directly to the user. It processes any scripting information, and passes the resulting HTML to the user as well.

This chapter helps you discover how PHP works with Google Web Services. I'm assuming that you already know something about PHP, but the first two sections suggest how to learn more about PHP. Because PHP runs on so many platforms, you'll also find suggested resources for getting and installing PHP for your particular server. These instructions require a little technical knowledge on your part, so make sure you understand the instructions before you perform them.

The examples in this chapter show how to use PHP to create a Google Web Services application. The first example provides simple instructions for accessing the Web service without any fancy application features. You'll also find an application that shows how to use PHP with MySQL, an open source database. In fact, you can download every piece of software in this chapter free and try out all of the examples without spending a penny—that's one of the benefits of using open source.

I've also provided a number of tips to help you with your PHP applications. You'll find that the open source support system is adequate, but you won't get the same level of hand-holding that you do with paid products such as Visual Studio. Open source solutions tend to require a motivated developer, so it might not be the right solution if you need a packaged approach that doesn't require a lot of fiddling on your part. With this in mind, the chapter also provides some ideas on where you can get help when you need it.

> **▶ NOTE**
>
> I'm using the Apache 2.0.47 Windows and PHP 4.3.3 versions for this chapter. You might notice some differences between these product versions and other versions available on the download sites. Because of the way PHP works, the example code should work fine on any newer version of Apache and PHP you choose to use. Older versions of both Apache and PHP could encounter problems when they don't support the features found in the current products.

Understanding the Benefits of Using PHP

PHP has a number of interesting benefits, especially for a company on a budget. Some people view PHP as essentially a hobbyist tool, but it's a full-fledged product that you can use for enterprise development as well (see the Builder.com article at `http://builder.com.com/5100-6371-1058656.html` for details). One of the biggest benefits is that PHP is essentially free because it's open source, as is the main Web server it runs on—Apache. All you need to do is download the required products and install them on your system. In fact, you'll find an amazing array of products you can use with Apache and PHP on the Apache Software Foundation site at `http://www.apache.org/`. Note that this site also keeps you informed about many of the conferences associated with the open source movement and many of the political issues as well.

Another important benefit of using PHP is that it runs just about anywhere. The Apache server comes in versions for Windows, NetWare, Linux, Macintosh OS/X, and most Unix systems. You can also find Apache support for larger systems such as the AS/400. In fact, there are few places that Apache doesn't run. Anywhere you can run Apache, you can likely run PHP. In the few cases you can't find a version of Apache to use for your copy of PHP, it's quite possible you can find a version of PHP that runs on another Web server for that platform.

PHP is relatively easy to transport from one system to another. Because PHP applications run as scripts (essentially text), any application you create for PHP on one platform is likely to work with a few tweaks on another platform. Google Web Services developers should find that PHP works especially well for multiple platforms. Problems can occur when you begin adding platform-specific features to an application to make it look nicer or perform better.

The creators of PHP have improved it a great deal since its initial release. For example, you no longer need Apache to run PHP (many Web sites and articles still say this is a requirement). See the "Downloading and Installing PHP" section for additional information on this topic. The open source community also provides regular patches for PHP, including the all important security patches. You can find these patches on the PHP download site. Because these patches receive an open review, many developers consider them better coded and more stable than the proprietary solutions available on the market.

Understanding the Usage of *Free* with Software

Free can be a subjective term. Free doesn't necessarily mean without cost. In many cases, you see the word *free*, but it doesn't mean that everything about a product is free. The problem is that I haven't come up with better terminology. The use of the term *free* has caused so much worry for users that some of them have sued vendors over the use of the term *free* because it really doesn't mean inclusively free for the entire product. This article sums up the situation: `http://www.infoworld.com/article/03/08/29/34FElinux_1.html`.

The political part of the equation comes from the uncertainty of cost. If you're Microsoft and you want to dissuade someone from buying Linux, then you make those costs as high as you can without losing support from the "independent" experts who will back up your claim. On the other hand, if you're a member of the open source community, you want to make those costs as low as possible without calling your sanity into question.

This chapter won't discuss the political issues that surround the concept of *free*. For the purposes of this book, free means the product won't cost anything to download. You still have to consider support, installation, and management costs as part of any solution you use.

Resources for Learning PHP

This chapter assumes that you already know how to use PHP and simply want to learn how to use it with Google Web Services. Consequently, the chapter doesn't include essential language instruction that you might need if you're a PHP novice. If you think you might want to learn to use PHP for your next Web application, the resources in this section will help. One of the first places you should look for PHP information is the PHP site at `http://www.php.net/manual/en/introduction.php`. Once you spend some time with the PHP tutorial, you'll also want to look at the PHP manual at `http://www.php.net/manual/en/index.php`. The manual tells you how to use various PHP commands.

> ▶ **NOTE**

The PHP materials come in languages other than English. All you need to do is change the two-letter language abbreviation in the URL to your language. For example, to see the PHP manual in Spanish, you'd use an URL of `http://www.php.net/manual/es/index.php` instead of the English URL provided in this chapter. German readers can use the `http://www.php.net/manual/de/index.php`, while French readers can use `http://www.php.net/manual/fr/index.php`.

The Webmonkey Web site has an excellent PHP tutorial (`http://hotwired.lycos.com/webmonkey/01/48/index2a.html?tw=programming`). Another tutorial will help you understand PHP and MySQL Usage (`http://hotwired.lycos.com/webmonkey/programming/php/tutorials/tutorial4.html`). However, you'll also want to view the other PHP topics on this Web site (`http://hotwired.lycos.com/webmonkey/programming/php/index.html`) to learn more about PHP and see how you can use it with other products such as Oracle.

A number of other sites also provide PHP tutorials. For example, the Free Webmaster Help.com site at `http://www.freewebmasterhelp.com/tutorials/php` provides a seven-part tutorial that includes information on using forms. You'll also find great articles and tutorials on the PHPBuilder site at `http://www.phpbuilder.com/`. The tutorials on Dev Shed (`http://www.devshed.com/Server_Side/PHP/`) are a little more advanced. The tutorials on this site help you discover how to work with the local hard drive and even create PDFs as output from your application. You'll also find a number of articles about error handling and other developer topics. However, you'll want to save this site as your last stop because many of the articles get quite detailed and you could find yourself lost quickly.

It's also helpful to have a good book on the topic. Take a look at *Creating Interactive Web Sites with PHP and Web Services* by Eric Rosebrock (Sybex, 2004). This book shows how to install and configure development and production platforms of Apache, PHP, and MySQL on both Windows and Linux systems, and teaches Web development with PHP from a problem-solving viewpoint. Also visit Eric's wildly popular Web site PHP Freaks (`http://www.phpfreaks.com`).

Downloading and Installing PHP

One of the first places you'll want to visit is the Webmonkey site at `http://hotwired.lycos.com/webmonkey/00/44/index4a.html?tw=programming`. Use this tutorial to get PHP set up on your system and learn a little about this product. This PHP tutorial will also introduce you to the language. Unfortunately, the tutorial is also a little outdated and many of the links no longer work. Here's a list of links you can use instead of the links provided with the Webmonkey article (the article information is still very good, so don't be concerned about the outdated links).

- Apache Server Download (`http://httpd.apache.org/download.cgi`)
- Apache Documentation (`http://httpd.apache.org/docs-2.0/`)
- PHP Download (`http://www.php.net/downloads.php`)
- PHP Manual (`http://www.php.net/manual/en/index.php`)

Because the Webmonkey article is a little outdated, you'll also want to spend time with the official PHP installation documentation found at `http://www.php.net/manual/en/installation.php`. Although this text isn't quite as readable as the Webmonkey version, it's definitely current. Make sure you base any installation decisions, such as whether to use Common Gateway Interface (CGI) or Internet Server Application Programming Interface (ISAPI), on the content of the official documentation.

> ▶ **TIP**
>
> Instead of installing Apache, PHP, and MySQL separately, you can use one of the package products on the market. For example, the Apache Friends site at `http://www.apachefriends.org/xampp-en.html` provides a product named XAMPP that includes all three products plus PERL. Best of all, this product is free and comes in versions for both Linux and Windows.

One thing you won't need to do to work with Google Web Services is add any extensions. All of the examples in this chapter work fine with the default extensions. You might need to add extensions to process the data, but it's a good idea to work with Google Web Services for a while using the default PHP configuration. Using the default configuration ensures you won't run into any extension-specific errors.

> ▶ **TIP**
>
> Like most programming languages, you'll find a variety of third party support sites for PHP. One of the better sites, ByKeyword.com (`http://www.bykeyword.com/pages/php.html`) includes a list of utilities to edit, manage, and even convert your PHP code. Make sure you also visit sites like Tucows (`http://tdconline.tucows.com/`). A simple search can net a list of useful shareware and freeware products you can use.

Don't get the idea that PHP only comes in versions for Apache users. It's true that many people use PHP with Apache, but you can also use it with Internet Information Server (IIS), Personal Web Server (PWS), and Xitami (among other servers). Many of the other servers require that you use the CGI version of PHP, but you can also get an ISAPI version for IIS. The ISAPI version will provide superior performance and a little more flexibility, as well as improved reliability and recoverability. If you want the ISAPI support, you must download the Zip version of the PHP file, not the installer version, which includes only the CGI files.

You can run into a number of issues with Apache that none of the documentation mentions. For example, you might run into a situation where Apache installs and even starts, but you can't access it. Make sure you don't have another Web server installed on the same system. The second Web server could make it difficult or impossible to access the Apache server. This problem is especially prominent on Windows systems because Microsoft simply assumes that every server should have IIS installed.

▶ **WARNING**

Make sure you take care of security when you set up Apache. Thawte is offering a free guide that shows how to secure your Apache server using a digital certificate. You can obtain the guide at `http://www.thawte.com/ucgi/gothawte.cgi?a=e39560143317026000`.

Google Web Services can accept either eXtensible Markup Language (XML) over Hyper-Text Transport Protocol (HTTP) or Simple Object Access Protocol (SOAP) requests from PHP; however, the SOAP requests are better documented. The choice of interface depends on what you plan to achieve with the Web service. In many cases, you can achieve acceptable results using the XML over HTTP approach with less coding and effort than using the SOAP approach. If you decide to use the SOAP approach, you'll need to download a SOAP library to use with PHP. You can find this library at `http://cvs.sourceforge.net/cgi-bin/viewcvs .cgi/nusoap/lib/nusoap.php`. This file must appear in a central location or in the same folder as your other application files.

Developing a PHP Search Application

Many developers will want to use PHP to create some type of search feature for their Web site. Yes, you can use the search engine provided by the Web server, but only if you have access to the server. When working with a hosted setup, you might not have such access and it might prove difficult to write a good search engine application. In addition, the search engines provided with many Web servers are inferior to the Google search engine. The PHP technique lets you create a site search engine that works for many needs. The following sections show two forms of this example—a simple best 10 results technique and a technique that extends the number of results to whatever Google can provide.

▶ **NOTE**

In general, you'll find this solution effective only if you have a site with moderate traffic. Remember that the Google license agreement limits you to 1,000 searches per day. It's possible to overcome this problem partially by using caching techniques (see the "Writing a PHP Application with Database Support" section for details). You can also request more searches per day from Google. In some cases, Google does provide a waiver for deserving individuals. Make sure you understand the ramifications of using Google Web Services before you devote a lot of time and effort to an application that will experience problems.

Using the Simple Search Technique

The example in this section assumes that you want to limit the search information to your site. It also presents the output as a table. Some developers prefer to use a tabular format for some types of search results because it lets the viewer scan the information quickly. Listing 7.1 shows a typical PHP site search. You'll find the complete source code for this example in the \Chapter 07\SimpleSearch folder of the source code located on the Sybex Web site.

Listing 7.1   **Creating a Site Search Using PHP**

```php
<?php
// Include the NuSOAP class.
include("nusoap.php");

// Get the input data as needed.
// Search term.
if ($_REQUEST["txtSearchTerm"] == null)
    $SearchTerm = "";
else
    $SearchTerm = $_REQUEST["txtSearchTerm"];
?>

<html>

<head>
  <title></title>
</head>

<body>

<form action="Your Web Site"
     id="SubmissionForm"
     method=get
     name="SubmissionForm">

   ... Other Form Related Code ...

</form>

<?php

if ($_REQUEST["Submit"] == "Submit")
{
   // Create an instance of the SOAP client.  This client must point
   // to the Google search site.  Don't attempt to create a client
   // that uses a proxy because it won't work with Google.
   $soapclient = new
   soapclient("http://api.google.com/search/beta2");
```

```php
    // Uncomment the next line to see debug messages
    // $soapclient->debug_flag = 1;

    // Set up an array with the parameters use for the call.  Make
    // sure you include your license key or the call will definitely
    // fail.
    $params = array(
        'key' => 'Your License Key',
        'q' => "{$SearchTerm} DataCon Services site:www.mwt.net",
        'start' => 1,
        'maxResults' => 10,
        'filter' => false,
        'restrict' => '',
        'safeSearch' => false,
        'lr' => '',
        'ie' => '',
        'oe' => '');

    // Invoke the method.  Include the method name, the list of
    // parameters, the namespace, and the SOAP action.
    $result = $soapclient->call("doGoogleSearch",
                                $params,
                                "urn:GoogleSearch",
                                "urn:GoogleSearch");

    // Display the total results.
    print_r("<p>Total Estimated Results: ");
    print_r($result[estimatedTotalResultsCount]);
    print_r("</p>");

    // Get the result array.
    $Results = $result[resultElements];

    // Display the actual results.
    print_r("<p>Actual Results: ");
    print_r(count($Results));
    print_r("</p>");
?>

<table border="1" cellpadding="5" width="90%">
    <tr>
        <th width="200pt">Title</th>
        <th width="100pt">URL</th>
        <th width="50pt">Size</th>
        <th>Snippet</th>
    </tr>

<?php

    // Process each result array element.
    for ($Counter = 0; $Counter < count($Results); $Counter++)
```

```
    {
        $IndSite = $Results[$Counter];
        print_r("<tr><td>");
        print_r($IndSite[title]);
        print_r("</td><td><a href=");
        print_r($IndSite[URL]);
        print_r(">Go To Site</a></td><td>");
        print_r($IndSite[cachedSize]);
        print_r("</td><td>");
        print_r($IndSite[snippet]);
        print_r("</td></tr>");
    }
}
?>

</table>
</body>
</html>
```

The code begins with a simple include() function call. The PHP examples in this rely on NuSOAP, so I've included the required PHP file in the example. If you use another SOAP product, you'll need to include whatever support it requires in your code.

Once the code imports the required SOAP support, it saves any data passed as parameters and creates an input form. The input form lets the user type a search phrase. The current setup for this form also lets the user request a search without any search phrase. In this case, the example returns a list of all pages on the site, which you could cache and use as a site map.

Creating the SOAP client comes next. The code performs three tasks. First, it creates the actual client. Notice that you must point the client at the Google search URL, rather than the Web Service Description Language (WSDL) file. Pointing at the WSDL file and using a proxy to make the method calls results in an error. (Other Web services do allow you to use a proxy— some developers might prefer this practice, which is why I specifically mentioned the problem here.) You can find an example of the failed WSDL setup in the \Chapter 07\NoWSDL folder of the source code on the Sybex Web site.

Second, the code creates an array of arguments. You must include all of the arguments in the array, even if you don't use a particular argument—the SOAP parser reports an error if you don't. Also, notice the order of the arguments in the example. In general, the order shouldn't matter, but you'll receive fewer errors if you use the order shown. Finally, notice that the q argument includes the $SearchTerm provided by the user, a special identifier, and the site parameter.

I have a problem searching my site with Google because another company hosts it and I haven't obtained a unique domain name. Consequently, my main page is at http://www.mwt .net/~jmueller. Many other small businesses and individuals find themselves in the same situation. It's important to remember that a site search accepts only the domain name for the site argument. This limitation means you can't use a site such as www.mwt.net/~jmueller. The /~jmueller portion of the URL is unacceptable. You can get around this problem by specifying your name, company name, or other unique key term as part of the title on every page. By combining the domain with the keyword, you can create a site search type that Google doesn't support directly.

Third, the code makes the call to doGoogleSearch(). Because the example uses the SOAP calling method shown, you must provide the method name, the list of parameters, the namespace, and the SOAP action as a minimum or the call will fail. One return from the call, $result contains the search results, along with statistics information Google provides.

> ▶ **TIP**
>
> It often helps to run a simple test of your SOAP setup before you begin adding too many features to your application. The \Chapter 07\Test folder of the example source code on the Sybex Web site contains a test application you can try. This example displays the raw results from a site search.

The application shows the estimated results provided by Google and the actual number of array elements returned next. A number of searches show that the estimatedTotalResultsCount field is inaccurate. Consequently, always use the count() function to determine the actual number of array elements.

The final piece of code displays the results on screen. The return values appear in the resultElements array and it usually works better if you place the elements in a separate variable as shown to make the information easier to handle. In this example, we only use the site title, URL, page size, and a descriptive snippet. Most users will get everything they need from these items. Figure 7.1 shows typical output from this example.

Notice that the snippet is short and normally includes the search terms in bold type. Generally, the snippet contains the kind of information you want. However, you might find that you have to include your own hints as part of a database or perform specific background searches to create snippets that are more informative.

Using the Multiple Search Technique

The multiple search technique is about the same as the simple search technique, except that you now have to keep track of pages. This technique introduces a few issues you need to consider when working with PHP and Google Web Services. You'll find the complete source code for this example in the \Chapter07\MultiResult folder of the source code located on the Sybex Web site.

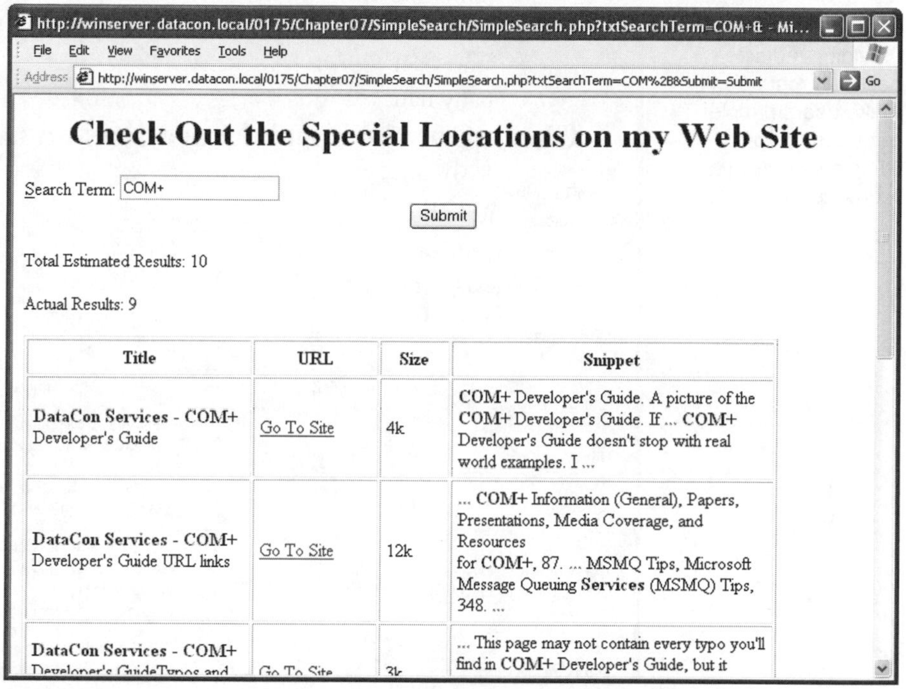

FIGURE 7.1:

You can get great results from a site-specific search.

Check Out the Special Locations on my Web Site

Search Term: COM+

Submit

Total Estimated Results: 10

Actual Results: 9

Title	URL	Size	Snippet
DataCon Services - COM+ Developer's Guide	Go To Site	4k	COM+ Developer's Guide. A picture of the COM+ Developer's Guide. If ... COM+ Developer's Guide doesn't stop with real world examples. I ...
DataCon Services - COM+ Developer's Guide URL links	Go To Site	12k	... COM+ Information (General), Papers, Presentations, Media Coverage, and Resources for COM+, 87. ... MSMQ Tips, Microsoft Message Queuing Services (MSMQ) Tips, 348. ...
DataCon Services - COM+ Developer's GuideTypos and	Go To Site	3k	... This page may not contain every typo you'll find in COM+ Developer's Guide, but it

Before you can track anything, you need to provide some means of saving the starting result number from page to page. The best way to do this is provide the user with a textbox that contains the current result number. Using this method lets you display the result number (so the user knows something has changed) and the simple tracking method shown in the following code.

```
// Create the starting page.
if ($_REQUEST["pvtStartIndex"] == null)
   $StartIndex = 1;
else
   if ($_REQUEST["Submit"] == "Forward")
      $StartIndex = $_REQUEST["pvtStartIndex"] + 10;
   else
      if (($_REQUEST["Submit"] == "Back") &&
          $_REQUEST["pvtStartIndex"] > 10)
        $StartIndex = $_REQUEST["pvtStartIndex"] - 10;
      else
        $StartIndex = $_REQUEST["pvtStartIndex"];
```

You need to increment or decrement the starting index variable, $StartIndex, to reflect the number of results that Google returns with each request. Normally, I request 10, the maximum that Google allows, to keep the number of requests to a minimum. If you find that you can't display 10 requests at a time, you'll need to increment the starting index by a different amount.

FIGURE 7.2:
Providing multiple pages of results will make users happier, but uses up your Google search requests.

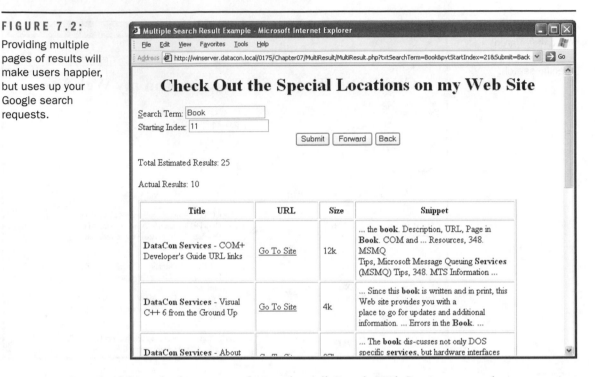

As part of the code change, you also need to tell Google Web Services to use the new starting index. This means modifying the $params array shown in Listing 7.1 to accept the $StartIndex variable as input. You must perform a cast of the variable as shown here to ensure Google Web Services will understand the request.

```
'start' => (Integer)$StartIndex
```

An odd thing happens when you don't perform the cast. Google doesn't report an error—it simply tells you there aren't any results. Look through the WSDL file and you'll notice that the start element has to contain a number, but the lack of a fault indication makes this a particularly difficult error to find.

All that you need at this point is two additional buttons (Forward and Back) and a textbox for display. Figure 7.2 shows typical output from this application.

Using MySQL as a Database

You'll probably want to improve the efficiency of your PHP application, at some point, by storing some data locally. It's likely that you'll use a database to perform this task. One of the more popular databases on the market is MySQL. It provides robust capability and the price is right. In addition, MySQL seems to enjoy better than average support from a cadre of developers who use it.

Like everything else in this chapter, MySQL is open source. Normally, you don't have to buy this product—just download it. However, in some situations you do need to buy a license, such as when you create an application for commercial (shrink-wrap) distribution where you'll realize a profit from the sale of the application. Make sure you understand the distribution requirements for MySQL by reading them at `http://www.mysql.com/downloads/index.html`.

The example in this chapter relies on MySQL 4.0, the latest production version at the time of writing, which you can download at `http://www.mysql.com/downloads/mysql-4.0.html`. You'll notice that MySQL comes in quite a few versions for various platforms including Linux, Windows, Solaris, FreeBSD, Mac OS X, HP-UX, IBM AIX, Novell NetWare, SCO OpenUnix, SGI Irix, and DEC OSF. You can also download the source code and create your own flavor of MySQL if necessary. The test system for this chapter uses the compiled Windows version with default settings applied by the installer. If you use some other form of MySQL, your screen shots will vary from mine.

Once you download the version of the product you need, install it according to the vendor directions. In most cases, this means starting the installer or unpacking the product and performing a manual install. The Windows Installer version is very easy to use—just double-click the executable that you download and follow the prompts.

Learning to use MySQL is relatively straightforward. You can find the complete product documentation at `http://www.mysql.com/documentation/index.html`. The documentation comes in two formats: PDF, for a printed version, or HLP, for a desktop electronic version. Part of the documentation is a tutorial that you'll find at `http://www.mysql.com/doc/en/Tutorial.html`. The vendor provides training and certification courses that you can learn about at `http://www.mysql.com/training-and-certification.html`. The Webmonkey site at `http://hotwired.lycos.com/webmonkey/programming/php/tutorials/tutorial4.html` provides an excellent online MySQL tutorial. Another good tutorial appears on the TAASC site at `http://www.analysisandsolutions.com/code/mybasic.htm`. In fact, you can find a number of tutorials on this product. In addition, take a look at *Mastering MySQL 4* by Ian Gilfillan (Sybex, 2003).

Writing a PHP Application with Database Support

One of the most important techniques you have at your disposal for creating a truly efficient Google Web Services environment is database caching. Google doesn't set any limits on the time you can store the data you retrieve, so it's theoretically possible that you'll only have to make each query once. Practically, you'll have to set a time limit on the data to ensure your data store doesn't get too old. However, depending on your research field, the storage time could be considerable. Even in the world of computer research, storage times of a month aren't uncommon.

The big question about this technique is whether it actually provides a benefit. Using a cache implies that someone makes the same query more than once. The "Caching as a Practical Performance Enhancing Technique" section of Chapter 5 discusses many of the issues surrounding caching. However, there's a significant difference in usage between a desktop application and a Web application.

You have to know how people use the Web site to make any assumptions about the benefits of caching. In many cases, you might not know the search habits of the people using your site. Public Web sites with ill-defined goals will experience the biggest problems because you can't narrow the focus of the search in any way. A boutique Web site that sells candles has a strong focus so you won't have a problem. On the other hand, a personal Web site that discusses every topic imaginable isn't a good candidate for caching because it's public and you can't narrow the focus of searches—people could literally search for anything.

It's also important to consider the size and scope of potential searches. Even if you intend to follow the Google licensing agreement, popular sites can stretch the limits on the number of searches per day. The only way to ensure your site meets the requirements is to narrow the search focus. Narrowing the focus does help you comply with license limitations and also means that users will receive more accurate search results for your particular site topic. A user can enter a generally understood term for your profession and the search narrowing additions you provide ensure the search results reflect the user's intent.

> ▶ **NOTE**
>
> You can run into problems with the 1,000 search daily limit on popular sites. At some point, you won't be able to narrow the focus of your searches any more without losing search capability. When this problem occurs, it's time to ask Google for an extension on the limit or find some other means of satisfying the user's search needs (including redirecting the user to the Google search site).

Caching can have additional benefits for Web applications. For example, you can use caching to reduce the number of Google requests for a site search because many people will request the same topics. A site search narrows the search scope to the local site by definition, so you can restrict the search criteria in that way and make caching worthwhile.

The most important consideration is that a local search encourages the user to look at additional content. When a user searches for information on the Google Web site, their attention might drift to other locations, making your site less effective—keeping the user on site means that they won't be as likely to move somewhere else. With all these pros and cons in mind, let's look at an example. The following sections describe how to create a basic cached application using PHP.

Setting Up the Database

Before you can begin using PHP with MySQL, you need a database. The `\Chapter 07\Data` folder of the source code located on the Sybex Web site contains a Structure Query Language (SQL) script called `GoogleData.SQL`. Copy this file into the `\MySQL\bin` folder of your server (assuming you used a default setup). At the command line, type **MySQL MySQL < GoogleData.SQL** and press Enter. Your system will pause for a moment and return to the command prompt. That's all you need to do to create the database for this example.

You can use the MySQL utility to verify the presence of the database, table, and data at the command line. Simply type **USE GoogleData;** and press Enter. If the `GoogleData` database is present, the utility will use that database. Type **SELECT * FROM DataStore** and press Enter. You'll see a lot of data stream by if the script successfully created the table and filled it with data. An easier way to achieve the same results on a Windows system is to use the `WinMySQL admin` utility shown in Figure 7.3. Simply select the Databases tab and you'll see the database, table, and associated fields.

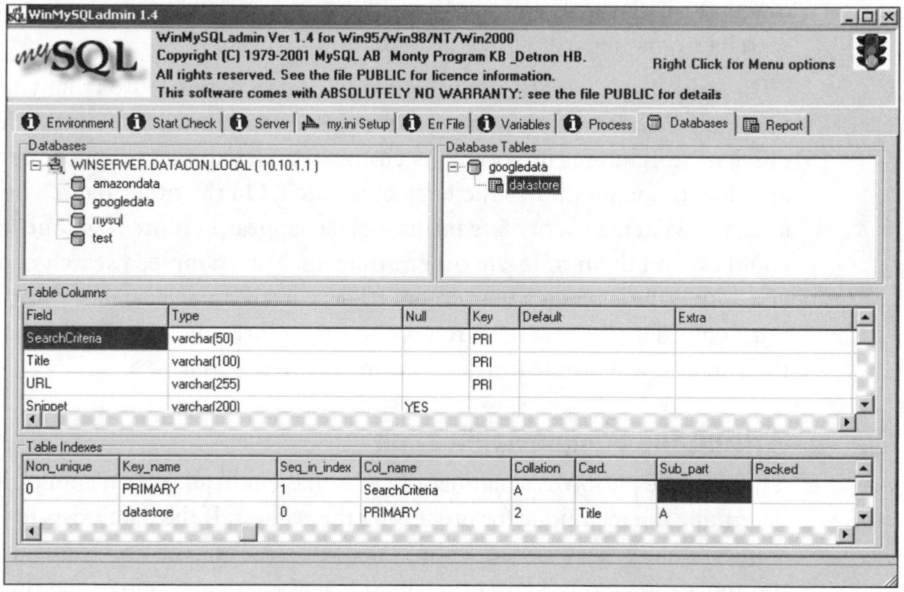

FIGURE 7.3:

The `WinMySQLadmin` utility validates the success of the script on a Windows machine.

It's important to understand how Google returns values and how you store them. In many cases, all you'll really need is the title, snippet, URL, and possibly the cached size of the data in the database. The database could also include a scanned date and other information that you provide as value-added content. This content won't affect your Google search—it's information you add after the fact to make the content of the database more valuable to you.

Depending on how you create the database and the fields you plan to use as keys, you'll run into a number of problems. For example, you can use the title, URL, and search criteria as primary keys for the database and still end up with duplicate values from Google Web Services. Consequently, when you perform a search for an item online, Google Web Services might return ten entries, but a refresh from the database will show only nine entries. The difference is that the original Google search returned a duplicate value that MySQL didn't store in the database. In reality, this feature is handy for automatically reducing the size of the result set to just the unique sites that Google finds.

Another issue to consider is the matter of how to identify the search criteria. The example defines each set of criteria as unique—even when it comes to the order of words. For example, a search for Visual Basic isn't the same as Basic Visual. Even though the words are the same, the order of the words is different. Try the terms using Google's advanced search and you'll notice that the order of the words does make a difference to Google, but does it make a difference to you? In some cases, you'll want to break the search phrase into component words, sort the words, and use the sorted version as the search criteria in the database. Using this technique, the user would receive the same results every time the same set of words appears as a search criteria, regardless of word order.

To expand on this idea, you might also want to define words that your search will ignore. Google generally ignores common terms such as *if*, but you could go further than that when efficient searching is important. A custom search engine can ignore common jargon terms in an effort to maintain the efficiency of a search. On the other hand, you might want to expand a search. When a user enters terms that can appear in more than one way, the search engine could expand them to locate other instances. For example, a search could look for both VB and Visual Basic when a user enters VB as part of the search criteria. Your database design must consider all of these search options to ensure you retrieve the same information from the database as Google provided during the live search.

Writing the Sample Application

The example performs a number of tasks inherent in all cached applications. First, it must determine the technique for processing the request. If the data exists in the database, then the application uses that source. If the data doesn't exist or the user wants to force a refresh, then the application has to make the request from Google. Second, when the application does make a request to Google Web Services, it places this information into the database. However, when using the database, the application builds an array that roughly simulates the array of result values returned by Google Web Services. Finally, the application uses the array (no matter the source) to display the information on screen. Listing 7.2 shows the first of these three steps. You'll find the complete source code for this example in the \Chapter07\CachedSearch folder of the source code located on the Sybex Web site.

Listing 7.2   Determining How to Process a Request

```php
if ($SearchTerm != null)
{
   // Create a database connection.
   mysql_connect("localhost")
   or die ("Cannot connect to the database.");

   // Select the database.
   mysql_select_db("GoogleData")
   or die ("The database doesn't exist or is inaccessible.");

   // Obtain the data.
   $Output = mysql_query("SELECT * FROM DataStore ".
                         "WHERE SearchCriteria = '$SearchTerm'");

   // Verify the data is in the database.
   if (mysql_num_rows ($Output) == 0 or $DoRefresh)
   {
      // Get the data.
      $result = GetData();

      // Display the total results.
      print_r("<p>Total Estimated Results: ");
      print_r($result[estimatedTotalResultsCount]);
      print_r("</p>");

      // Get the result array.
      $Results = $result[resultElements];
   }
   else
   {
      for ($Counter = 0;
          $Counter < mysql_num_rows ($Output);
          $Counter++)
      {
         // Get the display data.
         $Row = mysql_fetch_row($Output)
         or die ("No Data in Query Row.");

         // Get the current row of data.
         $Temp = array($Counter => array("title" => $Row[1],
         "snippet" => $Row[2], "URL" => $Row[3],
```

```
                    "cachedSize" => $Row[4]));

            // Add this data to the result set.
            $Results = array_merge($Results, $Temp);

            // If this is the first pass through the data,
            // include the scanned date.
            if ($Counter == 0)
                print_r("<label>Scanning Date: {$Row[5]}</label></br>");
        }
    }

    // Display the actual results.
    print_r("<label>Actual Results: ");
    print_r(count($Results));
    print_r("</label>");
?>
```

The application begins by creating a connection to MySQL using mysql_connect(). This connection remains active throughout the application. The code then uses the mysql_select_db() function to select the caching database. Both of these calls display a special message if they fail. At this point, the code uses mysql_query() to look for the data. A failure here simply means the data doesn't appear in the database. When the call fails or the user specifically requests a refresh ($DoRefresh is true) the code calls on GetData(), explained later in this section, to obtain the information from Google. Notice that the code displays the estimated number of results on return from the call. This information isn't available (or necessary) when working directly with the database. Finally, the code retrieves the result elements and places them in $Results.

When the database does contain the required information, the code must retrieve it one row at a time using mysql_fetch_row(). Unfortunately, the presentation of the data in the database is nothing like the data retrieved from Google, so the application has to build an array that approximates the Google result elements. The array_merge() function works nicely for this purpose.

One additional problem in using the database is that the data might be too old. The example handles this problem by displaying a scanned date when it retrieves data from the database. The user can choose to search online by checking the Force Refresh option. The final step is to display the actual number of results that appear on screen.

The application uses a special function, GetData() to retrieve the information from Google Web Services. This function isn't strictly necessary for the example, but placing the code in a separate location does become valuable when working with complex applications. Listing 7.3 shows the GetData() function.

Listing 7.3   **Getting the Data and Updating the Database**

```php
function GetData()
{
    global $SearchTerm;
    global $ProductType;
    global $StartIndex;

    // Create an instance of the SOAP client.  This client must point
    // to the Google search site.  Don't attempt to create a client
    // that uses a proxy because it won't work with Google.
    $soapclient = new
    soapclient("http://api.google.com/search/beta2");

    // Uncomment the next line to see debug messages
    // $soapclient->debug_flag = 1;

    // Set up an array with the parameters use for the call.  Make
    // sure you include your license key or the call will definitely
    // fail.
    $params = array(
    'key' => 'Your License Key',
    ... Other Arguments ...
    'oe' => '');

    // Invoke the method.  Include the method name, the list of
    // parameters, the namespace, and the SOAP action.
    $result = $soapclient->call("doGoogleSearch", $params,
                                "urn:GoogleSearch", "urn:GoogleSearch");

    // Get the result array.
    $Results = $result[resultElements];

    // Get the scanning time.
    $ScanTime = strftime("%y/%m/%d %H:%M:%S");

    // Remove the existing record (if any).
    mysql_query("DELETE FROM DataStore ".
                "WHERE SearchCriteria = '$SearchTerm'");

    // Process each result array element.
    for ($Counter = 0; $Counter < count($Results); $Counter++)
    {
        // Obtain the update values.
        $IndSite = $Results[$Counter];
        $Title = $IndSite[title];
        $URL = ($IndSite[URL]);
        $CachedSize = $IndSite[cachedSize];

        // Some sites don't include a snippet, so
```

```
        // check for the snippet length.
        if (strlen($IndSite[snippet]) == 0)

            // In many cases, sites that don't include
            // a summary.
            if (strlen($IndSite[summary]) > 0)
                $Snippet = $IndSite[summary];
            else
                $Snippet = "N/A";
        else
            $Snippet = $IndSite[snippet];

        // Create the query string.
        $UpdateQuery =
            'INSERT INTO DataStore (SearchCriteria, Title, URL, Snippet,
                Size, Scanned)
            VALUES ("' . $SearchTerm . '" , "' . $Title . '" , "' .
                $Snippet . '" , "' . $URL . '" , "' . $CachedSize
                . '" , "' . $ScanTime . '")';

        // Update the database.
        mysql_query($UpdateQuery);
    }

    return $result;
}
```

The function begins with a declaration of global variables. Make sure you include this declaration. PHP won't tell you when they aren't included and debugging for this particular program can become difficult.

As with other examples in the chapter, the next step is to create a SOAP client, define the arguments to access the Web service, and make the call to Google Web Services. The results appear in $result, which is returned to the caller for processing.

It's important to keep track of when you last scanned the data for a particular search. Otherwise, the data in your application becomes old and unusable. This application creates the $ScanTime variable and places the information in the database as part of a record insertion.

The code updates the database at this point. The first step is to delete any old records from the DataStore table to ensure the old data doesn't remain behind. The code then processes the results one element at a time. It places the data in variables, creates an update statement, and finally uses mysql_query() to perform the update.

The actual display code for this application is the same as the display code shown in Listing 7.1. The technique for displaying the data doesn't change, just the means for obtaining it. Figure 7.4 shows typical output from this application.

FIGURE 7.4:

Using cached search data has a number of benefits for online users.

Your Call to Action

This chapter demonstrates the techniques you can use to access Google with PHP. As with most applications, the idea is to keep the search local, rather than sending the user to the Google site. In addition, you can control the presentation and weighting of the data. However, PHP also opens the possibility of site-specific services—something you don't need to consider when working with some other languages.

You have some decisions to make at this point. The first is whether you want to use caching to reduce the number of Google Web service requests. Not only does caching provide better performance, but also it helps you keep within the confines of the Google licensing agreement. The downside is that you have to watch out for old data. It's also important to consider the kinds of input you want to allow and the orientation of the search. Make sure you provide some type of user feedback form (discussed in the "Adding Feedback to Your Application" section of Chapter 11) so that you can improve the quality of the search for users who might have different ideas on what they'd like to look for.

Chapter 8 moves from PHP to Java. You'll find that Java is another extremely popular choice. The Google Web Services Kit doesn't provide support for PHP, but it has good support for Java. Although Java isn't quite as easy as PHP to transfer from one platform to another, it's a more popular choice. In addition, you'll find that Java applications run faster because Java performs some of the interpretation required to run the application during a compile cycle. Java still doesn't run as fast as a native code application, but it's a very good choice.

Chapter 8

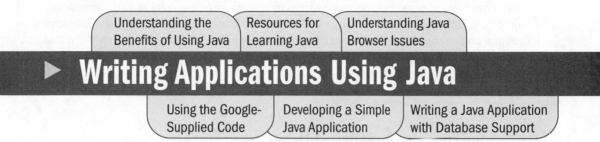

Understanding the Benefits of Using Java | Resources for Learning Java | Understanding Java Browser Issues

▶ **Writing Applications Using Java**

Using the Google-Supplied Code | Developing a Simple Java Application | Writing a Java Application with Database Support

Most people have heard about Java and many people have worked with it. Java appears on Web sites with some regularity because it lets Web designers create solutions that work with a number of browsers. Developers create Java applets for many Web-enabled applications as well as desktop applications. In short, Java appears in numerous places, so it's no wonder that you can use Java with Google Web Services too.

This chapter discusses techniques for using Java with Google Web Services. The examples show various strategies you can use to improve the user experience, while keeping the cost of development low. In general, you'll find many resources for using Java online. In addition, because Sun essentially owns Java, you'll find that it enjoys a level of support that most solutions can only dream about and openness not normally found with fully proprietary solutions.

However, using Java can become problematic in some cases. Java isn't fully proprietary, nor is it fully open. Consequently, some contention surrounds Java, and you need to consider the issues using Java can cause. (Read about these issues at http://www.infoworld.com/article/03/05/12/HNfowler_1.html.) This chapter doesn't examine these issues in detail, but it does provide enough information that you can learn more about the issues yourself and make a decision about the suitability of Java for your next application. As part of the Java overview, you'll also learn where you can find more information about the language. As with all other languages in the book, I assume you've already learned Java and performed the required software installation before you begin this chapter.

> **▶ NOTE**
>
> The examples in this chapter rely on the Java 2 Platform, Standard Edition (J2SE) version 1.4.2 available at `http://java.sun.com/j2se/1.4.2/download.html`. Older versions of the product might work, but you may need to modify the example code to exclude new features or functionality. In addition, I used the Windows platform for writing many of the applications and associated explanations. While the source code will work on any platform that supports the latest version of Java, you might need to modify some of the usage instructions slightly for other platforms.

Understanding the Benefits of Using Java

Java is popular because it can do so many things well. You can use Java on either the client or the server, or even both at the same time. This feature makes Java different from other solutions such as PHP because it provides flexibility in determining where an application runs. Unlike many other solutions, Java enjoys wide platform support, so a solution you create for one platform has a good chance of working on other platforms, too. In fact, you'll find numerous Java applications available for download that run on multiple platforms. For example, a single byte-code file (compiled code) can run on Macintosh OS X, OS/2, Unix, VMS, and Windows.

Many developers use Java for both desktop and Web-based applications, although most people equate Java with Web development where it's a much stronger presence. The fact that you can use it for multiple application types makes Java a good solution for many multi-environment scenarios. Even though you'd need to make changes to an application (desktop) to run it as an applet (Web), the changes are minimal compared to other languages. However, make sure you understand the limits of Java compared to platform-specific solutions such as Visual Basic before you decide to use it in more than one place.

Using Java for Web applications has many significant benefits. The most important benefit is that so many platforms support Java natively. You can develop Web-based applications using products such as Shockwave or Flash, but this solution often forces the Web site visitor to download a browser plug-in. Given Microsoft's recent loss of a lawsuit allowing plug-ins, using Macromedia Shockwave or Macromedia Flash might not even be an option in the future (see the eWeek article at `http://eletters.eweek.com/zd/cts?d=79-181-2-3-67152-23278-1` for details). Java applications generally work without any additional effort at all on the part of the user. In addition, Java is more capable than most other languages used for Web application presentation because it allows full interactivity between the client and server.

One feature that could be a benefit or a problem, depending on how you view it, is the fact that Java applications rely on a runtime engine that keeps them in a secure environment known as a sandbox. A Java application can only use the resources allotted to it by the runtime engine or Java Virtual Machine (JVM). This feature is beneficial because it improves security and makes it less likely that an errant Java application will cause other applications to fail (crash). The feature can cause problems by making it difficult to access resources the application needs to perform essential tasks such as writing data to the hard drive.

Another feature that you can view as a benefit or problem is the fact that Java tends to take a one size fits all approach to platform support. Yes, every platform requires a special JVM, but that JVM tends to have the same functionality as every other JVM. This means you face fewer problems porting Java applications from one platform to the next. In fact, except for text-based products such as PHP, Java is one of the easiest languages to port. However, the one size fits all approach also means that you'll experience problems using advanced features a specific platform has to offer. Microsoft tried to address the lack of platform-specific support in Java by (among other things) creating its own version of the JVM (see the "Understanding Java Browser Issues" section for details).

Resources for Learning Java

Learning any high-end language is difficult. However, some developers have complained that Java is one of the harder languages to learn because it lacks tools that other high-end languages provide. Sun is apparently aware of the complaints because it's promised to provide better tools (see the article at `http://www.infoworld.com/article/03/06/09/23NNjavaone_1.html` for details). Ease of use issues aside, Java is still a very powerful and flexible language, so you should honestly consider this solution for your next Google Web Services application. A single chapter can't show you everything about Java, so this section provides some resources where you can learn more.

▶ **TIP**

The court of public opinion on whether .NET or Java is the best solution to use for Web services is about split. According to a survey late in 2002 (see `http://www.infoworld.com/article/02/10/09/021009hndevsurvey_1.html?1010thap` for details), developers are spending equal time on both technologies. In short, both technologies are popular—you need to decide which one meets your needs best.

One of the best places to learn about Java is the Sun Web site at `http://java.sun.com/docs/books/tutorial/`. This site provides a good overview of Java and some great introductory material you can use to learn the language. For example, this tutorial explains the difference between a stand-alone application and an applet. Note that this Web site does provide separate instructions for Windows, Linux/Unix, and Macintosh developers. You might find it helpful to read the instructions for your platform of interest, and then quickly glance through the other two sections to pick up platform-specific issues.

If you need another basic tutorial, then look at "Brewing Java: A Tutorial" at http://www .ibiblio.org/javafaq/javatutorial.html. The author of this tutorial actually expanded it into a book that he also mentions on the site. If you find the whole concept of object-oriented programming with Java difficult to understand, you'll want to view the "Don't Fear the OOP" tutorial at http://sepwww.stanford.edu/sep/josman/oop/oop1.htm.

Choosing a Java Editor

The Sun tutorial suggests using Windows Notepad or a similar text editor, such as Notepad+ (http://www.mypeecee.org/rogsoft/), for creating your Java applet code. However, you should consider using a good Java editor to make the development experience a lot better. The Sun ONE Studio 4, Community Edition IDE mentioned in the tutorial isn't available for download any longer—Sun has replaced it with a 60-day demonstration version of Sun ONE Studio 5, Standard Edition. You can get the Sun ONE Studio 5, Standard Edition IDE at http://wwws.sun.com/software/sundev/. The advantage of using the official IDE is that Sun designed it for Java and the IDE provides Java-specific help.

In some cases, a third party product such as SlickEdit (http://www.slickedit.com/) is actually a better deal. The SlickEdit solution provides support for multiple languages, which means you only have to learn one editor. Although this is a shrink-wrapped application, you can obtain a limited use trial version from the company Web site.

You might also consider using a product such as jEdit (http://www.jedit.org/) because the same executable runs on Macintosh OS X, OS/2, Unix, VMS, and Windows. The author wrote this editor in Java and it points out the platform independence this language provides in a real world application. You'll find that jEdit has great community support, so you can download any of a number of add-on products for it. I used the jEdit editor to write the GoogleSearch and SimpleApplication examples in this chapter and found the color coding it provides extremely helpful. You can download this open source product free.

Another great IDE is JCreator (http://www.jcreator.com/). You can get the freeware version of the product and use it as long as you like. The professional version of the product is shareware, so you can download and use it free for 30 days. I also tried this editor while working on the DatabaseStore and SimpleApplication examples for this chapter. (The JCreator version of the SimpleApplication example appears on the Sybex Web site.) It's a great choice for developers who have worked with VBA or Visual Studio and are familiar with the IDE for those products. This is also one of the better editors for large projects because it helps you organize your project better and includes features such as a debugger.

An excellent beginner tutorial is Phil Heller's *Ground-Up Java* (Sybex, 2004). *Ground-Up Java* assumes no programming experience, but gets the reader up and running as a Java programmer quickly. The unique aspect of this book is the collection of powerful animated illustrations on the accompanying CD-ROM. They provide a crash-free environment to experiment with Java programming. The animated illustrations combined with the graded exercises that conclude every chapter and Phil Heller's clear explanations of concepts and techniques make *Ground-Up Java* a programming course and computer lab rolled into one.

Once you learn a little about Java, try some of the more advanced developer tutorials offered by Sun at `http://developer.java.sun.com/developer/onlineTraining/`. The tutorials on this site are diverse and some are complex, so make sure you understand the requirements for using the tutorial before you get too involved (the requirements normally appear as part of the tutorial's introduction). The feature I like most about this site is that all of the tutorials have dates, so you know how old the information is before you get started.

A number of third parties also provide advanced tutorials and this section doesn't even begin to list them all. One of the more interesting offerings is the Advanced Java/J2EE Tutorial at `http://my.execpc.com/~gopalan/java/java_tutorial.html`. This tutorial begins with a comparison of the various communication technologies (including Java/RMI, DCOM, and CORBA). You might also want to look at Java Coffee Break at `http://www.javacoffeebreak.com/` because it includes a wide range of tutorials (some advanced) as well as other resources.

Newsgroups can also provide essential information to the Java developer. One of the best newsgroups to try is `comp.lang.java`. Note that this newsgroup has numerous subfolders you'll also want to visit. For example, you can keep track of Java bugs on the `comp.lang.java.bugs` newsgroup. The `comp.lang.java` newsgroup enjoys broad support and some people even support it on their Web sites. For example, check out the comp.lang.java FAQ List at `http://www.ibiblio.org/javafaq/javafaq.html`. You can also try newsgroups such as `alt.comp.lang.java`. Make sure you check any vendor specific Java newsgroups groups such as `borland.public.jbuilder.java` when you use a particular product.

Understanding Java Browser Issues

As previously mentioned, you can use Java in a client, server, or mixed solution. The problem with developing either a client or mixed solution is that you have to consider the user's browser. The media has documented the combat between Sun and Microsoft over the JVM. (See the story at `http://archive.infoworld.com/articles/hn/xml/02/12/05/021205hnmsblames.xml?1205tham` as just one example.) Microsoft, as usual, decided to produce its own version of the JVM, which is incompatible with Sun's version. Some users might have this incompatible version installed, even though Sun won a lawsuit over the issue and Microsoft no longer produces it.

The latest twist in the battle is that some versions of Windows no longer come with the JVM installed, which means that the client can't run your Java application at all. In some cases, Microsoft is withdrawing products from the market earlier than anticipated to ensure they meet the court-ordered deadline for restricting distribution of their custom JVM solution (see the eWeek article at `http://eletters.eweek.com/zd1/cts?d=79-353-2-3-67152-42164-1` for details). Microsoft originally shipped Windows XP without a JVM, downloading the JVM on demand, rather than supplying it as a default (see the InfoWorld story at `http://archive.infoworld.com/articles/hn/xml/02/06/18/020618hnjavasupport.xml?0620thap` for details).

Sun is also active in the JVM battle. For example, the company is trying to get around the Windows JVM problem by signing individual companies to distribute the Sun version of the JVM (see the InfoWorld article at `http://www.infoworld.com/article/03/06/11/HNjavadell_1.html` for details). The two companies are still in court over this issue (see the story at `http://www.infoworld.com/article/03/04/03/HNmsorder_1.html`). Because of this contention, you can't be sure which version of the JVM a client has or even if the client has the JVM installed.

Even if the client has the JVM installed, crackers have made Java one of their tools of choice. Consequently, many people turn off support for the JVM in their browsers. This task is amazingly easy with products such as Internet Explorer. Because you don't know whether the client has the JVM installed, telling them to turn the JVM on in an error message is unlikely to produce the desired results in many cases.

Finally, it might seem like everyone would have a JVM installed and all the proper browser support, but that's not true. Many browsers simply don't have the required support. You can view the Webmonkey charts at the following locations for specific platform support of Java.

- Windows
  `http://hotwired.lycos.com/webmonkey/reference/browser_chart/index.html`

- Macintosh
  `http://hotwired.lycos.com/webmonkey/reference/browser_chart/index_mac.html`

- Linux
  `http://hotwired.lycos.com/webmonkey/reference/browser_chart/index_nix.html`

- Other
  `http://hotwired.lycos.com/webmonkey/reference/browser_chart/index_other.html`

The bottom line is that you have to know the client capabilities of the users of your application or develop a server-side solution. Java is a great solution because it's so flexible, but it also carries a number of problems that you might not run into with less flexible or less capable solutions. You need to decide whether the potential browser problems with Java are going to interfere with your Google Web Services application.

Using the Google-Supplied Code

The Google Web Services Kit provides a Java example as part of the package. This example helps you understand how to use Google Web Services, but isn't the best example of the power of Google Web Services. Even so, you'll want to view the example and the accompanying code to make your development experience easier. Using this example also helps you create a working Google Web Services setup on your machine so that you know any errors you see in your application aren't setup related. The following sections discuss the pre-setup requirements for the example and discuss how to use the Google-supplied example to your benefit.

Running the Demonstration Program

Google doesn't leave you out in the cold if you use Java—in fact, the Java support provided by Google is better than any other programming language. Google Web Services comes with an unassuming library in a file named GoogleAPI.jar. You'll find this file in the \GoogleAPI folder. The documentation for this library appears in the \GoogleAPI\javadoc folder. In general, you'll want to begin with the help-doc.html file to learn about the library and move on to the index.html file for reference purposes. The usage instructions for the demonstration portion of this library appear in ReadMe.txt, but the instructions are so difficult to understand that this section provides some pointers on trying the demonstration program.

The googleapi.jar file contains a number of interesting features—the most important of which is the Google Java wrapper located in com.google.soap.search.*. The documentation doesn't make the point clear, but this wrapper also includes a method you can use to test the API called GoogleAPIDemo(). You call the method from the command line using the Java interpreter. To learn what tasks the demonstration program can perform, you call the method by itself using a command line such as this one:

```
java -cp googleapi.jar com.google.soap.search.GoogleAPIDemo
```

In the current version of the API, you get a usage statement in return that includes the three request types: search, cached (page), and spell. Here's a typical usage line:

```
Usage: java com.google.soap.search.GoogleAPIDemo <client-key> (search <query> |
cached <url> | spell <phrase>)
```

The order of the information is important. For example, you can't place your developer license after the request type. In addition, the request type must appear before the request information, such as a list of keywords. You could use this command line entry to request a cached version of my home Web page:

```
java -cp googleapi.jar com.google.soap.search.GoogleAPIDemo Your-Developer-
License cached http://www.mwt.net
```

Note that you must replace Your-Developer-License with the license that Google provides. Because this example runs at the command line, the output also appears in the command window as text. Figure 8.1 shows typical output for the example application. Notice the application repeats all of the input information, along with the Google response. The Client Key field shown in Figure 8.1 is blanked, in this case, but you'll see your key as one of the request values.

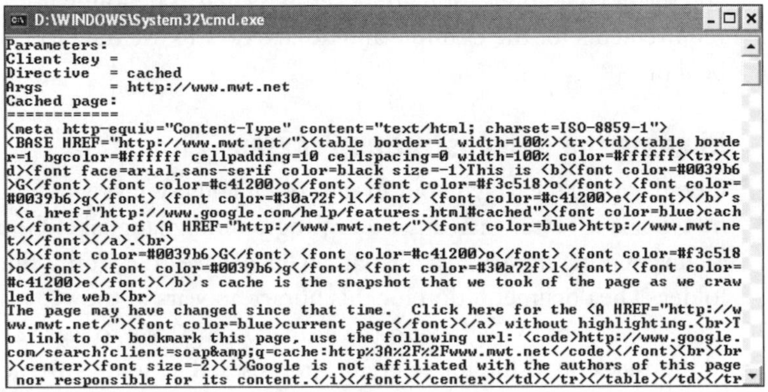

FIGURE 8.1:

The Google example program outputs text to the command window.

Using the Examples for Your Own Applications

The library that Google supplies doesn't just demonstrate the utility of Google Web Services—you can also use it to build your own applications. A big benefit of using the library is that you don't have to reinvent the wheel. Google has already created the essential pieces for you. All you need to do is create a reference to the library within your application as shown in Listing 8.1. You'll find the complete source for this example in the \Chapter 08\UseGoogleAPI folder of the source code located on the Sybex Web site. This code comes from the UseGoogleAPIFrame.Java source file. Note that there's additional code for starting the application that appears in the UseGoogleAPI.Java source, but not in this listing.

Listing 8.1   **Spelling Check with the Google Library**

```java
import java.awt.*;
import java.awt.event.*;
import java.net.*;
import javax.swing.*;
import javax.swing.table.*;
import com.google.soap.search.*;

public class UseGoogleAPIFrame extends JFrame
```

```
{
   ... Variable Declarations ...

   public UseGoogleAPIFrame()
   {
      // Get the display information.
      Display = getContentPane();
      Display.setLayout(new GridBagLayout());

      // Define the panel grid bag constants.
      ... See Listing for Details ...

      // Define the component grid bag constants.
      ... See Listing for Details ...

      // Create the Request panel.
      ... See Listing for Details ...

      // Create the Spelling input.
      lblSpell = new JLabel("Spelling Request:");
      lblSpell.setDisplayedMnemonic('S');
      pnlRequest.add(lblSpell, gbcComp);
      gbcComp.gridx = 1;
      txtSpell = new JTextField(20);
      txtSpell.setText("Soem Tetx is Misppelled");
      txtSpell.setToolTipText("Type the word or phrase to check.");
      txtSpell.setFocusAccelerator('S');
      pnlRequest.add(txtSpell, gbcComp);

      ... Other Request Display Items ...

      // Create the button handler.
      BtnHndl = new ButtonHandler();

      // Create the Response panel.
      ... See Listing for Details ...

      // Create the Correct Spelling output.
      ... See Listing for Details ...

      // Add the request and response setup to the main form.
      Display.add(pnlRequest, gbcPanel);
      gbcPanel.gridy = 1;
      Display.add(pnlResponse, gbcPanel);
   }


   // This class handles button click events.
   private class ButtonHandler implements ActionListener
```

```
    {
        GoogleSearch   Service; // Google Search Service Object.
        String         Result;  // Result of request.

        public void actionPerformed(ActionEvent AE)
        {
            // End the program.
            if (AE.getSource() == btnQuit)
                System.exit(0);

            // Issue a request and receive a response.
            if (AE.getSource() == btnTest)
            {

                try
                {
                    // Create the required SOAP objects.
                    Service = new GoogleSearch();

                    // Insert the request data.
                    Service.setKey(txtKey.getText());

                    // Get the result.
                    txtCorrect.setText(
                        Service.doSpellingSuggestion(txtSpell.getText()));
                }
                catch (GoogleSearchFault f)
                {
                    System.out.println("Error making spelling check.");
                    System.out.println(f.toString());
                }

            }
        }
    }
}
```

The code begins with the UseGoogleAPIFrame class code. The main() method creates an instance of this class and displays the result on screen. Most of the code in this class displays objects on screen that the user interacts with to call Google Web Services. Generally, you want to create a form that lets the user enter all of the required input information, along with a developer license when necessary. (You can also embed this information as needed.)

Along with the various inputs, the code defines a button handler of the ButtonHandler class that takes care of calling Google Web Services. The ButtonHandler class interacts with the response objects so the user can see the Google Web Services output. Finally, the UseGoogleAPIFrame class adds these objects to the display area. Figure 8.2 shows a typical example of output from this application.

The Google API works
well for many of the
requests you'll make.

To use the Google-supplied library, the ButtonHandler class code begins by creating a GoogleSearch object. The definition for this object appears in the com.google.soap.search library imported at the beginning of the code listing. Because the code is making a simple spelling request, it can use a string as output. The library also defines appropriate objects for other requests.

The actionPerformed() method begins by checking the type of button the user clicked. When the user clicks Quit, the system simply exits.

When the user clicks Test, the code begins by instantiating the GoogleSearch object, Service. This object includes entries for all of the Google Web Services request information—you won't use every property for every call. Most properties have default values so that you don't need to worry about providing a specific value for properties that your call doesn't use. The only property that you must define is the Key property that the code sets using the setKey() method. In this case, the code uses the doSpellingSuggestion() method to request a spelling check from Google Web Services and to return that value to the application using the txtCorrect.setText() method.

Notice that you must catch any errors that Google Web Services can generate. The library encapsulates all of the possible errors into a single GoogleSearchFault object. In most cases, this single fault approach works fine and you'll never need to do anything more. However, this approach is less explicit than using a low-level call where you can retrieve object-specific fault information. The "Developing a Simple Java Application" section describes an alternative approach that provides better fault information. The trade-off is that you must also perform more coding.

▶ NOTE

Your experiences with Google spell checking could vary depending on where you live. For example, many people spell color as colour. Google will always correct the spelling to color, even though both spellings are correct.

Developing a Simple Java Application

The "Using the Google Supplied Code" section of the chapter demonstrates an easy way to create a Google Web Services application using only the features provided with the Google Web Services Kit and your favorite Java development product. In most cases, this setup works fine because you can create a basic application without a lot of extra code or effort. However, this technique doesn't always work for several reasons:

- You need detailed error information.
- The application requires precise control over the session, especially communication with Google Web Services.
- The project uses more than one Web service or introduces other complexities the Google library doesn't support.
- Google updates its Web Services Description Language (WSDL) file to include other function calls that the library doesn't support.

You really won't run into these problems very often, but it's good to know that you have options when you do run into them. The sections that follow accomplish three tasks. First, you'll learn how to set up an alternate library for Google Web Services that does use the WSDL file directly so you can make use of any new features that Google provides. Second, the chapter demonstrates one of the better Java editors on the market so you can automate at least part of the programming process. Third, you'll see an example that demonstrates the low-level access technique that provides precise control over the communication environment.

> ▶ **TIP**
>
> You may soon have other options for working with Java code. According to an eWeek article (`http://www.eweek.com/article2/0,4149,1375757,00.asp`), Sun is working on a new editor for Java developers. This editor will feature Visual Basic style functionality that will make it easy to create Java applications.

Using an Alternative Library Setup

The library provided for Java use in the Google Web Services Kit is amazingly complete and usable. In most cases, you won't need to look any further than that library for your Java development needs. However, sometimes you do need the additional flexibility and capability provided by a third party library. This section shows how to create an alternative library setup that relies on the WSDL file provided with the Google Web Services Kit or one that you download from the Google site. You'll find all of the batch files and the resulting library in the `\Chapter 08\WSDL2Java` folder of the source code located on the Sybex Web site.

Make sure you get the latest versions of the Java Development Kit (JDK) and the Axis Simple Object Access Protocol (SOAP) provider. At the time of this writing, you can obtain the Java 2 Platform, Standard Edition (J2SE) version 1.4.2 at `http://java.sun.com/j2se/1.4.2/download.html`. All of the Apache Axis versions appear at `http://ws.apache.org/axis/`.

▶ **WARNING**

Do not use the Beta 3 version of Apache Axis—at least not on Windows, where it caused a number of errors including a nonreproducible system reboot. I used the Final 1.1 version for the book with good success.

Once you download all of the required support products, install them on your system. Theoretically, you don't have to worry about the installation order. However, I found that I obtained better results by installing the J2SE first and then the various Apache support files.

▶ **NOTE**

Do not follow the Apache Axis installation instructions unless you plan to create your own Web service. You only need the library files to create the Java files required for the client portion of Google Web Services. With this in mind, you can simply un-Zip the Axis files into a convenient directory of your hard drive.

Java must have access to the files required to build the SOAP stubs. This means that you must place the Axis files in the same folder as the WSDL file or you must create a class path for the library. You can use this second technique by adding the –classpath switch to the command line (edit the Client.Axis.BAT file to include it for Windows developers). The class path must include all of the JAR files located in the \Axis-1_1\Lib folder. When you receive a java.lang.NoClassDefFoundError message, it means that Java can't find the Axis libraries. If you experience this error, you must fix it before you proceed with the rest of this section.

Java takes a piecemeal approach to SOAP support. In addition to Axis, you also need XML parser support. The Axis documentation recommends using the Xerces-J parser found at `http://xml.apache.org/dist/xerces-j/`. You don't need the XML parser to create the SOAP stubs, but you do need it to create the example executable using the javac command. Again, make sure you provide a class path for the XML parser. You can find a sample batch file XercesCompile.BAT located in the \Chapter 08\WSDL2Java folder of the source code on the Sybex Web site that performs this step.

At this point, you might see a listing of errors. These errors occur because the capitalization of functions in the Axis-generated stubs differs from the capitalization of function calls in the Google example files. Generally, you must fix an entry in the Google SOAP files. For example, if you see an error for `class com.Google.soap.axis.GoogleSearchBindingStub`, you'll need to change the `GoogleSearchBindingStub.JAVA` file. All you need to do is compare the Axis capitalization to the Google capitalization to fix the error.

> ▶ **WARNING**

Don't attempt to change the automatically generated Axis files. These files appear in the \com\Google\soap\axis folder and reflect the current state of the Google WSDL files. When you generate these files again, all the errors you fixed earlier will reappear. Always change the Google example files.

Once the program compiles, you can run it. Make sure you include the class path, as you did for the other steps. The `RunExample.BAT` file located in the `\Chapter 08\WSDL2Java` folder of the source code on the Sybex Web site shows how to perform this step.

Configuring the JCreator Editor

The professional version of the JCreator editor can make working with Google Web Services a lot easier because it provides help with the various packages and libraries. You don't have to spend time working with batch files because the application compiles within the IDE. In addition, the debugger makes it easy to see how requests to and responses from Google Web Services work. To obtain all these benefits, you need to perform the following configuration steps.

> ▶ **NOTE**

The JCreator Web site currently includes two versions of the product: 2.5 and 3.0. In addition, you can download a freeware or professional product of each of these major versions. The examples in this chapter assume you have JCreator 3.0 Professional. The steps will also work with the freeware product, but won't work with either 2.5 product.

1. Create a new workspace using the File ➤ New ➤ Project command. You'll see a Project Wizard dialog box shown in Figure 8.3.

2. Select the Basic Java Application option and click Next. The wizard will ask you to provide a project path.

3. Type a name for the project (the example uses SimpleApplication) in the Name field and click Next. You'll see the Project ClassPath dialog box shown in Figure 8.4. Notice that this dialog box has two tabs JDK Profiles and Required Libraries.

4. Select the Required Libraries tab so you can add the Axis, Xerces, and custom Google libraries.

5. Click New. You'll see the Set Library dialog box shown in Figure 8.5. This dialog box can add either archives, such as those used for Axis and Xerces, or library paths, such as the one used for the custom Google library.

FIGURE 8.3:

Select a project type from the list of options.

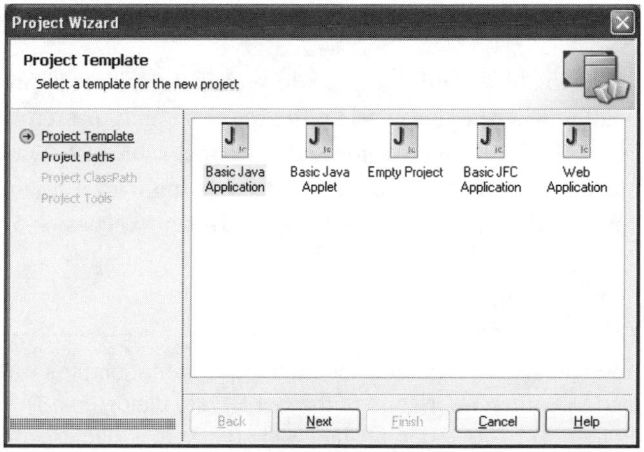

FIGURE 8.4:

Define one or more libraries as needed using the Required Libraries tab.

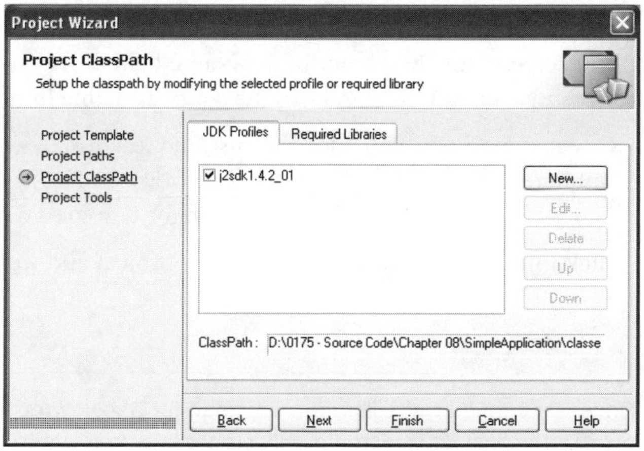

FIGURE 8.5:

Add library paths or archives using the Set Library dialog box.

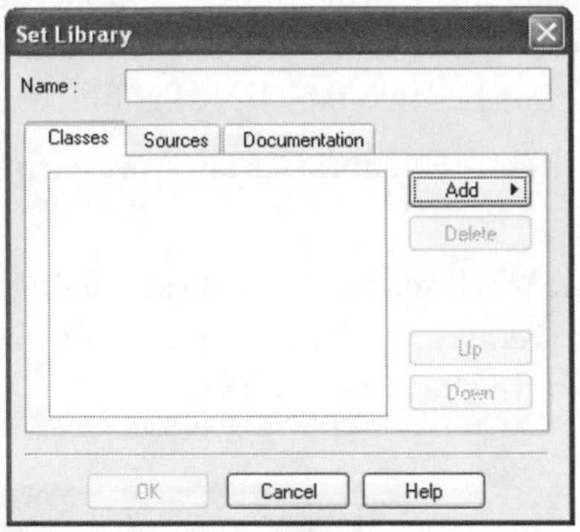

6. Select Add ➢ Add Path or Add ➢ Add Archive as appropriate. In both cases, you'll see a dialog where you can select the required path or archive file. When selecting the custom Google library path, choose the \Chapter 08\WSDL2Java\com folder because it's the top-level folder for the library. When working with Axis and Xerces, select all of the appropriate archive files in the \axis-1_1\lib or \xerces-2_5_0 folder.

> **▶ NOTE**
>
> You can also add source code and documentation files when available using the Sources and Documentation tabs of the Set Library dialog box. The Axis documentation files appear in the \axis-1_1\docs folder, while the Xerces documentation files appear in the \xerces-2_5_0\docs folder.

7. Type a name for the library in the Name field of the Set Library dialog box and click OK. JCreator will add the library to the list of available libraries for the project.

8. Repeat steps 5 through 7 for the custom Google, Axis, and Xerces libraries. When you complete the steps, check each of the library entries in the Project ClassPath dialog box. Figure 8.6 shows a typical library setup for Google Web Services.

9. Click Finish. JCreator will create a new project and workspace for you.

> **▶ TIP**
>
> Once you configure the libraries you need for Google Web Services, they're available for every other project you create. All you need to do is check the required libraries as shown in Figure 8.6.

FIGURE 8.6:

Make sure you always check the libraries that you want to use with your project.

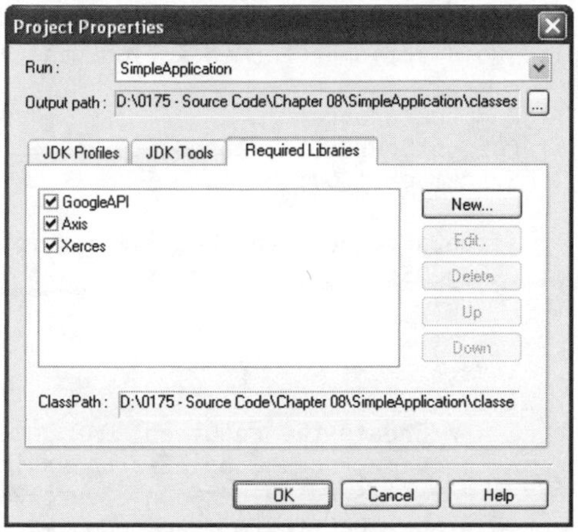

You've configured JCreator for use with Google Web Services at this point. These steps probably seem like a lot more work than simply typing what you need into a batch file, but it's also less error prone and somewhat easier to configure. Generally, you'll find modification and updates are much easier to perform using this editor.

> ▶ **NOTE**
>
> JCreator includes a `package myprojects.databasestore` or similar statement in the templates that it uses. In some cases, this statement prevents you from running the application from the command prompt. The examples in this chapter don't include the statement. As a result, you'll find the compiled code and `RunExample.BAT` file in the `classes` subfolder, rather than in the `classes\myprojects` subfolder as usual. Make sure you add this statement back in if you want to run the application from within the JCreator IDE.

Writing the Application

At this point, you have a custom library and a specially configured environment in which to work. The example in Listing 8.2 shows how to create a simple search using Google Web Services. The emphasis of this example (besides creating the search) is the use of a custom library. You'll find the complete source for this example in the `\Chapter 08\SimpleApplication` folder of the source code located on the Sybex Web site.

Listing 8.2   **Using a Custom Library**

```
// This class handles button click events.
private class ButtonHandler implements ActionListener
{
```

```java
... Variable Declarations ...

public void actionPerformed(ActionEvent AE)
{
   // End the program.
   if (AE.getSource() == btnQuit)
      System.exit(0);

   // Issue a request and receive a response.
   if (AE.getSource() == btnTest)
   {

      try
      {
         // Create the required SOAP objects.
         Service = new GoogleSearchServiceLocator();
         Port = Service.getGoogleSearchPort(
            new URL("http://api.google.com/search/beta2"));
         Result =
            Port.doGoogleSearch(
               txtKey.getText(), txtSearch.getText(), 0, 10, false,
               "", false, "", "", "");
      }
      catch(java.net.MalformedURLException e)
      {
         System.out.println("MalformedURLException error.");
         System.out.println(e);
      }
      catch(javax.xml.rpc.ServiceException e)
      {
         System.out.println("A ServiceException error occurred.");
         System.out.println(e);
      }
      catch(java.rmi.RemoteException e)
      {
         System.out.println("A RemoteException error occurred.");
         System.out.println(e);
      }

      // Clear the response table.
      for (int RCount = 0;
           RCount < 10;
           RCount++)
         for (int CCount = 0;
              CCount < 4;
              CCount++)
            tblResp.setValueAt("", RCount, CCount);

      // Retrieve the result elements.
      Elements = Result.getResultElements();
```

```
        // Output the result.
        for (int Count = 0;
            Count < Elements.length;
            Count++)
    {
        // Print out the information.
        tblResp.setValueAt(
            StringToText(Elements[Count].getTitle()), Count, 0);
        ... Other Response Table Entries ...
    }
    }
    }
}
```

The code begins by creating the objects used to access and store Google Web Services data. The Service object makes contact with Google Web Services. The Port object defines the actual conduit for information exchange. The Result object contains all of the data returned by Google Web Services, while the Elements object contains just the individual result elements. This setup is far simpler than many Web services, but it's still a little more complex than using the Google library.

You must create the SOAP objects within a try block. Notice that this example contains more catch clauses than the example in Listing 8.1. As expected, the additional error trapping means you must supply additional code, but you also gain the benefit of better error handling. Now you can determine whether an error is the result of a bad URL or something that has gone wrong with the service.

The code creates three SOAP related objects in this example. The Service object is actually instantiated as a GoogleSearchServiceLocator. The GoogleSearchServiceLocator class contains information about Google Web Services, such as the location of the default port. The code uses the Service object to create a port using the getGoogleSearchPort() method. The GoogleSearchServiceLocator class actually provides two forms of this method. The example shows how you can override the default port by supplying a specific port as part of the call. When you call getGoogleSearchPort() without any arguments, you get a port that uses the default settings. It's possible to check the default port using the getGoogleSearchPort-Address() method.

Once the code creates the Port object, it can make the call to Google Web Services using the doGoogleSearch() method. Unlike the Google library, you must supply values for each of the required arguments, even if the argument is blank. This call returns the GoogleSearch-Result object, Result.

The example doesn't output information contained within the upper level of the SOAP response—it concentrates instead on the individual search elements. With this in mind, the code clears the response table. It then places the result elements in `Elements` using the `getResultElements()` method. The `Elements` object is actually an array of `ResultElement` objects. Consequently, the code doesn't have to work very hard to discover the individual property values. As shown, all you need is the correct method call to retrieve the property value. Unfortunately, Google assumes that you want to display the information on a Web page, so you must remove the HTML tags and special characters from the output using the `StringToText()` method described later in this section. Figure 8.7 shows typical output from this application.

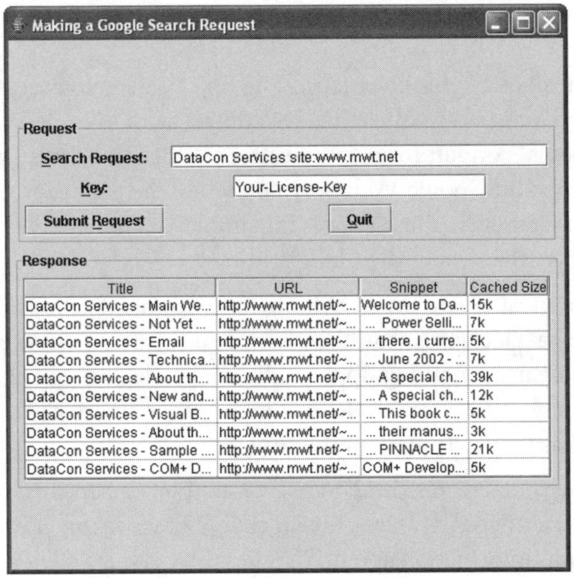

FIGURE 8.7:

A standard search works equally well with the Google or a third party library.

One of the interesting things about Google output is that you receive the actual output from the HTML page. This method of data retrieval adds HTML tags that won't render correctly with a desktop application. In addition, Google adds the <b> (bold) tag to highlight the keywords in the output. Listing 8.3 shows one technique you can use to remove the extra characters.

Listing 8.3   Replacing HTML Characters

```
public String StringToText(String Input)
{
    // Replace the bold tag.
    Input = Input.replaceAll("<b>", "");
    Input = Input.replaceAll("</b>", "");
```

```
    // Replace the single quote.
    Input = Input.replaceAll("&#39;", "'");

    // Replace the <br> tag.
    Input = Input.replaceAll("<br>", "");
    Input = Input.replaceAll("<br/>", "");
    Input = Input.replaceAll("<br />", "");

    // Return the results.
    return Input;
}
```

Fortunately, string replacement is easy in Java. All you need to use is the `replaceAll()` method in most cases. The problem is discovering how to remove the HTML tags. For example, the <b> tag has both an opening and a closing tag. In some cases, a Web page replaces common characters with special escapes, such as the ' sequence used for the single quote. Make sure you also consider permutations of some tags. Not every Web site uses the same form of the <br> tag, so you must replace the variations Web sites are likely to use.

Writing a Java Application with Database Support

Google is an amazingly fast search engine. However, it can't beat the speed of a local database connection. In addition, Google limits the number of calls you can make to Google Web Services during a single day. These two reasons, among others, make database storage of Google data viable. Storing data locally means you can get fast responses for common searches and you'll make fewer requests of Google Web Services.

> ▶ **NOTE**
>
> Using SQL Server with Java means using the Java DataBase Connectivity (JDBC) to Open DataBase Connectivity (ODBC) adapter, which is one of the reasons I chose this setup for the example. The JDBC–ODBC Bridge Driver supplied with the latest JDK complicates matters slightly, but not to the point of making a connection impossible. The example uses an ODBC Data Source Name (DSN) of StoreGoogle. You set up the DSN using the Data Sources (ODBC) applet normally found in the Administrative Tools folder of the Control Panel. You can learn how to use the ODBC Data Source Administrator various places online. The best place to start with SQL Server is the TechRepublic article at `http://techrepublic.com .com/5100-6268-5030474.html`. Another good source of information is the MSDN article at `http://msdn.microsoft.com/library/en-us/odbc/htm/sdkodbcadminoverview.asp`.

You'll need to work with this example in two parts. The first part handles the request from the database if possible. The second part makes the request from Google if the database doesn't contain the requested information or the information in the database is too old. List-ing 8.4 shows the essential code for the first part of this example—the listing isn't complete. You'll find the complete code for this example in the \Chapter 08\DatabaseStore folder of the source code located on the Sybex Web site. The macros and data to re-create the SQL database appears in the \Chapter 08\SQL Data folder of the source code located on the Sybex Web site.

Listing 8.4   **Handling the Initial Request**

```java
// This class handles button click events.
private class ButtonHandler implements ActionListener
{
    public void actionPerformed(ActionEvent AE)
    {
        ... Variable Declarations ...

        // End the program.
        if (AE.getSource() == btnQuit)
            System.exit(0);

        // Issue a request and receive a response.
        if (AE.getSource() == btnTest)
        {
            // Initialize the variables.
            Scanned =  new java.util.Date();
            Now =  new java.util.Date();
            SearchNum = "0";

            // Create an instance of the JDBC-ODBC Driver.
            try
            {
                Class.forName("sun.jdbc.odbc.JdbcOdbcDriver");
            }
            catch (java.lang.ClassNotFoundException e)
            {
                ... Handle Error ...
            }

            try
            {
                // Make a connection to the database.
                Con = DriverManager.getConnection("jdbc:odbc:StoreGoogle");

                // Define an executable statement.
                Stmnt = Con.createStatement();
```

```java
// Get a result set.
RS = Stmnt.executeQuery(
   "SELECT * FROM SearchQueries WHERE SearchQuery='" +
   txtSearch.getText() + "'");

// Verify the data exists.
if (!RS.next())
{

   // Make the request.
   GenerateRequest();

   // Exit the routine.
   return;
}
else
{
   // Get the SearchNumber value.
   SearchNum = RS.getString("SearchNumber");

   // Get the scanned date.
   Scanned = RS.getDate("DateScanned");

   // Convert the scanned date to a string.
   ConvDate = new SimpleDateFormat("dd MMMM, yyyy");
   txtScanned.setText(ConvDate.format(Scanned));

   // Add 24 hours to the scan date.
   TimeComp = Scanned.getTime();
   TimeComp = TimeComp + 86400000;
   Scanned.setTime(TimeComp);

   // Close the result set.
   RS.close();

   // If the data is too old.
   if (Now.after(Scanned))
   {
      // Remove the old records.
      Stmnt.executeUpdate(
         "DELETE FROM SearchQueries WHERE SearchQuery='" +
         txtSearch.getText() + "'");
      Stmnt.executeUpdate(
         "DELETE FROM Results WHERE SearchNumber='" +
         SearchNum + "'");

      // Make the request.
      GenerateRequest();

      // Return without processing the database.
```

```java
                    return;
                }
            }
        }
        catch (java.sql.SQLException e)
        {
            ... Handle Error ...
        }

        try
        {
            // Define an executable statement.
            Stmnt = Con.createStatement();

            // Create a new query for the results.
            RS = Stmnt.executeQuery(
                "SELECT * FROM Results WHERE SearchNumber='" +
                SearchNum + "'");

            // Clear the response table.
            for (int RCount = 0;
                RCount < 10;
                RCount++)
                for (int CCount = 0;
                    CCount < 4;
                    CCount++)
                    tblResp.setValueAt("", RCount, CCount);

            // Process the records.
            Count = 0;
            while (RS.next())
            {
                // Print out the information.
                tblResp.setValueAt(RS.getString("Title"), Count, 0);
                ... Other Table Entries ...

                // Go to the next row.
                Count++;
            }

            // Close the result set.
            RS.close();
        }
        catch (java.sql.SQLException e)
        {
            ... Handle Error ...
        }
    }
    }
}
```

The first step is to establish a connection with the database. As previously mentioned, this example relies on the JDBC–ODBC Bridge Driver to perform the required linkage between Java and SQL Server. The example shows a typical setup for this kind of database connection. Once the driver is instantiated, the code can use it to make the actual connection using the getConnection() method. The code also creates a standard statement with the execute-Query() method—one that it can use for queries made up of executable SQL statements. The first statement returns a recordset, RS, when the database contains the information needed. If the RS.next() method fails, the code knows the data doesn't exist in the database and calls the GenerateRequest() method to request the information from Google. Because the GenerateRequest() method also fills the screen with data, the routine exits.

The example relies on two databases, SearchQueries, which stores the main node data, and Results, which stores the individual links. These two tables are joined with the SearchNumber field. Once the code retrieves a record for SearchQueries, it retrieves the SearchNumber field using the getString() method. The SearchNum string holds the data for later use in retrieving the links.

The example must also determine whether the data in the database is too old. It retrieves the DateScanned field as a date using the getDate() method. The Scanned.getTime() method converts the date to a long and adds 86,400,000 milliseconds to it (24 hours). You can use any comparison you see fit, or even allow the user to make the decision based on the date displayed. The Now.after(Scanned) method determines whether the data is too old. If it is, the example deletes the old records from the database and makes the request using GenerateRequest().

At this point, the example knows that the database contains the required information and that the information isn't too old. It uses a technique similar to the one explained for Listing 8.2 to clear the current response table data and to display the new data on screen. Notice that this data comes from the Results table and that the code retrieves it using the executeQuery() method.

This discussion assumes that the database contains the required data. When the database can't provide the required information, the code must request it from Google Web Services. Listing 8.5 shows the request code.

Listing 8.5　　　**Creating the Request and Performing the Database Update**

```
public void GenerateRequest()
{
    ... Variable Declarations ...

    ... Initialize the variables...
```

```
try
{
   // Create the required SOAP objects.
   Service = new GoogleSearchServiceLocator();
   Port = Service.getGoogleSearchPort(
      new URL("http://api.google.com/search/beta2"));
   Result =
      Port.doGoogleSearch(
         txtKey.getText(), txtSearch.getText(), 0, 10, false, "",
         false, "", "", "");
}
   ... Handle Errors (See Listing 8.2 for Details) ...

// Set the scanned date.
Scanned = new java.util.Date();

// Convert the scanned date to a string.
ConvDate = new SimpleDateFormat("dd MMMM, yyyy");
txtScanned.setText(ConvDate.format(Scanned));

// Format the released date for use with SQL Server.
FormDate = new SimpleDateFormat("yyyy/MM/dd HH:mm:ss");


// Create the SearchQueries record.
try
{
   // Create a prepared statement with variables for
   // value entries. You must include one variable for
   // each database column.
   PState =
      Con.prepareStatement("INSERT INTO SearchQueries " +
                           "VALUES (?, ?, ?, ?, ?, ?, ?, ?)");

   // The database entries are 1-based, not 0-based. Use
   // the correct set method for each entry.
   PState.setString(1, Result.getSearchQuery());
   ... Other Prepared Statement Entries ...
   PState.executeUpdate();

   // Close this statement.
   PState.close();
}
catch (java.sql.SQLException e)
{
   System.out.println("SearchQueries Update Error");
   System.out.println(e);
}

// Get the search number of the newly created record.
try
```

```
{
    // Define an executable statement.
    Stmnt = Con.createStatement();

    // Get a result set.
    RS = Stmnt.executeQuery(
        "SELECT * FROM SearchQueries WHERE SearchQuery='" +
        txtSearch.getText() + "'");

    // Get the record.
    RS.next();

    // Get the SearchNumber value.
    SearchNum = RS.getLong("SearchNumber");

    // Close the result set.
    RS.close();
}
catch (java.sql.SQLException e)
{
    ... Handle Error ...
}

// Clear the response table.
... See Listing 8.4 for Details ...

// Retrieve the result elements.
Elements = Result.getResultElements();

// Output the result.
for (int Count = 0;
     Count < Elements.length;
     Count++)
{
    // Print out the information.
    tblResp.setValueAt(
        StringToText(Elements[Count].getTitle()), Count, 0);
    ... Other Response Table Entries ...

    // Create the Results record.
    try
    {
        // Make a connection to the database.
        Con2 = DriverManager.getConnection("jdbc:odbc:StoreGoogle");

        // Create a prepared statement.
        PState =
            Con2.prepareStatement("INSERT INTO Results " +
                                  "VALUES (?, ?, ?, ?, ?, ?)");

        // Use the correct set method for each entry.
```

```
        PState.setLong(1, SearchNum);
        ... Other Prepared Statement Entries ...
        PState.executeUpdate();

        // Close the statement and the connection after each update.
        PState.close();
        Con2.close();
    }
    catch (java.sql.SQLException e)
    {
        ... Handle Error ...
    }

  }
}
```

The Google Web Services request begins by creating the service and establishing a connection using a port through the getGoogleSearchPort() method. The code uses the resulting Port object to request the data from Google Web Services. On return from the call, Result contains the Google response in a series of variables, including some arrays. The code dissects this data and places the important information in the database.

One of the first tasks is to establish a scanning date. The code places the date in Scanned and also displays the information on screen. Notice the use for the ConvDate.format() method in this case. The code uses a similar technique to create a date in a format suitable for storage in SQL Server using the FormDate object.

You can interact with SQL Server using a number of techniques. However, when inserting a date into the database, you'll find the prepared statement technique shown here works exceptionally well because it can handle all kinds of data. The code uses the prepareStatement() method to create an insertion statement. It then uses various set methods, such as setString(), to fill the statement entries with data. Finally, the code makes the entry permanent using the executeUpdate() method.

Remember that the two tables are linked using the SearchNumber field. At this point, the code retrieves the SearchNumber value by making a query. You can't obtain this information in any other way. For this reason, you must make sure the queries in the database are unique or that you find some unique combination of entries to use to store the data. Otherwise, you can corrupt the linkage between the two tables.

The code processes the individual links next. The technique used is similar to the one in Listing 8.2. However, you also need to create the Results table entries. After the code outputs the link values to the response table, it creates a new connection to the database, creates a prepared statement, fills the statement with data, and executes the statement. The final step closes both the prepared statement and the database connection. If you don't perform this step, the example will fail with errors stating the connection is busy.

Your Call to Action

This chapter helps you understand how to use Java to build a Google Web Services application. In fact, the chapter discusses how to build several application types so you get a better idea of just how flexible Java is. The chapter has also pointed out hurdles you might encounter when building the application. Java is an outstanding language with amazing flexibility, but it also has significant problems that you can't overcome with ease. The important issue is to determine whether the benefits of using Java outweigh potential problems when you decide whether to use this language.

Begin your preparation for using Java by using the Web site URLs in the "Resources for Learning Java" section of the chapter. Once you know Java well enough, you're ready to look at the requirements for your application. Make sure you spend enough time considering the issue of whether the intelligence for your application will reside on the client or the server (or something in between). You also need to consider the server setup you want to use and decide what kind of functionality to build into your application. You might decide to start with something as simple as a search site so you can see how Google Web Services performs, as well as how you need to configure your setup for a more advanced application.

Chapter 9 moves development from desktop, laptop, notebook, and other large devices to the small, mobile devices that many people use today. These devices are lightweight, easy to carry, and generally allow the user to communicate everywhere. As great as these devices are for the general user, they're a problematic platform at best for the developer because you need to consider the limitations of such devices. Most mobile devices have small displays, lack full keyboard functionality, have limited memory, have reduced processing power, and have significant operating system limits. However, even with these problems, mobile devices can serve as an important platform for your Google Web Services application and Google certainly makes it easy to use these devices.

Chapter 9

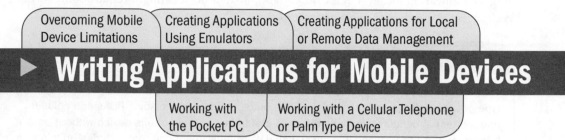

Overcoming Mobile Device Limitations | Creating Applications Using Emulators | Creating Applications for Local or Remote Data Management

▶ Writing Applications for Mobile Devices

Working with the Pocket PC | Working with a Cellular Telephone or Palm Type Device

Working with Google using a mobile device is a natural extension of the services that Google already provides. In fact, road warriors may well find themselves using a mobile device more often than their desktop machine to search Google. Google recognizes this need and provides access to its service using a specialized mobile interface. You can learn more about this interface at `http://www.google.com/options/wireless.html`. The two essential problems with this service are that Google supports a limited number of devices (no Pocket PC support) and imposes significant limitations on how you can search. The easiest way to overcome these limitations is to create mobile access for your specific needs using Google Web Services.

Mobile devices do present special problems for the developer, especially a developer using Google Web Services. The biggest problem is what to do with all the data Google returns with every request. Trying to fit all that information on a small screen isn't going to work, so you need to create prioritized displays. The request data presents a smaller problem, but is still something you need to consider. The first section of the chapter discusses the limitations you need to consider in light of the physical and operational characteristics of a mobile device.

It isn't always possible to test your Google Web Services application on the actual machine. Although you should test the application on an actual machine before you give it to anyone, using an emulator can greatly decrease development time and make the development process easier. The second section of the chapter discusses emulators.

Data management is also an issue. Many of the previous chapters of the book discussed scenarios where you can store data locally to improve performance. However, a mobile device doesn't stay in the same place, so using this technique can prove problematic. The third section of the chapter discusses techniques for local and remote data management options.

The remaining sections of the chapter discuss application development techniques for various devices. This chapter uses products such as Visual Studio .NET to show how to access Google Web Services using a mobile device. The mobile device you choose greatly affects the kind of development you perform. For example, a Pocket PC is perfectly capable of running an application locally. On the other hand, smaller devices might require some form of Web access through a custom server setup.

> **▶ NOTE**
>
> This chapter uses very specific terms for the various devices. A mobile device refers to any type of device the user can move from one place to another (including PDAs and cellular telephones). A cellular telephone refers to a standard version of this device without built-in intelligence. A Smartphone is a special kind of cellular telephone that includes built-in intelligence that a developer can program using a product such as Visual Studio .NET. A PDA is any kind of non–cellular telephone handheld device. For this book, the term PDA includes both Palm and Pocket PC devices. A Palm device specifically uses the Palm OS. A Pocket PC specifically uses some form of Windows. I won't discuss other PDA OSs in this book.

Understanding Mobile Device Limitations

Every device has limitations that you must consider. Whether those limits become a burden depends on what you plan to do with the device. The technique you use to perform a task is also a factor. Modern PCs have few limitations because vendors have increased their capabilities over the years. However, early PCs were so limited that developers worried about every byte of data. Mobile devices today are almost in the same position as early PCs—vendors simply haven't created ways to overcome problems with these small devices yet. Some of these problems might never go away because they have more to do with the limits of the humans using the device than the device itself. For example, you can place entire books on the head of a pin, but who can read them? Likewise, make the display of a mobile device too small and you encounter usage problems. The following sections discuss mobile device limitations of all types as they relate to Google Web Services.

Special Add-ons

Most vendors design PDAs as electronic versions of the calendar, address book, and personal note taker. Early versions of these products didn't include the mini–word processors and spreadsheets you'll find in modern versions. In fact, you can extend many PDAs to double as cameras, scanners, and other devices now with special add-ons. Other mobile devices, such as cellular telephones, have followed suit, but to a lesser degree.

The PDA isn't exactly a standard device to begin with. There are many hardware implementations, more than a few operating systems, and even different capabilities to consider. When users start adding features to their PDA, you may find that it's nearly impossible to determine what features you can rely on finding. In short, when you create a Google Web Services application for your company, try to standardize the device configuration. On the other hand, when you create an application that users outside the company can access, you need to provide a list of specific device requirements to reduce the potential for compatibility problems.

Generally speaking, you don't need special add-on devices to work with Google. You can normally type the information you need into the device, select a search, and receive the results you need. However, add-on devices can work to your advantage in a number of situations. For example, you could scan words into the search form instead of typing them. Given the limited typing potential of most of these devices, you'll find scanning comes in quite handy.

Theoretically, you could also use add-on devices to extend the range of your application. The "Using Google Web Services and Amazon Web Services Together" section of Chapter 11 describes techniques for combining these two Web services. You might not think you could perform this task using a mobile device, but it's relatively easy to do with careful programming. With a combined application, you could scan a UPC, ask Amazon to tell you more about the product (and perhaps provide a price comparison), and then use the information Amazon provides to extend the search using Google. Such a mobile application could help you make good buying decisions while standing in the store holding your PDA.

Networking

Distributed application development relies on a connection between the client and the server. Because most mobile devices have limited processing capability, distributed applications are especially important in this situation. It's easy to create a connection when you're working with a desktop machine. If you can't create a direct connection using a LAN, there are always alternatives such as using dial-up support. However, networking with a mobile device can prove problematic.

The networking problems fall into three categories that can affect your Google Web Services session. The first problem is the limited networking potential of devices such as cellular telephones. These devices have good connectivity, but you'll find it difficult to run custom Web applications using them because it's tough to add any form of security. You can't reliably determine the identity of the caller, secure the application, or ensure the integrity of the connection. Consequently, cellular telephones are good for downloading noncritical information or performing nonsecure queries.

Newer PDAs have much better processing capability than any cellular telephone and include good connectivity through a wireless connection. It's possible to provide a reliable identity check with higher end systems such as the Pocket PC. In addition, you can provide some level of application security. Unfortunately, you still can't secure the communication path between server and Pocket PC easily, so critical data could become compromised. You can perform most Google Web Services tasks, but might not want to perform online ordering because there's a possibility that someone could intercept the credit card numbers and identifying information.

> **▶ WARNING**
>
> Lest you think that hacking of the sort mentioned in this section falls into the urban legend category, hacking does happen regularly at the various Internet cafes such as Starbucks and McDonalds. In fact, hackers have standard tools to perform the task. Find out more in the Computerworld article at `http://www.computerworld.com/mobiletopics/mobile/story/0,10801,87523,00.html?f=x68`.

Older PDAs are far less capable than the newer products on the market. In some cases, you might not even have good networking capability. Some of these older models rely on an internal modem for communication. A few models I've see use an add-in card to provide a wired connection to the network. Although the wired connections of some older models are inconvenient for the user, they actually make it possible to create a very secure connection. A physical connection lets you secure the wire, the application, and provide full user credentials, but at the cost of user productivity. In general, you won't ever need to use one of these solutions with Google Web Services.

Operating System

The operating system you use for a mobile device affects the device functionality and your ability to interact with Google Web Services. Generally, you don't have a choice of operating system when it comes to your cellular telephone. Even the Smartphone comes with a single operating system choice and that operating system really isn't capable of providing more than Web application access. (You can create certain classes of local applications using Visual Studio .NET with the Smartphone, and we'll explore the Google Web Services perspective in this chapter.)

PDA users do have some choices to make, especially if you have a Pocket PC device at your disposal. Early versions of the Pocket PC used Windows CE. However, you can now find devices that come loaded with compact versions of Windows 2000 or Windows XP. No, you can't create a full desktop application for these devices, but the newer the operating system and the greater the device functionality, the better your chances are of creating an application that can perform most (perhaps all) tasks locally. Even Windows CE users can rely on local applications that use SOAP to communicate with Google Web Services using JavaScript (one of the options considered in this chapter).

> ▶ **TIP**
>
> Make sure you keep up-to-date with mobile device technologies by checking vendor sites often. For example, you can learn about updated capabilities for the Pocket PC and Smartphone devices by visiting Microsoft's site at `http://www.microsoft.com/windowsmobile/default.mspx`. Visit the Web site for your particular cellular telephone vendor to obtain cellular telephone updates. Finally, make sure you visit the Palm site at `http://www.palm.com/home.html`.

Early versions of the Palm are extremely limited and any hopes you have of creating a local application are dim (unless you want to do the equivalent of assembly language programming). These early versions require that you use a Web application to communicate with Google Web Services. Newer versions of the Palm offer greater functionality, and you'll probably find a strong third party market for development tools as these versions gain support. In the meantime, you can use the developer resources provided directly by Palm at `http://www.palmone.com/us/developers/` or rely on Web applications to access Google Web Services.

Screen Size

Many users have 17-inch or 19-inch monitors capable of a minimum of 1280 × 1024 resolution today. Developers have taken advantage of the screen real estate to create better applications that display more data at one time. Even Microsoft uses higher resolutions as a baseline for applications—many of their application screens won't fit on an 800 × 600 display anymore.

Everything you want to do with your PDA has to fit within a small screen space (320 × 200 pixels if you're using a Pocket PC model like the Casio Cassiopeia). That's a lot smaller than the typical computer screen. Developers working on cellular telephone applications have even less screen real estate—some models display just a few lines of information. In addition, some PDAs and most cellular telephones use black and white displays in place of color, so you can't even use the modern tricks to make the display look nicer. In short, mobile device screens tend to look a bit plain, and developers normally find themselves feverishly cutting their application screens down to size. However, with careful data sizing and information layout, you can create a perfectly acceptable display for Google Web Services requests and responses. The examples in this chapter demonstrate techniques for each device type.

Make sure you consider eXtensible Hypertext Markup Language (XHTML) for complex applications with many elements (http://www.w3.org/TR/xhtml1/). It helps you to display your application in segments with relative ease.

Other display options include using the Handheld Device Markup Language (HDML) (http://www.w3.org/TR/NOTE-Submission-HDML-spec.html) or Wireless Markup Language (WML) (http://www.oasis-open.org/cover/wap-wml.html). Both of these technologies use the concept of cards and decks to break up information into easily managed pieces. Of course, the mobile device you use has to provide support for these standards (most do) before you can use the tags within a document. Unfortunately, using any of these solutions normally prevents your Web application from appearing properly on a desktop machine.

Color

Developers have gotten used to seeing colors on their applications. Color dresses up a drab display and makes the application more fun to use. In addition, using color presents cues to the user. For example, many users associate green with a good condition and red with something bad. In short, most applications rely heavily on color today and with good reason.

Depending on the mobile device you use, you may not have any color at all. For example, many Palm models present the world in shades of gray. Many cellular telephones also represent all data using either black or white and don't even provide for shades of gray. (The newer picture cellular telephones are an exception to the rule and you might consider creating special software to accommodate them.) Even if a mobile device does provide color support akin to the Pocket PC, the developer still has to use color carefully.

The problem for mobile device users is that the screen is already small. If a user gets into an area with bright sunlight, seeing the screen might become impossible, especially if the screen contains colors that don't work well in such an environment. Fortunately, Google uses very little color and its Web page is somewhat plain—making its Web site useful for some mobile device applications. Even so, your application can provide extended functionality, choice of color support, and better device support.

Using color to display icons or to convey a message is still a good idea, even in the world of the mobile device. For example, a red icon could signal danger or tell the user to wait without using up screen real estate for words. Of course, you need to explain the meaning of the color changes within a manual or help file (preferably both). Make sure the users of your application actually have a device capable of displaying color before you use color to signify anything in the application (some devices display only shades of gray). In addition, you must exercise care in using color because colorblind users might not be able to interpret the application correctly.

User Interface

Cellular telephone users commonly have just a keypad as an interface device. In some cases, the vendor will also supply some control keys, including an arrow keypad, but that's about it. If you want to create a Google Web Services application for a cellular telephone, you need to consider these limitations.

Most PDA users rely on a pointer to do all of their work. Sure, a few PDAs do offer a keyboard and mouse as separate items, but most of these offerings are bulky and difficult to use. Pointer use is one of the reasons that you want to keep your application on one screen, or use multiple screens when necessary. Scrolling on a PDA screen is less than intuitive and requires some level of skill to master.

No matter what type of mobile device development you do, be sure to include some pointer friendly features. For example, try to make as many tasks use a single pointer option or numeric keypad input as possible. The user should be able to point to what they want and allow the mobile device to complete the input for them.

Pointer friendly programs also make tasks yes or no propositions. Again, this allows the user to accomplish the task with a single click, rather than writing something down. The point is to make the PDA as efficient as possible so the user doesn't get frustrated trying to do something easy.

Working with Emulators

An important consideration for this chapter is that Google offers data in response to a request. Handling the input and output is up to you. One of the problems that developers must solve when working with mobile devices is testing for multiple models. Unlike desktop systems, it's not always easy to determine whether an application will provide the correct presentation on a mobile setup. Each mobile device has different capabilities, installed software, and a host of other problem areas for the developer to consider.

Most developers turn to emulation software to help test their applications. An emulator provides the equivalent environment of the mobile device that it's supposed to model. I stress the word equivalent, because most of these emulators don't provide a complete picture of the mobile device environment. You can rely on an emulator to tell you whether the application fits within the screen area that the mobile device provides, but you can't rely on it to tell you about memory issues or whether a particular device has a piece of support software you need. (Some emulators, such as the one provided with Visual Studio .NET, are getting better about testing memory issues—vendors are aware of many of the emulator issues that developers face and are providing emulator support for these needs.) These other issues require testing on an actual device—something you should do for at least a subset of the mobile devices you want to support.

> ▶ **TIP**
>
> You don't need to buy every mobile device on the market—emulators can help you keep your costs under control. However, you should buy the devices that people in your organization use most often. Actual device testing is better than using emulators, but you can rely on emulators to help when your application won't be used by a particular mobile device very often.

The following sections describe four emulation software options. The first option is the built-in support that Visual Studio .NET 2003 provides. If you don't plan to use this IDE, you can skip the first section.

> ▶ **TIP**
>
> Keep apprised of the latest Microsoft mobility and embedded system developments at `http://msdn.microsoft.com/mobility/`. This Web site includes many of the links you'll need to download the latest Microsoft products to make your Google Web Services mobile application development easier.

I chose these options because they provide a broad range of support, and you can download at least evaluation units of all three emulators. Here are the download locations so that you can get your copies of the products before you begin this section. The following sections assume that you've downloaded the software required for the installation.

- Microsoft eMbedded Visual Tools 3.0 (2002 edition): `http://www.microsoft.com/downloads/details.aspx?FamilyId=F663BF48-31EE-4CBE-AAC5-0AFFD5FB27DD` (full development package) or `http://www.microsoft.com/downloads/details.aspx?FamilyId=25F4DE97-AE80-477A-9DF1-496B85B3D3E3` (emulators only) or `http://www.microsoft.com/downloads/details.aspx?FamilyID=2dbee84a-bd94-4167-b817-2b2e548b2e92` (older full development version)

- Openwave SDK: `http://developer.Openwave.com/download/`

- Smartphone: `http://www.yospace.com/spe.html`

> ▶ **TIP**
>
> You can also download the Microsoft Smartphone 2003 emulator at `http://www.microsoft` `.com/downloads/details.aspx?familyid=8fe677fa-3a6a-4265-b8eb-61a628ecd462`. This emulator requires eMbedded Visual C++ 4.0. The Microsoft eMbedded Visual Tools 3.0 (2002 edition) package does contain the Smartphone 2002 emulator. Likewise, you can find the Microsoft Pocket PC 2003 emulator for eMbedded Visual C++ 4.0 at `http://www` `.microsoft.com/downloads/details.aspx?FamilyId=9996B314-0364-4623-9EDE-` `0B5FBB133652`.

Visual Studio .NET Built-in Emulator

Visual Studio .NET 2003 comes with a built-in emulator you can use for various kinds of development. When you create a mobile project, the IDE automatically sets up the required emulator support as well. After you develop the application, use the Debug ➤ Start command to display the Deploy PocketPC dialog box shown in Figure 9.1.

To use the emulator, simply select the Pocket PC 2002 Emulator (Default) option and click Deploy. The IDE will copy the application to the emulator folder, start the emulator, and load your application. At this point, you can begin testing the application as you would any another .NET application.

The emulator is configurable. Use the Tools ➤ Options command to display the Options dialog box. Select the Device Tools ➤ Devices option to display the list of devices available for this project. Select the device you want to configure and click Configure. You'll see a Configure Emulator Settings dialog box similar to the one shown in Figure 9.2.

You can change features such as the display size and color depth. More importantly, you can set memory restrictions on the System tab so that the application can model the memory restrictions of the target device to an extent. Note that the default Visual Studio .NET setup has a number of emulators including the Pocket PC and Windows CE devices.

FIGURE 9.1:

Use the options in this dialog box to choose a deployment option.

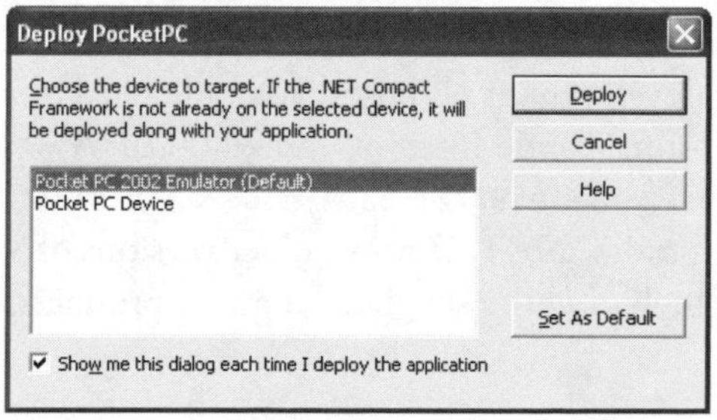

Configure the emulator to better model the mobile device you want to use.

> ▶ **TIP**
>
> Microsoft recently released the Visual Basic .NET Resource Kit, a must-have addition for mobile development. The kit offers additional samples and makes it much easier to create robust mobile applications. Learn more about this kit at `http://www.microsoft.com/downloads/details.aspx?FamilyId=EF4289B4-FFCB-40BD-9BFE-95256ABD0E13`.

Microsoft eMbedded Visual Tools

The Microsoft eMbedded Visual Tools option is free. All you need to do is download the product and unpack it into an installation directory. You have a choice of two versions on the Internet right now, but the URL at the beginning of this section points to the latest version of the product. Developers have reported fewer problems with the newer version of the emulators and it does model the device more accurately.

Earlier versions of the product create two folders: one named `Disk1` and a second named `Disk2`. If you have an earlier version of the product, the `Disk2` folder contains the three emulators and you can install them individually if desired by using the Setup program found in the individual emulation product folder. For example, if you want to install just the Pocket PC emulation, you can double-click the Setup program in the `\Mobile Development Tools\DISK2\PPC12SDK` folder. If you're using Visual Studio .NET 2003 or a language such as PHP for development purposes, you only need to install these emulators. You also need the Microsoft Mobile Internet Toolkit (`http://www.microsoft.com/downloads/details.aspx?familyid=ae597f21-b8e4-416e-a28f-b124f41f9768`) when you use an older version of Visual Studio .NET. Users of older versions of Visual Studio will need to install the whole package, including the supplied language products.

> ▶ **NOTE**
>
> The older versions of the emulators have a few problems. For example, the handheld PC emulation will sit in the upper left corner of your display and not move. However, it does provide a good environment in which to test your mobile application. Another potential problem with these emulators is that you can only run one of them at a time. Make sure you close an existing emulator before you start a new one. Generally, the new emulator will check for this problem and tell you to close the existing emulator. We'll discuss other emulator issues as the chapter progresses.

The latest version of Microsoft eMbedded Visual Tools uses a self-extracting executable. When you start the application, it unpacks the contents of the executable into a temporary folder. It then displays a series of dialog boxes that help you install eMbedded Visual Tools 3.0, Microsoft Windows SDK for Pocket PC 2002, and Microsoft Windows SDK for Smartphone 2002. The newer version only includes the Pocket PC and Smartphone emulators—you can separately download SDKs for the handheld and palm size emulators found in the older version of Microsoft eMbedded Visual Tools at `http://msdn.microsoft .com/downloads/list/handheldpc.asp`. The Smartphone SDK is only available for eMbedded Visual C++, so make sure you install this language if you want to create a Smartphone application.

When you finish installing everything, it's important to test each of the emulators to ensure you received a good installation. Open one of the sample projects to test the emulator when using the newest version of Microsoft eMbedded Visual Tools. If one of these emulators fails, rerun the setup program and select just that emulator for a reinstall. You need to run each emulator separately when using the older products. If one of the emulators fails to work, you can always uninstall just that emulator using the appropriate entry in the Add/Remove Programs applet. Reinstall the emulator using the required Setup program for that emulator in the `Disk2` folder. Figure 9.3 shows a typical Smartphone emulation.

OpenWave SDK

Like the Microsoft emulators, the Openwave SDK is also a free download, but the Openwave Web site offers plenty of opportunity to purchase products as well. The Openwave file you download is an executable, so double-clicking it starts the installation process. Simply follow the prompts to install the product. Most versions of the product require yes or no answers to each question.

FIGURE 9.3:

Test each of the emulators to ensure they work.

The Openwave Web site offers a number of versions of the product. I suggest you download the latest version of the product to ensure you get the latest features. However, the 5.1 version is also very capable and it includes a number of features not found in the 6.2.2 version used for this chapter. Figure 9.4 shows some of the optional features you can install with the 5.1 version. If you want to use Openwave as your development platform, you might want to download the 5.1 version (or both versions). The 6.2.2 version is most useful as an emulator only.

Once you get Openwave installed and have restarted your machine, you'll want to test this product. If you installed the 6.2.2 version, all you get is the emulator. To start the emulator, select the Start ➢ Programs ➢ Openwave SDK 6.2.2 ➢ Openwave SDK 6.2.2 HTTP option. You'll see an emulator similar to the one shown in Figure 9.5. The emulator automatically goes to the Openwave test site on first use, but you can change that location by opening the SDK Configuration dialog box using the Tools ➢ Options menu. Select the Browse tab and change the Homepage field.

FIGURE 9.4:

Select custom options as needed for your emulator setup.

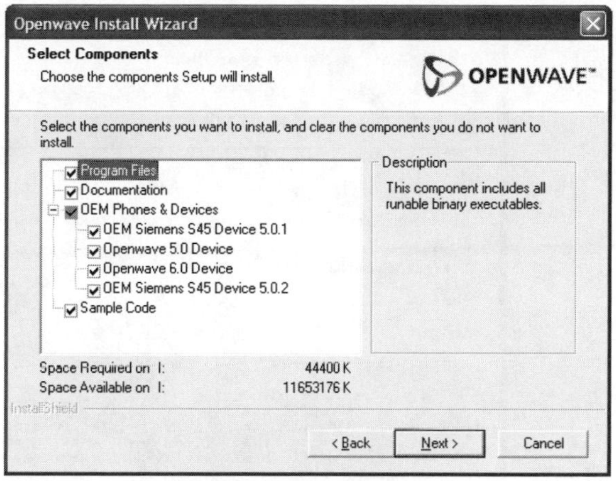

FIGURE 9.5:

Using the Openwave emulator means starting the associated IDE and entering an URL using a menu command. Image courtesy Openwave Systems Inc.

As previously mentioned, Openwave SDK 5.1 has more to offer than other versions of the product. Unlike some of the other emulators you'll use, this one is actually part of a development IDE. Select the Start ➢ Programs ➢ Openwave SDK 5.1 ➢ Openwave SDK 5.1 option to open an IDE similar to other IDEs you may have used in the past. However, for this book, the important feature is the emulator that appears in the right side pane. To use this feature, you'll need to use the Simulator ➢ Go to Address command, enter an URL in the Go to Address dialog box, and then click OK. Figure 9.6 shows a typical example of the Openwave emulator within the IDE.

FIGURE 9.6:

Use the 5.1 version if you need an IDE in addition to the emulator. Image courtesy Openwave Systems Inc.

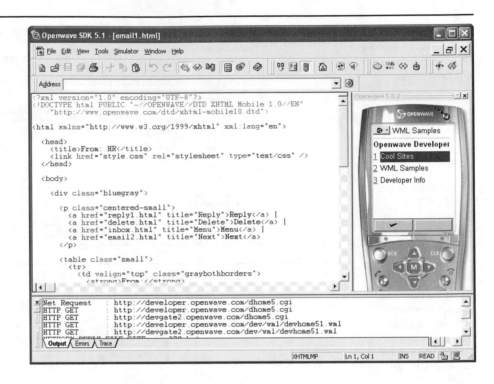

Smartphone

The Smartphone emulator is one of the timed usage options you can try. After you download the product, you can try it for anywhere from 5 to 15 days free (depending on the version you download), at which time your license will expire and the product will cease working. The Smartphone emulator is in a Zip that you download and unpack to a temporary folder. To start the installation process, double-click the setup application that appears in the Zip file (the actual name varies by Smartphone version number). Follow the prompts to install the product.

Now that you have the product installed, you can test it to see if it works. The first time you start this product, you'll see a dialog that requests your licensing details. This dialog box accepts your name, email address, and the key that you were sent in your email. (The company sends this key after you download the product from their Web site.) Make sure you use the information from the email because this step is quite picky.

You also have a choice of starting the product in Development or Display mode. The Development mode opens an IDE you can use to create applications. This mode also shows multiple forms of the emulation, as shown in Figure 9.7. These aren't the only emulators available. The number of emulation options provided surprised me—they're all available on the Workspace ➤ Add Emulator menu. This product also uses the concept of an emulator group. Figure 9.7 shows the default emulator group. A single test sends the same input to all of the emulators in a group—greatly reducing the time required for testing.

The Display mode opens a single emulator, as shown in Figure 9.8. Use this option when you want to fine-tune the display details of your application. Most of the emulators have a full view and several zoomed views. Figure 9.8 shows a full view.

FIGURE 9.7:
Create a complex emulator environment using the Smartphone Development mode.

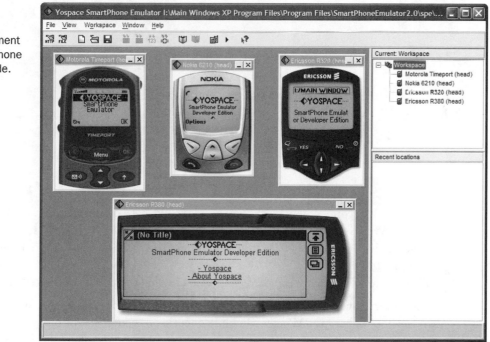

Designing for Local or Remote Data Management

Most programming chapters of this book have mentioned the need to store commonly used Google data locally to improve performance and provide a backup should the main connection to Google fail. A desktop application can rely on any of a number of Database Management Systems (DBMSs) to perform the task of storing this data for future use. Given the static connection a desktop system enjoys, you can assume the user will always have access to the data. Unfortunately, it's not possible to say the same thing about mobile devices. Mobile devices have dynamic connections that might not be available when you need them.

FIGURE 9.8:

Fine-tune the display details and perform final testing using the Display mode.

The lack of connectivity means you have to make hard choices about how to make your Google Web Services application perform well. You could still rely on a server-based DBMS to perform this task for you. For the purposes of this discussion, you can consider this a remote solution. It's remote because you can't count on a connection, and the mobile device might actually need to rely on a nonstandard connection to obtain the data (as when you're on the road).

An alternative for some devices is to use a product such as Microsoft SQL CE or Sybase iAnywhere. These DBMSs let you build a local connectivity solution that stores data short term on the local device. This solution tends to solve the problem of remote connectivity—the user can always count on the local data store. However, this solution also has problems. For one thing, you might not see as great a performance gain as you might anticipate—the limited memory and processing capacity device is now running your application and a DBMS. In addition, you'll find that many older devices aren't able to run either Microsoft SQL CE or Sybase iAnywhere. In short, you can't assume that database caching is even possible.

It might sound as if there aren't any good solutions for offline data storage for mobile devices. To some extent, that perception is true. However, you can use storage technology and improve both the functionality and performance of your mobile application incrementally. The best solution is to use local storage when the processing power and storage capability of the mobile device is up to the task. When you can't rely on the resources provided by the mobile device, use a Web application with server-based storage instead.

Developing for a Pocket PC

The Pocket PC is the most capable of the mobile devices you can use for a Google Web Services application. You can use local storage with this device and perform a multitude of tasks that some mobile devices can't, such as limited data analysis using the copy of Pocket Excel provided with the operating system. This platform even helps you create reports using Pocket Word. In sum, you can use a Pocket PC for most Google Web Services tasks—at least in a limited way.

> ▶ **TIP**
>
> You may have to search the Internet for some Pocket PC resources. However, you can find many Microsoft-supplied developer tools at `http://www.microsoft.com/windowsmobile/resources/downloads/developer/default.mspx`.

The following sections discuss three methods you can use to create applications for the Pocket PC: eMbedded Visual Tools, Visual Studio .NET, and third party tools (emphasizing PocketSOAP). Each of these methods has advantages and disadvantages that make it useful for a particular kind of application. For example, eMbedded Visual Tools provides the best compatibility. Even earlier versions of the Pocket PC can easily use the eMbedded Visual Tools option.

Using Older Microsoft Products

Many developers have used the eMbedded Visual Tools product provided by Microsoft to create applications for the Pocket PC over the years. You have a choice of using either Visual Basic or Visual C++ for the application. As previously mentioned, the main advantage to using eMbedded Visual Tools is compatibility. You don't need anything special to use this solution and it's likely that the resulting application will run on all versions of the Pocket PC as native code (rather than as a Web application).

The biggest disadvantage of this solution is that Microsoft created eMbedded Visual Tools at a time when SOAP wasn't part of the development strategy. You can overcome this issue with some Web services by issuing the request as a specially formatted URL using XML over HTTP (also known as REpresentational State Transfer or REST). Unfortunately, Google doesn't support this option, so you must use a third party product such as PocketSOAP to add SOAP capability to your eMbedded Visual Tools environment. The "Using Third Party Development Products" section of the chapter explains how to use PocketSOAP as part of a JavaScript application—the technique for using it with eMbedded Visual Tools is similar.

Using the .NET Compact Framework

The .NET Compact Framework offers a lot in the way of SOAP functionality. Using this product helps you create elegant Google Web Services applications with a minimum of fuss and without the need for third party solutions. However, the system you choose to support this application must have the .NET Compact Framework installed, which could result in memory problems for some older Pocket PCs. Listing 9.1 shows a typical example of a search routine that relies on the .NET Compact Framework. You'll find this example in the \Chapter 09\PocketPC folder of the source code located on the Sybex Web site.

Listing 9.1   **Creating a Google Request Using the .NET Compact Framework**

```
private void ApplicationTest_Click(object sender, System.EventArgs e)
{
    GoogleSearchService   Service;  // Search service routine access.
    GoogleSearchResult    Result;   // All of the results.
    ResultElement[]       Items;    // All of the search items.
    DataRow               DR;       // Output data.
    FrmDetail             Details;  // Detail form.

    // Create the search service.
    Service = new GoogleSearchService();

    // Make the call.
    Result = Service.doGoogleSearch(txtLicense.Text, txtKey.Text,
                            Convert.ToInt32(txtIndex.Text),
                            Convert.ToInt32(txtResults.Text),
                            false, "", false, "", "", "");

    // Process the main nodes.
    txtIndex.Text = Convert.ToString(Result.endIndex + 1);
    txtEstResults.Text = Result.estimatedTotalResultsCount.ToString();
    cbEstExact.Checked = Result.estimateIsExact;

    // Create the details form.
    Details = new FrmDetail();

    // Create a data set to store the data and associate
    // it with the grid.
    Details.DS = new DataSet("dsGoogle");
    Details.DS.Tables.Add("Results");
    Details.DS.Tables["Results"].Columns.Add("Title");
    Details.DS.Tables["Results"].Columns.Add("URL");
    Details.DS.Tables["Results"].Columns.Add("Snippet");
    Details.dgOutput.DataSource = Details.DS.Tables["Results"];

    // Process the result elements.
    Items = Result.resultElements;
    foreach (ResultElement Item in Items)
```

```
{
    // Add a row.
    DR = Details.DS.Tables["Results"].NewRow();

    // Add the data to the row.
    DR["Title"] = StringToText(Item.title);
    DR["URL"] = Item.URL;
    if (Item.snippet.Length > 0)
        DR["Snippet"] = StringToText(Item.snippet);
    else
        DR["Snippet"] = StringToText(Item.summary);

    // Display the row on screen.
    Details.DS.Tables["Results"].Rows.Add(DR);
}

    // Show the details form.
    Details.Show();
}
```

The example code looks similar to desktop versions of the code, but also reflects the requirements posed by mobile devices. For example, the application uses a main and a detail form to distribute the data. Even with this concession, the data is a little hard to read on the detail page, as shown in Figure 9.9.

FIGURE 9.9:

The detail page shows all of the links returned from the search.

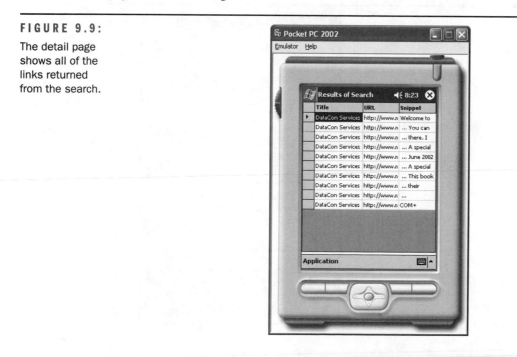

The example begins by creating a new `GoogleSearchService` object. The next step is to use the `doGoogleSearch()` method to obtain the search results. In this case, the application lets the user change the license key, the search phrase, the starting index, and the desired number of results. It's important to limit search criteria to those that the user can reasonably use on a small device or must change to make the application work.

Once the code obtains the results, it changes the required main page entries using values from the main nodes. Figure 9.10 shows typical output from this portion of the example.

The code creates the detail form next. The detail form must include two public objects—a `System.Windows.Forms.DataGrid` and a `System.Data.DataSet`. Visual Studio assumes that you want to keep these members private, but you can't access them properly without the change. You also need to add a reference to the `System.Windows.Forms.DataGrid` namespace to your application since a mobile application doesn't include this control by default.

To store the data in the details form, the code must create the `DataSet` dynamically and assign it to the `DataGrid`, `dgOutput`. Processing the result items is about the same as a desktop application. However, you must keep the display restrictions of a mobile device in mind. This example doesn't include the cached size of the page as part of the output since it's unlikely the mobile device user will store the information locally. The final step is to display the detail form using `Details.Show()`.

FIGURE 9.10:

The code automatically updates the main page with the estimated number of results and a new start index.

Using Third Party Development Products

You don't have to use a Microsoft solution for your Pocket PC. It's relatively easy to build a fully functional application using just a Web page and some JavaScript when you combine it with a third party SOAP solution. One of the better solutions on the market is PocketSOAP (http://www.pocketsoap.com/). This example relies on PocketSOAP, so you'll need to download a copy to use it. Listing 9.2 shows a typical solution using JavaScript. You'll find this example in the \Chapter 09\PocketPC folder of the source code located on the Sybex Web site.

Listing 9.2　　　**Creating a Google Request Using PocketSOAP**

```
function btnRequest_Click()
{
    var SOAPEnv;    // SOAP envelope
    var Transport;  // SOAP transport
    var Details;    // Details array holder

    // Create the envelope.
    SOAPEnv = new ActiveXObject("pocketSOAP.Envelope.2");
    SOAPEnv.SetMethod("doGoogleSearch", "urn:GoogleSearch");

    // Create a parameter to place within the envelope.
    SOAPEnv.Parameters.Create("key", "Your-License-Key");
    SOAPEnv.Parameters.Create(
        "q", "DataCon Services site:www.mwt.net");
    SOAPEnv.Parameters.Create("start", 0);
    SOAPEnv.Parameters.Create("maxResults", 10);
    SOAPEnv.Parameters.Create("filter", false);
    SOAPEnv.Parameters.Create("restrict", "");
    SOAPEnv.Parameters.Create("safeSearch", false);
    SOAPEnv.Parameters.Create("lr", "");
    SOAPEnv.Parameters.Create("ie", "");
    SOAPEnv.Parameters.Create("oe", "");

    // Send the request and receive the data.
    Transport = new ActiveXObject("pocketSOAP.HTTPTransport.2");
    Transport.SOAPAction = "urn:GoogleSearchAction";
    Transport.Send("http://api.google.com/search/beta2",
                   SOAPEnv.Serialize());
    SOAPEnv.Parse(Transport, "UTF-8");

    // Get the Details.
    RecData = new
        VBArray(SOAPEnv.Parameters.Item(0).Nodes.Item(4).Value);

    // Process each URL in turn.
```

```
    Output = "";
    for (Counter = RecData.lbound();
         Counter <= RecData.ubound();
         Counter++)
    {
      Output = Output +
               RecData.getItem(Counter).Nodes.ItemByName("URL").Value +
               "\r\n";
    }
    window.document.SampleForm1.Results.value = Output;
}
```

You could create the required message in a number of ways. The code shows the easiest technique that works reliably with Google Web Services. The example begins by creating a SOAP envelope using the `ActiveXObject()` method. The specific names of the object will change with PocketSOAP version, so you need to select the correct name for the version you're using (see the PocketSOAP help file).

At this point, you may think that you need to create the body of the message. The code performs this task using a different technique than usual. It adds the body elements to the envelope using the `SOAPEnv.Parameters.Create()` method. Notice that you pass the various values as the actual types that Google expects, rather than as strings. The serializer performs any required conversions and provides the required type information as part of the SOAP message.

Once the message is complete, the code creates a transport (connection) object. It adds a SOAP action to the transport and then uses the `Send()` method to send the message. The `Send()` method requires two arguments—an endpoint address and the serialized SOAP data found in `SOAPEnv`.

The code uses the `SOAPEnv.Parse()` method to retrieve the response from the `Transport` object. Although it isn't specifically required, you should provide the character encoding argument, UTF-8 as part of the call. Adding this information ensures the application output is usable. Unfortunately, the data within `SOAPEnv` isn't viewable immediately. The code places the data with `RecData` by creating a new `VBArray` based on the value of the `<resultElements>` node.

Gaining access to the result data as an array means that you can use standard array processing techniques to display the data. In this case, the code uses the `ItemByName()` method to access the `<URL>` element of the return data and place it within a string. The concatenated string appears on screen as the result data to the user. You can easily extend this technique to meet other needs, but the example shows the basics of working with PocketSOAP and Google Web Services.

Developing for a Cellular Telephone or Palm Type Device

Older versions of the Palm and most cellular telephones are so limited in processing capacity and memory that you really won't want to try to create a local Google Web Services application for them. The best alternative is to create a Web application that retrieves and formats the data for the device before passing it along. This example relies on a special ASP.NET application specifically designed for mobile devices. The server detects the device type and pages forms as needed to ensure each form appears correctly on the device.

▶ **TIP**

> Many developers wrongly assume that cellular telephones will remain limited devices. Many companies are working on advanced versions that will let users perform some advanced tasks. For example, Cisco recently released an IP cellular telephone with XML support. This device could allow a user full access to Google from any location. Read more about this new cellular telephone at http://www.eweek.com/article2/0,4149,1259848,00.asp. In addition, at least one company is working with Microsoft to include the Windows Mobile 2003 operating system in a cellular telephone (see the Computerworld story at http://www.computerworld.com/mobiletopics/mobile/story/0,10801,84923,00.html).

Listing 9.3 shows the essential code you need for this example. Make sure you look at the form setup for this example in the source code. You'll find this example in the \Chapter 09\ WebApp folder of the source code located on the Sybex Web site. It's also important to review the installation procedures found in the "Using the ASP.NET Applications in this Book" section of Chapter 6 when placing this code on your development machine.

Listing 9.3   **Creating a Web-based Google Web Services Application**

```
private void btnSubmit_Click(object sender, System.EventArgs e)
{
    GoogleSearchService  Service; // Search service routine access.
    GoogleSearchResult   Result;  // All of the results.
    ResultElement[]      Items;   // All of the search items.
    StringBuilder        SB;      // Contains the output data.

    // Create the search service.
    Service = new GoogleSearchService();

    // Make the call.
    Result = Service.doGoogleSearch(txtLicense.Text, txtKey.Text,
```

```
                                Convert.ToInt32(txtIndex.Text),
                                Convert.ToInt32(txtResults.Text),
                                false, "", false, "", "", "");

    // Update the index.
    txtIndex.Text = Convert.ToString(Result.endIndex);

    // Process the result elements.
    Items = Result.resultElements;
    foreach (ResultElement Item in Items)
    {
        // Blank the StringBuilder.
        SB = new StringBuilder();

        // Add the data to the row.
        SB.Append(StringToText(Item.title));
        SB.Append(" - ");
        SB.Append(Item.URL);

        // Add the data to the list.
        lstOutput.Items.Add(SB.ToString());
    }

    // Show the form.
    this.ActiveForm = Results;
}
```

The code begins as usual by creating a `GoogleSearchService` object. In this case, the variable `doGoogleSearch()` arguments are limited to the license, search phrase, starting index, and number of results. In a production application, you would probably hard code the license value for the user or make it configurable through a dialog box. The idea is to keep the number of entries small because the screen real estate is limited. In addition, all of the entries have default values. You don't want to force the user to type any more information than needed. One configuration option for this application should be a default search so the user can modify it as needed (or use it as presented on screen).

The application output is also very simple. The code places the data in a `StringBuilder` object, and then places this object in a list box. This is one case where you might want to limit the user to less than 10 entries. Experimentation shows that you can get four entries at most on a screen if you include the page title. It's possible to get up to eight short URLs on a screen, but they have to be very short. A good alternative, in this case, is to present the URLs one page at a time. Figure 9.11 shows typical output from this application.

FIGURE 9.11:
Typical output when working with a Web-based application. Image courtesy Openwave Systems Inc.

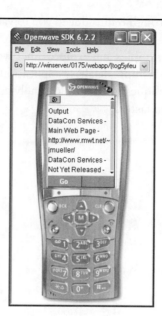

Your Call to Action

This chapter has helped you understand some of the mobile device options at your disposal. You shouldn't consider this chapter complete or comprehensive—mobile device development kits abound. This chapter only discussed some of the more popular options. However, the concepts in this chapter apply equally well to other kinds of mobile development and you can apply the lessons learned to other language products discussed in the book. For example, it's perfectly acceptable to create a mobile device solution using PHP or Java—all you need is a little inspiration.

Now that you have a little more perspective of what's possible, it's time to consider what types of mobile device you want to provide for your Google Web Services application. One mistake that developers make is to assume they must include support for every available device and that's simply not possible—at least not without a major investment in time and resources. A better path is to choose one or two devices to begin development and add additional devices as needed.

Chapters 4 through 8 introduced you to various language options. In each of these chapters, you learned how to access Google Web Services using various techniques. Now it's time to refine those examples and explore other ways to use Google Web Services. Chapter 10 takes you beyond simple database applications into refined database development. You also learn other techniques for creating a finely crafted application that helps users get the information they need faster.

Part III

▶ Refining Your Google Web Services Program

Chapter 10

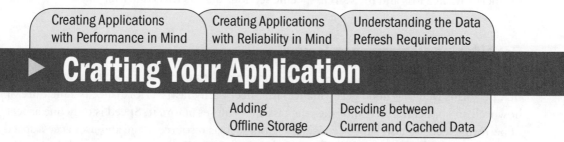

Creating Applications with Performance in Mind | Creating Applications with Reliability in Mind | Understanding the Data Refresh Requirements

▶ **Crafting Your Application**

Adding Offline Storage | Deciding between Current and Cached Data

All of the chapters so far have considered various ways to obtain data from Google. However, great applications do more than just get data—a developer crafts them to get the data efficiently, reliably, and quickly. For example, you could use multiple search techniques to compare results. In some cases, this cross tabulation technique produces search results targeted to a specific need. (See the "Conducting an Expansion Search" section of Chapter 1 for an example of using multiple searches to good effect.) Using the correct search to obtain multiple results makes your application more efficient, but not necessarily more reliable. Sometimes using multiple search techniques will fail to obtain every result because the cross tabulation process eliminates good results as well as those you don't need. Crafting an application means knowing what kind of interaction to perform with Google based on your specific needs.

This chapter assumes that you've read one or more of the preceding language-specific chapters (Chapters 5 through 9) and understand the concepts discussed in Chapters 1 through 4. This chapter answers the question of what comes next. You'll discover some of the concerns you need to address to move your application from *functional* to *usable*. In most cases, this means making your application efficient, reliable, and fast.

One of the major performance and reliability concerns you have to address is the use of databases in your application. Many of the examples in previous chapters showed how to create a database interface for your application so you can store information offline and therefore improve performance. However, the previous chapters left some questions unanswered, such as when to use database storage techniques to improve overall application performance. Sometimes, offline storage is more of a hindrance than a help.

You'll also learn about some new Google search techniques in this chapter. The reason these searches are important is that they help you look for data on Google in new ways. These searches can make your application more efficient or faster (sometimes both). However, you need to consider what you lose in the process. Sometimes the losses will add up to an effective performance loss and the search-specific sections discuss this issue too.

Considering Performance Issues

Some developers confuse the concept of performance with the idea of speed. An application that performs well (has good performance) isn't necessarily fast. Performance is a measure of how well an application accomplishes the task that you set before it. Speed is only one aspect of performance. You also have to consider factors such as resource usage and user access speed (efficiency). In addition, you often have to consider the effect of search repeatability and network bandwidth availability (reliability). The following sections discuss performance concerns for Google applications.

Addressing Speed Concerns

Speed measures how fast an application can perform a task. Many developers concentrate on this factor when developing an application because it's relatively easy to quantify. You can easily demonstrate that a particular coding change or technique improvement provides a corresponding increase in speed. Making changes that result in a speed increase is important when using a Web service such as Google Web Services because your application incurs a performance penalty when it requests the data.

Quantifying speed is relatively easy for most applications because the developer has control over the environment. On the other hand, getting, proving, and quantifying a speed increase with Google Web Services can prove elusive. For example, your application will always slow during peak activity periods on Google—you can't control this factor and it always affects the overall performance of your application. Consequently, long-term speed measurement is essential when working with Google Web Services. You need to consider whether a change actually provides a performance boost or Google Web Services just happened to provide faster results during the initial test. In addition, make one change at a time because you can't accurately measure the effects of multiple changes.

It's also important to consider the state of Google Web Services at the time of your test. Monitor the state of changes by visiting the developer forum at `http://groups.google.com/ groups?group=google.public.web-apis`. This newsgroup helps you keep up-to-date on changes that Google is making that could affect your application. (Google will also send you a newsletter with probable changes to Google Web Services.)

> ▶ **NOTE**
>
> This book doesn't even begin to address local application speed issues because the language you choose, application environment, and platform affect the speed of your application. Look in the language-specific chapters of the book for suggestions on third party resources you can use for that language. Writing code that executes quickly takes time, effort, and planning, so make sure you begin with a good application specification.

Initially, you might get the idea that you have to perform all kinds of weird programming to gain much of a speed increase. However, you can reduce all Google Web Services application speed improvements into five main areas.

Use the Fewest Possible Calls   A combination of optimized searches, explicit input, and data ordering usually serves to reduce the number of calls your application has to make to Google. Every call costs time, so even reducing the number of calls by one round-trip helps. It's important to remember that Google returns data in 10-record chunks, so you should optimize your searches around this number.

Handle Only the Required Data   Some developers parse and store every piece of data that a Web service has to offer with the idea that they might need the information later. In general, you only need to save the site title, URL, and snippet or summary to get good results with Google. In some cases, you might want to save additional information, such as the estimated number of results or the cached size of the page. The important element to consider is that every data manipulation costs time and resources, so you want to work with just the data you need to make your application work well.

Use Offline Storage Effectively   Don't assume that every application has to use offline storage or that you need to store everything offline. An application used to perform research might not benefit from offline storage as most requests are unique and data input is unlikely to repeat. In addition, an application that requires a source of constant updates might not benefit much from complete offline storage—you might want to store just the essentials for locating the data such as an URL. (See the "Using Offline Storage Effectively" section of this chapter for details.)

Improve the Local Application Speed   It's easy to become fixated on the speed of Google Web Services communication and forget local application requirements. The local application has a large effect on application speed. Consider items such as how fast the application makes a request. Because Google relies exclusively on SOAP, your communication choices are limited, but there are still ways to build the request more quickly if you eliminate unnecessary inputs. Consider special programming needs as well. For example, don't rely on Google to sort the data if none of the default sort criteria completely meet your needs—sort the data locally instead.

Define the Best Possible User Experience Many developers assume that fast code always results in a fast application. When a user spends considerable time trying to figure out your application, code execution speed becomes a nonissue. Always check user performance when you consider the speed of your application because the user is going to be the main choke point. Whenever you make the user fast, you gain a significant improvement in application speed (not to mention reducing support costs). Chapter 11 discusses this concept in detail.

> ▶ TIP
>
> Always use the current version of Google Web Services to get speed, efficiency, reliability, and request features. As Google improves its Web service, you'll see options for additional inputs and search types that will make your application faster.

Addressing Efficiency Concerns

Efficiency affects performance by modifying the resource requirements for the application. An efficient application uses resources to their fullest and therefore reduces the cost of using the application. Making an application efficient can improve application speed as well. For example, an application that uses memory efficiently won't have to rely on swap files or other memory enhancements as much, which usually results in a speed boost. However, an efficient application can just as easily slow performance. An application that uses disk storage rather than memory to improve overall system efficiency by freeing memory for other applications is almost certain to work slower than an application that relies exclusively on memory.

> ▶ NOTE
>
> It's important to understand that most performance tuning relies on assumptions that might not be true on the production system. The more control you exercise over the host machine, the better you can control the assumptions you make about performance tuning. Real systems run multiple applications, including background applications such as virus checkers. In addition, applications can experience problems such as memory leaks. Consequently, you need to make the best assumptions you can about the application environment and use those assumptions when tuning your application.

You'll also find that efficiency affects reliability. An application that uses resources conservatively is less likely to run out of resources to process the incoming Google data. Resource deprivation is a major cause of application crashes, so using resources carefully means your application is likely to crash less often.

A Google Web Services application developer only considers the client side of the data exchange because Google takes care of the server side. When a user makes a request, you must consider the efficiency of that request. Inefficient requests can cause Google to return more results than needed and reduce overall system performance. As a side effect, consider how inefficient requests will add to the load the Google Web Services servers must handle. When multiple developers create applications that perform requests inefficiently, server load increases, and could increase the time the user waits for responses.

One of the most important efficiency considerations is the effect of false starts on application efficiency. For example, Google normally lists a snippet for a Web site so you know what it contains before you actually click the link to view it. However, some Web sites use a summary instead, so the smart developer looks for both. You also need to consider the organization of the links—the way Google organizes them might not be the way that you need them. Sometimes it's better to have the user assign a weight to each link so that ordering becomes easier and more appropriate to that particular user's requirements.

▶ TIP

Some users will experience problems using the snippets that Google provides. In some cases, the snippet is too short—it doesn't provide enough information for the user to make a decision about the link. In other cases, the snippet appears in the middle of a sentence or incorporates pieces of multiple sentences, making it impossible to understand. A custom application could request the required information from Google, and then download amplifying information from the Web site to provide the user with better information.

Buffering the Data

Reliability measures several factors. For example, if you can satisfy a search only 80 percent of the time, then the application is only 80 percent reliable, ignoring other reliability factors. Likewise, an application that doesn't provide repeatable results within a given time and without any change in external factors (such as the technique Google uses to create the results) isn't very reliable. Data buffering can help increase reliability by making the results of a search available, even when the network connection to Google fails. In addition, data aging ensures the user obtains consistent results, but not outdated results.

Google, more than any other Web service, can benefit greatly from certain types of data buffering. You already know that Google only allows you to retrieve 10 results at a time. Consequently, most of the application displays in the book revolve around a display that provides 10 links. However, if you want for the user to click a button every time the application needs to retrieve additional links, user efficiency suffers. In general, it's better to request results before you actually need them. You can use one of two techniques to make buffering seamless.

The first approach is to display the links in pages. When using this technique, you build three buffers into the application. The first buffer holds the previous 10 links, the second the current 10 links, and the third the next 10 links. This way the user can page back and forth without experiencing a delay unless the paging is faster than the buffering process can work. Note that the first buffer won't hold any information on the first request because there isn't any previous information; likewise, the third buffer won't hold information on the last request because there isn't any additional information available.

The second approach is to scroll the data. When using this technique, you create one buffer with 10 or more results before the current link and a second buffer that holds the current link plus 10 or more additional links. This technique relies on the user scrolling through the results one link at a time. Because of the limitations that Google places on your use of the Web service, this technique is less efficient. You really do want to request pages in 10-link segments to reduce the number of calls your application makes.

No matter what buffering technique you use, it pays to place the buffering code in a separate thread. Whenever the user changes the current record, the application should create a thread to request more data as a background process. Making the request using this technique reduces the performance hit and makes the request process almost invisible to the user.

Listing 10.1 shows a typical example of the paged buffer approach. This listing shows only the essentials—the actual source code is much longer. You'll find the complete listing for this example in the \Chapter 10\BufferedPage folder of the source code located on the Sybex Web site.

Listing 10.1   **Using the Paged Buffer Approach**

```
// These variables track the current index number.
String    NextIndex;
String    PreviousIndex;

// This variable defines when an update is complete.
Boolean   IsUpdating;

private void btnTest_Click(object sender, System.EventArgs e)
```

```
{
    DataRow  NewData; // New data for SearchResults.

    // Wait until the update is complete.
    while (IsUpdating)
        lblUpdating.Visible = true;
    lblUpdating.Visible = false;

    // Create a thread to get the next results.
    Thread ReqThread = new Thread(new ThreadStart(NextRequest));

    // Determine which type of processing to perform.
    if (btnTest.Text == "&Test")
    {
        // Make the initial request.
        MakeRequest("SearchResults");

        // Get the next results by starting a thread to
        // perform the work.
        ReqThread.Start();

        // Continue by changing the button text.
        btnTest.Text = "&Next";

        // Enable the previous button.
        btnPrevious.Enabled = true;

        // Set the next index value.
        NextIndex = txtResults.Text;
    }
    else
    {
        // Verify there are more entries to obtain.
        if (Int32.Parse(NextIndex) < Int32.Parse(txtEstResults.Text))
        {
            // Set the current index value.
            PreviousIndex = txtIndex.Text;
            txtIndex.Text = NextIndex;
            NextIndex = Convert.ToString(
                Int32.Parse(NextIndex) + Int32.Parse(txtResults.Text));

            // Transfer the NextResults table to the SearchResults table.
            dsGoogle.Tables["SearchResults"].Clear();
            foreach (DataRow DR in dsGoogle.Tables["NextResults"].Rows)
            {
                NewData = dsGoogle.Tables["SearchResults"].NewRow();
                NewData.ItemArray = DR.ItemArray;
                dsGoogle.Tables["SearchResults"].Rows.Add(NewData);
            }

            // Get the next results by starting a thread to
```

```
            // perform the work.
            ReqThread.Start();
        }
    }
}

private void NextRequest()
{
    // We're updating.
    IsUpdating = true;

    // Request the next set of results. Place them in the NextResults
    // buffer table.
    if (Int32.Parse(NextIndex) < Int32.Parse(txtEstResults.Text))
        MakeRequest("NextResults");

    // Request the previous set of results. Place them in the
    // PreviousResults buffer table.
    if (Int32.Parse(txtIndex.Text) >= Int32.Parse(txtResults.Text))
        MakeRequest("PreviousResults");

    // Done updating.
    IsUpdating = false;
}
```

The example begins by creating a thread. The thread isn't executing, but it's available for later use. The thread code appears in the NextRequest() method shown later in this listing. As you can see, this method calls the MakeRequest() method. The MakeRequest() code is essentially the same as the code in Listing 6.5. All that I added was the ability to use more than one table to store the data.

The next step is to ensure the thread isn't updating the database. It's not an issue of reentrancy, but one of database usage. You must make sure that the client doesn't perform multiple updates of the same table. When the user clicks Next or Previous when an update is completing, the application displays a message. The message is cleared when the update process completes.

Whenever the user starts the application, the DataSet is empty, which means the code must fill it with data. Consequently, the code has two paths to follow. The first case occurs only when the user creates a new query; the second case occurs whenever the user moves between pages of the query results.

An initial query must fill the SearchResults table of dsGoogle, so the application calls MakeRequest() without using a thread. This initial request is the only time most users will need to wait for results. In most other cases, the data will already appear in one of the two caches. After the application fills the SearchResults table, the code starts the thread using ReqThread.Start(), which fills the two other tables in the background.

The code also makes a few other changes to the application at this point. The code replaces Test button with the Next button and enables the Previous button. Finally, the code sets the NextIndex value. This string holds the next index that the application will need to find.

Both the Previous and Next buttons operate the same, just in different directions in the query set. The first step is to verify that the query set contains additional links to process. Otherwise, the code could look for nonexistent index values. At this point, the code updates the three index values: PreviousIndex, txtIndex.Text (current), and NextIndex.

The data the user needs already appears in the NextResults table (PreviousResults if the user clicks the Previous button). The code simply clears the current SearchResults table data and fills it with the NextResults table data. Note the technique used in this case. Depending on the language you use, you might need to use other data transfer techniques. Finally, the code starts the thread. Again, this step fills the two cache tables in the background.

Considering Reliability Issues

Reliable application performance is essential if you plan to use Google Web Services for any type of business purpose. The "Buffering the Data" section explains how buffering affects reliability and therefore application performance. This section considers reliability from a user perspective.

Most people associate reliability with availability, but that's only part of the picture. When working with Google Web Services, you need to consider four reliability factors.

Availability of Data   Unless a user can access the Google data, using the application you create is useless. Fortunately, Google Web Services has a high availability rate, so most desktop applications will run fine even if you don't include backup data through a database. However, you need some form of local and/or remote database support for mobile applications where high availability is a requirement and a connection isn't always available.

Consistency of Results   Providing consistent results to application users is important. Consistency means including all data (or a standard response to all data outputs). Sometimes, Google won't provide an output that you need. For example, many links won't provide a directory category list (the <directoryCategories> element). If you feel that this information is important, you'll have to find an alternative means of providing the directory category list when the Web site doesn't. Consistency also means providing similar response times (when possible) and standard error notifications.

Accessibility of Google Site   You have to decide, at some point, whether you can tolerate any availability problems with Google Web Services because they'll eventually occur. On the day I wrote this information, my ISP experienced connection problems due to an overzealous road crew. Even though Google was probably accessible to someone, it wasn't available to me. To provide maximum reliability, you must provide a cache of some sort. In my case, I had a database full of searches that I'd performed over the last few days. No, it didn't have everything I needed, but at least I had some resources. However, this requirement doesn't always mean creating a database to hold the data, although that is one option. You can also use memory caches or disk-based browser caches. For that matter, your application can rely on the cache provided by a proxy server. The point is to provide some alternative, if you need it, for the few times that Google Web Services doesn't respond.

Availability of the Local Application Strange things can happen to an application between the time it leaves your development machine and when it appears on the user's machine. In general, you need to perform complete application testing on several (more is better) user machines that don't include all the features of your development machine. Make sure you test obscure as well as common features. For example, test every search type that your application supports. It's also important to test features such as the use of cached pages. Make sure you verify that the cached page feature works as needed so that the user doesn't have to wrestle with your application to get the desired results.

Considering the Data Refresh Requirements

Google doesn't require you to refresh your data. You can store the links you retrieve from Google as long as needed. In fact, you can build link histories if you want to provide a basis for analysis. However, you'll eventually need to refresh the data you receive from Google because the links will become outdated. The technique you use to refresh the data depends on how you're using the data within your application. A research firm that deals with relatively stable data might not need to refresh its links as often as someone who works with computers for a living. The stability of the data makes a difference in the technique used to refresh the data, as well as the refresh interval.

All of the examples in this book take a dynamic approach. The application checks the date that it last retrieved any data in the database from Google Web Services in response to a user request. If the data is too old, the application requests the information from Google Web Services. Unfortunately, this means that some users will observe an inconsistent delay in responses. You could also build a database of links and refresh those links every night at a convenient time—when no one is likely to need the information. The idea is to refresh the data at a convenient interval using the technique that best suits your organization.

Make sure you keep up with current Google policy regarding offline data storage. Although the licensing agreement doesn't currently require you to update your data, a future agreement might add this requirement. The reason that I mention this particular potential change is that most Web services do require you to update your data at regular intervals to ensure your application accurately represents that Web service.

Sometimes you need to consider the source of Google data. None of the links that Google provides are based on Google data. You can find more than a few books on the market that purport to help you change your Web page characteristics to make the Google search engine work in your favor. In a few cases, Web sites include search terms that have nothing to do with the content of their sites. Consequently, a link that looks like it has good information might not have any useful data. This is the reason that you want to maintain a personal database of good links when accuracy is essential and validate that database against Google at reasonable intervals.

You can't extend permanent storage to volatile information such as precise page content unless you work in an area of research where the data remains relatively stable. A Web page owner can update and modify data at any point, which would make your locally stored cache inaccurate. When your business depends on the accuracy of the data you derive from Internet sites, you need to keep that data updated to reflect changes in technology. As people learn new facts, they'll update their site to reflect these changes and you need to keep apprised of them. However, a local cache does afford you the opportunity to compare the page with your cached page to see what changed—reducing the time you spend researching new information.

Using Offline Storage Effectively

Many of the performance enhancements you can add to your Google Web Services application revolve around some type of offline storage. How your application uses offline storage makes a big difference in performance enhancement. In most cases the vendor and product you choose will determine factors such as reliability and availability. The following sections describe a few of the issues you need to consider as part of your offline storage strategy.

Choosing the Correct Offline Storage Strategy

All of the examples so far in the book have considered offline storage from the perspective of storing the Google data that an application needs to handle multiple requests for the same information. This technique is the most important strategy to learn from a speed and reliability perspective. However, it's not the only strategy to consider because some applications simply don't benefit from this approach.

Another offline storage technique to consider is the use of a database containing links, page titles, phrases, categories, or other information. You can associate the information with specific non-changing data such as a research topic description. This database can help users quickly identify previously researched information. Even if you can't save other information from Google Web Services, saving these values can improve user efficiency by reducing the number of research requests the user has to make.

Don't become fixated on output data when working with Google Web Services. All of the requests you make have value too. For example, you might create a database of recent request data to provide hints to the user. As the user fills in request data, your application can make suggestions for the next input value and reduce the chance the user will make an invalid request. Likewise, you can store requests that didn't work. Making a quick check for these requests before you send the data to Google will save a round-trip over the Internet and improve application speed. The application can also alert the user to the fact that the request won't work and make suggestions on how to change the request.

> ▶ **TIP**

Google provides the `<searchComments>` and `<searchTips>` elements to alert users to search conditions that didn't result in a valid return value. For example, a specific combination of search terms might not return any links. You can search these search combinations in a database and simply return the `<searchComments>` and `<searchTips>` values to the user, rather than waste time making a round-trip call to Google Web Services.

Selecting a Database That Suits Your Needs

The database-related examples in the book rely on one of three database managers: SQL Server, Microsoft Access, or MySQL. You can find many other alternatives—these are just a sampling of what's available. I chose these three database managers because they represent several steps in functionality, performance, ease of use, and cost. It's important to get a database manager that you can afford, that will perform the tasks you need it to do, and is easy enough to manage, so you might choose any of the myriad alternatives on the market.

SQL Server is the most expensive of the three, but it also provides the best functionality. Microsoft constantly touts the speed of SQL server, but it's a memory hog and can consume copious amounts of hard drive space. Given the complex tasks that SQL Server can perform, you might not find it as easy to use as Access, but the GUI-based tools do make it easier to use than the command line interface of MySQL.

Microsoft Access is probably the easiest of the database managers to use because it provides a single GUI interface where you manage everything. Some developers feel that Access is only useful for local databases, but many small businesses rely on Access as their only multiuser database manager. From a speed perspective, Access is probably the slowest of the three database managers. However, it's very easy on hard drive use and relatively light on memory use as well.

> ▶ **NOTE**
>
> You can use the Microsoft Data Engine (MSDE) as a substitute for SQL Server in some cases. It always works as a good alternative to SQL Server for local development. In some cases, you can also use MSDE as an alternative to SQL Server for groups of up to five people. Make sure that MSDE actually meets your needs before you spend time installing it—this product doesn't include all the features of SQL Server. Because MSDE relies on the same DLLs as SQL Server in many cases, you'll also want to apply any required patches to ensure the integrity of your system. Learn more about MSDE at `http://www.microsoft.com/sql/msde/default.asp`.

MySQL is the least expensive of the three database managers—you simply download your copy from a Web site. You'll find that this database manager is the hardest of the three to use because almost everything happens at the command line. Some middle-sized companies use MySQL because it has the speed required to handle larger applications. It's also relatively easy on memory use, but about equal with SQL Server when it comes to hard drive space requirements.

Considering Database Storage Alternatives

Don't assume that you need a database to provide the benefits of local storage. It's true that you need a database when the usage requirements are high or you need long-term storage of information. However, storing the Google data isn't exactly rocket science—you can use any of a number of alternatives. For example, the "Using a Script to Call an XSLT Page" section of Chapter 3 discusses a technique where you rely on the capabilities of a browser to process the Google data. In this case, the simple fact that the browser caches pages it downloads from the Internet is enough to improve performance for multiple calls for the same data—at least for the local user. Obviously, the browser caching solution won't work for multiple sessions if the user sets the browser to clear the cache after each session.

Sometimes you need something a little more substantial than the cache provided by a browser, but still don't need permanent storage. In these situations, you can use an in-memory solution. The simplest solution is an array or other memory structure. However, many languages also provide actual caches you can use and some vendors provide caches as part of their third party product. For example, the `DataSet` object provided with Visual Studio .NET is actually a form of in-memory cache, but it definitely has database functionality and you can link it to a physical database.

> ▶ **TIP**
>
> You can find a great article on caching techniques for PHP and Web services ("Caching With PHP Cache_Lite") at `http://www.devshed.com/c/b/PHP` or `http://www.devshed.com/c/a/PHP/Caching-With-PHP-Cache_Lite/`. This article considers important issues, such as using the browser cache and implementing server-based caching.

It's possible to get by without using a database even when you need some form of permanent storage. For example, you could store a list of home page links in an XML file. In fact, you can easily extend XML storage to entire requests or other types of permanent data. At some point, the performance of such a system is going to become problematic, but it works for small amounts of data for one user and could even work for a few users if you use a central storage location for the XML files.

Choosing between Current and Cached Data

Google caches Web pages as a means to obtain the data when the original source changes or becomes unavailable. You can use a cached version of a page for comparison purposes or when the site goes offline for some reason. I've often used cached pages to retrieve data that the original Web site no longer carries. The actual uses for cached pages are unlimited.

The problem with cached pages is that they contain old data. You can't depend on a cached page to provide current information you need to make a decision on a research requirement or business need. Consequently, you need to define when a cached page is acceptable or even required as part of your application setup. The user needs guidelines on how to best use this feature with your particular application. With this in mind, Listing 10.2 shows how to obtain cached data from Google Web Services and display it on screen. You'll find this example in the \Chapter 10\CachedPage folder of the source code located on the Sybex Web site.

Listing 10.2   **Obtaining Cached Data**

```
private void btnTest_Click(object sender, System.EventArgs e)
{
   GoogleSearchService  GSS;        // Interacts with Google.
   Byte[]               Response;   // The cached page.
   Char[]               CResp;      // A char array of the page.
   Int32                Counter;    // Loop counter.
   String               Results;    // The page as a string.
   StreamWriter         DataOut;    // Disk storage for data.
   Object               Blank;      // A blank object.
```

```
// Initialize the service.
GSS = new GoogleSearchService();

// Get the cached page.
Response = GSS.doGetCachedPage(@txtLicense.Text,
                               @txtCached.Text);

// Convert the cached data to a character array.
CResp = new Char[Response.Length];
for (Counter = 0; Counter < Response.Length; Counter++)
   CResp[Counter] = Convert.ToChar(Response[Counter]);

// Use the character array to create a string.
Results = new String(CResp);

// Save the string to a file.
DataOut = new StreamWriter(@txtOutput.Text);
DataOut.Write(Results);
DataOut.Close();

// Display the cached data on screen.
Blank = new object();
wbOutput.Navigate(@txtOutput.Text,
                  ref Blank,
                  ref Blank,
                  ref Blank,
                  ref Blank);
}
```

The code begins by creating the `GoogleSearchService` object, `GSS`, as usual. In this case, the request arguments are relatively simple, so all you need to do is request them from the user and input them directly to the `GSS.doGetCachedPage()` method call.

Unfortunately, the data you receive isn't ready to use. Google sends the data as a base 64 encoded data stream. (See the "Defining the Cache Request Arguments" and "Defining the Cached Page Results" sections of Chapter 4 for details on this process.) The example overcomes this problem by converting the resulting `Byte` array to a `Char` array. The .NET Framework provides the means to use a `Char` array as input to the `String()` constructor.

At this point, you have a string that contains the HTML for the Web site. Viewing this string shows that it contains the proper escapes for saving the data to disk. You can't simply place the information on screen and hope that someone will read it. Consequently, the code creates a `StreamWriter` object and uses it to place the data on disk.

The `wbOutput` object is a standard COM Microsoft Web Browser control. You can add the Web browser to your toolbox by selecting the Microsoft Web Browser option shown in Figure 10.1 from the Customize Toolbox dialog box (accessed by right-clicking the Toolbox and selecting Add/Remove Items from the context menu).

The IDE automatically builds the required interface code for you. However, the resulting `wbOutput.Navigate()` method requires entries for all of the arguments, even though you don't need to provide them to make the control work. The example gets around this problem by supplying a blank object as input that the control simply ignores. When the control navigates to the data saved on disk, it displays it as shown in Figure 10.2.

FIGURE 10.1:

You can use a standard Microsoft Web Browser control to display the results.

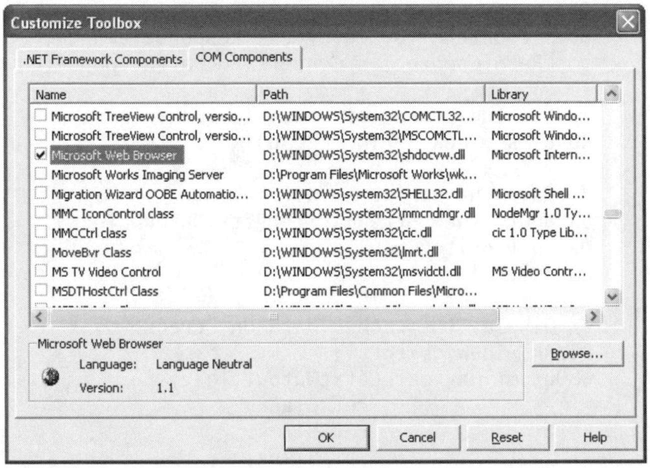

FIGURE 10.2:

Cached pages are relatively easy to use once you convert the data.

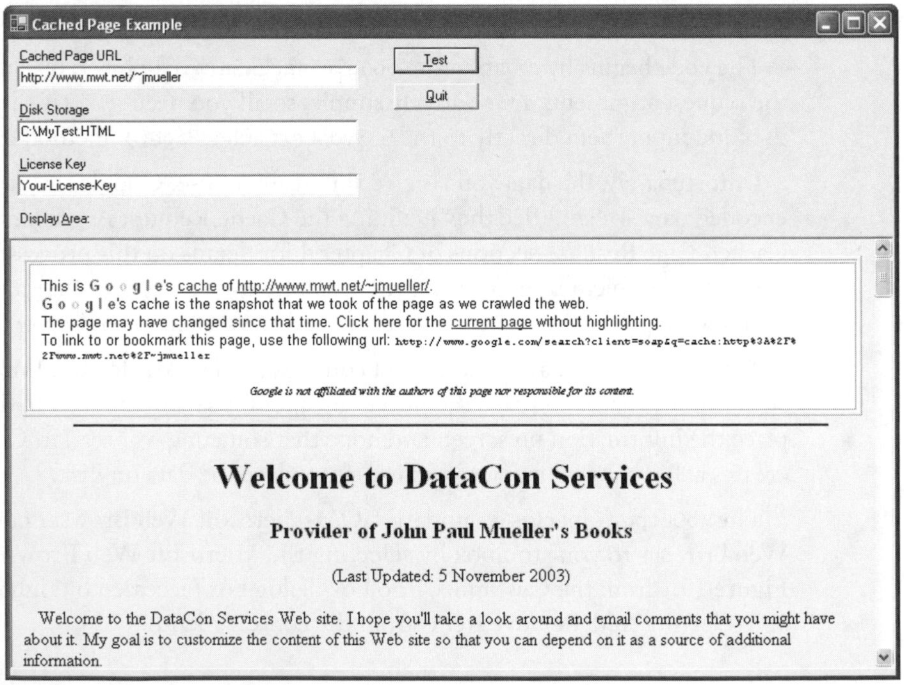

Your Call to Action

This chapter considers some of the fit and finish items for your Google Web Services application. Making your application reliable, efficient, and fast is important if you want to get the most out of the features Google Web Services provides. However, it's also important to remember that some choices are mutually exclusive—you might have to give up a little performance to obtain better application reliability.

While reading this chapter you considered options, not absolutes. The only absolute is your application needs. You need to use the information presented in this chapter to address your specific application needs. Consider elements such as the application platform and user environment as part of the option selection process. For example, a mobile device will probably give up a little reliability to ensure the application operates fast enough, but this isn't always a hard and fast rule. You might find that your particular mobile application helps locate sensitive information on Google (such as links for a product you want to buy) and therefore requires superior reliability.

Chapter 11 continues the process of honing your application. However, instead of considering the application requirements, Chapter 11 considers user requirements. Making an application faster may net you an overall gain in performance, but making the user faster always nets an overall gain in performance because user task speed is usually the critical performance factor for an application.

Chapter 11

Working with Specific Types of Users | Creating Flexible Interfaces | Developing for Users with Special Needs

▶ Other Refinements You Should Consider

Considering Privacy Issues | Letting the User Tell You about Your Application | Building Applications That Use More Than One Web Service

Building an application that works with Google Web Services means doing more than simply writing code that interacts with the Web service and making it perform well. The application requires other refinements, such as an easy to use interface and some means of providing feedback so you can continue to improve the application later. This chapter offers suggestions in both areas.

No matter what kind of application you write, you must consider the user's needs to ensure someone will actually use the application. Most developers realize that a Graphical User Interface (GUI) is better than a character mode interface and a few even realize that help is a requirement—not a nicety. A few developers understand that tooltips are also important and speed keys (shortcut keys) help users keep their hands on the keyboard so they can remain efficient. These elements, along with layout and design, are common to any application you might create. The market already has a number of good User Interface (UI) design books, so I won't replicate their information here (you'll find some of them listed in the "Selecting User Interface Design Resources" sidebar in the "Targeting a Specific User Type" section). This chapter helps you decide how to create a great interface for your Google Web Services application using a combination of general and specific coding techniques.

Along with specific interface requirements for your application, this chapter also considers helpful design decisions. For example, although no one requires you to address privacy issues, many users are beginning to request this functionality and might not visit your site more than once if you don't provide a privacy policy. In addition, it's important to personalize the user's experience with your site so you don't have to ask the same questions every time the user visits. A user might like to use a specific stylesheet with your Web site or request a specific setup for your application. Personalization helps users have a better experience and improves user efficiency.

Feedback is the most common feature that you'll use in this chapter because even a Web site that performs simple searches should include some type of user feedback form. Desktop applications also benefit from feedback, although far too few applications include this feature. The idea is to provide a means for a user to make a comment about your application immediately during use—when an idea, concern, or other comment is fresh and they're most likely to send it to you.

The final section of this chapter explores a new kind of application—one in which you combine two Web services. It may seem like a bit of a stretch today, but future applications may well make use of several Web services at a time. The functionality provided by a Web service is certainly easier to manage than building that functionality on your own. This application combines Google Web Services with Amazon Web Services to create a research application for products.

Targeting a Specific User Type

You'll invest a lot of time honing your Google Web Services application if you plan to present it to other people. For that matter, it doesn't hurt to hone your application even if you only plan to use it to meet your own needs. No matter who uses your application, you have to consider their needs or the user will quickly tire of the application and not use it. Targeting specific user types helps you design an interface that works well, meets the user's needs, and requires less maintenance time.

Many books and Web sites on application design target generic applications—the type that anyone could use. However, this book considers a more specific application type—one that relies on Google Web Services. Even so, the number of uses for applications in this group is quite large, so you need to consider your specific application. It's essential to consider how the user will interact with the application and the user's skill level. In fact, you should consider the following elements when targeting your application to meet a specific user's needs.

- The environment in which the application executes—Web applications often have different requirements than desktop applications.

- The device the user will use to access your application—mobile devices have strict limitations that will affect your user interface design.

- The user's skill level—advanced users require less help and will quickly tire of repetitive help offers.

- The input and output requirements for the application—complex applications (those with more input or output) could require multiple screens.

- The request parameters of the application—simple Google searches that don't use sorting are the easiest to accommodate.

- The user's expectations for the application—most users want to perform research of some kind.

- The availability of localized help—users of Web applications typically receive less help than users of desktop applications.

- The use of special features—a cached page is going to be harder to manipulate than a list of links.

Selecting User Interface Design Resources

Getting great user interface design references helps you get started faster and ensures you won't make as many mistakes during the design process. Typically, you'll find that books are better than Web sites for this kind of information because books have more space to cover contingencies that articles or other online resources can't discuss. However, don't discount Web sites—you might find something that meets a specific need. Newsgroups can help, but you need to state the design issues you want to overcome very clearly and take any advice with a grain of salt because the developer helping you might not have a clear picture of the issues.

You can find a number of good books online. The trick is to find a book that's either completely generic or meets the need of a specific environment. For example, if you want to design a Web application, then you might consider reading *Designing Web Usability: The Practice of Simplicity* by Jakob Nielsen (New Riders, 1999). Although Web developers could rely on this book, desktop developers can benefit most from *The Humane Interface: New Directions for Designing Interactive Systems* by Jef Raskin (Addison-Wesley, 2000) and *About Face 2.0: The Essentials of Interaction Design* by Alan Cooper and Robert Reimann (John Wiley & Sons, 2003). A good generic book that addresses interface design as a component of total application design is *Designing Highly Useable Software* by Jeff Cogswell (Sybex, 2004).

It's possible to find good help online. For example, the Microsoft User Interface site at `http://msdn.microsoft.com/nhp/default.asp?contentid=28000443` provides a wealth of information on topics as diverse as accessibility and Microsoft Agent. Dr. Jakob Nielsen presents a number of usability articles at `http://www.useit.com/alertbox/`. This monthly column provides continuing help with your application as user needs and expectations change. In some cases, you can even find online books such as *Task-Centered User Interface Design* by Clayton Lewis and John Rieman at `http://www.hcibib.org/tcuid/`. The authors offer this book as shareware, so make sure you support them if you use it.

Locating a newsgroup that offers advice on user interfaces isn't hard—it's hard to find good advice. Generally, you'll need to find a newsgroup that caters to your programming language and choice of device (such as the .NET Compact Framework for mobile devices at `microsoft.public.dotnet.framework.compactframework`). Some newsgroups, such as `comp.human-factors`, provide limited generic help should you need it. After many hours of searching, I couldn't find a suitable newsgroup devoted to the topic of user interfaces. Contact me at `JMueller@mwt.net` if you know of such a newsgroup and I'll post it on my Web site with the updates for this book.

It's relatively easy to use these criteria to build a profile of an individual user, but assessing the needs of multiple user types can become more difficult. In this case, you need to build a profile of each user type and then organize the users by priority. This exercise lets you determine how much weight to give each requirement. An advanced user who only uses the application once a month can easily turn off the extra help you provide to novice users (assuming that you provide a switch for turning the help off).

Sometimes several user types will conflict, making prioritization essential. For example, if most of your users will employ a cellular telephone to access the site, you might need to provide alternatives for the few desktop users who visit. In many cases, careful development will allow both groups to access the site—the desktop users might notice that the site is a little plain, but that's about it. The goal is to accommodate the needs of each group based on their level of access to your site—don't accommodate the needs of a small group to the detriment of the users who normally support your site.

Designing Flexible Interfaces

No matter how well you design your application, someone will complain that some feature doesn't work as expected. During my years of programming, I've personally seen arguments between users about order of fields on a form. One discussion about a screen degenerated into an intense argument about the order of name elements on the form (one user wanted last name first—the other wanted the first name to appear first). Users will grumble about every aspect of your application given a chance and you'll never satisfy all the users. Some developers solve the problem by giving up and creating the application they want. However, this solution probably works least often because the user's immediate reaction is that the developer isn't listening and lacks any form of human interaction skills.

Flexible user interfaces resolve the user problem by letting each user design the interface that meets their specific needs. Just how flexible you can make the interface depends on a number of factors including the application environment and the programming language you use. Making Web applications flexible is somewhat harder than for most desktop applications because many browsers lack the support required to move visual elements around and perform other manipulations the user would like. Depending on your programming skill, schedule, programming language, and patience, you can make some desktop applications so flexible that the user has control over every display element and the application will remember its configuration between sessions.

Let's start with something a little more reasonable than complete application configuration. Even the most mundane Web page allows configuration. For example, you can use Cascading Style Sheets (CSS) to format the Web page. Some browsers let the user substitute their CSS file for the default that you provide on your Web site—making it possible for the user to have complete control over the presentation of information even if you don't provide any other form of programming with the Web page. Some sites extend this principle by providing multiple CSS files. A simple cookie entry controls which CSS file the Web site uses when presenting information to the user. Desktop applications are even easier to control in this area. All you need is an Options dialog box containing the display element settings so the user can change them to meet specific needs. Most desktop applications already provide this feature. Make sure you save the user options in a file or other central location (such as the Windows Registry) if you offer this feature.

The next level of application configuration is component selection. For example, not every Google Web Services user will want to sort the output results. It might seem that simply ignoring the sort field would work, but unnecessary fields are annoying to some users. Again, Web pages can use a cookie to store a list of fields or controls the user doesn't want to see. You'll likely have to provide a configuration page to support this form of application setup—adding a simple link to the page to allow configuration usually works fine. Desktop applications can use an Options dialog box. Most desktop applications don't offer this feature—likely because the developer didn't think to offer the feature or assumed that everyone would want access to every field.

> **▶ NOTE**

Don't make every field on a form optional. A user will have to make some entries to perform even basic tasks. For example, a user can't perform a search without entering a search phrase, so the search phrase field isn't optional. However, hiding optional fields can make the application faster and easier to use. You might even find that you want to include some developer-only fields in the list that you control with special entries in the configuration file.

Web applications don't commonly use toolbars or special menus in the same way that desktop applications use them. However, both environments can benefit from some level of customization for both items. Quite a few desktop applications offer this feature. Generally, the user selects a special menu command that allows them to move menu or toolbar elements around, add new menu or toolbar options, or delete options the user feels aren't important. Trying to implement this feature on a Web site would be very hard, but doable if you use some technologies, such as ASP.NET. Make sure you offer a feature that returns everything to its default state in case the user makes a few too many changes.

The ultimate level of interface flexibility lets the user move controls around on screen. This feature lets one user place names in last name order and another user place them in first name order. Complete interface control is difficult to implement on a desktop application and likely impossible for a Web application. Applications that allow complete interface configuration are extremely rare. However, a Google Web Services application doesn't suffer from the level of complexity that some applications do, so this might be a viable solution in some cases. At least you can provide the user with enough flexibility to define precisely how the display appears so that your application works as efficiently for that user as possible.

▶ **NOTE**

If you plan to provide complete interface flexibility for your application, you should go all the way by allowing the user to change even mundane features such a font size and typeface. To an extent, you could even let the user change the button captions and control the color of the tiniest text element. It's even possible to let the user add graphics and perform other odd configuration changes given the right programming language, a platform that supports the changes, and enough time.

Addressing Users with Special Needs

This section of the chapter considers features that make an application easier to use for those with special needs. Don't automatically equate special needs with physical challenges faced by some people. As users age, they need better screens because their eyesight begins to fail. Older hands often suffer from arthritis and require more options for executing commands. Even someone who's very young can require help at the end of the day when a day full of eye-fatiguing research means using a display with larger type. With this in mind, the following sections describe things you can do to make your Google Web Services application more usable without a large investment in time or effort.

▶ **NOTE**

A section of a chapter can't possibly address every accessibility requirement. In addition, if you work for an organization that provides services to the government, you have certain legal requirements you must meet to address accessibility concerns. See my book, *Accessibility for Everybody: Understanding the Section 508 Accessibility Requirements* (Apress, 2003) for a complete treatment of this topic.

Adding Hints for Desktop Applications

Desktop applications commonly rely on hints to help a user understand their operation. For example, when you see a letter of a field underlined, you realize that pressing Alt+<key> selects that field. If the developer has wisely selected a different letter for each field, every field is a single key combination away. The use of speed keys helps touch typists work faster by allowing them to keep their hands on the keyboard, rather than use a mouse. However, speed keys also help those who can't use a mouse at all. In this case, the user has a choice of pressing Tab multiple times to locate the field or using a speed key to access it—the speed key is preferable because it's faster and requires fewer key presses. (Make sure you set the order of the tabs as well so the user progresses in a logical manner when pressing Tab.) Adding speed keys to your application takes moments—all you need to do is type an ampersand in front of the letter you want to use for the speed key for most Windows languages.

Another common hint that also serves an accessibility need is the tooltip. Adding a tooltip for each control lets you explain the purpose of that control using a single sentence. If the user needs additional information, they can refer to the online help, but this feature usually provides enough information so that a trip to the help file isn't necessary. From an accessibility perspective, a screen reader or other piece of accessibility software normally reads the information in the tooltip to the user. Consequently, the tooltip helps users with vision needs build an image of the application and its functionality in their mind. The technique used to add a tooltip to an application depends on the language product used. For example, Visual Studio .NET developers can rely on the simple addition of a `ToolTip` control to make the tooltip addition. The `ToolTip` control adds a new ToolTip property to each of the other controls—just type the text you want to appear in the tooltip. The desktop applications in this book contain both speed keys and tooltips to ensure anyone can use them.

> ▶ **NOTE**

Always try to support the accessibility features provided by the operating system. For example, Windows supports a number of accessibility features, including the use of high contrast displays for users with special visual needs. Some of these features, such as support for a screen reader, are so easy to implement that there's never a good reason not to implement them. Other features, such as the use of the Windows ShowSounds, can incur a higher cost in programming time because most programming languages don't support the feature.

Platforms such as Windows include a number of operating system–specific accessibility features as well. Windows includes a high contrast setting that displays images in just a few colors using large fonts. The display makes it a lot easier for people with less than perfect vision to see the display. However, many people with normal vision also use the setting at the end of a hard day when a standard display is apt to give them a headache. The problem for developers is that the high contrast setting tends to make labels and other text elements on a form difficult or impossible to see because the element consumes too much space. Figure 11.1 shows a typical example of this problem.

FIGURE 11.1:

High contrast displays can make some information unreadable.

I chose this particular dialog box because it demonstrates two common problems. First, the information in the middle of the display is garbled—unreadable for the most part. Second, the application-specific text didn't size with the change in high contrast setting, so the application user receives minimum benefit. Generally, you can avoid problems with the high contrast display by testing this setting with your application. All you need to do is open the Accessibility Options applet in the Control Panel, select the Display tab, and click Use High Contrast. Click OK and you'll see your display change to a high contrast representation. Note that Windows supports a number of high contrast configurations, so you might want to try out several with your application.

One of the biggest problems with Google Web Services is that it provides a wealth of data—too much in some cases. It's easy to overwhelm someone with special needs with data they'll never use. The problem isn't quite as noticeable with many Web applications because the Web presentation format can reduce the problem. However, desktop applications can suffer significant information overload problems. In some cases, you'll need to present details one at a time or on separate displays to keep the display focused on the essentials.

Adding Hints for Web Applications

Web applications use many of the same hints used by desktop applications, but the techniques for creating the hint differ. As with desktop applications, one of the more important hints is the use of speed keys. You implement a speed key using a combination of special text formatting and HTML tag attributes, as shown in the following code for a label.

```
<label id="Input">
    <span style="TEXT-DECORATION: underline">I</span>nput:
</label>
<input id="InputVal"
       type=text
       value="Hello World"
       name="InputVal"
       accesskey="I"
       title="Type the input string."
       autocomplete=on/>
```

The user needs to know which Alt+<key> combination to use to access the field, so the `style` attribute for the label is important—it underlines the target key. The `accesskey` attribute defines the speed key for the field associated with the label. The `title` attribute defines the tooltip text. When the user hovers the mouse over the input, the browser displays a tooltip, just like a desktop application. Use the `autocomplete` attribute to control the use of automatic completion for the field. Some fields benefit from this setting because the user is likely to type the same text more than one time, but for other fields automatic completion is a nuisance because the user will never type the same text twice.

Images require a little special handling because you can't easily determine whether the user can see the image or not. In this case, you don't use the `title` attribute because that would display a tooltip. In most cases, you'll use the `alt` attribute, as shown here, to provide a description of the image.

```
<img align="middle"
     src="OddImage.gif"
     alt="This image contains the words, 'An Odd Image'."
     height=130
     width=130/>
```

It's easy to use the `ProductDescription` field returned in the `ProductInfo` structure for the `alt` attribute text in most cases. You'll find an example of an accessible Web page in the

\Chapter 11\AccessibleWeb folder of the source code found on the Sybex Web site. Try this page out in a browser to see how your browser reacts to it. In most cases, browsers do provide support for accessibility features—at least the basic features described in this section.

The example is a little plain. Generally, you should avoid adding too much formatting to your Web page if you can help it, but most of us like a little color and some formatting to make the page interesting. You can follow some basic guidelines to avoid causing accessibility problems while you dress up the page. For example, use CSS to avoid formatting problems. Someone with special needs can substitute a CSS file of their choosing that makes the page easier to read and you still get the formatting you want. Make sure your page is compliant by testing it with any of a number of online testers such as Bobby (http://bobby.watchfire.com/bobby/html/en/index.jsp).

Considering Color-Blind Users

Before you read any further, it's important to understand that color blindness doesn't mean the viewer can't see color. What a color-blind viewer sees is the wrong color. A red or green dot might appear brown or some other color. Generally, the viewer can still see the object so long as you don't surround it with the color their eyes substitute for the real color of the object. In addition, not everyone has the same kind of color blindness. Most doctors agree there are three main forms of color blindness to consider (read the explanation of the types of color blindness at http://webexhibits.org/causesofcolor/2.html for details).

Because Google returns raw data and not color, you have a choice about the color content of your desktop application or Web site. Even so, you might want to add a little pizzazz to your presentation and that usually means adding color. You can find information about working around color-blindness issues on a number of Web sites, but here are three exceptional sources.

- Can Color-Blind Users See Your Site? (http://msdn.microsoft.com/voices/hess10092000.asp)

- Color Vision Color Deficiency (http://www.firelily.com/opinions/color.html)

- Visicheck (http://www.vischeck.com/vischeck/vischeckImage.php)

The first two sites tell you about color blindness and provide example images that show how things appear to someone with a particular kind of color blindness. The third site lets you check your image for color blindness—all you need is a Web site URL. You can use this site to check an entire Web page by grabbing a screenshot of the Web site and uploading it to your site. The same technique works for desktop applications.

Designing for Privacy Issues

Privacy has become a major concern because the news contains numerous stories of personal information misuse. One of the major misuses of personal information is identity theft, but that's by no means the largest misuse. Many users also feel that gathering personal information for marketing purposes without permission and full disclosure of how the requestor will use the information is also a major misuse of personal information. People don't want to suffer through a barrage of unwanted sales calls as witnessed by the proliferation of "No Call" lists both locally and nationally. In fact, many people are taking positive steps to take back their personal information or at least block further attempts to acquire new information. The proliferation of spyware blockers shows that users are becoming aware of covert attempts by some Web sites (including pop-up advertisements) to steal data from their systems.

Personal information covers a range of topics today. Most developers recognize that name, address, telephone number, and other personally identifying information is private. However, users don't want developers to know a lot of other information that some developers see as belonging to the public domain. For example, some developers will try to get the `Referrer` (the previous Web page), `User-Agent` (the browser type, version, and host operating system), and `From` (the user's email address) headers of the user's browser. Brisk sales of products such as Norton Internet Security demonstrate that users don't want developers to collect this information. An interesting side effect of this battle between user and developer is that even though the user is using a new version of products such as Internet Explorer and Netscape, the Web site often reports that the user has an outdated version of the product. You can easily avoid collecting browser information through careful design and by following standards. The Webmonkey chart at `http://hotwired.lycos.com/webmonkey/reference/browser_chart/index.html` helps you understand which design features to avoid based on browser compatibility.

Even with the best design, however, you'll eventually encounter a situation where you want to use cookies (assuming the user has their browser set to accept cookies). Many users realize that cookies aren't inherently evil, but they also realize that a Web site could use cookies for nefarious purposes. All the pop-up ads that you see floating around on your favorite Web site are one reason that people are suspicious. Some of these vendors follow people around to the various sites they visit and keep track of their movements. However, you can overcome the fears of most users by maintaining a privacy policy and including special tags for that policy on your Web site. The most common way to publish and use a privacy policy is Platform for Privacy Preferences (P3P). The World Wide Web Consortium (W3C) sponsors this technique and you can read about the six easy steps for implementing P3P on your Web site at `http://www.w3.org/P3P/details.html`. The P3P standard (`http://www.w3.org/TR/P3P/`) also contains a wealth of information you should review.

> ▶ **NOTE**
>
> The example in this section uses the IBM P3P generator (http://www.alphaworks.ibm.com/tech/p3peditor). The W3C site lists several other generators—I chose this particular generator because it comes with a 90-day free trial. Your code might turn out different from mine if you use another generator for your code. For some reason, the IBM P3P generator doesn't work with the current version of the Java Runtime Environment (JRE)—version 1.4.2. IBM recommends using the 1.3.1 version of the JRE that you can download at http://java.sun.com/j2se/1.3/.

Your privacy statement will consist of several files, including at least one P3P file that you create using the P3P generator and an XML reference file. A good generator will also help you create a generic privacy summary that you can use for queries from the user and a compact policy statement you can use in the response headers of pages that contain cookies. If you own the server you use for the Web page, you can place the privacy information in the \w3c folder of the Web site. It's also possible to create linkage between the privacy information and your Web page using a <link> tag similar to the one shown here.

```
<link rel="P3Pv1" href="http://www.mwt.net/~jmueller/p3p.xml">
```

The problem comes in when you don't own the server that hosts your Web page—the situation for many people, including small business owners. Internet Explorer 6 has several levels of cookie protection built in. The highest level will likely reject your privacy information because Internet Explorer relies exclusively on the compact policy statement supplied as part of the response headers. Adding the compact policy statement is relatively easy if you own the server. Listing 11.1 shows an alternative you can try when you don't own the server, plus some test code you can use to verify the results. You'll find the complete source code for this example in the \Chapter 11\Privacy folder of the source code located on the Sybex Web site.

Listing 11.1   **Adding a Compact Policy to a Web Page**

```html
<html>
<head>
<meta http-equiv='P3P'
      content='policyref="http://www.mwt.net/~jmueller/p3p.xml",
      CP="NOI DSP COR NID CURa OUR NOR NAV INT TST"'>
<title>Privacy Demonstration</title>
<script>
function SetCookie()
{
    var  UserCookie; // Stores the user name.

    // Create the username cookie.
```

```
        UserCookie - "UserName=" + escape(InputVal.value);

        // Add the cookie to the document.
        document.cookie = UserCookie;

        // Tell the user the cookie was saved.
        alert("The cookies were saved.");
    }

function ReadCookie()
{
    var  ACookie; // Holds the document cookie.
    var  Parsed;  // Holds the split cookies.
    var  Name;    // The user name.

    // Get the cookie.
    ACookie = unescape(document.cookie);

    // Split the cookie elements.
    Parsed = ACookie.split("=");

    // Get the user name.
    Name = Parsed[1];

    // Display the name.
    alert("Your name is: " + Name);
}
```

The <meta> tag at the beginning of the code is the essential addition to your application. The http-equiv attribute tells the server what kind of response header to add. Some servers don't honor this attribute, so this solution might not work completely in all cases. The content attribute tells the client where to locate the privacy policy for your Web site—it works much the same as the <link> tag discussed earlier in this section. Finally, the CP attribute defines the compact policy for your server. Most tools, such as the IBM P3P Policy Editor shown in Figure 11.2, tell you what these codes mean and generate a text file containing them for you.

The test code consists of two functions attached to buttons on the example form. The first creates a cookie and attaches it to the document. The second retrieves the cookie stored in the document and displays the results on screen. Neither function is that exciting, but this is enough code to create an error with Internet Explorer 6 if the compact policy isn't accepted. You must have a compact policy in place and Internet Explorer 6 must accept it if you want users to use the high privacy setting. However, even if Internet Explorer 6 decides that it won't accept the compact policy, having a privacy policy in place and set up using the information provided in this section lets the user rely on the medium high privacy setting. Although the medium high setting isn't quite as comfortable as the high setting, it's much better than the low setting your Web site would require if it didn't have a privacy policy.

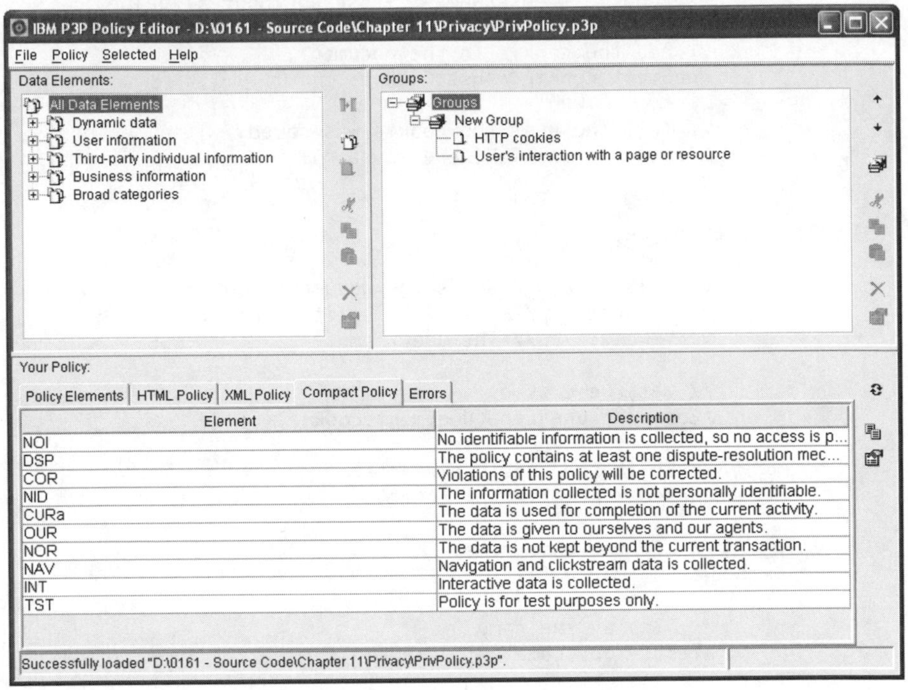

FIGURE 11.2:

Make sure you generate a compact policy for Web pages that have cookies.

Adding Feedback to Your Application

Most people have an opinion. The opinion doesn't have a right or wrong value—it's simply how they feel about a particular topic. Getting an honest opinion from people can be difficult, but you can do it. When the topic concerns your application or Web site, the need to get an honest opinion is essential. Otherwise, changes you make to an application or Web site as the result of user feedback is going to be off target—you want to target the users of your site to ensure they have a great experience.

When you mix interaction with another application, Google Web Services in this case, the problems of getting honest feedback intensify. You need to consider whether the feedback relates to your application, a connectivity issue caused by an ISP, the user's environment, or Google Web Services (among other things). It's not always easy to sort even a good opinion into the right area.

► **TIP**

Don't assume that every positive feedback message you receive means that you're doing everything right with your application. Some people will tell you positive things to obtain benefits they might not normally receive or simply because they don't want to hurt your feelings. Likewise, not every negative message is an indictment against your programming practices. Sometimes a user will have a bad day and decide to take it out on you because you're the nearest target that can't attack back. Deciphering feedback often means reading the message several times and deciding just how it affects your application (or whether it affects your application at all).

The following sections discuss user feedback. This information reflects issues you need to consider when working with Google Web Services. For example, it discusses some of the problems of sorting information into the right area for consideration.

Designing User Feedback

One of the problems in getting good user feedback is designing the form so that it elicits a response, especially from users who don't normally express themselves well. A nebulous question, such as "How do you feel about this search?" won't net you a very good response. You need to direct the user to the kind of input you want, without contaminating the user's response. For example, "Does the search help you find the information you need on my Web site, or do you find yourself using alternative search techniques?" offers the user a choice and makes them think about alternatives. The question is still specific enough that even a shy user can provide an answer. Offering yes, no, and other (with a comment field) lets the shy user off the hook, but also lets vocal users state their answers in precise terms.

The simplest method for obtaining user feedback on a Web page is to create a form and send it to your email (or other location). Although this method does require a little interpretation, it has the advantage of allowing you to get feedback almost free. If you use a programmable email reader such as Microsoft Outlook, you can write a macro to interpret and save the results for you. Otherwise, the careful use of form values will let you read the report with a little effort. Listing 11.2 contains an example of a simple form that works with almost all browsers even if the user has turned off scripting support and cookies. You'll find the complete source code for this example in the \Chapter 11\SimpleRespForm folder of the source code located on the Sybex Web site.

Listing 11.2   **A Simple, Low-cost Feedback Form**

```html
<!DOCTYPE HTML PUBLIC "-//W3C//DTD HTML 4.0 Transitional//EN">
<html>
<head>
<title>Simple Response Form</title>
<meta name="vs_targetSchema"
      content="http://schemas.microsoft.com/intellisense/ie5">
</head>
<body>

<!-- Display a heading. -->
<h1 align=center>Simple Response Form</h1>

<!-- Define the form and anticipated action. -->
<form action="mailto:JMueller@mwt.net?subject=Test Message"
      method=post
      name=SimpleRespForm
      enctype="text/plain">

<!-- Ask about search engine performance. -->
<label>Did the search engine work as you expected?</label>
<input type=hidden
       name="Q1"
       value="Search Engine"/><br/>
<label>Yes</label>
<input type=radio name="1A" value="Y"/><br/>
<label>No</label>
<input type=radio name="1A" value="N"/><br/>
<label>Other</label>
<input type=radio name="1A" value="O"/><br/>
<label>Additional comment (40 characters max):</label><br/>
<input type=text name="1E" maxlength=40/><p/>

<!-- Ask about link descriptions. -->
<label>Were the link descriptions easy to understand?</label>
<input type=hidden
       name="Q2"
       value="Link Description"/><br/>
<label>Yes</label>
<input type=radio name="2A" value="Y"/><br/>
<label>No</label>
<input type=radio name="2A" value="N"/><br/>
<label>Other</label>
<input type=radio name="2A" value="O"/><br/>
<label>Additional comment (40 characters max):</label><br/>
```

```
<input type=text name="2E" maxlength=40/><p/>

<!-- Submit the form to email. -->
<input type=submit value="Send" accesskey="S"/>
</form>
</body>
</html>
```

For anyone who has spent considerable time working with Web pages, this might look like old technology crying for a makeover. However, this technique works quite well. I didn't include the accessibility information in this example for the sake of clarity. You could also dress it up a bit using Cascading Style Sheets (CSS). The underlying example, however, is easy to understand.

The focus of this example is the `<form>` tag. Notice that the `action="mailto:JMueller@mwt`
`.net?subject=Test Message"` attribute defines my email address as the destination for the data in the form. In addition, the email subject is Test Message. By giving each survey a different name, you know precisely where the user took the survey and what to expect as input. Most developers would stop here and complain about the results received in their email (a rather unattractive attachment). By adding the `enctype="text/plain"` attribute, you can change the output to something that is easy to parse using any script and not all that hard to read using the email application's preview pane, as shown in Figure 11.3.

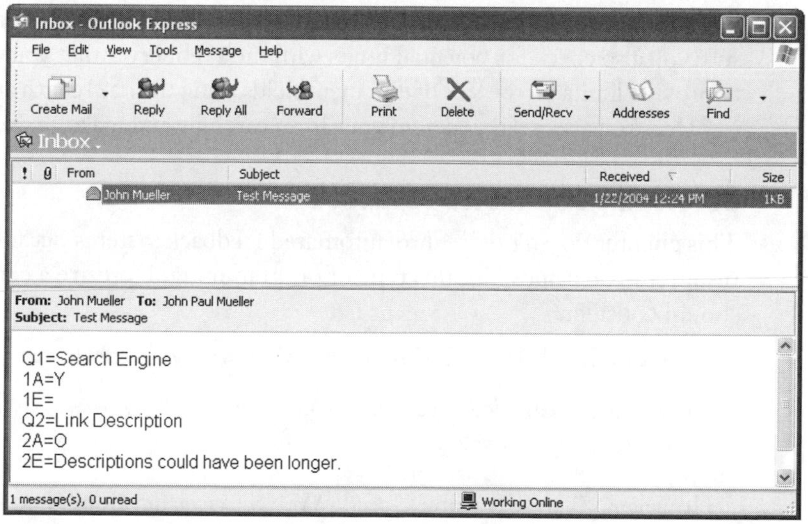

FIGURE 11.3:

Encoding your survey form correctly lets you read it directly in email.

> ▶ **TIP**
>
> Many developers don't understand the `mailto:` URL very well. The problem is that the proto-col doesn't appear very often on Web pages and most Web pages don't use the full potential of the `mailto:` URL. You can use most of the same fields with a `mailto:` that you use with an email program including such features as cc and bcc. You can find several good resources about the `mailto:` URL on the Internet. One of the better places to look is the Web Design Guides site at `http://www.ssi-developer.net/design/mailto.shtml`. Another good place to look for tips of this sort is the Ezine-Tips.com site at `http://ezine-tips.com/articles/format/20001020.shtml`.

Each of the entries in the email has a corresponding tag in the form that has the name attribute shown. Notice how the example separates the questions using a hidden `<input>` tag like this:

```
<input type=hidden
        name="Q1"
        value="Search Engine"/><br/>
```

The value you provide should include a reminder about the question content. In this case, I provided a reminder that the question asks whether the user found every product needed.

The main problem with using this technique is content size. Forms can have a 255-character limit on the amount of data they can send, although this limit is apparently uncommon. (Make sure you also check for potential limits with the Web server that you use.) This means you have to provide limits on the size of comment fields using the `maxlength` attribute, as shown in List-ing 11.2. You also need to design your form carefully and make answers terse whenever possible.

Developing Automated Feedback

This chapter doesn't delve into automated feedback systems because there are a number of resources you can use for this type of programming. Here are a couple of resources you should consider.

User Feedback HTML Form   `http://www.bytesworth.com/learn/html00009.asp`

Creating Feedback Forms for WAP Sites   `http://www.aspfree.com/articles/1137,1/articles.aspx`

However, given that many Google Web Services developers want to provide a research resource, making the feedback page friendly is critical. In general, the more you automate the feedback to make things easier for your company, the fewer users will be able to use the feedback system. This issue is especially true of form-based Web feedback because many users now turn off scripting, cookies, applets, and plug-ins for fear their systems will download viruses or experience other problems. Automation usually requires some level of client and server scripting, along with cookies and even plug-ins.

> ▶ **TIP**
>
> Some ISPs consider user feedback forms so important that they make them part of the documentation for their service. For example, check out the AT&T site at `http://www.att.com/style/wc_feedback.html`. This site tells how to create a user feedback for using the special features of the AT&T servers. Your ISP might provide similar services that you can use to make development of automated pages easier.

The problem even occurs with desktop applications. Some vendors make feedback available as part of a Help menu option. In most cases, the feedback form works and sends the information to the vendor (usually over the Internet). However, problems arise when the vendor assumes the user has a permanent connection to the Internet—many users use dial-up connections. Fortunately, Google Web Services developers can assume that the user has some kind of Internet connection (even if it's through a proxy server) because otherwise their application won't work at all.

Using Google Web Services and Amazon Web Services Together

Today, many people develop applications for individual Web services. We're past the stage where Web services are completely new, but now that businesses are beginning to accept Web services (see the eWeek story at `http://www.eweek.com/article2/0,4149,1455562,00.asp` for details), they're looking at them as single applications. This stage in the development of Web services will eventually pass too. At some point, developers will realize that the true power of Web services is in combining the functionality that each Web service provides into a new form—a cohesive whole. At least one intrepid developer is already making strides in this area. Make sure you review the Authorama site at `http://www.authorama.com/` for details on how this application is put together.

> ▶ **NOTE**
>
> This chapter doesn't contain very much information about Amazon Web Services. For a complete discussion of this valuable Web service, get my book, *Mining Amazon Web Services: Building Applications with the Amazon API* (Sybex, 2004). You can also learn more on the Amazon site at `http://www.amazon.com/gp/browse.html/103-5753584-4315028?node=3435361`.

This section of the chapter creates a simple application that uses resources provided by both Google and Amazon to research a Universal Product Code (UPC). The two Web services work very well together, in this case, because they both provide a piece of information a user is likely to need. Amazon Web Services tells the user the product name, which vendor produces the product, and the Amazon price. In addition, the user could obtain product reviews from Amazon. Google Web Services takes the user further by providing a list of links about the product. You can't currently look for a product using UPC on Google Web Services, so this Web service can't do the job alone. Likewise, Amazon Web Services can't provide related links. By combining the two Web services, you get a much better view of what this product is all about. Listing 11.3 shows a typical example of how these two Web services can work together. You'll find the complete source code for this example in the \Chapter 11\CombinedServices folder of the source code located on the Sybex Web site.

Listing 11.3   Combining Amazon Web Services with Google Web Services

```
private void btnTest_Click(object sender, System.EventArgs e)
{
    UpcRequest            Request; // The UPC of the CD.
    AmazonSearchService   AServe;  // Amazon Search Service
    ProductInfo           PI;      // Returned information.
    GoogleSearchService   GServe;  // Search service routine access.
    GoogleSearchResult    Result;  // All of the results.
    ResultElement[]       Items;   // All of the search items.
    DataRow               DR;      // Output data.

    // Create the service.
    AServe = new AmazonSearchService();

    // Create and define the request.
    Request = new UpcRequest();
    Request.devtag = txtTag.Text;
    Request.mode = txtMode.Text;
    Request.tag = "webservices-20";
    Request.type = "lite";
    Request.upc = txtUPC.Text;

    // Get the data.
    PI = AServe.UpcSearchRequest(Request);

    // Add data to the appropriate places on screen.
    txtASIN.Text = PI.Details[0].Asin;
    txtAvailability.Text = PI.Details[0].Availability;
    txtPrice.Text = PI.Details[0].ListPrice;
    txtManufacturer.Text = PI.Details[0].Manufacturer;
    txtName.Text = PI.Details[0].ProductName;
    txtReleaseDate.Text = PI.Details[0].ReleaseDate;
    lblURL.Text = PI.Details[0].Url;
```

```csharp
// Now that we have Google search criteria, create the
// search service.
GServe = new GoogleSearchService();

// Make the call.
Result =
   GServe.doGoogleSearch(
      txtLicense.Text,
      txtName.Text + " " + txtManufacturer.Text,
      0, 10, false, "", false, "", "", "");

// Clear the dataset of previous results.
dsGoogle.Tables["SearchResults"].Clear();

// Process the result elements.
Items = Result.resultElements;
foreach (ResultElement Item in Items)
{
   // Add a row.
   DR = dsGoogle.Tables["SearchResults"].NewRow();

   // Add the data to the row.
   DR["Title"] = StringToText(Item.title);
   DR["URL"] = Item.URL;
   if (Item.snippet.Length > 0)
      DR["SnippetOrSummary"] = StringToText(Item.snippet);
   else
      DR["SnippetOrSummary"] = StringToText(Item.summary);
   DR["CachedSize"] = Item.cachedSize;

   // Display the row on screen.
   dsGoogle.Tables["SearchResults"].Rows.Add(DR);
}
}
```

Before you do anything else, you need to add two Web references to your application. The first, `http://api.google.com/GoogleSearch.wsdl`, is for Google Web Services, while the second, `http://soap.amazon.com/schemas3/AmazonWebServices.wsdl`, points to Amazon Web Services. You'll also need to reference the two Web services at the beginning of the code module like this:

```csharp
using CombinedServices.com.amazon.soap;
using CombinedServices.com.google.api;
```

Now that you have the proper references in place, it's time to look at the code. Remember, all the code has to go on when it starts is a UPC. You would normally hard code the license numbers into the code. The user also has to supply a product category, music, in this case, but you could theoretically hard code that information too. The inputs you require depend entirely on how the user will interact with the application and how the two Web services interact.

The code begins by creating an Amazon Web Services connection. Creating the service is about the same as working with Google. However, the next step is different. Amazon supports a number of complex request types, each of which requires a special request object. In this case, the code creates a `UpcRequest` object to hold the Amazon data. This data includes the developer tag (essentially the same as the Google license), a product mode (such as music or books), an associate tag (in case you want to sell products through Amazon), the kind of search you want to perform (lite or heavy), and the UPC. The code sends all this information to Amazon Web Services using the `AServe.UpcSearchRequest(Request)` method call.

At this point, the `ProductInfo` object, `PI`, holds all of the data that Amazon provides for this particular request. The example doesn't use all of the information, but does provide a good representation of the information, as shown in Figure 11.4. In this case, the important information includes the product name, manufacturer, release date, availability, and price. In addition, the application provides an Amazon-specific identification number and an URL that the user can click to buy the product online.

Now that the application knows more about the product, it can perform a search for it using Google. The code instantiates the Google Web Service object, `GServe`, and uses it as many of the examples have in this book. However, you'll quickly notice that except for the

FIGURE 11.4:

Typical output from the combined Web services application

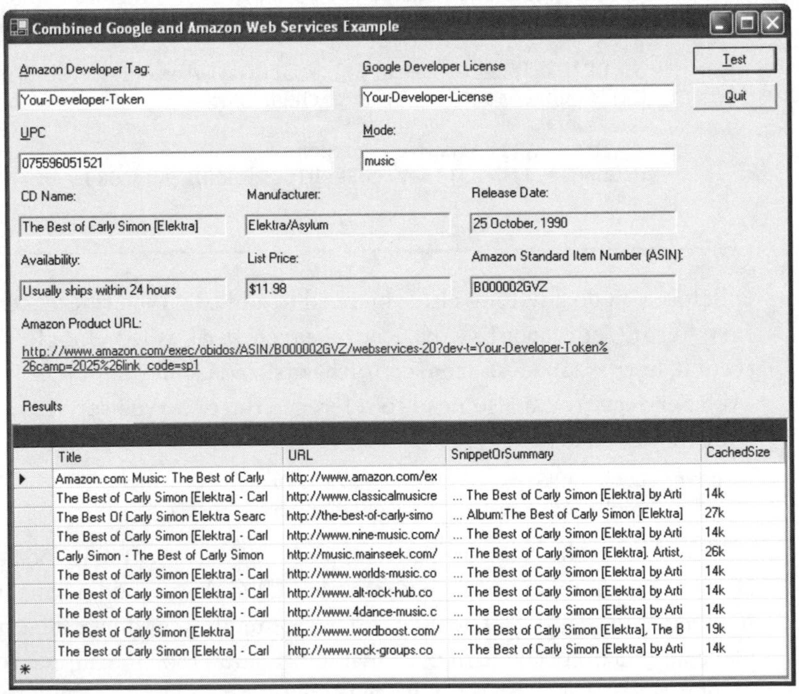

required developer license, Google Web Services doesn't receive any input from the user. All of this input comes from Amazon, yet the user is the beneficiary of the output, as shown in Figure 11.4.

The code makes the search request as normal and fills the dataset with the resulting Web site titles, URLs, snippets, and cached sizes. The output appears in a grid, as shown in Figure 11.4. Now the user can search online to learn more about the product before buying it. Imagine a retail kiosk that uses this setup to help buyers make good decisions without sales staff support. In addition, a user could easily load such an application on a Pocket PC or access it as a Web application using a Palm. Now a store experience need not include the dread that follows some purchases. A user is always informed about the product.

Your Call to Action

This chapter helps you discover some of the user-related elements of creating a Google Web Services application. Building a great application isn't a matter of simply presenting information on screen. The technique you use for presentation turns an adequate application into one that users really enjoy. The chapter also discusses the idea of combining Web services. This idea isn't all that new—developers have combined applications in the past. However, it's important to examine this concept again in light of Web services. Instead of combining applications on a single machine or network, you're now combining applications that could exist anywhere in the world. This concept is another expansion of user-centric computing. Applications that combine the functionality of multiple resources make life easier for the user and therefore improves user productivity and efficiency.

The essential nugget of knowledge you can take from this chapter is that the user is important. Whether you have good communication skills or not, the user depends on you to create an application that not only works well but also meets specific needs. It's up to you to decide to put the user first and make your application both useful and friendly. Empowering the user is one way to gain an order of magnitude in application performance and efficiency.

Congratulations! You've reached the last chapter of the book. However, your journey should also include the appendices for this book. Appendix A helps you locate useful third party utilities. Use Appendix B to ensure your application meets all of the Google licensing requirements. Finally, use Appendix C to learn about breaking Google Web Services news—new technologies made available as this book went to press. If you've read from the beginning to the end of the book, you know that it covers a lot of ground. I encourage you to continue to use the book as a reference. Google Web Services is a truly remarkable undertaking and I'd love to hear about your experiences with it. Make sure you contact me at JMueller@mwt.net if you have any questions about this book. Also, look on my Web site at http://www.mwt.net/~jmueller/ for updates and additional information.

Appendix A

Finding Additional Google
Web Services Resources

Seeing Demonstrations
Created by Others

▶ Helpful Third Party Resource Sites

Locating Other
Interesting Web Sites

Using the Office
2003 Add-on

Throughout the book, you discovered a number of resources that would help you perform some tasks with less effort or faster. In some cases, a product added the special functionality required to make Google Web Services access possible. I usually placed the special products in a separate section or used them to demonstrate a particular type of Google Web Services access. The book also references a number of Web sites that feature special information—these helpful Web sites normally appear as part of notes or tips. This appendix is an extension of all those special sections, notes, and tips—it contains a number of helpful third party resources that will make your Google Web Services experience better.

Of course, this appendix begs the question of why these third party products and sites don't appear in the main part of the book somewhere. In many cases, these products fulfill a special need that I didn't demonstrate in the book or they duplicate a functionality that you'll already find in the book. This appendix contains additional information that I thought you would find helpful, but didn't find a place in the main part of the book for whatever reason.

I'm always on the lookout for great third party products, and I like to know about Web sites with helpful information. These sites often appear in my newsletter (sign up at http://www .freeenewsletters.com/). I also provide them as updates to the book on my Web site at http://www.mwt.net/~jmueller/. If you know of a special third party product or Web site that has special information that would help users of this book, please let me know by writing to me at JMueller@mwt.net.

Google Web Services–Specific Web Sites

Google Web Services has been so successful that many language vendors are beginning to take notice, as well as a number of third parties. The following list presents a few of the most interesting places to find Google Web Services information. However, you should also check with the vendor that creates your programming language product and look around at other third party solutions too. For example, the "Microsoft Office 2003 Add-on" section describes how Microsoft is adding Google Web Services support to their Office product.

Dev Shed Articles on Google Web Services
http://www.devshed.com/index.php?option=search&searchword=Google%20API

SoapWare.org
http://www.soapware.org/directory/4/services/googleApi

Using the Google API with Radio and Frontier
http://radio.userland.com/googleApi

XML-RPC Gateway for the Google API
http://www.xmlrpc.com/googleGateway

Demonstration Web Sites

Sometimes a demonstration is better than any amount of descriptive text. Most of the demonstrations I've seen on the Internet are simple, at this point, but the potential for creating some very interesting Web applications is definitely there. The following Web sites provide demonstrations you can try online.

CapeSpeller 1.0
http://capescience.capeclear.com/google/spell.shtml

Google by Email
http://capescience.capeclear.com/google/

Google2RSS
http://www.razorsoft.net/weblog/stories/2002/04/13/google2rss.html

GoogleBox ASP
http://www.edazzle.net/#googlebox

GoogleBrowser
http://www.kasei.com/google/browse

Google Graph Browser
http://traumwind.de/soap/

Google Outline Browser

http://radio.outliners.com/googleOutlineBrowser

Loading OPML Documents

http://w3future.com/html/opmlloader.html#rel=http///www.soapware.org/

> ▶ **NOTE**
>
> An Outline Processor Markup Language (OPML) document uses an XML-based format for exchange of outline structured information. Designing a Web page or other document as an outline makes it easier to understand in many cases. You can learn more about this technology at http://opml.scripting.com/spec.

Mail 2 Google

http://www.ohardt.com/mail2google/

Spell Checker for JEdit

http://www.paradox1x.org/archives/00000421.shtml

Swingin' Google

http://davidwatson.org:8086/2002/04/20.html#a90

One Web site deserves a special mention because the developer has created a production-quality Google Web Services application. However, this application doesn't stop at providing Google information—it also uses Amazon Web Services, which makes this site quite interesting. You can learn more about the developer at http://blog.outer-court.com/archive/2003_06_21_index.html. The application appears at http://www.authorama.com/. Figure A.1 shows typical output from this Web site—the Google output appears on the left and the Amazon output on the right.

Web Sites That Provide Other Facts You Should Know About

You'll find helpful Web sites in every chapter of the book. However, some Web sites didn't quite fit in any of the chapters, yet they supply useful information for your Google Web Services experience. For example, the "Sending Special Characters Using URL Encoding" section of Chapter 3 discusses the need to URL encode special characters before you send a request to Google Web Services. Equally important is the need to *escape* special characters in some types of HTML and XML output by converting them to numeric sequences. The quote (') and double quote (") often cause problems, as do the angle brackets (<>). You can escape these characters as &#39, &#34, &#60, and &#62. The HTML Character Codes site at http://home.online.no/~pethesse/charcodes.html contains a good list of these codes.

This production Web site relies on output from two Web services.

Web accessibility is an extremely important topic and I hope that you take it as seriously as I do. You can find multitudes of statistics on Web sites that specialize in accessibility such as http://www.w3.org/1999/05/WCAG-REC-fact. An ExtremeTech article entitled "The State of Web Accessibility" (http://www.extremetech.com/article2/0,3973,11774,00.asp) says it all by stating that accessibility is for everyone—the 180 posts for this article provide some interesting insights as well. These additional Web sites provide some pointers you can use to make your site accessible and yet keep development costs to a minimum.

Policies Relating to Web Accessibility

http://www.w3.org/WAI/Policy/

Safe Web Colors for Color-Deficient Vision

http://more.btexact.com/people/rigdence/colours/

Usability and Accessibility—Everyone Learning

http://www.cdlr.tamu.edu/dec_2002/Proceedings/david_peter.pdf

Once you learn about Web services and understand how valuable they can be, you'll want to try out other Web services to learn whether they can help you with your application. One of the most interesting places to learn about new Web services is the Macromedia Flash site at http://www.flash-db.com/services/.

Sometimes you can find individual sites that include some Google Web Services material. I like browsing these sites because many of them include insights and perspectives you won't find on mainstream sites. Of course, some of them just repeat material you find elsewhere. Here are a few of the more interesting selections.

Charon Internet Tutorials
http://www.charon.co.uk/content.aspx?CategoryID=4

How to Use the Google API in Movable Type
http://www.10500bc.org/code/mt_howto_googleapi.php

Integrating Google Web Services with Your Notes Databases
http://www-10.lotus.com/ldd/today.nsf/lookup/AWSintegration_pt3

Steve Sharrock's ASPAlliance Contributions
http://authors.aspalliance.com/shark/

Windley's Enterprise Computing Weblog
http://www.windley.com/2002/07/18.html

Microsoft Office 2003 Add-on

Most Microsoft Office users will need to use the VBA programming techniques found in Chapter 5 to access Google Web Services. However, Office 2003 users have an alternative solution that works in some cases. Microsoft is creating a new add-on for the Research Task Pane that should be available when you read this. This add-on lets you perform research on Google without ever leaving the Office environment. You can find the add-on at http://www.office.microsoft.com/marketplace.

This add-on provides a customizable interface. Generally, you'll interact with this add-on much as you interact with the Google Web site, but you can also create a custom application to define the interface you want. You can find additional details at:

Google Sample
http://msdn.microsoft.com/library/en-us/rssdk/html/rsSamplesGoogle.asp

Gadgetopia
http://www.gadgetopia.com/2004/01/16/MicrosoftOffice2003ResearchLibrary.html

Creating Your Own Research Service for the Microsoft Office 2003 Research Library
http://www.devx.com/codemag/Article/18214?trk=DXRSS_XML

Customizing the Microsoft Office 2003 Research Task Pane
http://msdn.microsoft.com/library/en-us/dno2k3ta/html/odc_customizingtheresearchpane.asp

Appendix B

▶ Google License Checklist

This appendix discusses some of the requirements you must fulfill to use Google Web Services. The purpose of this appendix is to help you create a checklist to ensure you meet the legal requirements—the appendix doesn't tell you about your legal rights, act as a legal guide, or provide anything that would normally require a lawyer. I often create checklists of this sort for my own use and find that many other people find them useful too. The main reason I create these checklists for myself is that they make it easier for me to determine whether an application I create fulfills the basic requirements of the license. If you do have questions about the legal requirements, make sure you contact Google (api-support@google.com) to ensure you understand your role completely. In addition, although this appendix is current as of the date of writing, Google could change the licensing agreement at any time—you must make sure that you keep current on all of the requirements.

> ▶ **WARNING**
>
> Google assumes that you've given them permission to use any ideas you share when you send a message to Google Support or upload messages to their developer's newsgroup. In short, if you don't want Google to use your ideas, then don't tell Google about them.

General Requirements

The following topics discuss usage requirements of the licensing agreement. This section discusses general issues, such as what you can do with the Google Web Services. Because Google didn't use numbering in the licensing agreement, the sections follow the general order of the agreement, but you can't match them to a specific paragraph. For example, the first two sections that follow appear as part of the "PERSONAL AND LEGITIMATE USES ONLY" section of the licensing agreement.

Creating a Single Developer License

Working with Google Web Services is fun and profitable. The examples in this book demonstrate you can do a lot with the functionality that Google Web Services provides today, and Google only plans to increase this functionality in the future. Some developers might feel the call limits create development problems and that it would be nice to have multiple developer licenses. Google makes it clear that they only want to issue one developer license to each person. When you think about it, this restriction is the best way to ensure that everyone gets a chance to use Google Web Services and that the Google severs don't become overwhelmed by too many calls. When you do make an application available for public use, you can request that the application user get their own license (as many of the applications in the "Demonstration Web Sites" section of Appendix A do).

Using the Google API for Private Needs

This particular isn't quite as restrictive as you might think. Look through the list of applications in the "Demonstration Web Sites" section of Appendix A and you'll see a list of diverse applications that developers have made available for general use. In all cases, you must obtain a developer license to use these applications, so each user of the application is using it privately. Yes, it's stretching the rule a bit, but Google hasn't mentioned this kind of release so far.

You do need to observe two rules when creating an application. The first is that you can't create an application for general sale. For example, you couldn't create a shrink-wrapped application and sell it to someone. A private application means one that you haven't developed for sale to other people. The second is that you can't create an application that competes with the services that Google provides. This restriction is sensible considering Google needs to remain financially solvent to continue providing the Web service.

Making Calls That Don't Exceed Limits

Google notes that you can make calls using any method that it supports—as you see in the book, that list is relatively short, but you can make calls using a variety of languages and techniques. You can make calls to Google Web Services any time day or night, 7 days a week. Those are the good things you should simply file somewhere.

However, Google is a business and its customers come first. When you use Google Web Services for development, you're a developer, not a customer. It's not too surprising that Google places some limits on the resources you can use. These limits ensure customers can access the Web site and get good service. In addition, it means that all developers get a fair share of the available resources. Google asks that you not exceed 1,000 calls per day. This limitation is the reason that I manually execute each request, rather than perform the task through code.

Always Observe the Requirements of the Law

Most people realize that you can't use information you receive from Google as a bludgeon to hurt someone else. Google doesn't want to get involved in the long running feud between you and your neighbor. They're being nice enough to let you use the data generated on their site for any of a number of useful purposes. All they ask in return is that you don't violate the law—whatever the law is in your country.

It's also important to consider Google's rights when you create your application. An application that violates Google's proprietary rights is going to attract the wrong kind of attention. In short, don't do things like claim you created the information displayed by your application when Google obviously provided it to you.

Display Requirements

This section discusses display issues, such as how you can present Google Web Services information in your application. The important consideration in this section is that Google realizes that you want to add value to the content, but they also have to maintain the integrity of the content they supply to you.

Selecting a Formatting Method

You can display the data in any format you choose so long as you don't break one of the rules in this agreement. For example, you can display text in bold or in an odd font if you want, but you have to follow the rules for using text.

Altering the Text

Some Google content gets rather long and you might not be able to display all of the text on one page of your Web site. You can shorten the text as needed to make it easier to display. However, you can't change the text. You can remove formatting, such as the HTML formatting codes, but you can't modify the text in such a way that the content is altered.

Leaving Proprietary Information in Place

Google will provide the copyright and trademark symbols with their content as needed. You must leave these symbols in place. The same holds true for any notices or other identifying information. There really isn't a good reason to modify any of this information.

Getting Written Permission to Use the Google Logo

As long as you follow all of the rules that Google provides, you can tell other people that your application uses Google. In fact, Google encourages you to mention that you've used Google Web Services to develop your application. It's free advertising and any good business knows that advertising promotes more activity. However, you can't use the Google logo without written permission.

Although the licensing agreement doesn't provide a reason for this action, Google likely wants to ensure that any application containing their logo meets high standards and represents Google Web Services well. Whatever the reason, adding the Google logo to your application can attract additional interest. If you plan to create a public application similar to those listed in Appendix A, you'll probably want to seek Google's written permission to use their logo.

Intellectual Property Issues

The checklist portion of this appendix discusses development issues. However, you need to consider the entire licensing agreement before you make your application public. For example, you have to consider ownership rights. While you do own the rights to any application you create, you need to consider the data you obtain from Google as part of the application picture. Google doesn't give up any rights to its intellectual property. Since intellectual property rights are figuring in a number of legal cases right now, it's important to keep track of how you use Google property in your application. Google grants you certain rights, but those rights could change at any time. Google spells out ownership rights in the "INTELLECTUAL PROPERTY" section of the licensing agreement.

Google also provides you with access to some of its trademarked material in order to promote the Google connection to your application. Obviously, Google doesn't want you to use its trademarked material in a way that would cause problems. For example, you couldn't use the trademarked material on a Web site that disparages other people based on sex, religion, or ethnic origin (among other things). Although the usage requirements in the agreement don't spell out every good use of the trademarked material, they do spell out a few of the ways that you can't use the material. As usual, make sure you contact Google if you have any questions about how to use the trademarked material.

You'll find that Google, like most large companies, is very conscious of its public appearance. This means you have to exercise care in spelling out your relationship with Google. Saying that you're Google's main representative, when you're just using its Web service, isn't a good idea. Generally, it's best to keep a low profile and simply say that some information presented with your application comes from Google Web Services.

Appendix C

Understanding the
Google Viewer

▶ Late Breaking Google Web Services News

Using Numeric
Searches

Considering
RSS Feeds

This appendix brings you late breaking news about Google Web Services as of the time of this writing. With many products, there are definite breaks in the development cycle so you can say one version is complete and another is beginning. The Web makes it easy to create products that have a continuous development cycle—there aren't any real versions to consider. Google Web Services falls into this category.

The following sections describe some of the latest Google Web Services features. Many of these features are new additions to the search engine itself that you'll eventually access using special calls with the Web service. In most cases, these features don't appear as part of the Web service today. These new features make Google more useful by helping you do more with less effort. You'll also find that these new features make it easier for you to create robust applications that fulfill more user needs.

Google Viewer

The Google Viewer is a new tool that lets you view the results of a Web search as a slideshow. The benefit of this approach is that you can see the Web pages without actually visiting them. In short, you view the search results graphically, rather than working with a text description. Of course, the slideshow includes the usual snippet so you can see where the search terms come into play.

Using this technique does make searching faster when you're looking for complex information but slows things down considerably when you need something simple. For example, when you need to find a Web page with a table or other feature that you remember seeing during previous research, this technique can help you find it faster. On the other hand, when you're looking for a site that offers a very specific piece of information and you don't care what format the site uses, then this feature probably won't help much. You can learn more about this feature at `http://labs .google.com/gviewer.html`.

Numeric Searches

When you use the standard Google search engine to look for numbers, you can't be sure what you'll find. Numeric information is critical in today's society, but it's also meaningless, in most cases, without a frame of reference. In short, you need a search that adds a frame of reference so the number has meaning. According to an InfoWorld article (`http://www.infoworld.com/article/04/01/13/HNgoogletools_1.html`), a new Google numeric search will have this capability. You'll be able to perform searches for UPS, FedEx, and U.S. Postal Service packages based on a tracking number. You can also perform tasks such as checking the status of an airline flight based on the flight's numeric information.

This feature will appear as part of Google Web Services as soon as it's released. Unfortunately, the feature wasn't available for testing as of the date of writing. It will likely be available at some point after this book appears in print.

An Overview of RSS Feeds

A Rich Site Summary (RSS) feed is a kind of publishing service. A Web site that wants to make all or part of its content generally available to the public finds an RSS publisher. Users subscribe to this RSS publisher when they want to receive certain types of information. The information often appears on Web sites as part of a headline news feature. Most vendors use this kind of information publication for news, events, headlines, project updates, discussion group excerpts, and even corporate news.

Google doesn't provide RSS feeds directly, but a number of third party developers do. For example, you can obtain RSS feeds of the latest Google news using the Google News RSS Feeds located at `http://googlenews.74d.com/`. These feeds are updated every 15 minutes and make you aware of new information on the Google News Service. You could couple such a feed with Google Web Services to provide a full-featured description of the latest events as part of your application. To use the RSS feed all you need to do is load an URL, such as `http://googlenews.74d.com/rss/google_world.rss` for world news, into an XML document.

Once the document loads into the local document, you can parse it into any form needed for your application. The data adheres to a standard format that includes a description of the RSS feed, as well as individual items that describe the content you'll find in the Google New site. Figure C.1 shows a typical example of the output for the world news site.

The problem with RSS feeds is that it normally requires special software to use or at least an understanding of XML to create your own RSS reader software. You can find a number

of RSS readers on the Internet. For example, the intraVnews reader found at `http://www
.intravnews.com/` integrates with Microsoft Outlook. In fact, you can find a lengthy list of
RSS readers at `http://directory.google.com/Top/Reference/Libraries/Library_and_
Information_Science/Technical_Services/Cataloguing/Metadata/RDF/Applications/
RSS/News_Readers/`.

Don't get the idea that RSS feeds have to be limited to the Google News Service. For
example, the d2r site at `http://www.dynamicobjects.com/d2r/archives/002304.html`
discusses how the author created an RSS feed based on Google Web Services and a query.
You can actually use this RSS feed to monitor changes to the query result so you can detect
new links as they appear. Another such RSS service is Google.rss at `http://rajivraj
.europe.webmatrixhosting.net/google/googlerss.html`.

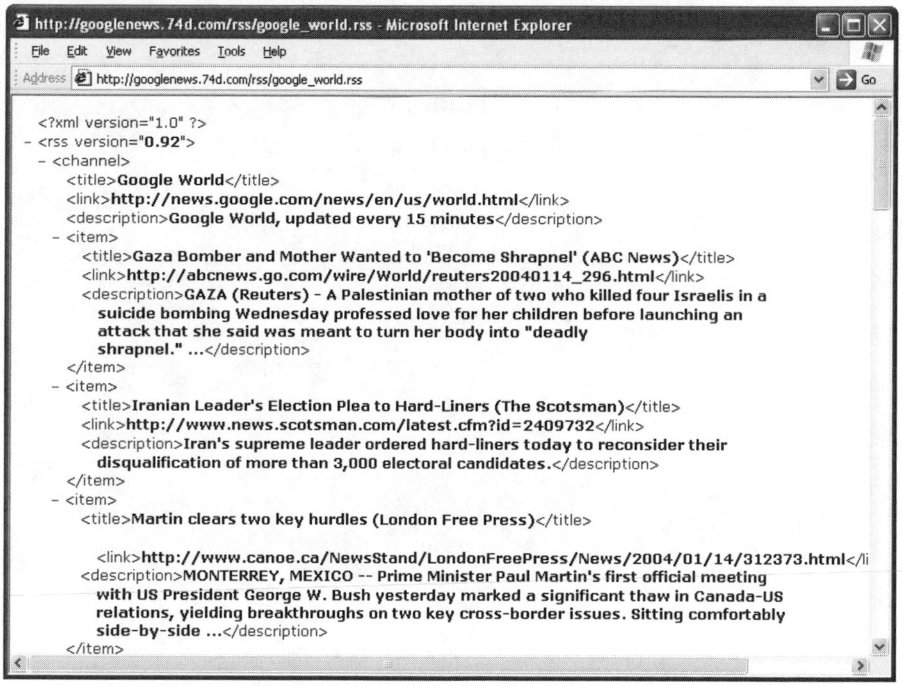

FIGURE C.1:

RSS feeds rely on spe-
cially formatted XML.

▶ Glossary

This book includes a glossary so that you can find terms and acronyms easily. It has several important features you need to know about. First, every acronym in the entire book appears here—even if there's a better than even chance you already know what the acronym stands for. (The book does exclude common acronyms such as units of measure and most file extensions because these terms are easy to find in other sources, and most people know what they mean.) This way, there isn't any doubt that you'll always find everything you need to use the book properly.

Second, these definitions are specific to the book. In other words, when you look through this glossary, you're seeing the words defined in the context in which they're used in this the book. This might or might not always coincide with current industry usage since the computer industry changes the meaning of words so often.

Finally, I've used a conversational tone for the definitions here in most cases. This means that the definitions might sacrifice a bit of puritanical accuracy for the sake of better understanding. The purpose of this glossary is to define the terms in such a way that there's less room for misunderstanding the intent of the book as a whole.

What to Do If You Don't Find It Here

While this glossary is a complete view of the words and acronyms in the book, you'll run into situations when you need to know more. No matter how closely I look at terms throughout the book, there's always a chance I'll miss the one acronym or term that you really need to know. In addition to the technical information found in the book, I've directed your attention to numerous online sources of information throughout the book and few of the terms the Web site owners use will appear here unless I also chose to use them in the book. Fortunately, many sites on the Internet provide partial or complete glossaries to fill in the gaps:

Acronym Finder   `http://www.acronymfinder.com/`

Free Online Dictionary Of Computing (FOLDOC)   `http://nightflight.com/foldoc/`

Microsoft Encarta   `http://encarta.msn.com/`

TechDis Accessibility Database   `http://www.niad.sussex.ac.uk/glossary.cfm`

Webopedia   `http://webopedia.internet.com/`

yourDictionary.com   `http://www.yourdictionary.com/`

Let's talk about these Web sites a little more. Web sites normally provide acronyms or glossary entries—not both. An acronym site only tells you what the letters in the acronym stand for, it doesn't provide definitions to explain what the acronym means in everyday computer use. The two extremes in this list are Acronym Finder (acronyms only) and Webopedia (full-fledged glossary entries).

Acronym Finder has the advantage of providing an extremely large list of acronyms from which to choose. At the time of this writing, the Acronym Finder sported 164,000 acronyms. Many of the acronyms have nothing to do with computers—making Acronym Finder an excellent resource for acronyms of all types.

Most of the Web sites that you'll find for computer terms are free. In some cases, such as Microsoft's Encarta, you have to pay for the support provided. However, these locations are still worth the effort because they ensure you understand the terms used in the jargon-filled world of computing.

Webopedia has become one of my favorite places to visit because it provides encyclopedic coverage of many computer terms and includes links to other Web sites. I like the fact that if I don't find a word I need, I can submit it to the Webopedia staff for addition to their dictionary, making Webopedia a community supported dictionary of the highest quality.

One of the interesting features of the yourDictionary.com Web site is that it provides access to more than one dictionary and in more than one language. If English isn't your native tongue, then this is the Web site of choice.

A

Accessibility   A measure of a user's ability to interact with an application. For example, applications should provide both mouse and keyboard access to every control to ensure the user can reach the control for use. In addition to direct user support, an application should support all devices without providing specialized support for a particular device unless necessary. A Braille input device should receive no special treatment beyond that required for a keyboard.

Active Server Pages (ASP)   A special type of scripting language environment used by Windows servers equipped with Internet Information Server (IIS). This specialized scripting language environment helps the developer create flexible Web applications that include server scripts written in a number of languages such as VBScript, JavaScript, JScript, and PerlScript. The use of variables and other features, such as access to server variables, helps the developer create scripts that can compensate for user and environmental needs as well as security concerns. ASP uses HTML to display content to the user. Recent extensions to ASP in the form of Active Server Pages eXtended (ASPX) provide a broader range of application support functionality, improved debugging, new features such as "code behind," and improved performance. Note that you need to install the .NET Framework to use ASPX pages.

ActiveX Data Object (ADO)   A local and remote database access technology that relies on Object Linking and Embedding - DataBase (OLE-DB) to create the connection. ADO is a set of "wrapper" functions that make using OLE-DB and the underlying OLE-DB provider easier. ADO is designed as a replacement for Data Access Objects (DAO) and as an adjunct to Open DataBase Connectivity (ODBC).

ADO   See ActiveX Data Object

API   See Application Programming Interface

Applet   A helper or utility application that normally performs a task within a specialized environment such as a browser or as part of an operating system. Java is one of the most commonly used languages for creating applets for browser applications. Another example is the Control Panel applications used to configure Windows. In both cases, the applications perform a limited task within a specialized environment.

Application   The complete program or group of programs. An application is a complete environment for performing one or more related tasks.

Application Programming Interface (API)   A method of defining a standard set of function calls and other interface elements. It usually defines the interface between a high-level language and the lower level elements used by a device driver or operating system. The ultimate goal is to provide some type of service to an application that requires access to the operating system or device feature set.

Array   A structure that acts like an in-memory database. An array provides random or sequential access each element by number (also called a subscript). Arrays normally contain a single dimension. In some cases, arrays provide multi-dimensional access to data. A multidimensional array has the same number of elements in each sub-array in a given dimension. Jagged arrays treat each dimension as a separate sub-array, which means that each sub-array can contain a different number of elements.

ASP   See Active Server Pages

AT&T   American Telephone and Telegraph

Attribute   An attribute expresses some feature peculiar to an object. When referring to a database, each field has an attribute that expresses what type of information it contains, the length of the field, the field name, and the number of decimals. When referring to a display, the attribute expresses pixel color, intensity, and position. In programming, an attribute can also specify some type of object functionality, such as the method used to implement security.

B

Bandwidth   A measure of the amount of data a device can transfer in a given time. For example, the amount of data a processor can send to memory every second. In many cases, bandwidth also considers software limitations, such as the estimated bandwidth of an Internet connection.

BBB   Better Business Bureau

Binary   1. A numbering system that only uses two digits: 0 and 1. 2. A method used to store worksheets, graphic files, and other nontext information. The data store can appear in memory, but most often appears in a file on disk. While you can use the DOS TYPE command to send these files to the display, the contents of the file remain unreadable. Other binary files include programs with extensions of EXE, DLL, or COM.

Boolean   A method of determining whether a statement is true or false using rules of logic. Boolean values are often used to help a computer determine whether it needs to take a certain course of action based on current system or application conditions.

Browser   A special application, such as Internet Explorer, Opera, or Netscape, normally used to display data downloaded from the Internet. The most common form of Internet data is the HTML (HyperText Markup Language) page. However, modern browsers can also display various types of graphics and even standard desktop application files such as Word for Windows documents directly. The actual capabilities provided by a browser vary widely depending on the software vendor and platform.

Browser Plug-in   An external application that a browser calls to help it perform certain tasks. For example, the browser could call on the application to display a specific file type such as a PDF. The browser plug-in can take the form of a library or a stand-alone application. In many cases, browser documentation will also refer to them as helper applications.

Buffer   The area in memory where program variables, data, or executable code is stored. Buffers often act as a means of caching data or code. For example, word processing applications will normally read more than one page from a document to improve performance. The application stores pages in addition to the one currently viewed by the user in the buffer until needed. Buffering is also used in applications where long request delays are anticipated, such as applications based on Web services.

C

CAD   See Computer-Aided Drafting

Cascading Style Sheets (CSS)   A method for defining a standard Web page template. This may include headings, standard icons, backgrounds, and other features that would tend to give each page at a particular Web site the same appearance. The reason for using CSS includes speed of creating a Web site (it takes less time if the developer doesn't have to create an overall design for each page) and consistency. Changing the overall appearance of a Web site also becomes as easy as changing the style sheet instead of each page alone. CSS is also a standards supported technology, so it represents an easy method for developers to create Web pages that will work in standards-compliant browsers. There are several versions of CSS due to the standards process—using the most recent version of CSS is usually the best idea.

Cache   A storage area for data, code, or other resources normally associated with memory or a special file on a hard drive. Both hardware and applications rely on the cache to improve performance.

CD   Compact Disc

CD-ROM   See Compact Disc Read-Only Memory

CGI   See Common Gateway Interface

Client   The requestor and recipient of data, services, or other resources from a file or other server type. This term can refer to a workstation or an application. Often used in conjunction with the term "server," this is usually another PC or an application.

CLR   See Common Language Runtime

COM   See Component Object Model

Common Gateway Interface (CGI)   One of the more common methods of transferring data from a client machine to a Web server on the Internet. CGI is a specification that defines how a Web server can launch EXEs and communicate with them. A developer normally writes a GCI application using a low-level language such as C or Practical Extraction and Reporting Language (PERL). CGI receives input through the standard input device and output data through the standard output device. There are two basic data transfer types. The user can send new information to the server or can query data already existing on the server. A data entry form asking for the user's name and address is an example of the first type of transaction. A search engine page on the Internet (a page that helps the user find information on other sites) is an example of the second type of transaction. The Web server normally provides feedback for the user by transmitting a new page of information once the CGI application is complete. This could be as simple as an acknowledgment for data entry or a list of Internet sites for a data query.

Common Language Runtime (CLR)   The engine used to interpret managed applications within the .NET Framework. All Visual Studio .NET languages that produce managed applications can use the same runtime engine. The major advantages of this approach include extensibility (you can add other languages) and reduced code size (you don't need a separate runtime for each language).

Common Object Request Broker Architecture (CORBA) This protocol describes data and application code in the form of an object. This is the Object Management Group's (OMG) alternative to Microsoft's Component Object Model (COM). Although CORBA is incompatible with COM, it uses many of the same techniques as COM to create, manage, and define objects. CORBA was originally designed by IBM for inclusion with OS/2.

Compact Disc Read-Only Memory (CD-ROM) An optical storage technology used to store up to 650MB of permanent data. The optical media includes a reflective surface that the reader interprets as a 1. When a special writer burns a hole in the media, the reader sees the corresponding location as a 0. The combination of 0's and 1's forms the basis for interpreting the data.

Compiler A program that converts English-like statements into machine instructions in an executable or intermediate form. In some cases, the executable code can run without assistance on the host machine (called a native executable). In other cases, the intermediate code requires compilation into an executable form. This secondary form can rely on an interpreter, such as Beginner's All-Purpose Symbolic Instruction Code (BASIC), or runtime engine, such as Java, or it can use a secondary compiler or linker to change an object format into a standard native executable (C).

Component Object Model (COM) A Microsoft specification for a binary-based, object-oriented code and data encapsulation method and transference technique. It's the basis for technologies such as OLE (Object Linking and Embedding) and ActiveX (components and controls). COM is limited to local connections.

Computer-Aided Drafting (CAD) A special type of graphics program used for creating, printing, storing, and editing architectural, electrical, mechanical, or other forms of engineering drawings. CAD programs normally provide precise measuring capabilities and libraries of predefined objects, such as sinks, desks, resistors, and gears.

Connectivity A measure of the interactions between clients and servers. In many cases, connectivity begins with the local machine and the interactions between applications and components. Local Area Networks (LANs) introduce another level of connectivity with machine-to-machine communications. Finally, Wide Area Networks (WANs), Metro Area Networks (MANs), intranets, and the Internet all introduce further levels of connectivity concerns.

Cookie One or more special files used by an Internet browser to store site-specific settings or other information specific to Web pages. The purpose of this file is to store the value of one or more variables so that the Web page can restore them the next time the user visits a site. A Webmaster always saves and restores the cookie as part of some Web page programming task using a programming language such as JavaScript, Java, VBScript, or CGI. In most cases, this is the only file that a Webmaster can access on the client site's hard drive. The cookie could appear in one or more files anywhere on the hard drive, depending on the browser currently in use. Microsoft Internet Explorer uses one file for each site storing a cookie and places them in the Cookies folder that normally appears under the main Windows directory or within a user specific directory (such as the \Documents and Settings folder). Netscape Navigator uses a single file named COOKIE.TXT to store all of the cookies from all sites. This file normally appears in the main Navigator folder.

CORBA See Common Object Request Broker Architecture

Cracker A hacker (computer expert) who uses their skills for misdeeds on computer systems where they have little or no authorized access. A cracker normally possesses specialty software that allows easier access to the target network. In most cases, crackers require extensive amounts of time to break the security for a system before they can enter it. Some sources call a cracker a black hat hacker.

CSS See Cascading Style Sheets

D

DAO See Data Access Objects

Data Access Objects (DAO) An older data access technology introduced by Microsoft that relies on the Microsoft Access JET engine for local data access. DAO does not provide remote access features; although, some programmers have been able to establish unreliable connections with it. ActiveX Data Objects (ADO) and Object Linking and Embedding - DataBase (OLE-DB) have largely replaced this technology.

Data Source Name (DSN) A name assigned to an Open Database Connectivity (ODBC) connection. Applications use the DSN to make the connection to the database and gain access to specific database resources such as tables. The DSN always contains the name of the database

server, the database, and (optionally) a resource like a query or table. Many database technologies such as Object Linking and Embedding - DataBase (OLE-DB) rely on the use of DSN connection information.

Database Management System (DBMS) A method for storing and retrieving data based on tables, forms, queries, reports, fields, and other data elements. Each field represents a specific piece of data, such as an employee's last name. Records are made up of one or more fields. Each record is one complete entry in a table. A table contains one type of data, such as the names and addresses of all the employees in a company. It's composed of records (rows) and fields (columns), just like the tables you see in books. A database may contain one or more related tables. It may include a list of employees in one table, for example, and the pay records for each of those employees in a second table. Sometimes referred to as a Relational Database Management System (RDBMS) that includes products such as SQL Server and Oracle.

DBMS See Database Management System

DCOM See Distributed Component Object Model

DDE See Dynamic Data Exchange

Delimiter 1. A special symbol or symbols used to separate text. For example, many programming languages use the single (') or double (") quote to separate text elements. 2. A boundary between two different objects. The boundary normally consists of a special symbol or group of symbols. A delimited file contains variable length records. Each field normally uses a comma as a delimiter. Each record normally uses a carriage return as a delimiter.

Developer License   A special identifier issued by an organization to allow access to a resource such as a Web service. For example, Google issues a developer license to Google Web Services developers. The developer supplies this license for identification purposes when creating a Google Web Services application.

Digital Subscriber Line (DSL)   A term used to refer to any of a number of technologies that allow higher communication rates over standard telephone lines than normally allowed using standard modems. DSL is normally used between a remote location such as a home or office and the switching station or ISP. It isn't used between switching stations. Types of DSL include asynchronous DSL (ADSL), symmetric DSL (SDSL), and high bit-rate DSL (HDSL). The technologies vary by their ability to pack data onto the copper line, distance from the switching station, and other characteristics. ADSL allows communication from 1.5 Mbps to 9 Mbps downstream (to the remote connection) and 16 Kbps to 640 Kbps upstream (from the remote connection). SDSL allows communication up to 3 Mbps in both directions. HDSL allows communication up to 1.544 Mbps in both directions.

Digital Video Disc (DVD)   A high capacity optical storage media with capacities of 4.7GB to 17GB and data transfer rates of 600KBps to 1.3GBps. A single DVD can hold the contents of an entire movie or approximately 7.4 CD-ROMs. DVDs come in several formats that allow read-only or read-write access. All DVD drives include a second laser assembly used to read existing CD-ROMs. Some magazines will also use the term *digital versatile disc* for this storage media.

Distributed Component Object Model (DCOM)   A transport protocol that works with the component object model (COM), and is used for distributed application development. This protocol enables data transfers across the Internet or other non-local sources, but is usually limited to a Local Area Network (LAN) or Wide Area Network (WAN) environment. DCOM adds the capability to perform asynchronous, as well as synchronous, data transfers between machines. The use of asynchronous transfers prevents the client application from becoming blocked as it waits for the server to respond.

DLL   See Dynamic Link Library

DSL   See Digital Subscriber Line

DSN   See Data Source Name

DVD   See Digital Video Disc

Dynamic Data   Information that changes regularly due to internal or external events, as a result of the nature of the data, or consistent with a systematic or mathematical progression. For example, an application can provide automatic updates as it detects changes in the underlying data used for presentation. Many research sources, such as the Internet, now rely on dynamic data to reduce the effects of data aging.

Dynamic Data Exchange (DDE)   1. The capability to place data from one application on the Windows clipboard and paste it from the clipboard into another application. A user can cut a graphics image created with a paint program, for example, and paste it into a word processing document. After it's pasted, the data doesn't reflect the changes made to it by the originating application. The source and target applications must provide DDE functionality for this technology to work. They must also support the data formats required for the information exchange. 2. A method of communicating with an application that supports DDE when the application allows requests for data or services. The communication parameters include the application, the topic of the conversation, and a DDE message. In most cases, the DDE message consists of a series of menu or macro sequences that perform the desired task.

Dynamic Link Library (DLL) A specific form of application code loaded into memory by request. It's not executable by itself like an EXE is. A DLL does contain one or more discrete routines that an application may use to provide specific features. For example, a DLL could provide a common set of file dialogs used to access information on the hard drive. More than one application can use the functions provided by a DLL, reducing overall memory requirements when more than one application is running. DLLs have a number of purposes. For example, they can contain device-specific code in the form of a device driver. Some types of COM objects also rely on DLLs.

E

ECMA See European Computer Manufacturer's Association

Emulator A specialized application that provides the same features and functionality as the target

device. The device on which the emulator runs is normally more capable than the emulated device. For example, emulators commonly enable a developer to test applications designed for use on Personal Digital Assistants (PDAs) using the standard PC.

Error Trapping The additional code required to detect, analyze, repair, report, and overcome errors in an application. An error trapping routine normally locates the precise origin of the error, determines the error type, and defines a course of action for repairing the error when possible. If the application can't recover, the error trapping routine helps the application fail gracefully after reporting the source and cause of the error to the application user.

European Computer Manufacturer's Association (ECMA) A standards committee originally founded in 1961. ECMA is dedicated to standardizing information and communication systems. For example, they created the ECMAScript standard used for many Web page designs today. You can also find ECMA standards for product safety, security, networks, and storage media.

eXtensible Access Control Markup Language (XACML) A technique for creating secure Web service data communication. This standard lets developers add specialized XML tags to their code that define the security policy for data communication needs such as a Web service. Many developers view XACML as the next step beyond Security Assertions Markup Language (SAML). In fact, XACML is a high-level protocol that relies on SAML to perform many of the low-level tasks.

eXtensible Hypertext Markup Language (XHTML)
A cross between eXtensible Markup Language (XML) and HyperText Markup Language (HTML) specifically designed for Internet devices such as Personal Digital Assistants (PDAs) and cellular telephones, but also usable with desktop machine browsers. Since this language relies on XML, most developers classify it as an XML application builder. The language relies on several standardized namespaces to provide common data type and interface definitions. XHTML creates modules that are interpreted based on a specific platform's requirements. This means that a single document can serve the needs of many display devices.

eXtensible Markup Language (XML) 1. A method used to store information in an organized manner. The storage technique relies on hierarchical organization and uses special statements called tags to separate each storage element. Each tag defines a data attribute and can contain properties that further define each data element. 2. A standardized Web page design language used to incorporate data structuring within standard HTML documents. For example, you could use XML to display database information using something other than forms or tables. It's actually a lightweight version of Standardized Generalized Markup Language (SGML) and is supported by the SGML community. XML also supports tag extensions that allow various parts of a Web-based application to exchange information. For example, once a user makes a choice within a catalog, that information could be added to an order entry form with a minimum of effort on the part of the developer. Since XML is easy to extend, some developers look at it as more of a base specification for other languages, rather than a complete language.

eXtensible Markup Language Remote Procedure Call (XML-RPC) A technique for passing XML requests to a Web server that mimics the method calling strategy used by older technologies such as Distributed Common Object Model (DCOM) and Common Object Request Broker Architecture (CORBA). The client constructs an XML document with the required arguments as nodes in a specialized RPC format and transmits it to the server using a transport such as HyperText Transfer Protocol (HTTP).

eXtensible Style Language (XSL) This term is also listed as eXtensible Stylesheet Language by some sources. XSL is a technology that separates the method of presentation from the actual content of either an eXtensible Markup Language (XML) or HyperText Markup Language (HTML) page. The XSL document contains all of the required formatting information so that the content remains in pure form. This is the second style language submitted to the World Wide Web Consortium (W3C) for consideration. The first specification was for Cascading Style Sheets (CSS). XSL documents use an XML-like format.

eXtensible Style Language Transformation (XSLT)
The language used within the eXtensible Style Language (XSL) to transform the content provided in an eXtensible Markup Language (XML) file into a form for display on screen or printing. An XSL processor combines XML content with the formatting instructions provided by XSLT and outputs a new document or document fragment. XSLT is a World Wide Web Consortium (W3C) standard.

F

Fault Tolerance   The ability of an object (application, device, or other entity) to recover from an error. For example, the fault tolerance provided by a transaction server allows a network to recover from potential data loss induced by a system or use failure. Another example of fault tolerance is the ability of a Redundant Array of Inexpensive Disks (RAID) system to recover from a hard drive failure.

File Transfer Protocol (FTP)   One of several common data transfer protocols for the Internet. This particular protocol specializes in data transfer in the form of a file download or upload. The site presents the user with a list of available files in a directory list format. An FTP site may choose DOS or UNIX formatting for the file listing, although the DOS format is extremely rare. Unlike HTTP sites, an FTP site provides a definite information hierarchy using directories and subdirectories, much like the file directory structure used on most workstation hard drives. Generally, FTP transfers require a special application, but some browsers now include this capability. FTP transfers occur without encryption, so security is an issue unless the owner of the FTP site encrypts the individual files.

Filtering   The act of removing unnecessary information from a data stream, data store, or response set. For example, when you receive data from a Web service, the response set will likely contain data you don't need for the current application. In most cases, applications use filtering to make the resulting output easier to understand and less complex.

FTP   See File Transfer Protocol

G

GIF   See Graphics Interchange Format

Graphics Interchange Format (GIF)   One of several standard file formats used to transfer graphics over the Internet. There are several different standards for this file format—the latest of which is the GIF89a standard you'll find used on most Internet sites. CompuServe originally introduced the GIF standard as a method for reducing the time required to download a graphic and the impact of any single-bit errors that might occur. A secondary form of the GIF is the animated GIF. It allows the developer to store several images within one file. Between each image within the file are one or more control blocks that determine block boundaries, the display location of the next image in relation to the display area, and other display features. A browser or other specially designed application will display the graphic images one at a time in the order in which they appear within the file to create animation effects.

Graphical User Interface (GUI)   1. A method of displaying information that depends on both hardware capabilities and software instructions. A GUI uses the graphics capability of a display adapter to improve communication between the computer and its user. Using a GUI involves a large investment in both programming and hardware resources. 2. A system of icons and graphic images that replace the character mode menu system used by many older machines including "green screen" terminals that are connected to mainframes and sometimes to cash registers. The GUI can ride on top of another operating system (such as DOS, Linux, and

Unix) or reside as part of the operating system itself (such as the Macintosh and Windows). Advantages of a GUI are ease of use and high-resolution graphics. Disadvantages include cost, higher workstation hardware requirements, and lower performance over a similar system using a character mode interface.

GUI   See Graphical User Interface

H

Hacker   An individual who works with computers at a low level (hardware or software), especially in the area of security. A hacker normally possesses specialty software or other tools that allows easier access to the target hardware or software application or network. The media defines two types of hackers which include those who break into systems for ethical purposes and those who do it to damage the system in some way. The proper term for the second group is crackers (see *cracker* for details). Some people have started to call the first group "ethical hackers" or "white hat hackers" to prevent confusion. Ethical hackers normally work for security firms that specialize in finding holes in a company's security. However, hackers work in a wide range of computer arenas. For example, a person who writes low-level code (like that found in a device driver) after reverse engineering an existing driver is technically a hacker. The main emphasis of a hacker is to work for the benefit of others in the computer industry.

Handheld Device Markup Language (HDML)   A technology that predates most standardized efforts, such as the Wireless Access Protocol

(WAP), for transmitting Internet content to cellular telephones. It's a proprietary language that users can only view using OpenWave browsers. The associated transport protocol is the Handheld Device Transport Protocol (HDTP). A user types a request into the phone, which is transferred to a gateway server using HDTP. The gateway server translates the request to HTTP, which it sends to the Web server. The Web server provides specialized HDML content, which the gateway server transfers to the cellular telephone using HDTP. To use this protocol, the Web server must understand the text/x-hdml Multipurpose Internet Mail Extensions (MIME) type.

Handheld Device Transport Protocol (HDTP)   A specialized set of rules for sending requests and receiving responses using a mobile device such as a cellular telephone or Personal Digital Assistant (PDA). This transport provides the same services as HTTP, but with the needs of mobile devices in mind.

HDML   See Handheld Device Markup Language

HDTP   See Handheld Device Transport Protocol

Hierarchical   1. A method of arranging data within a database that relies on a tree-like node structure, rather than a relational structure. 2. A method of displaying information on screen that relies on an indeterminate number of nodes connected to a root node. 3. A chart or graph in which the elements are arranged in ranks. The ranks usually follow an order of simple to complex or higher to lower.

Hit   The successful completion of a task or goal. This term is normally associated with searches where a single hit is one search result. It's also used in context with Web pages, where one person visiting the site is considered a hit.

HTML   See HyperText Markup Language

HTTP   See HyperText Transfer Protocol

HyperText Markup Language (HTML)   1. A data presentation and description (markup) language for the Internet that depends on the use of tags (keywords within angle brackets <>) to display formatted information onscreen in a non-platform-specific manner. The non-platform-specific nature of this markup language makes it difficult to perform some basic tasks such as placement of a screen element at a specific location. However, the language does provide for the use of fonts, color, and various other enhancements onscreen. There are also tags for displaying graphic images. Scripting tags for using scripting languages such as VBScript and JavaScript are available, although not all browsers support this addition. The <OBJECT> tag addition allows the use of ActiveX controls. 2. One method of displaying text, graphics, and sound on the Internet. HTML provides an ASCII-formatted page of information read by a special application called a browser. Depending on the browser's capabilities, some keywords are translated into graphics elements, sounds, or text with special characteristics, such as color, font, or other attributes. Most browsers discard any keywords they don't understand, allowing browsers of various capabilities to explore the same page without problem. Obviously, there's a loss of capability if a browser doesn't support a specific keyword.

HyperText Transfer Protocol (HTTP)   One of several common data transfer protocols for the Internet. HTTP normally transfers textual data of some type. For example, the HyperText Markup Language (HTML) relies on HTTP to transfer the Web pages it defines from the server to the client. The eXtensible Markup Language and Simple Object Access Protocol (SOAP) also commonly rely on HTTP to transfer data between client and server. It's important to note that HTTP is separate from the data it transfers. For example, it's possible for SOAP to use the Simple Mail Transfer Protocol (SMTP) to perform data transfers between client and server.

I

IDE   See Integrated Development Environment

IETF   See Internet Engineering Task Force

IIS   See Internet Information Server

Integrated Development Environment (IDE)   A programming language front end that provides all the tools you need to write an application through a single editor. The IDE normally includes support for development language help, access to any tools required to support the language, a compiler, and a debugger. Some IDEs include support for advanced features such as automatic completion of language statements and balloon help showing the syntax for functions and other language elements. Many IDEs also use color or highlighting to emphasize specific language elements or constructs. Older DOS programming language products provided several utilities—one for each of the main programming tasks. Most (if not all) Windows programming languages provide some kind of IDE support.

Integrated Services Digital Network (ISDN)   A term used to refer to any of a number of technologies that allow higher communication rates over standard telephone lines than normally allowed using standard modems. ISDN can also use digital telephone lines in addition to the normal voice telephone lines. The basic transmission rate of ISDN is 64 Kbps. However, a special variant called B-ISDN can tranmit data at 1.5 Mbps. The line is normally divided into a number of channels. A Basic Rate Interface (BRI) supports two 64 Kbps B channels for transmitting data and a D channel for transmitting control information. A Primary Rate Interface (PRI) supports 23 B channels (United States) or 30 B channels (Europe) and one D channel.

Internationalized Application   An application that contains code or other resources necessary to make the output seen by the user appear in one or more languages. In most cases, this also means modifying date and monetary format to the form used by that culture.

Internet Engineering Task Force (IETF)   The standards group tasked with finding solutions to pressing technology problems on the Internet. This group can approve standards created both within the organization itself and outside the organization as part of other group efforts. For example, Microsoft has requested the approval of several new Internet technologies through this group. If approved, the technologies would become an Internet-wide standard performing data transfer and other specific kinds of tasks.

Internet Information Server (IIS)   Microsoft's full-fledged Web server that normally runs under the Windows Server operating system. IIS includes all the features that you'd normally expect with a Web server: FTP and HTTP protocols along with both mail and news services. Older versions of IIS also support the Gopher protocol; newer versions don't provide this support because most Web sites no longer need it.

Internet Server Application Programming Interface (ISAPI)   A set of function calls and interface elements designed to make using Microsoft's Internet Information Server (IIS) easier. Essentially, this set of API calls provides the programmer with access to the server itself. This technology makes it easier to provide full server access to the Internet server through a series of ActiveX controls, without the use of a scripting language. There are two forms of ISAPI: filters and extensions. An extension replaces script-based technologies like CGI. Its main purpose is to provide dynamic content to the user. A filter can extend the server itself by monitoring various events like user requests for access in the background. You can use a filter to create various types of new services like extended logging or specialized security schemes. Most developers use technologies such as Active Server Pages (ASP) in place of ISAPI because these technologies are easier to use. For example, ASP makes it easy to modify a file without the need to recompile it. However, ISAPI is still used for speed critical applications such as the Simple Object Access Protocol (SOAP) listener used by some SOAP implementations.

Internet Service Provider (ISP)   A vendor that provides one or more Internet-related services through a dial-up, Digital Subscriber Line (DSL), Integrated Services Digital Network (ISDN), or other outside connection. Normal services include email, newsgroup access, full Internet Web site access, and personal Web page hosting.

ISAPI   See Internet Server Application Programming Interface

ISBN   See International Standard Book Number

ISDN   See Integrated Services Digital Network

ISP   See Internet Service Provider

J

J2SE   Java 2.0 Standard Edition

Java DataBase Connectivity (JDBC)   A method of providing database interoperability similar to Open Database Connectivity (ODBC). This form of connectivity is Java specific, and other applications require a JDBC-ODBC bridge to provide the necessary interoperability between the two systems. JDBC always uses SQL statements to request data from the database manager. Although ODBC is language independent, it has limited platform support. JDBC is language specific but runs on any platform that supports Java.

Java Development Kit (JDK)   A special set of application development tools, resources, example code, help files, and other resources designed to help a programmer create Java applications. The JDK normally contains a full set of development tools and a copy of the Java Runtime Enviroment (JRE). However, most developers will require one or more third party solutions to create a complex Java application. For example, unlike many languages today, Java doesn't provide SOAP support, so the developer would require a third party library to create an application that relies on SOAP.

Java Runtime Environment (JRE)   Another name for the Java Virtual Machine (JVM). This set of files provides Java support on the host machine, allowing it to run Java applications.

Java Virtual Machine (JVM)   The application used to interpret the Java language originally developed by Sun Microsystems. This includes both text and byte code .CLASS files containing common routines. Java is similar to C++, but eliminates many of the complex programming constructs and uses a more restrictive security scheme. Many operating systems have a Java Virtual Machine including most versions of Windows, Mac OS, and Unix. The use of text files means that Java applets can run on any number of operating system platforms without modifications, but the use of an interpreter implies slower execution speed.

JDBC   See Java DataBase Connectivity

JDK   See Java Development Kit

JRE   See Java Runtime Environment

JVM   See Java Virtual Machine

K

Keyword A term used for a specific purpose. For example, a researcher can use one or more keywords to perform a search for specialized data. A developer can use keywords to write an application. An accountant could use keywords to create equations within a spreadsheet. The keyword is set apart from other words in that it provides specialized functionality.

L

LAN See Local Area Network

LCID See Locale Identifier

Local Area Network (LAN) Two or more devices located in a relatively small physical area connected together using a combination of hardware and software. The devices, normally computers and peripheral equipment such as printers, are called nodes. A NIC (network interface card) provides the hardware communication between nodes through an appropriate medium (cable or microwave transmission.) The actual connection is provided through cables, in many cases, but can also rely on radio waves, infrared, and other technologies. There are two common types of LANs (also called networks). Peer-to-peer networks allow each node to connect to any other node on the network with shareable resources. This is a distributed method of files and peripheral devices. A client-server network uses one or more servers to share resources. This is a centralized method of sharing files and peripheral devices. A server provides resources to clients (usually workstations).

Locale Identifier (LCID) A number that uniquely identifies a country, language, or other nationalistic information. An application, online resource, or data manager uses the LCID to provide specific information, services, or resources in a form that the user can understand. For example, many applications support more than one language and the application would use the LCID to change the prompts to match the user's language.

Loop A method of running repetitive instructions. Most languages implement several kinds of loop instructions that include specific counts or Boolean terminations. An example of a specific count loop is the for structure supported by most languages, which processes a set of instructions a specific number of times and then stops. An example of a Boolean termination is the while structure that continues processing instructions until the terminating condition meets a specific requirement such as variable equality.

M

Marshal The act of making data created by one object accessible and acceptable to another object. The process of marshaling usually includes moving the data from one memory space to another memory space. The marshaling process could also include some type of data conversion. The type of data conversion depends on the requirements of both objects and the data types that they support.

Microsoft Database Engine (MSDE) This term also appears as Microsoft Desktop Engine and Microsoft Data Engine in various publications. MSDE is a miniature form of SQL Server that enables developers to create a test database application. Microsoft designed this engine for use by one person, usually the developer; however, you can potentially use it for up to five people. The developer accesses MSDE through a programming language Integrated Development Environment (IDE) or using command line utilities. In some cases, MSDE is also used to provide access to a remote copy of SQL Server. Some third party products, such as MSDE Query, provide a Graphical User Interface (GUI) for MSDE.

MIME   See Multipurpose Internet Mail Extensions

MSDE   See Microsoft Database Engine

MSDN   Microsoft Developer Network

Multipurpose Internet Mail Extensions (MIME) The standard method for defining the content of Internet messages. This standard allows computers to exchange objects, character sets, and multimedia using email without regard to the computer's underlying operating system. MIME is defined in the Internet Engineering Task Force (IETF) Request for Comment (RFC) 1521 standard.

N

Network Interface Card (NIC)   The device responsible for allowing a workstation to communicate with servers and other workstations. It provides the physical means for creating the connection. The card plugs into an expansion slot in the computer. A cable that attaches to the back of the card completes the communication path.

NIC   See Network Interface Card

Node   1. A single element in a file that might contain a number of leaf elements. The file normally couples nodes into a hierarchical structure, such as the structure used by the eXtensible Markup Language (XML). Some database systems also use the hierarchical structure of nodes and leaves to make data easier or faster to locate. 2. A single element in a network. In most cases, the term *node* refers to a single workstation connected to the network. It can also refer to a bridge, router, or file server. It doesn't refer to cabling, passive, or active elements that don't directly interface with the network at the logical level.

Non-connected Mode   A state in which the client can't communicate with the server. Most applications don't provide support for a non-connected mode unless they also provide some type of caching. For example, an application that normally communicates with a database over a network usually needs to maintain a connection to the database to operate. In some cases, applications support non-connected mode by establishing a local cache of data found at a remote resource, such as a Web service, by storing common data in a local database.

O

Object Linking and Embedding (OLE)   The process of packaging a file name or data, server name (generally an application), and any required parameters into an object, and then placing this object into the file created by another application. For example, a user could place a graphic object within a word processing document or spreadsheet. OLE supports both linking (placing a pointer to the source data in permanent storage in the target file) and embedding (placing the actual data into the target file). When you look at the object it appears as if you simply pasted the data from the originating application into the current application, which is similar to Dynamic Data Exchange (DDE). However, the data object created by OLE automatically changes as you change the data in the original object (provided you use the linking portion of the technology). It also contains the intelligence to know which application created the data. Generally, you can start the originating application and automatically load the required data by double-clicking on the object.

Object Linking and Embedding - Database (OLE-DB)
A low level database access technology that relies on COM and a vendor supplied OLE-DB provider rather than the SQL used by Open DataBase Connectivity (ODBC). OLE-DB is designed to work with both remote and local databases. In addition, it can access database managers that don't rely on SQL, such as those found on mainframe computers. OLE-DB and ODBC are cooperative, rather than competing data access technologies. OLE-DB, when coupled with ActiveX Data Objects (ADO), is designed to replace older database technologies such as Remote Data Objects (RDO) and Data Access Objects (DAO).

ODBC   See Open Database Connectivity

ODP   See Open Directory Project

OLE   See Object Linking and Embedding

OLE-DB   See Object Linking and Embedding - Database

Open Database Connectivity (ODBC)   One of several methods for exchanging data between DBMSs. In most cases, this involves three steps: installing an appropriate driver, adding a source to the ODBC applet in the Control Panel, and using specialized statements, such as Structured Query Language (SQL), to access the database.

OPML   See Outline Processor Markup Language

Open Directory Project (ODP)   A Web site directory originally created by Rich Skrenta as GnuHoo. The directory originally used volunteer editors to enter Web site names, categories, and descriptions into a database. Netscape acquired the directory on 17 November 1998 and renamed it ODP. A number of search engines, such as Google, Netscape Open Directory, Netscape What's Related, Lycos, HotBot, Dogpile, Thunderstone, Mars Society, and Linux.com Links use ODP as a source of Web site information.

Outline Processor Markup Language (OPML)   An XML-based format for exchange of outline structured information in Web pages or other documents. Each entry represents a different level of the document hierarchy. Designing these documents as an outline makes them easier to understand in many cases.

P

P3P   See Platform for Privacy Preferences

Palm   A mobile, handheld device normally associated with office tasks such as maintaining an address list or appointment calendar. The Palm uses the Palm operating system. Although this device lacks the processing power of higher end devices such as the Pocket PC, most office workers prefer its small size and long battery life.

Parameter   A value received by a function or procedure from another function or procedure, the command line, or some other source.

Parse   The act of reducing a string or other data structure to its constituent parts. For example, spreadsheets normally break words and numbers apart using the spaces between them as the break point. Developers use a multitude of application programming techniques to perform data element parsing and some object technology even includes a Parse() method.

PDA   See Personal Digital Assistant

PERL   See Practical Extraction and Report Language

Personal Digital Assistant (PDA)   A small hand-held device such as a Palm Pilot or Pocket PC. These devices are normally used for personal tasks such as taking notes and maintaining an itinerary during business trips. Some PDAs rely on special operating systems and lack any standard application support. However, newer PDAs include some level of standard application support, because vendors are supplying specialized compilers for them. In addition, you'll find common applications included, such as browsers and application office suites that include word processing and spreadsheet support.

Personal Web Server (PWS)   A less capable version of Internet Information Server (IIS) that's designed to provided limited Web access on an intranet. PWS isn't designed to provide the same level of services as IIS, but it does provide enough capability for a small company intranet or for a developer's test setup.

PHP   PHP Hypertext Processor

Platform   A description of the combination of software and hardware used to create a computing system. For example, many users use a combination of the Windows operating system and an Intel processor. The combination often appears as the Wintel platform. In some cases, a discussion will only use the operating system as the basis for a platform. A developer might create applications only for the Windows platform. The use of the term *platform* is often ambiguous and requires the actual platform type to make the meaning clear.

Platform for Privacy Preferences (P3P)   A Worldwide Web Consortium (W3C) sponsored technique for ensuring privacy through specialized programming techniques. The specification defines methods of communicating information requests, use, storage technique, and requirements to the requestor. The requestor then decides whether the requirements are acceptable and optionally transfers the necessary information.

Portable Network Graphic (PNG)   A graphics file format (pronounced ping) similar to the Graphics Interchange Format (GIF) used for Internet graphics. This graphics format is newer than the GIF and many developers consider it superior because it uses a newer compression mechanism. Many developers use the PNG file format because it doesn't rely on patented technology as the GIF format does.

PNG   See Portable Network Graphic

Pocket PC   A mobile, handheld device used to perform any of a number of computing tasks. A Pocket PC normally runs some form of advanced mobile operating system such as Windows CE or Windows XP. Most developers differentiate a Pocket PC from a Palm handheld device by the enhanced processing power, greater number of features, and larger display of the Pocket PC. A Pocket PC is also bulkier than a Palm, making it less suitable for some applications.

Point of Presence (POP)   An access point to the Internet normally associated with physical access such as a modem connection.

POP   See Point of Presence

Practical Extraction and Report Language (PERL)
Originally designed as a report generation language for the Internet, PERL has found other uses as well for more general Internet programming needs. PERL is normally an interpreted scripting language.

PWS   See Personal Web Server

Q

Quantum Computer   A new technology device that relies on subatomic reactions (quantum mechanics) to perform calculations or other computer-oriented tasks. Unlike current computer technology, a quantum computer is quaternary (having four states), rather than binary (having two states). Generally, quantum computers will be extremely small and fast and won't follow the rules of physics used by current computer technology.

R

RAID   See Redundant Array of Independent (or Inexpensive) Disks

RDO   See Remote Data Objects

Recordset   The result of a query on one or more tables of a database. A recordset contains a single result set consisting of a single table. The recordset relies on a connection with the DBMS in order to perform data exchange and update.

Redundant Array of Independent (or Inexpensive) Disks (RAID)   A set of interconnected drives that reside outside the server in many cases, but are connected to the server through cabling. Workstation RAID setups tend to reside in the workstation cabinet. There are several levels of RAID. Each level defines precisely how the data is placed on each of the drives. In all cases, all the drives in a group share responsibility for storing the data. They act in parallel to both read and write the data. In addition, there is a special drive in most of these systems devoted to helping the network recover when one drive fails. In most cases the user never even knows that anything happened, the "spare drive" takes over for the failed drive without any noticeable degradation in network operation. RAID systems increase network reliability and throughput.

Regression Search   A search in which the user or search engine begins with the result data and looks for the information used to create the results. For example, the search could begin with the word *salt* and end up with pages that describe the interaction of sodium and chloride.

Remote Data Objects (RDO)   An older Microsoft database technology that provides access to remote data using a set of Component Object Model (COM) objects similar to those found in technologies such as Data Access Objects (DAO) and Open DataBase Connectivity (ODBC). This technology relies on database providers to support multiple database products.

Remote Procedure Call (RPC)   One of several methods for accessing data within another application. RPC is designed to look for the application first on the local workstation, and then across the network at the applications stored on other workstations.

REpresentational State Transfer (REST)   A technique for passing data to a Web service using one or more arguments as part of an URL. Each argument represents an XML node that the client would normally pass as an XML document. This technique is also known as XML-over-HTTP. The input to the Web server is a standard URL with arguments, while the output is an XML document. Some developers use this technique to reduce the coding required to obtain Web service output on less capable devices or on Web sites.

REST   See REpresentational State Transfer

Rich Site Summary (RSS)   A technology that enables a content creator to register content with a publisher using specially formatted eXtensible Markup Language (XML) data. Subscribers access the content through the publisher. Content creators use this technology, originally developed by Netscape, to output information such as news feeds, product announcements, events, and other items of general or specific interest. Also known as Resource Description Framework (RDF) Site Summary.

RPC   See Remote Procedure Call

RSS   See Rich Site Summary

S

SAML   See Security Assertions Markup Language

Safe Search   A Google search in which links with pornographic content are minimized or excluded whenever possible.

Schema   A formal method for describing the structure of a database, storage technology, or data transfer technique such as XML. The schema defines the requirements for constructing the object in question. For example, a schema for a relational database would include information on the structure of tables, fields, and relations within the database.

Script   Usually associated with an interpreted macro language used to create simple applications, productivity enhancers, or automated data manipulators. Most operating systems support at least one scripting language. You'll also find scripting capability in many higher end applications such as Web browsers and word processors. Scripts are normally used to write small utility type applications rather than large-scale applications that require the use of a compiled language. In addition, many script languages are limited in their access to the full set of operating system features.

SDK   See Software Development Kit

Search Terms   One or more keywords combined with Boolean logic and specialized search conditions to form a phrase that expresses a search. For example, when using Google, the search term *DataCon Services –VBA site:www.mwt.net*, would locate all links that included the term *DataCon Services*, but wouldn't include *VBA*, on the *www.mwt.net* domain.

Secure Sockets Layer (SSL)   A digital signature technology used for exchanging information between a client and a server. Essentially an SSL-compliant server will request a digital certificate from the client machine. The client can likewise request a digital certificate from the server. Companies or individuals obtain these digital certificates from a third party vendor like VeriSign or other trusted source that can vouch for the identity of both parties.

Security Assertions Markup Language (SAML)   A technique for securing XML-based data communications that depends on the use of specialized tags. This technology defines mechanisms to exchange authentication, authorization, and non-repudiation information between client and server. It relies on a single sign-on technique to ensure the user doesn't receive constant requests for authentication information. SAML follows a four step process in which the caller makes a service or resource request, the SAML server requests authentication information, the SAML server uses the authentication information to open a session with the remote server, and finally, the caller receives an URL to use to access the service or resource.

Security Token   A number or other unique symbol used to identify a requestor (user or other entity). The security token acts as a key that allows a requestor to obtain resources from a secure location.

Serializer   Specialized software used to convert data chunks, such as a string or a file, into individual bits for transmission to a remote location. The act of serializing data makes it possible to transfer large quantities of data as individualized bits and then reconstruct the original form at the remote location.

SGML   See Standard Generalized Markup Language

Simple Mail Transfer Protocol (SMTP)   One of the most commonly used protocols to transfer text (commonly mail) messages between clients and servers. This is a stream-based protocol designed to allow query, retrieval, posting, and distribution of mail messages. Normally, this protocol is used in conjunction with other mail retrieval protocols like point of presence (POP). However, not all uses of SMTP involve email data transfer. Some Simple Object Access Protocol (SOAP) applications have also relied on SMTP to transfer application data.

Simple Object Access Protocol (SOAP)   A Microsoft-sponsored protocol that provides the means for exchanging data between COM and foreign component technologies like Common Object Request Broker Architecture (CORBA) using XML as an intermediary. SOAP is often used as the basis for Web services communication. However, a developer could also use SOAP on a LAN or in any other environment where machine-to-machine communication is required and the two target machines provide the required infrastructure.

SLN   See Solution File

Smartphone   A special form of the cellular telephone that normally includes a larger display, better processing capabilities, and more memory. The Smartphone makes some types of advanced development possible. However, a Smartphone doesn't posses the same capabilities of some handheld devices such as the Pocket PC or Palm. Some programming environments, such as Visual Studio .NET, provide special support for the Smartphone.

SMTP   See Simple Mail Transfer Protocol

SOAP   See Simple Object Access Protocol

Software Development Kit (SDK)   A special add-on to an operating system or an application that describes how to access its internal features. For example, an SDK for Windows would show how to create a File Open dialog box. Programmers use an SDK to learn how to access special Windows components such as the Component Object Model (COM) or the Media Player.

Solution File (SLN)   The file used by Visual Studio and other development environments to store application settings such as special file views and a list of the files contained within the application. The solution file is the central storage location for application-specific information that doesn't affect the actual application code.

SSL   See Secure Sockets Layer

Standard Generalized Markup Language (SGML)   A specification for defining document format

originally created for the publishing industry. Most developers consider SGML too complex for standard display purposes. However, both XML and HTML are based on SGML.

Static Data   Information that doesn't change. For example, many Web sites provide static data output; the information remains the same from visit to visit.

Stop Words   Search terms that Google doesn't recognize as appropriate. Most small words such as "to" and "the" are stop words. Words that contain numbers and the numbers themselves are stop words. Adding a + (plus sign) in front of the stop word tells Google to consider it as one of the search terms.

Structured Query Language (SQL)   Most Database Management Systems (DBMSs) use this language to exchange information. Some also use it as their native language. SQL provides a method for manipulating data controlled by the DBMS. It defines which table or tables to use, what information to get from the table, and how to sort the information. A typical request will include the name of the database, table, and columns needed for display or editing purposes. SQL can filter a request and limit the number of rows using special features. Developers also use SQL to manipulate database information by adding, deleting, modifying, or searching records. IBM research center designed SQL between 1974 and 1975. Oracle introduced the first product to use SQL in 1979. SQL originally appeared on mainframe and minicomputers. Today it's a favorite language for most PC DBMS as well. There are many versions of SQL.

SQL   See Structured Query Language

T

Tag   A generic term that refers to the specialized combination of keywords and punctuation used in a markup language such as HyperText Markup Language (HTML) or eXtensible Markup Language (XML). In many cases, the tag appears as a tag pair. For example, <H1>My Header</H1> contains a tag pair, <H1>, and associated text. The <H1> tag designates a level 1 header.

TCP/IP   See Transmission Control Protocol/Internet Protocol

Transaction Identifier   A number or other indicator used to identify a data exchange between client and server. The transaction identifier serves to maintain the link between individual transactions.

Transmission Control Protocol/Internet Protocol (TCP/IP)   A standard communication line protocol (set of rules) developed by the U.S. Department of Defense. The protocol defines how two devices talk to each other. TCP defines a communication methodology where it guarantees packet delivery and also ensures the packets appear at the recipient in the same order they were sent. IP defines the packet characteristics.

U

UI   See User Interface

Unicode Transformation Format (UTF)   A standardized method of representing characters both printed and abstract using codes. Other forms of character representation include ASCII. Some sources also abbreviate this term as Universal Character Set (UCS) Transformation Format.

Uniform Resource Identifier (URI)   A generic term for all names and addresses that reference objects on the Internet. An URL is a specific type of URI. See Uniform Resource Locator (URL).

Uniform Resource Locator (URL)   A text representation of a specific location on the Internet. URLs normally include the protocol (http:// for example), the target location (World Wide Web or www), the domain or server name (mycompany), and a domain type (com for commercial). It can also include a hierarchical location within that Web site. The URL usually specifies a particular file on the Web server, although there are some situations when a Web server will use a default filename. For example, asking the browser to find http://www.mycompany.com, would probably display the DEFAULT.HTM or INDEX.HTM file at that location. The actual default filename depends on the Web server used. In some cases, the default filename is configurable and could be any of a number of files. For example, Internet Information Server (IIS) offers this feature, so the developer can use anything from an HTM, to an ASP, to an XML file as the default.

Universal Product Code (UPC)   A 12-digit numbering system used to uniquely identify products of all types. The UPC is normally accompanied by a bar code that makes the number computer readable using scanning technology. A central agency manages the number list and each country has one agency that manages the pool of numbers assigned to that country. For example, the Uniform Code Council (UCC) manages the 12-digit numbers for North America. A UPC contains three groups of numbers: company prefix (6 digits), item reference number (5 digits), and check digit (1 digit). The 13-digit European Article Numbering (EAN) system is compatible with UPC to a point; all systems that read EAN can also read UPC, but the reverse isn't always true.

UPC   See Universal Product Code

URI   See Uniform Resource Identifier

User Interface (UI)   The portion of an application that contains user accessible controls and data manipulation elements. The user interface for a Windows application is commonly composed of buttons, text boxes, static text, graphics, and other design elements.

URL   See Uniform Resource Locator

UTF   See Unicode Transformation Format

V

VBA   See Visual Basic for Applications

Visual Basic for Applications (VBA)   A true subset of the Visual Basic language. This form of Visual Basic is normally used within applications in place of a standard macro language. Normally, you can't create stand-alone applications using this language in its native environment; however, you could move a VBA program to Visual Basic and compile it there.

W

W3C   See World Wide Web Consortium

WAN   See Wide Area Network

WAP   See Wireless Access Protocol

Web Services Description Language (WSDL)   A method for describing a Web-based application that is accessible through an Internet connection, also known as a service. The file associated with this description contains the service description, port type, interface description, individual method names, and parameter types. A WSDL relies on namespace support to provide descriptions of common elements such as data types. Most WSDL files include references to two or more resources maintained by standards organizations to ensure compatibility across implementations.

Wide Area Network (WAN)   An extension of the Local Area Network (LAN), a WAN connects two or more LANs together using a variety of methods. A WAN usually encompasses more than one physical site, such as a building. Most WANs rely on microwave communications, fiber optic connections, or leased telephone lines to provide the internetwork connections to keep all nodes in the network talking with each other.

Wireless Access Protocol (WAP)   A method of providing secure access for mobile devices of all types to Web-based application content through a gateway. The underlying technology works much like Handheld Device Markup Language (HDML), but using standardized and secure access techniques. This technology supports most mobile networks including Cellular Digital Packet Data (CDPD), Code-Division Multiple Access (CDMA), Global System for Mobile Communications (GSM), and Time Division Multiple Access (TDMA). Supported mobile device operating systems include PalmOS, EPOC, Windows CE, FLEXOS, OS/9, and JavaOS. The technology can support pages in either Wireless Markup Language (WML) or HyperText Markup Language (HTML) format; however, WML is preferred because it better supports mobile device requirements.

Wireless Markup Language (WML)   An XML-based language used to communicate with Wireless Access Protocol (WAP) devices such as cellular telephones or personal digital assistants (PDAs). Most cellular telephones provide support for WML. The pages are served in a manner similar to that used by the Handheld Device Markup Language (HDML).

WML   See Wireless Markup Language

World Wide Web Consortium (W3C)   A standards organization essentially devoted to Internet security issues, but also involved in other issues such as the special <OBJECT> tag required by Microsoft to implement ActiveX technology. The W3C also defines a wealth of other HTML and XML standards. The W3C first appeared on the scene in December 1994, when it endorsed SSL (Secure Sockets Layer). In February 1995, it also endorsed application-level security for the Internet. Its current project is the Digital Signatures Initiative—W3C presented it in May 1996 in Paris.

WSDL   See Web Services Description Language

X

XACML   See eXtensible Access Control Markup Language

XHTML   See eXtensible Hypertext Markup Language

XML   See eXtensible Markup Language

XML-RPC   See eXtensible Markup Language Remote Procedure Call

XML Schema Definition (XSD)   The portion of the eXtensible Markup Language (XML) specification that defines data types and other data elements. Most browsers and other applications use XSD to verify the XML document. XSD is also related to a Web site containing such information by use of XML parsers. A designer can create a custom XSD for use with a particular application.

XSD   See XML Schema Definition

XSL   See eXtensible Style Language

XSLT   See eXtensible Style Language Transformation

Z

Zip   A file that acts as a container for other files. The Zip normally provides some level of data compression to make the resulting package smaller than the individual files. Some operating systems such as Windows XP provide built-in support for the Zip file. However, in many cases, you need to buy or download an application that provides the Zip file functionality.

Index

Note to the Reader: Throughout this index, **boldfaced** page numbers indicate primary discussions of a topic. *Italicized* page numbers indicate illustrations.

H

T

Official DevX Books from SYBEX®

.NET PROGRAMMING 10-MINUTE SOLUTIONS

by A. Russell Jones and Mike Gunderloy
ISBN: 0-7821-4253-2 • US $29.99

Based on the popular question-and-answer feature of the DevX website, these ten-minute solutions fill the gaps in your knowledge. From them, you'll learn a lot about the realities of programming with .NET technologies, whether you're writing database applications, web applications, or desktop applications.

JAVA™ PROGRAMMING 10-MINUTE SOLUTIONS

by Mark Watson
ISBN: 0-7821-4285-0 • US $34.99

Java Programming 10-Minute Solutions provides direct solutions to the thorny problems you're most likely to run up against in your work. Especially when a project entails new techniques or draws you into a realm outside your immediate expertise, potential headaches abound. With this book, a veteran Java programmer saves you both aggravation and—just as important—time.

.NET DEVELOPMENT SECURITY SOLUTIONS

by John Paul Mueller
ISBN: 0-7821-4266-4 • US $39.99

.NET Development Security Solutions uses detailed, code-intensive examples—lots of them—to teach you the right techniques for most scenarios you're likely to encounter. This is not an introduction to security; it's an advanced cookbook that shows experienced programmers how to meet tough security challenges.

DEVELOPING KILLER WEB APPS WITH DREAMWEAVER MX® AND C#™

by Chuck White
ISBN: 0-7821-4254-0 • US $39.99

Written for both web page designers and Internet programmers, this unique book guides your transition from using Dreamweaver as a designer's tool to a developer's tool and IDE. Find out how Dreamweaver MX, when combined with Visual C#, becomes a rapid application development tool.